39.95

A CLINICIAN'S GUIDE
TO MAINTAINING AND ENHANCING
CLOSE RELATIONSHIPS

D1733359

DATE DUE

A CLINICIAN'S GUIDE TO MAINTAINING AND ENHANCING CLOSE RELATIONSHIPS

Edited by

JOHN H. HARVEY
University of Iowa

AMY WENZEL
University of North Dakota

2002

LAWRENCE ERLBAUM ASSOCIATES, PUBLISHERS
Mahwah, New Jersey   London

Lawrence Erlbaum Associates, Inc., Publishers
10 Industrial Avenue
Mahwah, New Jersey 07430

Cover design by Kathryn Houghtaling Lacey

Library of Congress Cataloging-in-Publication Data

A clinician's guide to maintaining and enhancing close relationships / edited by John H.
Harvey, Amy Wenzel
    p. cm.
  Includes bibliographical references and index.
  ISBN 0-8058-3631-4 (alk. paper) – ISBN 0-8058-3632-2 (pbk. : alk paper)
    1.   Interpersonal relations. 2. Family psychotherapy. I. Harvey, John H., 1943-II.
  Wenzel, Amy.

  HM1106 .C53 2001
  302—dc21

                                2001042313

Printed in the United States of America
10 9 8 7 6 5 4 3 2 1

Contents

Maintaining and Enhancing Close Relationships: Linking   1
Theory With Practice
    Amy Wenzel and John H. Harvey

PART I: THEORETICAL LINKS TO PRACTICE

1   Issues in Ebb and Flow: Management and Maintenance   13
       of Relationships as a Skilled Activity
       Masahiro Masuda and Steve Duck

2   Hurtful Messages in Family Relationships: When   43
       the Pain Lingers
       Anita L. Vangelisti and Katheryn Maguire

3   The Application of Attachment Theory to Individual   63
       Behavior and Functioning in Close Relationships:
       Theory, Research, and Practical Applications
       Leonard J. Simms

4.   Couples' and Children's Functioning in Families: 81
       Toward a Family Perspective on Relationship
       Maintenance and Enhancement
       E. Mark Cummings and Marybeth Graham

5.   Relationship Maintenance and Enhancement   105
       in Stepfamilies: Clinical Applications
       *Lawrence H. Ganong, Marilyn Coleman, and Shannon
       Weaver*

PART II: PSYCHOPATHOLOGY AND CLOSE RELATIONSHIPS

6. The Empirical Underpinnings of Marital Therapy for Depression
Sammy F. Banawan, Heather A. O'Mahen, Steven R. H. Beach, and Melanie H. Jackson   133

7. The Effects of Postpartum Depression on Close Relationships
Karin E. Larsen and Michael W. O'Hara   157

8. Anxiety Disorders and Relationships: Implications for Etiology, Functionality, and Treatment
Lydia C. Jackson and Amy Wenzel   177

9. Characteristics of Close Relationships in Individuals With Social Phobia: A Preliminary Comparison With Nonanxious Individuals
Amy Wenzel   199

10. When One Marital Partner Is an Alcoholic
Sara L. Dolan and Peter E. Nathan   215

PART III: PREVENTION AND INTERVENTION

11. The Role of Clinicians in the Prevention of Marital Distress and Divorce
Natalie D. Monarch, Scott G. Hartman, Sarah W. Whitton, and Howard J. Markman   233

12. Integrating Insight-Oriented Techniques Into Couple Therapy
Douglas K. Snyder   259

13. Forgiveness: Toward a Public Health Approach to Intervention
Frank D. Fincham and Steven R. H. Beach   277

PART IV: COMMENTARIES

Maintaining Relationships in the Millennium 303
Pepper Schwartz

The Relevance of the Biological Dimension 313
and Biopsychosocial Therapy in Maintaining
and Enhancing Close Relationships
Len Sperry

Author Index 321
Subject Index 337

Maintaining and Enhancing Close Relationships: Linking Theory With Practice

Amy Wenzel
University of North Dakota

John H. Harvey
University of Iowa

In the past 10 years, we have witnessed a substantial increase in the number of theoretical and empirical investigations into the maintenance and enhancement of close, romantic relationships. Rather than focusing on how relationships form or dissolve, this literature attempts to track the course of relationships over time. Further, rather than considering how unique or stressful life circumstances enhance or disrupt relationships, this literature targets the everyday behaviors, expressions of love, and cognitive styles that characterize successful long-term romantic relationships. To date, this line of research generally has been conducted in the realm of social psychology and communications studies. We felt it important to bring this approach to practitioners who treat couples in distressed relationships. It is our hope that this volume will provide insight into ways clinicians and patients can work collaboratively to enhance relationships rather than only to prevent further deterioration.

In a companion volume to this one (*Close Relationships: Maintenance and Enhancement*), a number of distinguished scholars outlined theories and applications of the manner in which close relationships are maintained and enhanced. Several themes that might be useful to clinicians emerged from that compilation. For example, Mills and Clark (2001) put forth a view of close relationships as those that are communal in nature. That is, close relationships will be successful to the extent that individuals meet the needs of their partner without expecting a benefit in return. Mills and Clark be-

I

lieve that communal behaviors result in both members of the dyad feeling cared for by the other. Although such an approach might be difficult to explore with distressed couples early in therapy, it is an approach that might be useful to consider after acute conflict subsides. Using this theory as a foundation, clinicians might work with couples to identify instances of communal behaviors, explore the positive affect associated with being on the giving and receiving end of a communal exchange, and monitor relationship satisfaction as a function of the extent to which a couple adopts this orientation.

According to a theory by Rusbult, Olsen, Davis, and Hannon (2001), commitment, rather than satisfaction or investment, is the strongest predictor of relationship persistence. They regard commitment as having three components—intention to persist, psychological attachment, and a cognitive orientation to being in the relationship for the long term. Many couple interventions include components that focus on these cognitive and affective dimensions. Rusbult and her colleagues base their work on an *interdependence* theory; the key to that theory is that many situations arise in relationships in which "the immediate well being of one person is incompatible with the immediate well being of the partner and relationship" (p. 88). They suggest that relationship distress might be related to problematic interdependence situations just as much as to individual variables, such as poor social skills or a blaming attributional style. Thus, they call for couple therapists to modify the problematic interdependence structure as well as attend to individual variables that interfere with relationship functioning.

Specific recommendations for the maintenance and enhancement of close relationships also were posited by a number of contributors in the companion volume. For example, Simpson, Ickes, and Orina (2001) described *empathic accuracy* as a relationship maintenance strategy in which one partner accurately identifies the thoughts and feelings of his or her partner. Although it is intuitive to regard empathic accuracy as a uniformly positive relationship maintenance strategy, Simpson and his colleagues provided evidence that it is harmful in situations in which the relationship is seriously threatened. In such cases, the relationship is maintained by *not* using empathic accuracy so that one partner can sustain a positive view of the other. In addition, Aron, Norman, and Aron (2001) illustrated the importance of couples engaging in novel, exciting activities together in order to grow both individually and relationally. Sahlstein and Baxter (2001) made the important point that the nature of relationships changes over time, often encompassing a number of contradictory elements. This work indicates that periodically defining levels of commitment and trust in close relationships contributes to their maintenance and enhancement. Acitelli's (2001) research demonstrated that attending to relationships, or putting effort into them, is important in maintaining satisfaction. However, she noted that women attend to relationships by thinking and talking about them, whereas men attend to relationships by sharing activities and spending time together. A couple therapist might provide psychoeducation about this gender difference and work toward both members of a dyad acknowledging the other's attempt at attending and practicing both of them.

Thus, the theoretical work included in the companion volume clearly has implications for the manner in which clinicians encourage maintenance and enhancement strategies in their therapeutic work with clients. The goal of the present volume is to provide specific suggestions for clinicians as to how to link this theory with clinical practice. The volume is divided into three sections. The first section includes five chapters that outline specific theoretical approaches to the maintenance and enhancement of close relationships and specify the manner in which these constructs are useful clinically. Not only does this section include work pertaining to close relationships that include two romantically involved individuals, but it also incorporates research about parent–child relationships and relationships in stepfamilies. The second section includes five chapters that illustrate the manner in which psychopathology disrupts the maintenance and enhancement of close relationships. Although it is well known that depression has an adverse effect on close relationships, very little research has been conducted on the effects of other types of psychopathology on relationship functioning. This section represents an attempt to accumulate the little knowledge we have in this area and make preliminary recommendations for treatment and future research. The third section includes three chapters on prevention and intervention strategies for relationship distress. One chapter reviews preventative strategies that focus on the maintenance and enhancement of close relationships [Monarch, Hartman, Whitton, & Markman], whereas the other two chapters describe innovative interventions for couples who are already distressed. Section IV concludes the book with some commentary by Len Sperry and Pepper Schwartz.

The importance of the everyday ebb and flow of relationships is captured in the chapter by Masuda and Duck. They make the important point that communication is only as strong as the shared meaning within the unique relationship culture. For example, independent observers could categorize a particular couple's communication style as adaptive, but if one individual cannot build an understanding of the other's thoughts and behaviors, then that communication style does not work for the relationship culture they have built. Moreover, partners need to practice appropriate relational maintenance skills in order to sustain attraction. Masuda and Duck regard conflicts as a part of the normal ebb and flow of relationships, and they review several adaptive and maladaptive conflict management strategies. In fact, even dissolution can be considered part of the ebb and flow if adaptive communication skills are used to redefine their new relationship as ex-partners. This chapter makes the important point that communication within relationships, for both major and mundane events, is cumulative in establishing a relationship culture that provides a shared meaning for both individuals in the dyad. In a therapeutic context, that relationship culture could be seen as a source of strength and stability that has been developed from many years of shared experiences. A couple intervention, then, could capitalize on that shared relationship culture as a basis for an exploration of relationship distress and the implementation of behavior change.

Vangelisti and Maguire explore the manner in which individuals cope with hurtful messages from family members, an issue that often arises in couple and family therapy. They suggest that individuals respond in one of two ways when a family member makes a hurtful remark—either they forgive the family member more easily than would be expected by the nature of the comment, or they harbor negative feelings and distance themselves from the family member who made the comment. In preliminary analyses of a study investigating these patterns of responding to hurtful remarks, Vangelisiti and Maguire find that satisfaction with the relationship accounts for much of the relation between the tendency to view a family member as hurtful and a tendency to withdraw from that relationship. The tendency of an individual to forgive his or her family member for making a hurtful comment is related to high levels of satisfaction with the relationship and low levels of perceived frequency and proclivity of hurtful statements. Thus, this research demonstrates that the tendency to forgive family members for making hurtful comments is clearly related to the maintenance and enhancement of close relationships. Vangelisti and Maguire anticipate the importance of incorporating forgiveness strategies into couple interventions, an issue addressed by Fincham and Beach in this volume.

The chapter by Simms illustrates the prominent role that attachment theory has played in conceptualizing typologies of close, romantic relationships in adults. He summarizes the well-established finding that adults can be classified into attachment styles (e.g., secure, avoidant, anxious–ambivalent) in much the same manner as infants were in early investigations of mother–infant relationships. In general, individuals who are characterized by a secure attachment style tend to be quite satisfied in their relationships, reporting high levels of trust, commitment, intimacy, and longevity. Conversely, individuals who are characterized by an insecure attachment style tend to report lower levels of these characteristics. Thus, it is not difficult to conclude that couples in which both members of the dyad are securely attached are generally successful in maintaining and enhancing close relationships. Simms reviews literature relating attachment styles to communication skills, sexuality, and conflict resolution strategies, three issues that are prominent foci of couple interventions. Attachment theory provides a sound basis for the process of examining patterns of interactions in close relationships as well as more general maladaptive interpersonal styles in the context of both individual and couple therapy. As Simms describes, clinicians can create new learning experiences to reshape the attachment styles of insecurely attached individuals, and couple therapy based on this approach helps the partners of insecurely attached individuals to provide a secure base as they explore and modify their interpersonal tendencies.

Cummings and Graham adopt a systems perspective to examine the manner in which couple conflict affects children's functioning. Quite simply, it appears that couple conflict, particularly conflict characterized by high levels of negative emotional responses in children, is strongly related to children's externalizing and internalizing behavior. Moreover, couple conflict is predictive of parent–child relational disturbances, such as those associated with insecure attachment. This chapter makes the important contribution of describing conflict management strategies that not only serve to maintain close relationships but also reduce the negative effects on couples' children. For example, Cummings and Graham normalize the anger experience and suggest that it is detrimental to avoid anger or conflict because children are unable to model effective conflict resolution strategies. In addition, they make specific recommendations for the intake and assessment as well as treatment planning based on these principles. In all, this chapter illustrates that conflict is a normal part of all relationships and, when handled constructively, it not only serves to maintain healthy relationships, but it also contributes to the emotional well being of children.

Ganong, Coleman, and Weaver apply their theoretical work on relationship maintenance and enhancement in stepfamilies to make several practical suggestions for clinicians. They outline four main reasons why stepfamilies have relationship problems—Members (1) lack relationship maintenance skills; (2) neglect relationship maintenance; (3) do not respond to other members' relational maintenance strategies; and (4) do not know how to use relational maintenance skills in a stepfamily context. Common interventions for these difficulties include education, teaching communication skills, encouraging members to spend quality one-on-one time with one another, clarifying expectations, validating feelings, and modifying expectations. This chapter reminds us of the importance of intervening at a family, rather than an individual, level when the presenting problem involves multiple layers of relationships, loyalties to particular family members, and expectations. Although maintaining and enhancing close relationships with many stepfamily members at times might seem daunting, Ganong and his colleagues demonstrate that these relationships can be quite satisfying when the new family creates a culture that has been shaped by all of its members.

In the opening chapter on the nature of close relationships in individuals with psychopathology, Banawan, O'Mahen, Beach, and Jackson review a substantial body of evidence demonstrating that depressed individuals tend to report lower levels of marital satisfaction than nondepressed individuals. They propose a number of mediators for this relation, including poor problem-solving skills, negative reinforcement of depressive behaviors versus other negative relationship behaviors, psychological abuse, sensitivity to criticism, and a lack of perceived social support. They frame the depression-relationship dissatisfaction relation in terms of a stress generation model by reasoning that depressed individuals create stress in relationships because of their pathology, and they exacerbate this relationship stress by reacting negatively to it. Banawan and his colleagues indicate that marital therapy is useful both in reducing depressive symptomatology and increasing relationship satisfaction, especially in individuals who perceive their relationship as playing a major role in their depression. They describe a number of specific techniques that are useful in working with couples in which one partner is distressed, such as enhancing perceived partner commitment and increasing intimacy. Although studies in this area to date generally have examined interventions addressing relationship distress, it will be important for future research to consider the manner in which relationships can be maintained and enhanced when one partner has a chronic mood disorder.

As illustrated in the chapter by Larsen and O'Hara, postpartum depression is an instance of psychopathology that is intricately related to the well being of the relationship with one's partner. Although existing research clearly indicates that women with postpartum depression tend to have distressed partner relationships, to date there have been no systematic recommendations of ways to maintain and enhance this relationship during pregnancy and the postpartum period. Thus, it will be important for researchers to describe protective factors (e.g., positive attributional style, high level of communication skills) that not only preserve the partner relationship, but also withstand the onset of postpartum depression. Further, Larsen and O'Hara review an extensive literature that has examined the relation between postpartum depression and problematic mother–infant relationships. It appears that distressed mother–child relationships emerge from subsequent depressive episodes rather than from the initial postpartum depressive episode that occurs when the child is an infant. Nevertheless, psychoeducational and skill-building interventions would be useful in helping the postpartum depressed woman to demonstrate competence in maintaining and enhancing the mother–child relationship throughout child development.

Jackson and Wenzel examine both the manner in which anxiety affects the maintenance of close relationships and also the manner in which maladaptive relationships affect the development of anxiety disorders. They suggest that the unique relationship culture often serves to maintain an individual's symptoms of anxiety, as the nonanxious partner generally benefits by having control in the relationship, and the anxious partner generally benefits by being able to avoid situations that cause discomfort. Relationship conflict often results when the nonanxious spouse becomes frustrated with the lifestyle constraints dictated by the anxious partner's disorder or when the roles in the relationship change, such as when the anxious spouse's symptoms begin to improve in treatment. This chapter illustrates that few structured approaches exist that target the treatment of a distressed relationship when one member of the dyad has an anxiety disorder. However. Jackson and Wenzel review evidence indicating that involving an anxious individual's partner as a coach in the treatment of an anxiety disorder is efficacious, sometimes more so than individual therapy for anxiety. Jackson and Wenzel call on researchers to examine basic characteristics of the close relationships of individuals with anxiety disorders that will help clinicians to determine when individual and when couple interventions are appropriate. By examining specific strengths and weaknesses that are characteristic of these relationships, clinicians can promote strategies for the maintenance and enhancement of relationships in the context of an anxiety disorder.

Wenzel's chapter is the first known study to examine the nature of close, romantic relationships in individuals with social phobia. Social phobia is an anxiety disorder characterized by excessive fears of negative evaluation, scrutiny, and interaction with others. Because of their interactional fears, it is logical to suspect that social phobic individuals would have disrupted close relationships. Confirming this hypothesis, Wenzel reports that individuals with social phobia endorsed a more negative relationship attributional style, less emotional and social intimacy, and a more insecure attachment style than nonanxious individuals. On the other hand, individuals with social phobia appeared to be as adept as nonanxious individuals at practicing aspects of minding their close relationships, which Harvey and Omarzu (1997) have indicated are related to successful maintenance and enhancement. We hope that clinicians will find this information useful, as relationship distress is one of the primary reasons individuals present for psychotherapy, and individuals with psychopathology often are characterized by a high degree of social anxiety, if not a diagnosis of social phobia.

In the final chapter on the nature of close relationships in individuals with psychopathology, Dolan and Nathan consider the interpersonal sequelae of alcoholism. They discuss a number of ways in which alcohol interferes with close relationships, including communication difficulties caused by alcohol-related cognitive deficits and social skills deficits, aggression, and sexual dysfunction. Interestingly, they reviewed evidence suggesting that in some cases, relationships in which one of the partners is an early-onset alcoholic are more satisfying than relationships in which one of the partners is a late-onset alcoholic (presumably less severe than early-onset alcoholism). Dolan and Nathan speculate that this finding is due to the fact that the nonalcoholic partner formed the relationship with the alcoholic individual when s/he was already drinking; thus, there were clear expectations about the role that alcohol would play in these relationships. Similar to what Jackson and Wenzel described with anxiety disorders, treatment that includes a nonalcoholic partner as a coach tends to reduce symptoms of psychopathology as well as increase relationship satisfaction. This chapter serves as a reminder that alcohol consumption should be included as part of a comprehensive assessment of relationship functioning and that treatment should address symptoms of alcohol abuse as well as resultant relationship distress.

Monarch, Hartman, Whitton, and Markman review an extensive literature describing the prevention of marital distress. Divorce prevention programs address risk factors such as dysfunctional relationship beliefs, negative communication patterns, parental divorce, religious dissimilarity, marrying after having known each other for a short period of time, premarital cohabitation, low or differing levels of education, and young age at marriage. Conversely, these programs also enhance protective factors, such as commitment and time spent for fun, friendship, and sensuality, which are factors we view as being related to maintaining and enhancing close relationships. Monarch and her colleagues describe a number of empirically validated divorce prevention programs and suggest criteria that one might consider in selecting a prevention program to implement with one's patients. They make the important point that clinicians should remain up to date with the current literature on divorce prevention programs so that they administer their program in the most efficacious manner possible.

Snyder's chapter on insight-oriented couple therapy illustrates the importance of alleviating relationship distress by understanding the developmental context in which interpersonal patterns occur. Although skills-oriented psychotherapy is useful in working through acute crises and presenting problems, the examination of long-standing relational tendencies in each partner is crucial in identifying and modifying maladaptive patterns of interactions that recur in the relationship. Examination of these dispositions promotes empathy and acceptance among partners and provides the impetus for partners to engage in new, more adaptive behaviors. Snyder demonstrates that this approach to couple therapy promotes longer-lasting change than traditional behavioral approaches to couple therapy. We view this therapy as being especially useful in moving couples from a state of distress into a position in which they are able to work on enhancing their relationships without the risk of vulnerability or injury.

In an exciting new intervention for relationship distress, Fincham and Beach describe the manner in which forgiveness can be used as a tool to increase acceptance and satisfaction and decrease negative affect in relationships. They review evidence that suggests forgiveness increases well-being by decreasing hostility (and associated adverse health outcomes), repairs relationships so that social support is able to be utilized, and reduces symptoms of psychopathology. Their model of their forgiveness intervention requires that individuals "acknowledge a transgression, identify that it is appropriate to feel negatively about being victimized, assert their right to better treatment, and [be willing] to relieve the debt incurred by the transgressor" (p. 290). This mode of intervention can be administered in the community by paraprofessionals or even take the form of an online self-help intervention. As Fincham and Beach note, transgressions inevitably occur in relationships, and forgiveness is crucial in preventing a relationship from deteriorating after these events. This chapter provides useful information as to how a clinician might explore forgiveness in the context of individual psychotherapy and illustrates that forgiveness is a central construct in maintaining and enhancing close relationships.

Several themes emerge from these chapters that are relevant to the clinician's role in maintaining and enhancing close relationships. First, it is clear that the relationship culture is central in maintaining relationships through shared experiences and in creating distress when it reinforces symptoms of psychopathology and maladaptive interactional styles. Although we regard the accumulation of shared experiences as a strength that characterizes close romantic relationships perhaps more than any other type of relationship, it certainly poses a challenge to clinicians when the culture that has emerged consists of negative attributes such as hostility, mistrust, or even violence. Divorce prevention programs play a crucial role in providing education and skills that prevent the relationship culture from developing along a maladaptive trajectory. Moreover, both insight-oriented couple therapy and interventions focused on forgiveness, although they intervene after damage has already occurred, prescribe useful techniques to overcome a problematic relationship culture. We believe that it is important for clinicians to assess the relationship culture and interpret presenting problems and complaints in the context of the shared experience of the couple.

Another theme that emerges from these chapters is that adult attachment styles have major implications for the adaptivity of close relationships. Although insecure attachment styles predispose individuals to having problematic close relationships, there is evidence that these styles can be modified in an individual or couple therapy format (Johnson & Greenberg, 1995; Johnson & Whiffen, 1999). We suspect that the assessment and understanding of adult attachment style will be increasingly important in promoting acceptance and understanding among couples in distressed relationships, and we encourage clinicians to conceptualize cases with this framework in mind.

To date, most couple interventions involve the teaching of skills to manage conflict, clarify expectations in times of distress, and generally repair damaged relationships. Most often, couples participate in therapy no longer than it takes to resolve their presenting problem. Unfortunately, there is evidence that as many as 50% of couples are considered distressed only 2 years after they complete couple interventions, and as many as 25% are functioning at a level that is lower than when they initially presented for therapy (Jacobson, 1989). Thus, we argue that couple interventions not only should provide skills to diffuse acute conflict, but they also should facilitate maintenance and enhancement strategies once the presenting relationship difficulties subside. Such strategies might be those that promote affective restructuring and insight into the developmental context of functioning in close relationships, as Snyder describes in his chapter. In addition, the protective factors that Monarch and her colleagues discuss in divorce prevention programs clearly appear to promote the enhancement of relationships. It might be useful to view couple interventions as composed of a hierarchy of goals: addressing conflict related to specific issues; and promoting skills to maintain and enhance the quality of the close, romantic relationship. We eagerly await the next generation of couple intervention research that incorporates both of these themes.

REFERENCES

Acitelli, L. K. (2001). Maintaining and enhancing a relationship by attending to it. In J. H. Harvey & A. Wenzel (Eds.), *Close relationships: Maintenance and enhancement* (pp. 153–167). Mahwah, NJ: Lawrence Erlbaum Associates.

Aron, A., Norman, C. C., & Aron, E. N. (2001). Shared self-expanding activities as a means of maintaining and enhancing close romantic relationships. In J. H. Harvey & A. Wenzel (Eds.), *Close relationships: Maintenance and enhancement* (pp. 47–66). Mahwah, NJ: Lawrence Erlbaum Associates.

Harvey, J. H., & Omarzu, J. (1997). Minding the close relationship. *Personality and Social Psychology Review, 1*, 223–239.

Jacobson, N. S. (1989). The maintenance of treatment gains following social learning-based marital therapy. *Behavior Therapy, 20*, 325–326.

Johnson, S. M., & Greenberg, L. S. (1995). The emotionally focused approach to problems in adult attachment. In N. S. Jacobson & A. S. Gurman (Eds.), *Clinical handbook of couple therapy* (pp. 121–141). New York: Guilford.

Johnson, S. M., & Whiffen, F. (1999). Made to measure: Adapting emotionally focused couple therapy to partners' attachment styles. *Clinical Psychology: Science and Practice, 6*, 366–381.

Mills, J., & Clark, M. S. (2001). Viewing close romantic relationships as communal relationships: Implications for maintenance and enhancement. In J. H. Harvey & A. Wenzel (Eds.), *Close relationships: Maintenance and enhancement* (pp. 13–25). Mahwah, NJ: Lawrence Erlbaum Associates.

Rusbult, E., Olsen, N., Davis, J. L., & Hannon, P. A. (2001). Commitment and relationship maintenance mechanisms. In J. H. Harvey & A. Wenzel (Eds.), *Close relationships: Maintenance and enhancement* (pp. 87–113). Mahwah, NJ: Lawrence Erlbaum Associates.

Simpson, J. A., Ickes, W., & Orina, M. (2001). Empathic accuracy and preemptive relationship maintenance. In J. H. Harvey & A. Wenzel (Eds.), *Close relationships: Maintenance and enhancement* (pp. 27–46). Mahwah, NJ: Lawrence Erlbaum Associates.

Sahlstein, E. M., & Baxter, L. A. (2001). Improving commitment in close relationships: A relational dialectics perspective. In J. H. Harvey & A. Wenzel (Eds.), *Close relationships: Maintenance and enhancement* (pp. 115–132). Mahwah, NJ: Lawrence Erlbaum Associates.

THEORETICAL LINKS
TO PRACTICE

1

Issues in Ebb and Flow: Management and Maintenance of Relationships as a Skilled Activity

Masahiro Masuda
Steve Duck
University of Iowa

This chapter explores relational maintenance from the point of view of the everyday *ordinariness* of relationships, such that when they are maintained, ordinariness is maintained. Most approaches to maintenance (Canary & Stafford, 1994) are based on the assumption that conflict and argument are sites that produce a need for maintenance and resolution of relationship difficulties, but we disagree. Conflict, argument, and resolution are special and atypical instances of maintenance of relationships, the everyday ordinariness of routine activity being the basis of many real-life conflicts anyway. Also, although special issues of conflict management constitute extraordinary occasions for management and maintenance of relationships, most of life is ordinary. Yet, ordinariness itself presents many simple, routine, and unconscious ways to maintain and manage relationships. The skills of relationship are not specific to special conflicts and arguments but impinge on and derive from abilities to handle "the everyday" also, a point that is all too often overlooked.

We, therefore, agree with Acitelli (2001) who uses the term "maintenance" to refer not to "repair" but to keeping the relationship running *well*. This notion of maintenance therefore largely overlaps conceptually with the notion of relationship satisfaction. We also explore relational maintenance from the point of view of the skills involved in sustaining routine everyday behavior, because recognizing, polishing, and repairing such skills may be addressed through clinical solutions.

Everyone with competency at conducting relationships has a number of implicit skills: awareness of the skills of interpersonal relating as these are valued in a particular culture or in the local social context where the relationship is played out; the ability to enact those relating skills within different specific relationships; awareness of the fact that maintaining a relationship is a persistent, if not constant, task; and the ability to maintain course and speed as conditions ebb and flow in the normal tides of life.

In this chapter, we consider these needs in the context of the variation in happenings that constitute life's experiences for all human beings whether or not they are clinical patients. Routinely, people encounter others in moods that are different from last time of meeting; people themselves have bad days and good days; the stress of dealing with a small child or work subordinate can differ from day to day and hour to hour; neighbors and colleagues can be irritating one day and pleasant the next; and feelings for a spouse or close romantic partner can vary in type and intensity according to the activities or circumstances of the moment but without changing the underlying relationships. We do not claim that life is completely chaotic, merely that there are daily variations and patches of turbulence that are routinely managed in relationships particularly and in life in general. A person's skill in handling this variety and the person's frame of mind for managing turbulence and change can each be significant influences on subsequent feelings of competence or incompetence, satisfaction or depression, and resentment or contentment. Those people who report a "happy marriage" or "difficulty with relationships" are, we assume, reporting their *summary* perceptions of a variety of experiences. The nature of their choice of summary terms, choices of metaphors, and style of speech may themselves be indicative of something from which a clinician can derive insights into a patient's state of mind (McCall, 1982). Someone who reports a relationship as "an empty shell" is having a different psychological experience from someone who reports it as a cage.

Our chapter is thus strongly based on the two notions of the ordinary and variability. Both of these, in their own ways, confront the relational partners with challenges to manage the relationship—perhaps alone and perhaps in concert with others, but always under the eye of the social network. Any discussion of the skills of relating must differentiate between those skills that are (1) generalized within the culture, (2) those that are instantiated and enforced in local networks with whom the two partners come into frequent contact, and (3) those that are negotiated privately by the parties themselves. The ability to negotiate the tensions between these three audiences, representing different levels of standard for competence, is a further skill of maintaining and managing a relationship. We propose that skills are often relationally and personally idiosyncratic and situated within contexts where their appropriateness may best be judged according to the goals of participants and observers (Spitzberg, 1993). Relational behaviors and skills are thus not simply universally applicable in ways that take no account of such contexts, but they require the subskill of recognizing the applicability of rules to particularized circumstances.

Some general skills are assumed in relating, particularly in public places or when the partners are expecting to be observed by other people. For example, a typical assumption will be that one should follow cultural norms of polite behavior in public (Goffman, 1959), although the negotiation of behaviors in private will be part of the special topical skill that creates a sense of uniqueness in the relationship. For example, cruelty is not accepted as a normal mode of public conduct of relationships, but in private, sadomasochism may be part of a couple's sexual practice. This may be one reason why, as noted by Aron, Dutton, Aron, and Iverson (1989), all romantic couples feel that their relationship is *unique*, despite the fact that it appears to the outside public observer as a prototypical embodiment of general patterns of both behavior and feeling.

To present a clinically relevant assessment of relationship maintenance, therefore, the present chapter must explore the nature of "good" or "poor" communication both in general and in specific circumstances. We should also differentiate between those "skills" that apply to public behavior and those that involve private negotiation. Those communicators labeled "poor" by observers who apply the general standard may nevertheless regard each other positively, because they either hold one another to a different standard from the general one, or make allowances in some way, or simply behave in private in ways that the normative standard does not acknowledge. On the other hand, some patients may lack the insight to comprehend that their personal behaviors are insufficiently responsive to the requirements of these different norms or of other people. Failure to recognize these relational subtleties is, of course, a classic symptom of such clinical conditions as borderline personality, anorexia, or depression (Segrin, 2000), and part of the clinical treatment might involve defocusing from self in order to enhance requisite awareness (Duck, 1991). However, many distressed couples exhibit signs of interpersonal misunderstanding simply because of different expectations generated in their family of origin (for example, a partner from one family may have learned to express anger by social withdrawal whereas the other may expect to express it openly and be nurtured—conflicting styles that lead to increased mutual misunderstanding; Gray, 1992).

Forms of relational behavior that are generally regarded as skilled (e.g., particular forms of behavior during relational dissolution, such as saving the other's "face" by blaming a dissolution on one's own changing needs rather than the partner's attributes) may in fact be unskilled if one assumes that skilled relating always produces dyadic satisfaction. As Spitzberg

(1993) indicates, there are dialectics of incompetence and, for example, some "lies" are skillful (e.g., keeping a birthday surprise secret) whereas some truths are best skillfully concealed (e.g., where a partner's new hair style looks terrible). The important issue for deciding whether behavior is skilled or not is the *partnership standard* within the relationship and the *shared meaning* that the partners have about each other's behavior in the context of that relationship once relationship maintenance is seen as relationship satisfaction. Traditional views of social skill therefore need reevaluation (cf. Burleson, Kunkel, Samter, & Werking, 1996) to ensure that the "public view" or only the perspective of the person outside the relationship is not taken as the gold standard for judgment of its merits. If the relationship is satisfying, then a level of skill has been achieved that is satisfactory to partners/insiders even if, to the outsider, the standard appears not to have been reached. For example, as Duck (1984) noted, personal satisfaction can be derived from a "good" dissolution as much as from a good repair, even though the societal standard assumes that any relationship dissolution is a relational failure.

LOCATION OF SKILL

The prior discussion raises the question of whose judgment of skill matters most. We prefer to place clinical evaluation of maintenance relative to the goals and achievements of the performer. This means that evaluation of skill cannot be applied only by an observer simply as a representative of the culture at large but only by someone who has become fully conversant with the personal goals of the partners also. This latter point is one reason why women and men see maintenance behaviors as carrying different weight (Acitelli, 1993, 2001), because their personal goals in talking about relationships are quite different. It is not so much the occurrence of the behavior itself that matters but the ways in which meaning is attached to it, or to its absence, by each person. For instance,

> the meaning of the strategy (whether it is seen as planned or routine) can vary depending on [factors such as] gender [and] marital status. . . . A man may interpret a woman's talking about the relationships as a strategic maintenance . . . and feel threatened. A woman may see such talk as routine, something she enjoys doing without the intent of pointing out problems or consciously maintaining the relationship. On the other hand a man may see the need to share activities together in order to strategically maintain the relationship, while his female partner may not interpret such activity the same way. (Acitelli, 2001, p. 154)

Accordingly, the notion of competence may be variously assessed (Spitzberg, 1993; Spitzberg & Cupach, 1984) and when one asks, "What is a 'competent' relational partner like?" the question is not an easy one to answer.

In most cases, relational maintenance is implicitly assessed by researchers in terms of an individual's or a couple's satisfaction with the relationship or with the partner, for example, Spanier's (1976) widely used Dyadic Adjustment Scale. According to such a judgment standard, therefore, a "competent" partner would be one who satisfies his or her partner and maintains a relationship in a way that leads both parties to express high levels of satisfaction in the relationship and in one another.

In the climate of the present age where "communication," broadly conceived, is regarded as the basis of good relating, and "good communication" is seen in popular culture as a panacea (Gray, 1992), one would normally expect that couple satisfaction will itself be equated with "communication," loosely understood. Assessment of partners' abilities to communicate with each other would also be assumed to be part of their satisfaction with each other and to help them to maintain their relationship (Gottman, 1994). If satisfactory maintenance of the relationship (i.e., stabilizing it at its present level of intimacy) is a goal of a relationship, then partners who have absorbed the prescriptions of their surrounding culture will articulate satisfaction with their communication as one part of their commentary. However, stability—as distinct from growth or dissolution—of a relationship is not always the desired state. Furthermore, communication is notoriously hard to conceptualize in a convincing way despite the fact that in clinical settings, decent communicative skills are often a prerequisite for patients' improvement.

Communication competence is sometimes measured by five separate means: (1) the effectiveness of a particular communication in satisfying partners; (2) its efficiency (such as in successful management of relational conflicts); (3) its role in managing or expressing the emotions of romantic partners; (4) its instrumentality in accomplishment of other goals; (5) its symbolic force in maintaining relationships, through its "mere occurrence" (that is to say, partners miss it when talking is absent, but do not particularly notice it when it is present—Duck, Rutt, Hurst, & Strejc, 1991). Furthermore, communication is significant in the management of a satisfactory dissolution of relationships as well as in management of their continuance (maintenance). Maintenance and dissolution sound like antonyms, but the notion of competence brings them together and reveals, as we indicated above, that they are two sides of the same coin: successful management of a particular relational process, as judged by the two partners.

Successfully managed relational processes thus need to be judged largely by reference to relational partners' intentions or expectations. Of course, partners' plans and expectations can range from the long-term strategic ("We will get married one day") to lower-level plans about specific daily relational activities ("It is my turn to do the dishes and I had better do them if I am to maintain relational equity"). However, such plans are rarely perfectly logical. Relational partners cannot anticipate exactly when there will be turning points in their relationship, and indeed the turning points that are often researched (e.g., Baxter & Bullis, 1986; Graham, 1997) are most often retrospective constructions rather than foreseeable events with predictable consequences. Certainly, turning points are identified by retrospective reports in all cases with which we are familiar (Huston, 1994; Huston, Surra, Fitzgerald, & Cate, 1981; Surra, Arizzi, & Asmussen, 1988). Thus, it is almost impossible to evaluate whether or not a particular communication is competent before its consequences are observed. Events that are meaningful for relational development cannot be acknowledged as meaningful until they actually have occurred and the relational partners share their evaluations with each other.

In other words, evaluation of a relational communication as skilled depends substantially on the ability of the participants to identify and designate its outcomes as such. On the other hand, such recognition is not all that counts. "I just happened to be there at the right time" is the sort of phrase uttered by a person who unintentionally becomes a hero in an emergency. Observers may praise the person for heroic actions that were in the broader sense unplanned, and hence the person's competence and skill are equated simply with the outcome: a successful rescue. A failed attempt could nevertheless also be seen as a competent and skilled effort, despite the outcome, if the behavior was logically or empirically appropriate from the view of skilled experts.

Thus, the evaluation of communication as competent in the maintenance of relationships is not straightforward. Acts of communication are not to be judged solely on their perceived consequences, because even otherwise competent actions can fail to achieve a desired goal. Appropriately skilled efforts may nevertheless be derogated or praised according to whether they result in failure or success. Therefore, successful maintenance of relational processes does not necessarily require the successful accomplishment of goals. If relational behavior is successful, its effectiveness brings relational partners a desired result; but even if unsuccessful, it can help partners to construct understanding of each other's behavior that could feel satisfying. For instance, partners' increased insights into one another's thought processes can in themselves produce therapeutic benefits in distressed couples (Gottman, 1994). In this case, success of communication derives from relational partners' joint activity in a process of meaning-making relative to their desired or intended relational processes. Effectiveness is achieved by relational partners' greater sense of sharing meanings for their relationships, and appropriateness is assessed in terms of the meaningfulness of the behavior to relational partners. In other words, satisfaction is an indicator of meaningfulness of a particular relational process.

Another way in which private interactions are skilled is through exhibition of Relationship Awareness (Acitelli, 1993) by means of which partners demonstrate to each other their thinking about interaction patterns, comparisons or contrasts between self and partner in the relationship, or thoughts about their couplehood or the relationship as an entity. These processes enable partners to achieve shared meanings about their relationship including the nature of their relationship and each other's self.

Such a view "locates" at least a part of satisfying relational maintenance at the dyadic or personal level rather than the public cultural level. For example, some relational skills help relational partners manage each other's relational self by jointly attaching the same meanings to it. Through such things as personalized idiomatic communication, like private nicknames for people or relational acts (Bell, Buerkel-Rothfuss, & Gore, 1987; Bombar & Littig, 1996; Bruess & Pearson, 1993; Hopper, Knapp, & Scott, 1981), romantic partners present their private selves as lovers to each other and yet simultaneously exclude other people from the relational space because those audiences will not understand the references coded into the private language.

This sort of internal, expressive, and dyadic communication skill in relationships represents the status of relationships and simultaneously constitutes relational processes for the partners. Of course, such skills change as a relationship progresses, until it reaches a state beyond which it does not proceed. Communication skills, at the early stages of development, identify relational partners' feelings for each other and also demonstrate two other things: one's perception or acceptance of the partner as one's romantic partner, and one's presentation of self to the partner as one partner's romantic partner. When one or both of the partners do[es] not make this sense of the other's relational behaviors, the relationship is not yet stable and partners make their relational process meaningful by seeking development, agreement, or dissolution. Romantic partners' personal idioms are not formed through telepathy but are negotiated through their everyday routine verbal or nonverbal communication. Lovers' communication is not mysterious but practical, with a practical need to meet the other partner's expectations.

What distinguishes compatible relationships from their incompatible counterparts is whether or not partners can adapt to perceived communication gaps. As Gottman (1994) points out, conflict management without flexibility about alternative solutions decreases partners' satisfaction with romantic relationships, because one partner's contemptuous criticism makes the other partner react defensively and finally withdraw from further interactions. Gottman thus points out that it is not conflict itself but problematic communication styles in conflict management that harm personal relationships. Conflict is a normal phenomenon, and we cannot imagine a superhuman communication skill that would prevent all conflict between partners. However, in the practical world, we seek to identify the communication skills and relational practices that bring relational partners back on the right tracks—"tracks" in the plural—because the role of communication is to help partners create as many alternatives as possible and provide them with a wide range of appropriate behaviors in their relationship. The behavioral appropriateness is assessed by (1) the appropriateness of communication and (2) the appropriateness of perception of partner.

The latter layer of communication activity depends on the fact that successful relational management originates also in partners' sensitivity to their "cultures" and use of cultural rules to carry out the instantiation of affection and courtship. We describe "cultures" as a plural because romantic relationships are embedded in at least three cultures: (1) One is the culture of the society at large (cf. Shotter, 1992); (2) the second is the directly accessible community of networked others in which the couple is raised and lives out a romance (Klein & Milardo, 1993, Parks, 1997); (3) the third is the unique dyadic culture that they create through their relational processes and that we have so far given most attention (Baxter, 1987; Wood, 1982). However, these three aspects of culture interact with each other. The idiosyncratic level must be presented to the intermediate and the larger group; the larger legitimatizes some personal idiosyncrasies as potential new prototypes of romantic interactions as the society evolves. Relational communication between the dyad and the network sustains the relationships by making a relationship's idiosyncratic skill evident to other people and so providing a sounding board for its acceptability. For instance, couples may consult friends about their relationship dynamics and ask whether their behavior is normal, acceptable, or within the realm of their friends' experience. In other words, the effective audience for maintaining personal relationships is not society at large but the community of friends and associates directly accessible to the persons day by day. Social attractiveness is meaningful only within the relatively homogeneous community in which members share the same comprehension of reasonable conduct (Feingold, 1988).

Once the acceptability of their own personally created relational particularities is accepted, this skill is recognized as a more prototypical skill, and then it becomes more meaningful to other people (Farr & Moscovici, 1984; Fehr & Russell, 1991; Flick, 1995, for the discussion about people's understanding of the unfamiliar; Russell, 1991, for discussion of identification of prototypes). Part of a successful intervention with distressed couples, for example, is ensuring that partners enact a relationship that is personally satisfying but also follows a form that will be supported by family or other network members.

ATTRACTION AND RELATIONAL MANAGEMENT

Attraction is still one important aspect of relational work that promotes the initiation of romantic relationships and adds to meaning-making within it. Classic research regarded attractiveness as a stimulus that is merely perceived and then processed by prospective partners, but more recent views have portrayed it as a competence in the presentation of self as a partner. What is the difference between attractiveness as stimulus and attraction as communicative maintenance of relationships? Actually, this issue was one of the first questions posed in attraction research, with Perrin (1921) distinguishing between static beauty (e.g., physical structure, as it were) and dynamic beauty (e.g., delicacy of movement, self-care, grooming). Unsurprisingly, we would equate "attractiveness as stimulus" with static beauty and "attraction as communicative skill" with the competent elements of relational maintenance that we explore here.

Attractiveness in general, usually the static sort, has been frequently studied and found to be broadly, but not unreservedly, advantageous. Attractive persons are more likely to be chosen as dating partners and be perceived as favorable persons in terms of their personalities (Berscheid, 1994). Moreover, attractiveness gives such people bargaining power over their less attractive romantic partner. The more attractive partners are able to obtain secure higher status in their relationships (Berscheid, 1994). Nonetheless, physically attractive persons are occasionally overlooked as "beyond reach" by potential partners and in fact lead much less exciting social lives than most people suppose (Reis, Nezlek, & Wheeler, 1980).

Because such studies focus on the relatively unchanging features that may bring people together initially, such as physical beauty, other factors have been typically explored by scholars seeking to understand the successful development of a real romantic relationship over time (e.g., Burgess & Huston, 1979). Such studies often focus on comparison level (CL), that is, the benchmark for the assessment of costs and benefits in relationships at large, or comparison level for alternatives (CL_{alt}), that is, the benchmark level of expectation that a person has of finding a relationship that is better than the present one. Our question is "Whose property is this benchmark?" Social exchange theory explains that each romantic partner sets a personal CL and a CL_{alt} for cost–benefit analysis, based on their own past experiences and societal values assigned to the relationship (Thibaut & Kelley, 1959). Such comparison levels are a partner's individual personal benchmarks that reflect only to some extent the culture at large. Relevant to dyadic conduct, however, is romantic partners' communicative attempts to understand each other's comparison level. Actually, without working together to set agreed benchmarks, no one is able to satisfy his or her partner, because everyone has unique goals and needs.

In personal relationships, a partner is not an abstract or average representative of the society but a real and unique person with individual aspirations and expectations. In actual everyday interactions, consideration of partner's personal comparison level is indispensable for making evaluations of the outcome of the relationship as satisfactory. Therefore, a failure in a romantic partner could be attributed less to changes in attractiveness of a person's personal characteristics and more to a failure to share a partner's values in the romantic relationship. In other words, the failure is not due to imbalance in both partners' physical attractiveness levels but to a communicative incompatibility between them about their needs and expectations. The moral of this line of research is that partners can maintain their relationship and their sense of equity in a relationship by talking about their expectations and needs (Acitelli, 1993). Therefore, persons have to learn or be trained to listen deeply to one another, putting aside personal expectations, clarifying carefully and sensitively what the other person is trying to say, with the purpose of increasing mutuality of understanding. Skillful communication is thus not the exchange of resources but the process of reaching an understanding and perhaps an agreement about the value of those resources (Duck, 1994b).

Of course, we cannot establish such agreements with our potential romantic partner until we start a relationship with this person, and this initial step most probably depends on a mixture of individual and cultural standards. However, any increase in intimacy in a relationship is the result of skillful negotiation. Recognizing a certain person as attractive is not the same as becoming romantically attached to that person (although some stalkers apparently do not recognize this fact; Cupach, Spitzberg, & Carson, 2000). As the research on the matching hypothesis implies (Murstein, 1972), an attractive person may be at a disadvantage in that he or she may be left aside as beyond the reasonable reach of the attracted person. The matching hypothesis presumes that moderately or less attractive (in terms of physical attraction) people avoid an attractive target person because their initial expectation is to be rejected by that person (Feingold, 1988; Murstein, 1972). In other words, a really attractive person may involuntarily declare inaccessibility. For this reason, attractiveness can create dysfunctionality if the attractive person assumes no need for proactive relational maintenance. In short, the naive but popular assumption (represented in many magazines, romance quizzes, and dating agencies) that successful relationships are predicates of positive personal characteristics rather than of successful maintenance strategies is incorrect. Therefore, attractiveness as assessed by the culture at large is not always meaningful for actual personal relationships, because it sometimes prevents the (statically) attractive people from developing prospects of getting to a phase of dynamic attraction with their potential partners. Thus, the key element in maintaining relationships is communication skill.

Communication skills have too often been seen as synonymous with social skills that are socially and culturally defined. In general, social skills mean one's ability to perform behaviors appropriate to cultural norms and one's knowledge of behavioral scripts in context (Argyle, 1975). If a person acquires sufficient social skills in intimate relationships, this person is able to meet a partner's expectations and make the relationship develop smoothly and maintain it satisfactorily. Therefore, partners with poor skills (such as shyness, speech dysfluencies, inappropriateness of language, such as frequent profanity—Winters & Duck, 2000) have been recognized as losers in the "love for sale" market. However, Burleson and Denton's (1992) research corrects this assumption. They compared "skilled" couples' marital satisfactions with those of "unskilled" couples. The "skills" in their study mean the ability to take the spouses' perspectives accurately, to create and use sophisticated, comforting, informative, persuasive, and regulative messages, and to develop and achieve more complex goals appropriate to the situations. However, they could not find significant differences in satisfaction between these two types of couples. Given such research findings, Burleson and Samter (1994) argue that it is not each partner's individual skill but the similarities in the level of both partners' communication skills that affect the maintenance of satisfaction in close relationships.

The totality of the relational partners' view of their relationship contributes to the maintenance of their relationship, and it is similarity of values and of deep understanding of each other's meaning systems that enables partners to share fully in their relationship. Here, similarity does not mean similarity in demographic characteristics or attitudes towards the relationship but similarities in relational experiences and future plans as well as routine behavior-like scripts (Duck, 1994b). Similarity in understandings of relational processes maintains relationships because each relational act is recognized as meaningful to the relationship partner (Acitelli, 2001). It is important to recognize that a personal relationship is a joint act that lasts for a period; a relational act is not just a one-time occurrence, but it happens repeatedly in a different or transformed way through communication of various sorts. However, such changes do not bewilder relational partners, who can identify variations within the range of relational acceptability; this identification is a practical management of dialectical tensions between stability and change (Baxter & Montgomery, 1996). It is relational partners' shared meaning that brings them this maintenance skill, via satisfaction derived from the ability to deal smoothly with relational problems.

So, what constitutes the range of appropriate maintenance skills? In the initial stage of romantic relationships, the range contains social skills that are based strongly on public cultural norms in partners' network members, because romantic partners do not invent a unique way of interactions before the relationship starts. Those who do not have skills or do not know appropriate behaviors in particular situations tend to fail in the initiation of romantic relationships with the unfamiliar target persons or who fail to realize limits around the behaviors that most members of the culture recognize as appropriate. For instance, one of the authors previously introduced the following personal experience as a good example of unskilled relational effort that would be broadly recognized as such:

> An example from my personal experience of this difficulty happened when I was in hurry once and running to an appointment. One of my pupils, an awkward young woman with minor behavioral problems, rushed up to me in the drizzle and thrust into my hand a piece of birthday cake wrapped in a paper bag. Evidently she had just celebrated her 21st birthday, had a secret crush on me and was trying to start something going. Soggy birthday cake in the drizzle when I was in a rush would seem like a pretty poor way to start, but she clearly did not realize this. Not everyone knows how to "read" the situation and to reserve the attempt at friend-making until a suitable moment. (Duck, 1991, pp. 34–35)

Most of us recognize this 21-year-old woman as poorly skilled. If we had been friends of hers, we could have advised her not to do what she did. We would have pointed out the following five points that support our judgment of her incompetence: (1) In the drizzle, most people do not like walking, let alone standing and holding a conversation; (2) Most people do not go out when it is a bad weather unless they have something to do; (3) Most people feel a bit insulted when they are given a piece of leftover birthday cake; (4) Most of us recognize that an ordinary paper bag is not a suitable wrapping for a gift; (5) Most of us do not customarily expect to celebrate the birthday of someone with whom we have little relational connection. We attribute ineptness here because we have learned how to read situations and how to choose appropriate behaviors contingent on the situations. This woman's behavior was outside the range of normative appropriateness.

As the French proverb has it, however, "To know all is to forgive all." We could reinterpret the prior episode by making allowances for the woman's behavior based on our understanding and acceptance of her intent; alternatively, if we knew her well, we might make such allowance "because that's how she is" and we have come to accept the eccentricity as endearing in some way. Waiting in the drizzle represents her good intentions and positive feelings. A piece of leftover birthday cake might have been intended as a very personal and unique present. Her wish to share it meant that the recipient was specially chosen. Also, a paper bag might have signified that she was free from vanity. If her behavior is understood in this way, then in terms of its personal context it is very meaningful. What is lacking is the full personal understanding that makes the interpretation sustainable, and the donor omitted the steps necessary to maintain the possibility of this interpretation. What motivated this woman is located within the range of appropriate behavior between people who know one another well, but her expression of inclusiveness lacked the necessary precursive steps. It was very unlucky for her that there was no one who previously shared the same range of appropriate behaviors for the initiation of romance, and that the target unfortunately had insufficient time to include her behavior in the range of appropriate behaviors by reflecting on them, because he was in a hurry. The challenging environment prevented them from further communication. Furthermore, he also did not have a chance to normalize her range of appropriateness by letting her understand that her behavior was not suitable. Again, there is a rule: Read the situation and make its treatment appropriate to the relationship that exists between the participants.

CONFLICT MANAGEMENT

Does conflict cause romantic relationships to deteriorate? In order to deal with such a question, we need to combine the previous points about relationship maintenance, whether at individual, social, or cultural levels. As our earlier example of unsuccessful rescue shows, some social contexts prescribe a very narrow range of appropriate behaviors. Therefore, whether or not those behaviors might result in success, the performers' appropriate behaviors are regarded as skillful. Even in close relationships, there are some situations that limit the range of appropriateness. On the other hand, in close relationships, we have some situations in which we can negotiate the range of appropriateness with our partners. Thus, in any discussion of maintenance of relationships there arises the constant interplay between the dyadic, social, and cultural levels of interaction through which partners must negotiate a relational form that satisfies not only their own dyadic needs but is also acceptable to their immediate social network and society at large. For these reasons, such issues as conflict management cannot be seen as merely individual or dyadic activity but as something that plays to the network as "referees" (Klein & Johnson, 2000; Klein & Milardo, 1993) and during which "maintenance of relationships" is created not only dyadically but also occasionally by people in the network.

As Lloyd and Cate (1985) note, certain sorts of conflict are typically destructive (e.g., conflicts about the other person's personal habits), but other sorts of conflict are actually productive of relationship enhancement (e.g., conflict about role assignment in the relationship and discussion of its internal dynamic). The general consensus of researchers appears to be that it depends on how relational partners manage their conflicts. None of us is able to prevent all kinds of any conflicts with our relational partners, because these appear to be a routine part of relationships. However, it is not impossible to prevent the reoccurrence of the same conflicts or the subsequent conflicts caused by the initial one. Canary, Cupach, and Messman (1995) point out that "conflict behaviors do not appear to have a direct influence on relational outcomes; rather, people first interpret conflict behaviors in terms of how appropriate and effective the partner was, and these interpretations filter the effects due to conflict behavior" (p. 107). In general, conflicts between romantic partners are characterized by partners' short-term or long-term loss of togetherness due to incompatibilities between both partners' values or interests in their relationships (Cahn, 1990, 1992; Canary, Cupach, and Messman, 1995). An extremely serious cause of conflicts in romantic relationships is marital transgression by one or both partners' violation of the social norms of monogamy (Metts, 1994). However, in most cases, interpersonal conflicts are due to partners' temporarily impaired communicative behaviors (Cahn, 1990). The relational behaviors by which partners assert their disagreements with their partners, identify and solve the problems that cause the disagreements, and express their dissatisfaction with the relationships may temporarily stray beyond the boundaries for acceptable variation. Conflicts do not originally derive from partners' negative intentions to damage their partners or relationships but from variation from previously established bandwidths for behavior (Duck & Wood, 1995). Therefore, relationship conflict itself is not inherently harmful for relationship maintenance; rather, it has potential to facilitate the maintenance of romantic relationships if it is properly managed, because "conflict plays a critical role in the ways in which people come to understand how social interaction functions to promote individual needs within personal relationships" (Canary et al., 1995, p. 2).

Relational conflict in a narrow sense signifies a relational challenge that originates in atypical departures from normalized conduct of positive regard (Duck & Wood, 1995). In such an impaired relationship experience, partners need management skills that normalize their relational interactions; in other words, partners make efforts to turn their atypical conducts into ones that are prototypical to their relationship. Theoretically, prototypes are "construed to resemble instances which are complete with all their attributes, even those that are irrelevant to category membership" (Ginsburg, 1988, p. 33). Therefore, romantic couples are flexibly able to identify any of their challenges with their relationship's prototypes, some exemplary interactions that represent their relationship well. Thus, we contend that successful management of this type of conflict involves communication as a catalyst to enhance interactions between romantic partners and help them jointly reconstruct their sense of relational stability or personal chemistry. By this means they increase shared meanings, which are different from each other's personal meanings before their conflict. The result of this sort of conflict is therefore a strengthened relational compound, to pursue our metaphor.

Such conflict management communication requires that both relational partners have positive regard towards each other despite conflict about topic on the one hand and the existence of negative regard for partner on the other hand are often confused. Duck and Wood (1995) define two types of relational challenges deriving from prototypical conducts: difficulty, which is based on positive regard, and inherently negative relations, which is based on negative regard (as in an enemyship, Wiseman & Duck, 1995). In other words, prototypical relational interactions do not require relational partners to have unconditional positive regard for each other, because mutual recognition of *negative* regard is elemental for enemies (because enemyship is a stable but negative relationship and enables enemies to establish consistent and foreseeable negative relationships). Such a relationship is theoretically possible (Wiseman & Duck, 1995) even though sufficient empirical research evidence has not yet been reported. In most cases, romantic relationships that have been undermined by increasingly negative regard are easily dissolved because such relationships dissatisfy romantic partners who are still psychologically or socially tied up in their relationships. So far as satisfaction is one of the well-studied criteria for comfort with a relationship, it is reasonable to presume that positive regard must underlie successful conflict management. Because a relational conflict is often based on unshared meanings including different goals evident in behaviors that are not in themselves intended to harm the relationship, partners' positive regard cannot necessarily be assumed to turn negative during the management of a conflict. It is their behaviors that turn (temporarily) negative, not necessarily their feelings towards each other. On the other hand, most prototypical relational challenges on negative regard can be seen as transitional processes towards either "difficult relationships" with positive regard, or toward dissolution of the relationship. It may be difficult to establish enemyship without organizational, sociocultural, or socioemotional constraints.

Romantic partners' intentionality in their conflict management is based on their positive regard for one another. Many research findings have presented the data that personal relationships are stabilized if both partners cooperatively and gently solve their problems by reconfirming and resetting their mutually shared goals rather than seeking and sticking to individual interests. Therefore, partners should not avoid their partners or conflict management if they want to avoid the future deterioration of their relationships (Cahn, 1992; Canary et al., 1995; Cate & Lloyd, 1992). For instance, Canary and his associates (Canary & Cupach, 1988; Canary & Spitzberg, 1987, 1989) defined three strategies of conflict management communication: integrative strategies, which are prosocial and oriented to relational goals, such tactics as seeking areas of agreement, expressing trust in the partners, and negotiating alternative solutions through open and friendly discussions; distributive strategies, which are competitive, antisocial, and oriented to individual goals, such tactics as faulting the partners, asking hostile questions, presumptuously attributing the problems to the partners' characteristics, seeking unilateral behavioral changes from the partners, and showing aggression with insults, threats, and sarcasm; and avoidant strategies, which avoid direct conflicts and minimize the conflictual tensions, such tactics as shifting the focus of conversations, and expressing dissatisfaction ambiguously by irritating the partners (e.g., teasing the partners, making the partners feel jealous, and so on). These latter actions allow prolonged intrapsychic processes of brooding and self-reflection that simultaneously imply the absence of sharing of these feelings or perceptions with the partner and therefore builds up a meaning for the blamed behaviors that is not seriously challenged. Brooding builds on and inflames itself (Duck, 1984, 1994a). Canary and his associates showed that integrative strategies brought more satisfaction to the partners and were perceived as more appropriate and efficient by the partners than their distributive or avoidant counterparts. Therefore, appropriate conflict management is not to find a way to judge which partner is right or to remove an alleged cause of the problem any more than to pretend to ignore the problem. We argue that "integrative" is not synonymous with "compliant." Constructing relational goals does not signify reading each other's face to imagine each other's goals—that is the only first step toward the relational goals. The integration of each other's individuals goals requires communicative processes in order to make the two partners' perspectives realign with each other (Duck, 1994b).

Good conflict management is a communicative process in which romantic partners explore common goals to surmount the difficulties of their relationship and share some common beliefs about reasonable ways to achieve such goals. Therefore, these forms and manners of relationship conflict enhance partners' mutuality. However, it is important that no one suggests that romantic partners should invent conflicts in order to get to know their partners better. Indeed, some romantic partners adopt mock negativity as a part of their idiomatic communication and enjoy teasing their partners (Bell et al., 1987), and some even agree to mock warfare with their partner just for excitement (Sternberg, 1998). However, our definition of relationship conflict does not categorize these instances as real relationship conflict, because such pseudonegativity does not go wrong until the partners get tired of such negativity and denote it as an appropriate interactional style for the present. So long as pseudonegativity represents typical communication based on positive regard for each other, romantic couples will not lose their togetherness. However, real conflict would occur once these romantic partners perceive that their partners' negativity deviates from the range of appropriateness that they have coconstructed.

In our view, relationship conflict occurs when both partners' range of appropriateness does not overlap in their interpretation of a particular behavior or incident. Because everyday life is filled with variation, unpredictability, and uncertainty, it is normal that relational partners confront an unexpected event and notice the discrepancy between each other's interpretation of the event. It is also normal that routine communicative behaviors suddenly obtain different meanings and become inappropriate (e.g., profanity may be acceptable at home but not when dining with friends, and so could provoke arguments on the drive home after the meal because it signifies a relational violation, Winters & Duck, 2000). Whereas personal relationships are not rigid but fluid, relationship maintenance is not characterized by accumulation of knowledge about partners but by "ongoing practical improvisation" (Baxter & Montgomery, 1996, p. 76). Relationship conflict can happen even if relational partners make maximum effort to prevent it, because conflict arises when such effort is no longer effective without updating the bandwidth of appropriateness. In this sense, romantic relationships are similar to automobiles; even the most careful drivers are not exempted from tuning up their cars and having their wheels brought back into alignment. Relationship conflict functions as a sign that notifies relational partners of the time for realignment.

In their exhaustive review on the research on relationship conflict, Canary, Cupach, and Messman (1995) point out the equivocality about the effects of avoidant communication and conclude that "avoidance can be either functional or dysfunctional for a relationship, depending on how it is manifested and what the shared relational norms dictate" (p. 138). Indeed, it is true that many satisfied relational partners usually avoid confrontation and that relationship stability is not necessarily a product of both partners' accurate perceptions of mutual agreement (Cahn, 1992, for review). If relational partners' temporary disagreement does not cause any consequent problems that may cause another conflict, avoidance could be a clever strategy. However, if the initial conflict does not die away, the partners are more likely to perceive that their problem gets worse. McCullough et al. (1998) analyzed the process of forgiveness in personal relationships, and they concluded that the more the partners liked their partners, the more likely they were to ruminate over the problems; however, their data implied that such ruminations would motivate the dissatisfied partners to take revenge on their partners who had hurt them. Cloven and Roloff (1991) presented data that suggest that prolonged thoughts about conflicts increase the perceived severity of the conflicts and the likelihood of blaming the partners, unless the problems are solved by integrative conflict management communication. Unsolved initial conflicts are very harmful especially for romantic relationships. For instance, Lloyd and Cate (1985) point out both romantic partners' love and satisfaction with their partners are damaged by the prolonged conflicts that were initiated by female partners. Once romantic partners lose the feeling of togetherness with their partners, their conflict management becomes much more difficult. The lack of intimacy tends to make the conflicts more escalated and lets partners include other issues in their current conflict including their complaints about conflict management communication (Gottman, 1994; Rands, Levinger, & Mellinger, 1981). Furthermore, avoidance connotes an imbalance in power dynamics between romantic partners. Roloff and Cloven (1990) point out that avoidance is the conflict management communication for those romantic partners who perceive that their partners have superior alternatives and those who believe that their own alternative romantic partners are superior to the current partners'. In other words, avoidance is inherently destructive because it implies that at least one partner of the romantic relationship is ready to disengage from the relationship.

Avoidance is an ineffective maintenance strategy as it is destructive to the romantic relationship. In her theoretical model of reactions to unsatisfactory relationships, Rusbult (1987) names avoidance as "Neglect" and classifies it into destructive responses as well as "Exit," which means dissolution. On the other hand, she posits two types of constructive response to relational dissatisfaction: "Voice," that is, active solutions including discussions about the problem, compromise, requests for professional help, and so on, and "Loyalty," passive solutions such as waiting for improvement. Indeed, it may be ideal that both "Voice" and "Loyalty" work together in conflict management; however, we need to point out the risk of "Loyalty," which may actually become "Neglect." For example, "Loyal" partners in abusive relationships are likely to interpret their relationships as normal romantic relationships with difficulties based on positive regards and to justify their partner's violence by blaming themselves for such difficulties. We argue that "Loyalty" without shared relational goals is identical to "Neglect"—avoidance strategies in conflict management. Here, stability of relationships is problematic. Such abusive relationships are not necessarily stabilized by partners' interdependency due to the lack of alternative partners. If this explanation is correct, abusive relationships would not entrap those who obtain sufficient social and economical resources. However, Rosen (1996) points out that some women who are socially and economically independent continue to stay in their abusive relationships. Her data show that these women rely on their "romantic fantasies," which justify their male romantic partners' violence. One of those dangerous "fantasies" is "Beauty and the Beast Fantasy," in which abused women "seemed to be under the illusion that they could be the ones who could save their boyfriends from their insecurities or mold them into kind and sensitive partners" (Rosen, 1996, p. 162). Marshall and Vitanza (1994) call attention to the danger of the entrapment with myths regarding physical abuse in romantic relationships. In the real world, it is very unlikely that the abusers naturally and voluntarily begin to acknowledge their misdeeds and reform. Harvey (1995) also argues that it is very harmful to believe that romantic partners' physical aggression is excused by nonrelational factors such as alcoholism and substance abuse, hormone balance and physiological phenomena, and socioeconomical statuses.

Practitioners need to prevent the abused partners' "Loyal" (Rusbult, 1987) from being loyal to such dangerously optimistic fantasies and myths that divert them from constructive negotiation with the abusive partners. It is notable that romantic partners' shared meanings about their relationships do not unconditionally benefit both partners. As we noted earlier, relationship maintenance requires both partners have positive regard for each other; however, the partners in abusive relationships self-deceptively regard their relationships as *"relationships with inherent difficulties based on positive regard"* (Duck & Wood, 1995). From the external view, however, inherent difficulties in abusive relationships are not actually inherent at all. Abuse is not inherent in prototypical romantic relationships. Therefore, therapists help the abused change their relational construct from prototypical to atypical. Based on Duck and Wood's (1995) framework, this process sounds like creation of another "conflict" rather than solution of the conflict. However, partners of impaired relationships need to know that their typical interactions are not prototypical but atypical. Once partners perceive that their relationships are atypical, they are able to seek alternative relational constructs for a new prototypical relational interaction that can be accepted by their network members and culture at-large. Furthermore, they gain another alternative strategy to handle the "conflict": They can change their view of their partners' intentionality in their atypical relational interactions. Duck and Wood (1995) define atypical challenges on the basis of negative regard as "Spoiling" characterized by betrayal and revenge. Especially for the abused partners, recognition of the "Spoiling" is very important for the maintenance of themselves rather than their relationships. As Duck (1984) points out, repair of personal relationships does not necessarily mean repair of impaired or broken relationships; repairing processes primarily enable relational partners to repair themselves as persons who have been damaged by their relationships. Paradoxically, therefore, dissolution is a possible strategy of relationship repair—for not only abusive relationships but also other dysfunctional relationships. When dissolution is itself the road to repair, it is very important that romantic partners maintain their shared meanings about their past romantic relationships, as we discuss next.

DISSOLUTION

Even though relational dissolution is culturally assumed to be the result of significant lack of mutual communication skills, it has also been classified as skillful maintenance, in that there are times when it promotes the integrity of the individual, even if at the expense of the relationship (Duck, 1984), as in the case of abusive relationships, for instance. Practitioners' goals are not always therefore to prevent relationship dissolution, but also to establish whether dissolution may in fact be a better option for one (or both) partner(s) enmeshed in a dysfunctional relationship. It can be a relational process that requires appropriate communication skills to accomplish it smoothly and satisfactorily. Wilmot, Carbaugh, and Baxter's (1985) work emphasizes the importance of mutuality in dissolutive processes. Their result also shows that Verbal Indirectness [attempts to end the relationship without an explicit statement of the goal, as for example in a discussion of the "state of the relationship"] is a better termination strategy than Nonverbal Withdrawal [for example, saying nothing but avoiding contact] and Verbal Directness [direct and unambiguous statements of a desire to withdraw from a relationship]. Compared with the latter two, those who had used Verbal Indirectness in their termination of romantic relationships reported the least regrets about the communication strategies that they chose. At first glance, both Verbal Indirectness and Nonverbal Withdrawal seem backhanded strategies of dissolution. However, Verbal Indirectness tends to bring about positive outcomes because it does not mean avoidance; Verbal Indirectness decreases the degree of intimacy from romantic level to nonromantic by eliminating communication that is specific to romantic partners. Unlike Nonverbal Withdrawal, which is nothing more than avoidance, Verbal Indirectness may enhance de-escalation of the romantic relationship, which can be the pathway to friendship after the breakup (Banks, Altendorf, Greene, & Cody, 1987). Why is Verbal Indirectness the optimal strategy of relationship disengagement? Unfortunately, how Verbal Indirectness functions has not yet been clarified. However, researchers have identified disadvantages of the other two: Verbal Directness is so blunt that the action apparently boomerangs and produces negative reactions for both partners; and Nonverbal Withdrawal is so impolite and ambiguous that the action strongly discourages both partners from further interactions (Metts, 1992; Wilmot et al., 1985). On the other hand, Verbal Indirectness enables both partners to reassess their current states of their relationships through their indecisive communicative processes—gradually, incrementally, and mutually. It is notable that we do not argue that relationship disengaging communication should be ambiguous; what we emphasize is that relationship dissolution requires both partners of communication skills that do not hastily limit both partners' options and degrees of freedom, because dissolution should be accomplished by both partners' mutual agreement and adaptation, which require of them plenty of time.

Why does it take time to dissolve romantic relationships with minimal distress? It is because dissolution is not a one-time event but a process, a series of events. Dissolution consists of several phases (Baxter, 1984, 1985; Duck, 1982; Lee, 1984). Therefore, it is very difficult to identify universal skills that prevent partners from unpleasant outcomes. Although we have just noted that Verbal Indirectness may be the optimal strategy (Wilmot et al., 1985), another study presented data that some verbally direct tactics such as justification of breakup decrease depression after dissolution (Banks et al., 1987). Verbal Directness is suitable for one phase but may not be for another, based on Duck's (1982) four-phase model of relationship dissolution. His stage model of relational dissolution suggests that different communication behaviors are suitable for different phases of dissolutive processes. Indeed, there are several complex, but interrelated, phases to dissolution that involve skillful adaptation, communication, and mutual adaptation—not only of the concerned individuals but also of their networks (Duck, 1982). Duck's four-phase model of romantic dissolution consists of Intrapsychic, Dyadic, Social, and Grave-dressing phases. Directness is not appropriate in the first, Intrapsychic, phase in which at least one partner silently evaluates the state of the relationship and ponders whether or not to maintain it. Direct reference to dissolution surfaces in the second, Dyadic, phase when the partners confront one another with their concerns. When dissolution reaches the Social phase, network members become involved mostly as consultants and advisors about the relationship and its handling. The fourth, Grave-dressing, phase is when partners need to account for their break-up to themselves and to their social network members. The fourth phase is one more clinically significant phase of relational breakup, where persons re-evaluate or re-establish a sense of self-worth and of their value as potential future partners for other people.

Recent theoretical frameworks confirm that dissolution is composed of several phases. Battaglia, Richard, Datteri, and Lord's (1998) recent research interestingly found that multiple phases of dissolutive processes are cultural scripts; dissolution requires partners to perform a series of communicative behaviors. It is notable that Battaglia et al. argue that not single phases but the whole set of phases are culturally defined as appropriate communicative strategies. In other words, the enactment of a series of multiple phases is itself a skill (Lee, 1984). Battaglia et al. also found out that some communicative behaviors (e.g., showing their lack of interest, keeping distance, trying to work out the problems in relationships) repetitively appeared in different phases. This finding supports the recent approaches to dissolution that assume that it develops through cyclic alterations of separation (e.g., keeping distance) and integration (e.g., working things out; Conville, 1988; Masheter & Harris, 1986).

Of course, phase models are not the only tools for investigating the ways in which persons maintain psychological health through communication. Metts (1992) proposes a new theoretical framework named the Face-work Model of Disengagement, based on Goffman's (1971) face management and Brown and Levinson's (1987) politeness theory. Metts' model shows that the appropriate communicative skill is determined by the severity of of-fense in the situation and the degree of politeness that the person wants to present. Her application of face-work to dissolution explains how romantic partners adapt to their relationship challenges and how they negotiate their relational selves, which are accountable to each other. Therefore, her model is another approach to the dissolution as transformation of relationship and of changes in the meanings that are shared in the relationship. In other words ⁺he primary objective of theories and research on dissolutive communication skills is to explain which communicative behaviors help romantic partners make sense of their dissolutive processes, that is, their joint redefinition of their relationship.

We conclude this section by referring to the necessity of communication skills for dissolution. First, dissolution of romantic relationships is not just a problem for romantic partners themselves but also for their network members; the loss of romantic partners sometimes mean the subsequent loss of friends associated with the former romantic partners (Johnson & Leslie, 1982; Milardo, 1982). Romantic partners need to minimize their partners' distress if they want to continue their friendships with mutual friends whom they share with their partners and also maintain good reputations among these people (Metts, 1992, 1997). Appropriate communication skills for relationship dissolution are essential for those romantic partners who want or need the maintenance of their relationships as friendships (Banks et al., 1987; Metts et al., 1989). Especially, divorced couples with children need to establish and manage functional ex-spousal relationships as co-parenting partnerships (Ahrons, 1994).

Second, even if romantic partners do not want further interactions with their partners and mutual network members, they still need proper skills in order to protect themselves from potential subsequent troubles. As noted in recent investigations into stalking (Cupach, Spitzberg, & Carson, 2000; Emerson, Ferris, & Gardner, 1998), one of the largest categories of stalkers is former romantic partners who do not accept a breakup initiated by their partners. Currently, it is still difficult to profile characteristics of those who are very likely to be stalkers. Indeed, some of them may suffer from erotomania or paranoia; however, others have been normal and decent until their painful breakups. In other words, any single romantic breakdown has potential to make the dissatisfied partner begin to pursue his or her heartbreaker for another negotiation or even revenge.

Although it sounds obvious, there are many research findings that emphasize the importance of mutuality in the dissolution of romantic relationships. When romantic partners cannot control the dissolutive processes of their romantic relationships, they tend to suffer from psychological distress (Frazier & Cook, 1993; Sprecher, Felmlee, Metts, Fehr, & Vanni, 1998), and this tendency is salient in male partners (Fine & Sacher, 1997; Helgeson, 1994). Given these findings, it is sensible advice to say "If you don't want to feel miserable, you'd better take the initiative in breaking up your romantic relationship as soon as possible." From our view, which attaches importance to shared meanings, however, such a competitive strategy would not help either or both partners. The initiators' neglect of communication strategies that are appropriate to their partners deprived not only the poor partners but also the intiators themselves of the opportunity to make sense of their breakups and to access their partners' thoughts of sense-making processes. Perhaps, the initiators of dissolution "win" their love games at the time of breakups; later, however, some of them may feel indebtedness derived from their own reassessment of their acts as cruel (Wilmot et al., 1985). Guilt forces the initiators to face a dilemma: Whereas guilt enhances their communal attachment to the partners whom they hurt, it also make them want to avoid direct interactions with the partners (Baumeister, Stillwell, & Heatherton, 1994). Therefore, some of them need justifications of their breakups in order to make them feel better (Banks et al., 1987). However, if the initiators made sufficient effort to share their relationship dissolution with their former partners, they would be free from such complicated intrapsychic processes of rumination. As we have noted in other parts of this chapter, rumination harms relationships and individuals. Because personal relationships are not individuals' property but both partners' jointly shared constructs, once partners lose accessibility to their partners, their problems associated with their relationships cannot be solved any longer.

CONCLUDING REMARKS

So, what are communication skills for relationship maintenance? Anything that keeps a relationship in existence, anything that lets the relationship go as it goes, and anything meaningful for the relationship—this is our answer to this question, trivial as it sounds. However, the key here is that partners who are able to maintain their relationships by making sense of their relational interactions do the best. Therefore, a practitioner's role is subtly to assist the unique sense-making processes. Relational partners' day-to-day interactions are trivial from the viewpoint of outside observers; however, the partners naturally acquire the skills that transform such trivial communicative interactions into meaningful activities that sustain their relationships. Unless the partners begin to recognize their trivial interactions as trivial or meaningless, they do not need practitioners' help to maintain their relationship. However, it is notable that the communication skills of the relational partners in trouble are those same skills that enable them to resume trivial, everyday talk with their partners. Everyday talk is essential to any personal relationship "because it continues to embody partners' understanding or shared meaning, and it continues to represent their relationship to one another in ways that each accepts and is comfortable with, or which 'ratify' the relationship" (Duck, 1994a, p. 54). As we note in this chapter, communication based on partners' individual unshared goals tends to hinder the partners' relationship maintenance; when they keep talking, they keep a relationship growing.

As we have indicated, communication skills in dissolution processes are as important as those in other relational processes in helping both partners reach a sense of understanding of their relational worlds. Relationships are not established and maintained only because of specific social constraints or particular purposes; relationships are important in themselves. We relate to others because of this important human fact. Therefore, we disagree with the idea that "romantic relationships are sustained and restored to the extent partners desire and create barriers to dissolution" (Attridge, 1994, p. 142). Do people have to prepare for their dissolution when they initiate their romantic relationships? We do not think so. These social and psychological barriers (such as family and coworkers) are just some of the resources that justify relationships. These barriers would not work unless both partners agree on their significance, because it is such exterior influences, rather than private preferences of partners, that "mark out" what is an inappropriate relationship or inappropriate behavior in a relationship (Duck & VanderVoort, 2001). Thus, we suggest that the major task for clinicians is to realign the meanings that partners have or share about their relationship's end. If one partner's evaluation of the meaning of the relationship is not matched by the other, it is harder for them both to make sense of the other person's behaviors after the dissolution.

People dissolve their romantic relationships simply because they are not able to cooperatively define their relationships as romantic relationships any longer. Therefore, we emphasize the importance of communication skills for dissolution that help them redefine their new relationships with ex-romantic partners. We believe that romantic partners need communicative processes of dissolution even if they have no plan of further interactions, because we assume that the lack of redefinition may nullify the whole meanings of the relationships that romantic partners have jointly constructed. As Sprecher and Fehr (1998) point out, dissolution traumatizes ex-partners when it is not socially acknowledged. If ex-partners think that the dissolution is not even acknowledged by their partners, it would be much more painful than it should be. As Duck (1982, 1984) notes, final dissolution is only a part of longer-term relational process that bring about the end of the relationship.

REFERENCES

Acitelli, L. K. (1993). You, me, and us: Perspectives on relationship awareness. In S. W. Duck (Ed.), *Individuals in relationships [Understanding relationships processes 1]* (pp. 144–174.) Newbury Park, CA: Sage.

Acitelli, L. K. (2001). Maintaining and enhancing a relationship by attending to it. In J. H. Harvey & A. Wenzel (Eds.), *Close, romantic relationships: Maintenance and enhancement*. Mahwah, NJ: Lawrence Erlbaum Associates.

Ahrons, C. R. (1994). *Good divorce: Keeping your family together when family comes apart*. New York: HarperCollins.

Argyle, M. (1975). *Bodily communication*. London: Methuen.

Aron, A., Dutton, D. G., Aron, E., & Iverson, A. (1989). Experiences of falling in love. *Journal of Social and Personal Relationships, 6*, 243–257.

Attridge, M. (1994). Barriers to dissolution of romantic relationships. In D. J. Canary & L. Stafford (Eds.), *Communication and relational maintenance* (pp. 141–164). San Diego: Academic Press.

Banks, S. P., Altendorf, D. M., Greene, J. O., & Cody, M. J. (1987). An examination of relationship disengagement: Perceptions, breakup strategies and outcomes. *Western Journal of Speech Communication, 51*, 19–41.

Battaglia, D. M., Richard, F. D., Datteri, D. L., & Lord, C. G. (1998). Breaking up is (relatively) easy to do: A script for the dissolution of close relationships. *Journal of Social and Personal Relationships, 15*, 829–845.

Baumeister, R. F., Stillwell, A. M., & Heatherton, T. F. (1994). Guilt: An interpersonal approach. *Psychological Bulletin, 115*, 243–267.

Baxter, L. A. (1984). Trajectories of relationship disengagement. *Journal of Social and Personal Relationships, 1*, 29–48.

Baxter, L. A. (1985). Accomplishing relationship disengagement. In S. W. Duck & D. Perlman (Eds.), *Understanding personal relationships* (pp. 243–265). London: Sage.

Baxter, L. A. (1987). Symbols of relationship identity in relationship cultures. *Journal of Social and Personal Relationships, 4*, 261–280.

Baxter, L. A., & Bullis, C. (1986). Turning points in developing romantic relationships. *Human Communication Research, 12*, 469–493.

Baxter, L. A., & Montgomery, B. M. (1996). *Relating: Dialogs and dialectics*. New York: Guilford Press.

Bell, R. A., Buerkel-Rothfuss, N., & Gore, K. (1987). "Did you bring the yarmulke for the Cabbage Patch kid?" The idiomatic communication of young lovers. *Human Communication Research, 14*, 47–67.

Berscheid, E. (1994). Interpersonal relationships. *Annual Review of Psychology, 45*, 79–129.

Bombar, M., & Littig, L. W. (1996). Babytalk as a communication of intimate attachment: An initial study in adult romances and friendships. *Personal Relationships, 3*, 137–158.

Brown, P., & Levinson, S. C. (1987). *Politeness: Some universals in language usage*. Cambridge, UK: Cambridge University Press.

Bruess, C. J. S., & Pearson, J. C. (1993). "Sweet pea" and "pussy cat": An examination of idiom use and marital satisfaction over the life cycle. *Journal of Social and Personal Relationships, 10*, 609–615.

Burgess, R. L., & Huston, T. L. (Eds.). (1979). *Social exchange in developing relationships*. New York: Academic Press.

Burleson, B. R., & Denton, W. H. (1992). A new look at similarity and attraction in marriage: Similarities in social–cognitive and communication skills as predictors of attraction and satisfaction. *Communication Monographs, 59*, 268–287.

Burleson, B. R., Kunkel, A. W., Samter, W., & Werking, K. J. (1996). Men's and women's evaluations of communication skills in personal relationships: When sex differences make a difference— and when they don't. *Journal of Social and Personal Relationships, 13*, 143–152.

Burleson, B. R., & Samter, W. (1994). A social skills approach to relationship maintenance: How individual differences in communication skills affect the achievement of relationship functions. In D. J. Canary & L. Stafford (Eds.), *Communication and relational maintenance* (pp. 61–90). San Diego: Academic Press.

Cahn, D. D. (1990). Intimates in conflict: A research review. In D. D. Cahn (Ed.), *Intimates in conflict: A communication perspective* (pp. 1–22). Hillsdale, NJ: Lawrence Erlbaum Associates.

Cahn, D. D. (1992). *Conflict in intimate relationships*. New York: Guilford Press.

Canary, D. J., & Cupach, W. R. (1988). Relational and episodic characteristics associated with conflict tactics. *Journal of Social and Personal Relationships, 5,* 305–325.

Canary, D. J., Cupach, W. R., & Messman, S. J. (1995). *Relationship conflict: Conflict in parent–child, friendship, and romantic relationships*. Thousand Oaks, CA: Sage Publications.

Canary, D. J., & Spitzberg, B. H. (1987). Appropriateness and effectiveness perceptions of conflict strategies. *Human Communication Research, 14,* 93–118.

Canary, D. J., & Stafford, L. (Eds.). (1994). *Communication and relationship maintenance*. New York: Academic Press.

Cate, R. M., & Lloyd, S. A. (1992). *Courtship*. Newbury Park, CA: Sage Publications.

Cloven, D. H., & Roloff, M. E. (1991). Sense-making activities and interpersonal conflict: Communicative cures for the mulling blues. *Western Journal of Speech Communication, 55,* 134–158.

Conville, R. (1988). Relational transitions: An inquiry into their structure and functions. *Journal of Social and Personal Relationships, 5,* 423–437.

Cupach, W. R., Spitzberg, B. H., & Carson, C. L. (2000). Toward a theory of obsessive relational intrusion and stalking. In K. Dindia & S. W. Duck (Eds.), *Communication and personal relationships* (pp. 131–146). Chichester, UK: Wiley.

Duck, S. W. (1982). A topography of relationship disengagement and dissolution. In S. W. Duck (Ed.), *Personal relationships 4: Dissolving personal relationships* (pp. 1–30). London: Academic Press.

Duck, S. W. (1984). A perspective on the repair of personal relationships: Repair of what, when? In S. W. Duck (Ed.), *Personal relationships 5: Repairing personal relationships* (pp. 1–23). London: Academic Press.

Duck, S. W. (1991). *Friends, for life,* 2nd ed., in UK [*Understanding personal relationships,* in USA]. Hemel Hempstead, UK/New York: Harvester-Wheatsheaf/Guilford.

Duck, S. W. (1994a). Steady as (s)he goes: Relational maintenance as a shared meaning system. In D. J. Canary & L. Stafford (Eds.), *Communication and relational maintenance* (pp. 45–60). San Diego: Academic Press.

Duck, S. W. (1994b). *Meaningful relationships: Talking, sense, and relating*. Thousand Oaks, CA: Sage Publications.

Duck, S. W., Rutt, D. J., Hurst, M., & Strejc, H. (1991). Some evident truths about conversations in everyday relationships: All communication is not created equal. *Human Communication Research, 18,* 228–267.

Duck, S. W., & VanderVoort, L. A. (2001). Scarlet letters and the marking of relationships as inappropriate. In R. Goodwin & D. Cramer (Eds.), *Inappropriate relationships*. Mahwah, NJ: Lawrence Erlbaum Associates.

Duck, S. W., & Wood, J. T. (1995). For better for worse, for richer for poorer: The rough and the smooth of relationships. In S. W. Duck & J. T. Wood (Eds.), *Confronting relationship challenges [Understanding relationship processes 5]* (pp. 1–21). Thousand Oaks, CA: Sage Publications.

Emerson, R. M., Ferris, K. O., & Gardner, C. B. (1998). On being stalked. *Social Problems, 45,* 291–314.

Farr, R. M., & Moscovici, S. (Eds.). (1984). *Social representations*. Cambridge, UK: Cambridge University Press.

Fehr, B., & Russell, J. A. (1991). Concept of love viewed from a prototype perspective. *Journal of Personality and Social Psychology, 60,* 425–438.

Feingold, A. (1988). Matching for attractiveness in romantic partners and same-sex friends: A meta-analysis and theoretical critique. *Psychological Bulletin, 104,* 226–235.

Fine, M. A., & Sacher, J. A. (1997). Predictors of distress following relationship termination among dating couples. *Journal of Social and Clinical Psychology, 16,* 381–388.

Flick, U. (1995). Social representations. In J. A. Smith, R. Harré, & L. Van Langenhove (Eds.), *Rethinking psychology* (pp. 70–96). London: Sage Publications.

Frazier, P. A., & Cook, S. W. (1993). Correlates of distress following heterosexual relationship dissolution. *Journal of Social and Personal Relationships, 10*, 55–67.

Ginsburg, G. P. (1988). Rules, scripts and prototypes in personal relationships. In S. W. Duck (Ed.), *Handbook of personal relationships* (1st ed., pp. 23–39). Chichester, UK: Wiley.

Goffman, E. (1959). *Behaviour in public places*. Harmondsworth: Penguin.

Goffman, E. (1971). *Relations in public: Microstudies of the public order*. New York: Harper & Row.

Gottman, J. M. (1994). *What predicts divorce?* Hillsdale, NJ: Lawrence Erlbaum Associates.

Graham, E. E. (1997). Turning points and commitment in post-divorce relationships. *Communication Monographs, 64*, 350–368.

Gray, J. (1992). *Men are from Mars, women are from Venus*. Clarion: New York.

Harvey, J. H. (1995). *Odyssey of the heart: The search for closeness, intimacy and love*. New York: Freeman.

Helgeson, V. S. (1994). Long-distance romantic relationships: Sex-differences in adjustment and breakup. *Personality and Social Psychology Bulletin, 20*, 254–265.

Hopper, R., Knapp, M. L., & Scott, L. (1981). Couples' personal idioms: Exploring intimate talk. *Journal of Communication, 31*, 23–33.

Huston, T. L. (1994). Courtship antecedents of marital satisfaction and love. In R. Erber & R. Glimmer (Eds.), *Theoretical frameworks for personal relationships* (pp. 43–65). Hillsdale, NJ: Lawrence Erlbaum Associates.

Huston, T. L., Surra, C. A., Fitzgerald, N. M., & Cate, R. M. (1981). From courtship to marriage: Mate selection as an interpersonal process. In S. W. Duck & R. Glimmer (Eds.), *Personal relationships 2: Developing personal relationships* (pp. 53–88). New York: Academic Press.

Johnson, M. P., & Leslie, L. (1982). Couple involvement and network structure: A test of the dyadic withdrawal hypothesis. *Social Psychology Quarterly, 45*, 34–43.

Klein, R. C. A., & Johnson, M. (2000). Strategies of couple conflict. In R. M. Milardo & S. W. Duck (Eds.), *Families as relationships*. Chichester, UK: Wiley.

Klein, R. C. A., & Milardo, R. (1993). Third-party influences on the development and maintenance of personal relationships. In S. W. Duck (Ed.), *Social contexts of relationships [Understanding relationship processes: Volume 3:]* (pp. 55–77). Newbury Park, CA: Sage Publications.

Lee, L. (1984). Sequences in separation: A framework for investigating the endings of personal (romantic) relationships. *Journal of Social and Personal Relationships, 1*, 49–74.

Lloyd, S. A., & Cate, R. M. (1985). The developmental course of conflict in dissolution of premarital relationships. *Journal of Social and Personal Relationships, 2*, 179–194.

Marshall, L. L. & Vitanza, S. A. (1994). Physical abuse in close relationships: Myths and realities. In A. L. Weber & J. H. Harvey (Eds.), *Perspectives on close relationships* (pp. 263–284). Needham Heights, MA: Allyn & Bacon.

Masheter, C., & Harris, L. (1986). From divorce to friendship: A study of dialectic relationship development. *Journal of Social and Personal Relationships, 3*, 177–190.

McCall, G. J. (1982). Becoming unrelated: The management of bond dissolution. In S. W. Duck (Ed.), *Personal relationships 4: Dissolving personal relationships* (pp. 211–232). London: Academic Press.

McCullough, M. E., Rachel, K. C., Sandage, S. J., Worthington, E. L., Brown, S. W., & Hight, T. L. (1988). Interpersonal forgiving in close relationships: II. Theoretical elaboration and measurement. *Journal of Personality and Social Psychology, 75*, 1586–1603.

Metts, S. (1992). The language of disengagement: A face-management perspective. In T. L. Orbuch (Ed.), *Close relationship loss: Theoretical approaches* (pp. 111–127). New York: Springer-Verlag.

Metts, S. (1994). Relational transgression. In W. R. Cupach & B. H. Spitzberg (Eds.), *The dark side of interpersonal communication* (pp. 217–239). Hillsdale, NJ: Lawrence Erlbaum Associates.

Metts, S. (1997). Face and facework: Implications for the study of personal relationships. In S. W. Duck (Ed.), *Handbook of personal relationships* (2nd ed., pp. 373–390). Chichester, UK: Wiley.

Metts, S., Cupach, W., & Bejlovec, R. A. (1989). I love you too much to ever start liking you. *Journal of Social and Personal Relationships, 6,* 259–274.

Milardo, R. M. (1982). Friendship networks in developing relationships: Converging and diverging social environments. *Social Psychology Quarterly, 45,* 163–171.

Murstein, B. I. (1972). Physical attractiveness and marital choice. *Journal of Personality and Social Psychology, 22,* 8–12.

Parks, M. R. (1997). Communication networks and relationship life cycles. In S. W. Duck (Ed.), *Handbook of personal relationships* (2nd ed., pp. 351–372). Chichester, UK: Wiley.

Perrin, F. A. C. (1921). Physical attractiveness and repulsions. *Journal of Experimental Psychology, 4,* 203–217.

Rands, M., Levinger, G., & Mellinger, G. D. (1981). Pattern of conflict resolution and marital satisfaction. *Journal of Family Issues, 2,* 297–321.

Reis, H. T., Nezlek, J., & Wheeler, L. (1980). Physical attractiveness and social interaction. *Journal of Personality and Social Psychology, 38,* 604–617.

Rusbult, C. E. (1987). Responses to dissatisfaction in close relationships: The Exit–Voice–Loyalty–Neglect model. In D. Perlman & S. W. Duck (Eds.), *Intimate relationships: Development, dynamics, deterioration* (pp. 209–238). London: Sage.

Roloff, M. E., & Cloven, D. H. (1990). The chilling effect in interpersonal relationships: The reluctance to speak one's mind. In D. D. Cahn (Ed.), *Intimates in conflict: A communication perspective* (pp. 49–76). Hillsdale, NJ: Lawrence Erlbaum Associates.

Rosen, K. H. (1996). The ties that bind women to violent premarital relationships: Processes of seduction and entrapment. In D. D. Cahn & S. A. Lloyd (Eds.), *Family violence from a communication perspective* (pp. 151–176). Thousand Oaks, CA: Sage.

Russell, J. A. (1991). In defense of a prototype approach to emotion concepts. *Journal of Personality and Social Psychology, 60,* 37–47.

Segrin, C. (2000). Interpersonal relationships and mental health problems. In K. Dindia & S. W. Duck (Eds.), *Communication and personal relationships* (pp. 95–112). Chichester, UK: Wiley.

Shotter, J. (1992). What is a "personal" relationship?: A rhetorical–responsive account of "unfinished business." In J. H. Harvey, T. L. Orbuch, & A. L. Weber (Eds.), *Attributions, accounts, and close relationships* (pp. 19–39). New York: Springer-Verlag.

Spanier, G. B. (1976). Measuring dyadic adjustment: New scales for assessing the quality of marriage and similar dyads. *Journal of Marriage and the Family, 38,* 15–28.

Spitzberg, B. H. (1993). The dialectics of (in)competence. *Journal of Social and Personal Relationships, 10,* 137–158.

Spitzberg, B. H., & Cupach, W. R. (1984). *Interpersonal communication competence.* Beverly Hills, CA: Sage.

Sprecher, S. (1994). Two sides to the breakup of dating relationships. *Personal Relationships, 1,* 199–222.

Sprecher, S., & Fehr, B. (1998). The dissolution of close relationships. In J. H. Harvey (Ed.), *Perspectives on loss: A sourcebook* (pp. 99–112). Philadelphia: Brunner/Mazel.

Sprecher, S., Felmlee, D., Metts, S., Fehr, B., & Vanni, D. (1998). Factors associated with distress following the breakup of a close relationship. *Journal of Social and Personal Relationships, 15,* 791–809.

Sternberg, R. J. (1998). *Love is a story: A new theory of relationships.* New York: Oxford University Press.

Surra, C. A., Arizzi, P., & Asmussen, L. (1988). The association between reasons for commitment and the development and outcome of marital relationships. *Journal of Social and Personal Relationships, 5,* 47–63.

Thibaut, J. W., & Kelley, H. H. (1959). *The social psychology of groups.* New York: Wiley.

Wilmot, W. W., Carbaugh, D. A., & Baxter, L. A. (1985). Communicative strategies used to terminate romantic relationships. *Western Journal of Speech Communication, 49*, 204–216.

Winters, A. M., & Duck, S. W. (2000). You ****!!! Swearing as an aversive and a relational activity. In R. Kowalski (Ed.), *The underbelly of social interaction: Aversive interpersonal behaviors* (pp. 59–77). Washington, DC: American Psychological Association Books.

Wiseman, J. P., & Duck, S. W. (1995). Having and managing enemies: A very challenging relationship. In S. W. Duck & J. T. Wood (Eds.), *Confronting relationship challenges [Understanding relationship processes 5]* (pp. 43–72.). Thousand Oaks, CA: Sage.

Wood, J. T. (1982). Communication and relational culture: Bases for the study of human relationships. *Communication Quarterly, 30*, 75–83.

2

Hurtful Messages in Family Relationships: When the Pain Lingers

Anita L. Vangelisti
Katheryn Maguire
University of Texas at Austin

If you talk with anyone long enough about their family relationships, you will find that, at some point, their feelings have been hurt by family members. They may describe the hurt they experienced as minor, or they may portray it as major and life-changing. They may say that their feelings were quick to pass, or they may talk as if the emotional pain they experienced continues to plague them. They may have forgiven the person who hurt them long ago, or they may continue to hold that individual in disdain. Being hurt by family members, in short, is a common experience, but some people feel their relationships with family members have been irreparably damaged by the hurt they have felt, whereas others seem to set aside their hurt feelings in favor of fostering close family ties.

What is it that encourages certain individuals to "forgive and forget" the emotional pain they have experienced in their family? Why do some people distance themselves from family members who hurt them, while others maintain relatively intimate relationships? Certainly, part of what distinguishes those who carry permanent scars from the hurtful interactions they have with family members from those who do not lies in the nature of the interaction—being told by a parent that you "never should have been born" probably creates more relational damage, on average, than being called "carrot top" by a sibling. Yet, there are cases when the nature of the interaction seems to make little difference—when a seemingly innocuous statement is considered by a recipient as devastating or when a particularly brutal comment is treated as harmless. In these situations, the way people conceptualize the hurtful statement (e.g., as frequently occurring or as atypical) and the way they perceive their family (e.g., as vindictive or as well-meaning) may influence the tendency of individuals to forgive family members who hurt them.

The purpose of this chapter is to explore whether a family environment that is seen as particularly hurtful (e.g., one in which hurtful interactions are viewed as commonplace) can influence the responses people have to family members who hurt them. To provide a backdrop for the discussion, the qualities that make families a unique context for the elicitation of hurt feelings are described. Then, a brief commentary follows concerning the social elicitation of hurt. Next, the findings of studies demonstrating the importance of people's cognitions about hurtful interactions are reviewed. Finally, an investigation is described exploring the relevance of individuals' perceptions of their family to their tendency to forgive family members who caused them pain.

Families as a Unique Context for Hurt

Families represent a unique context for social interaction (Booth, 1991). The fact that a hurtful comment or question came from a family member can either sharpen or soften its blow. At least two qualities of family relationships illustrate why this might be the case. First, family relationships are involuntary (Galvin & Cooper, 1990). Family members have little, if any, choice about their associations with each other. Children do not get to choose their parents, nor parents their children. Even in situations when family members say things to each other that are incredibly hurtful, they retain their relational status. In some cases, because it is so difficult to "opt out" of family relationships, individuals may have an incentive to downplay the impact of any single hurtful comment on their relationship. It may be more functional for these people to reason that an extremely hurtful statement or question did not affect their relationship than to admit that their mother, father, or sibling said something to them that caused them so much pain. In other cases, people may focus on and even exaggerate any hurt they feel precisely because it was elicited by a family member. The involuntary nature of their family relationships may make any hurtful interaction they have with family members more salient. People who feel "trapped" in relationships that were not of their choosing may amplify the effects of hurtful messages they have received from family members in part as a means to underline their own lack of agency (e.g., "If I had the chance, I never would have chosen a father who would say something like that.").

It also is important to note that the involuntary nature of family associations usually means that people have few relational alternatives to their family. It is difficult, if not impossible, to replace family members. Even when people adopt surrogate parents, siblings, or grandparents, they often qualify their relationship with those individuals (e.g., "Well, she's not my *real* grandmother . . ."). Because the alternatives people have to their family relationships are extremely limited, they may be motivated to minimize the influence that any single hurtful comment has on their family relationships. Knowing they are "stuck" with family members may encourage them to make the best of those relationships and, thus, to de-emphasize the impact of hurtful comments. It also is possible, however, that individuals place more, rather than less, weight on hurtful things their family members say. Being aware that they cannot readily replace a family member may encourage them to be hypervigilant of any hurtful behavior that could threaten or damage the relationship.

The second quality that may influence the impact of hurtful comments or questions on family relationships is the lengthy history that most family members share. Theorists argue that personal relationships are defined by the presence of interconnected activity over time and by the experience of diverse activities (Kelley, Berscheid, Christensen, Harvey, Huston, Levinger, McClintock, Peplau, & Peterson, 1983). To the degree that family relationships fit this definition, they should create a unique context for perceiving and interpreting hurtful communication. If a hurtful comment represents a relatively small proportion of family members' experience together, they may not place much emphasis on it. Because they feel that the statement or question is atypical, they may be more willing to forgive the person who hurt them. If, however, hurtful comments represent a large part of family members' interactions, or if a single hurtful statement violates a strongly held relational maxim, the impact of the comment on family relationships may be substantial. In this type of situation, the hurtful message(s) may be seen as so frequent or so egregious as to be unforgivable.

The Elicitation of Hurt

The elicitation of hurt feelings is an interpersonal event. People feel hurt because they believe they have been emotionally injured by something another individual said or did (Folkes, 1982; L'Abate, 1977; Leary, Springer, Negel, Ansell, & Evans, 1998; Vangelisti, 1994). The social processes by which hurt is evoked can be explained, in part, by appraisal theory.

Appraisal theorists would suggest that hurt, like other emotions, is evoked as a consequence of people's assessments of a particular event or situation (e.g., Lazarus, 1991: Ortony, Clore, & Collins, 1988; Scherer, 1984). Before they experience an emotion, people must perceive a stimulus event and evaluate any effect it might have on their well-being. The evaluations individuals make concerning the influence of the event are termed by most theorists as *appraisals* and typically are categorized into two relatively general types. Lazarus (1991) has labeled these as primary and secondary appraisals. *Primary appraisals* focus on the extent to which the stimulus event interferes with individuals' goals and their existing patterns of behavior. *Secondary appraisals* involve people's ability to address the event and any outcomes associated with it.

Both primary and secondary appraisals are closely linked to the social environment in which the original stimulus event took place. Those who adhere to appraisal theory suggest that the social context influences individuals' appraisals in at least two ways. First, it may serve as *background information*. People draw on their prior experiences when they appraise how an event will affect their goals or whether they will be able to deal with any outcomes associated with the event. In families, this background information is extensive. Individuals bring a rich history of experiences to any stimulus event they encounter involving members of their family. Thus, for example, when siblings find themselves saying things that hurt each other, their appraisals of the situation include their thoughts and feelings about prior hurtful episodes as well as the other social interactions they have had with each other over the years. A second way that the social environment affects appraisals is that it provides *foreground information*. Any stimulus event takes place within a particular social context. Social information is part of what comprises the event—it is in the foreground and, as a consequence, is inextricably linked to the appraisals people make concerning the event. When family members hurt each other, they do so within a social environment. If parents say something hurtful to their child in a public setting, the child will appraise the situation differently than he or she would if the same comment was made in a private setting. Similarly, if the hurtful statement is made in front of the child's peers, the appraisal he or she makes will be different than it would if the statement was made in the presence of the parents' friends.

Although most theorists acknowledge that appraisals are influenced by the social environment, they often provide a limited view of the social processes related to emotion. Appraisal theorists suggest that the evaluations people make concerning the social environment determine the nature of individuals' emotions. However, the elicitation of emotion does not always occur in such a direct, linear fashion. Instead, as Parkinson (1997) notes, emotions "are not only reactions to interpretations of events but also modes of social action and communication" (p. 75). The social context is used by individuals to make appraisals, but appraisals also comprise the social environment. Given this, another way that the social context can shape appraisals is by creating an opportunity for new information, and thus new appraisals, to emerge. Such *emergent information* comes from interactions people have with others about their appraisals or about the stimulus event. These interactions may take place prior to the event (e.g., grandparents may talk to their grandchildren about how to avoid hurting others' feelings), simultaneous with it (e.g., parents may intervene in a hurtful interaction between siblings), or after it has occurred (e.g., children may discuss their hurt feelings with parents). Regardless of when the interactions occur, they affect appraisals and, as a consequence, influence the way people feel.

The elicitation of hurt feelings, in short, is inextricably tied to appraisals people make of their social environment. When people feel hurt, they assess something another person said or did as a transgression—they believe another person caused them emotional pain. Of course, individuals may respond to a perceived transgression with other emotions such as anger (Weiner, 1986: Weiner, Amirkhan, Folkes, & Verrette, 1987) or even guilt (Vangelisti & Sprague, 1998). However, several factors distinguish appraisals that evoke hurt from those that elicit other emotions. Hurt, for example, is what theorists call an emotion "blend" (Weiner, personal communication, June, 1995): It involves a mix of both sadness and fear. Individuals who feel hurt are sad because they perceive they have been emotionally injured. At the same time, they are fearful because they believe they are vulnerable to being harmed (Kelvin, 1977). This aversive combination of sadness and fear, along with the knowledge that they may be vulnerable to further harm, often encourages people to distance themselves from the source of their pain (Vangelisti & Young, 2000).

Responses to Hurt

A number of scholars have argued that responses to emotion can be described broadly in terms of individuals' proclivity to either approach or avoid the source of their feelings (Fox & Davidson, 1984; Gray, 1987; Horney, 1945). Frijda (Frijda, 1986; Frijda, Kuipers, & ter Schure, 1989) more specifically theorizes that every emotion is associated with a particular state of action readiness. He suggests that when people feel an emotion such as hurt, they are primed to take action. The action they take involves engaging or disengaging from interaction with the environment.

Because hurt involves a sense of being vulnerable to emotional harm, it is associated with a tendency to disengage from the context in which it was elicited. Those who are hurt, in other words, experience a readiness to distance themselves from the person they see as the source of their feelings. In an effort to protect themselves from further pain, they may create what Helgeson, Shaver, and Dyer (1987) call "a rift" in their relationship with the individual who hurt them.

Of course, the degree to which people actually engage in such relational distancing varies. Some people cut off all interaction with the person who hurt them; others opt to stay close, even when it is likely they will be hurt again and again by the same individual. A readiness to disengage from a particular social context does not necessarily mean that people will enact the behaviors that will lead to distancing. Heightened action readiness does not directly translate into particular responses to emotion (Frijda, 1986; Lazarus, 1991; Oatley, 1992). Indeed, research suggests there are at least two factors that influence people's tendency to distance themselves from the source of their emotional pain. One of these is whether the individuals who are hurt perceive their pain was elicited intentionally. The other involves the degree to which people who are hurt see the hurtful behavior as part of an ongoing pattern.

Hurt and Perceived Intentionality. Individuals' perceptions about whether their hurt feelings were evoked intentionally appear to affect their tendency to distance themselves from the person who hurt them. In two studies (Vangelisti & Young, 2000), people were asked to describe an interaction in which someone said something that hurt their feelings and to report whether or not the other person intentionally hurt them. The studies' findings indicated that individuals who judged something another person said to them as intentionally hurtful felt the comment had more of a distancing effect on their relationship than did those who perceived the comment as unintentionally hurtful.

Why would hurt that is evoked intentionally encourage relational distancing? The response to this question lies, in part, in the cues people use to judge intentionality. Researchers note that individuals employ several different types of information when they evaluate others' intent (Malle & Knobe, 1997; Thompson, Armstrong, & Thomas, 1998; Weiner, 1995). People typically assess whether the relevant behavior involves volition (choice), forethought (planning), foreseeability (awareness of the outcomes associated with the behavior), and valence (desirable outcomes). Given this, when individuals judge a hurtful comment as intentional, they likely believe the person who hurt them chose to make the comment, planned it, was aware of the pain it would cause, and felt the outcomes associated with making the statement or asking the question were desirable.

Because comments that are perceived as intentionally hurtful involve free choice, planning, awareness, and even desire, the emotional pain they evoke may be greater than the pain elicited by statements or questions that are seen as accidental. Indeed, research confirms that this is the case: Individuals who believed another person intentionally hurt their feelings reported experiencing more intense hurt than did those who perceived their feelings were evoked unintentionally (Vangelisti & Young, 2000). Inasmuch as comments seen as intentionally hurtful elicit more intense emotional pain, people may opt to decrease their vulnerability. Those who appraise a statement or question as intentionally hurtful may decide to protect themselves by distancing themselves relationally from the individual who hurt them.

Hurt as an Ongoing Pattern. On average, statements or questions that are perceived as intentionally hurtful are associated with greater relational distancing than are those viewed as unintentionally hurtful. However, comments seen as unintentionally hurtful can do a great deal of harm to people's relationships. If, for example, a parent inadvertently hurts his or her children, but does so frequently over a long period of time, the children very well may take steps to avoid the repeated emotional pain. Even if they perceive their hurt is elicited unintentionally, the children may begin to distance themselves relationally from that parent.

Previous research suggests that, indeed, comments perceived as unintentionally hurtful vary in terms of the effect they have on interpersonal relationships (Vangelisti & Young, 2000). More specifically, statements or questions that were viewed as part of an ongoing pattern of hurtful communication were associated with greater relational distancing than were those that were seen as isolated incidents. Individuals who perceived they frequently were hurt by someone were relatively likely to distance themselves from that person. Similarly, those who reported that the person who hurt them had a general tendency to hurt others were likely to engage in relational distancing—regardless of whether they perceived their hurt was elicited intentionally.

Hurt in the Family

Although previous research provides some hints about what might encourage people to distance themselves from family members who hurt them, the hints it provides are tenuous. The findings summarized to this point do not distinguish family relationships from other sorts of associations. Hurtful comments made by family members, however, can operate differently than those made by friends, acquaintances, or romantic partners (Vangelisti & Crumley, 1998). People may be quite willing to distance themselves from an acquaintance who says something that hurts their feelings, whereas they may be much more hesitant to distance themselves from a family member who says the very same thing.

Prior research does not account for at least two factors that may affect people's tendency to distance themselves from family members who hurt them. First, it does not consider the influence that the family context may have on people's interpretations of hurtful statements or questions. Findings suggest that people's perceptions of those who hurt their feelings affect the degree to which individuals may engage in relational distancing. Yet, people's perceptions of individual family members are formed and maintained in the context of the family. Families may create a unique environment for interpreting and responding to hurtful communication. When family members, as a group, are perceived as frequently hurting each other or as having a general tendency to elicit hurt, relational distancing may be a relatively common response to hurt feelings. Alternatively, in families that often evoke hurt, members may act as if they are "immune" to emotional pain. People who belong to such families may become accustomed to receiving verbal barbs and, as a consequence, may not engage in relational distancing when they are hurt.

Second, previous studies do not account for the notion that relational distancing may be constrained in the context of the family. Because family members have a rich history together, it may be difficult for them to give up any intimacy or closeness they have shared. Even when members are not very close, they may be reluctant to change the attitudes and feelings they have about each other. In such cases, the familiarity and the small rewards that these family members receive from the intimacy they do share may be enough to discourage any relational distancing. Furthermore, a lack of relational distancing does not necessarily mean that people do not have ill feelings toward members of their family. People who fail to distance themselves from someone who hurt them do not necessarily forgive the transgressor. Because family members often are very interdependent—for example, they share activities, space, and social networks—they may opt to stay close while, at the same time, harbor a degree of anger and resentment.

It also is important to note that people's satisfaction with their family relationships may create a backdrop for interpreting and responding to any hurtful comments received from family members. Research on romantic couples has repeatedly demonstrated that people who are highly satisfied with their relationships view their partner's negative behavior in less negative ways than do those who are dissatisfied (e.g., Fincham, 1985; Grigg, Fletcher, & Fitness, 1989; Holtzworth-Munroe & Jacobson, 1985). Theoretically, those who are satisfied have reason to maintain positive illusions about their relationships (Murray, Holmes, & Griffin, 1996), whereas those who are dissatisfied do not. If a similar pattern holds for family relationships, individuals who are highly satisfied with their family may interpret hurtful comments in less negative ways than those who are relatively dissatisfied. As a consequence, they may be less likely to distance themselves from a family member who hurt them and more likely to forgive.

Initial Evidence for the Influence of a Hurtful Family Environment

To begin to address some of these issues, a study was conducted examining individuals' perceptions of their family environment, the degree to which they engaged in relational distancing when they were hurt by a family member, and their tendency to forgive family members who caused them pain (Vangelisti & Maguire, in progress). One hundred seventy-one participants completed a questionnaire that required them to describe an interaction in which a family member said something that hurt their feelings. They were asked to rate the intensity of their hurt feelings, report the degree to which the interaction made them feel more distant from the individual who hurt them, and note whether the person who hurt them did so intentionally. Participants also completed a measure of marital satisfaction (Huston, McHale, & Crouter, 1986) that was modified to assess family satisfaction (see, e.g., Vangelisti & Crumley, 1998), a measure of forgiveness (McCullough, Worthington, & Rachal, 1997), and a series of items that were designed to evaluate the degree to which the family environment was hurtful (e.g., "My family members often hurt each other's feelings," "There are times when my family members enjoy hurting each other's feelings," "I can think of many times when my family members chose to hurt each other's feelings"). The latter three measures were randomized to minimize order effects.

Preliminary Analyses. Prior to assessing the potential links between individuals' perceptions of their family environment, relational distancing, and forgiveness, the items measuring people's perceptions of their family environment were examined. More specifically, they were submitted to a principal components factor analysis to explore whether the data were characterized by any underlying factors. The eigenvalues and a scree plot were used as criteria to determine the optimal solution. Two factors, accounting for 68.57% of the variance, emerged from the analysis. The first factor was labeled *frequency*. It was comprised of items assessing how often family members hurt others or how typical it was for family members to hurt others' feelings. The second factor was called *proclivity*. The items representing this factor focused on family members' inclination to hurt others. The summed scales derived from these factors were used to measure people's perceptions of their family environment. Table 2.1 includes the relevant factor loadings and the α reliabilities of the summed scales associated with each of the two factors.

In addition to examining the measure tapping individuals' perceptions of their family environment, the reliabilities of the remaining scales were assessed. The α coefficient for the measure of relational distancing was .79. For family satisfaction, it was .93 (the r between the main scale items and the global satisfaction rating was .66).

Main Analyses. To provide an initial glimpse of the associations between people's perceptions of their family environment and their responses to a family member who hurt them, Pearson correlations were calculated. As expected, there was a significant positive association between

TABLE 2.1
Factor Analysis of Items Assessing Hurtful Family Environment

	Factor Loadings	
Item	Frequency	Proclivity
It is typical of my family members to hurt each other's feelings.	.91	
My family members often hurt each other's feelings.	.90	
My family members frequently hurt other's feelings.	.80	
My family members don't hurt each other's feelings often.*	.66	
There are times when my family members enjoy hurting each other's feelings.		.80
Sometimes my family members think it's fun to hurt each other's feelings.		.80
I can think of many times when my family members chose to hurt each other's feelings.		.76
I expect my family members to hurt each other's feelings.		.69
A lot of people have been hurt by my family members' behavior.		.67
alpha coefficients	.88	.85

*Item was reverse coded.

the *frequency* with which hurt was elicited by the family and the degree to which individuals distanced themselves from a family member who said something hurtful to them ($r(169) = .16, p < .02$). There also was a significant positive link between the family's *proclivity* to hurt others ($r(165) = .15, p < .03$) and relational distancing.

The pattern of associations between individuals' views of their family environment and their tendency to forgive a family member who hurt them also was examined. Findings indicated that there was a significant negative correlation between the *frequency* with which family members tended to hurt each other and forgiveness ($r(167) = -.41, p < .001$). Similarly, a negative link emerged between forgiveness and the *proclivity* of family members to hurt others ($r(164) = -.32, p < .001$).

Because individuals' satisfaction with their family relationships may influence the way people understand and respond to hurtful comments made by family members, additional analyses were conducted. Hierarchical regressions were used to test whether, when satisfaction was controlled, there were still significant associations between people's perceptions of their family environment and both relational distancing and forgiveness. In one analysis, relational distancing was the dependent variable; in the other, the dependent variable was forgiveness. In both analyses, family satisfaction was controlled by entering it as the first step in the equation. The two family environment scales—*frequency* and *proclivity*—were entered in the second step and served as the independent variables. Results suggested

TABLE 2.2
Beta Coefficients and R^2 Change for Prediction
of Relational Distancing and Forgiveness

Predictor	Beta	R^2 Change
Relational Distancing		
Step 1		.03*
family satisfaction	−.11	
Step 2		.01
frequency	.04	
proclivity	.09	
Forgiveness		
Step 1		.12**
family satisfaction	.17*	
Step 2		.07**
frequency	−.08	
proclivity	−.26**	

*$p < .05$
**$p < .01$

that when family satisfaction was controlled, the associations between relational distancing and both *frequency* and *proclivity* became negligible ($F_{change}(2, 160) = .86$, *ns*). By contrast, controlling for family satisfaction affected only one of the two associations between the family environment scales and forgiveness ($F_{change}(2, 159) = 6.89$, $p < .001$). The *frequency* with which family members hurt others was associated with forgiveness, but the *proclivity* of family members to elicit hurt feelings was not (see Table 2.2).

Although relational distancing and forgiveness are associated ($r(166) = −.47$, $p < .01$), they appear to operate in different ways. To further explore the interplay between individuals' tendency to distance themselves from a family member who hurt them and the degree to which they forgave that family member, another series of analyses was conducted. The goal of these analyses was to look at respondents who varied in terms of distancing and forgiveness and assess how they felt about their family and how they perceived their family environment. First, a median split was used to categorize both relational distancing and forgiveness into high and low groups. Then, the two resulting categorical variables were crossed so that four groups emerged: low distancing, low forgiveness; low distancing, high forgiveness; high distancing, low forgiveness; and high distancing, high forgiveness. Finally, a series of ANOVAs was conducted to explore possible variations among the four groups with regard to people's family satisfaction, the *frequency* with which they felt their family elicited hurt, and the *proclivity* of their family to hurt others. The findings revealed significant differences among the categories due to all three dependent variables: family satisfaction ($F(3, 128) = 8.93$, $p < .001$), *frequency* ($F(3, 128) = 8.47$, $p < .001$), and *proclivity* ($F(3, 125) = 6.13$, $p < .001$). Post hoc analyses further suggested that, in each case, there was a significant difference between two groups: low distancing, high forgiveness and high distancing, low forgiveness. Not surprisingly, people who reported low distancing and high forgiveness were more satisfied with their family relationships ($M = 6.23$, $SD = .82$) than were those who said they engaged in high distancing and low forgiveness ($M = 5.17$, $SD = 1.37$). Those reporting low distancing and high forgiveness also noted that their family elicited hurt less frequently ($M = 2.15$, $SD = 1.12$) and had less of a proclivity to hurt others ($M = 1.90$, $SD = 1.13$) than did individuals who engaged in high distancing and low forgiveness ($M = 3.42$, $SD = 1.82$ and $M = 2.85$, $SD = 1.56$, respectively).

In addition to the differences between these two groups, several other interesting distinctions emerged. For instance, people who said they engaged in high distancing and high forgiveness ($M = 6.20$, $SD = .87$) were more satisfied, noted that their family elicited hurt less frequently ($M = 2.17$, $SD = 1.22$), and reported their family had less of a proclivity to hurt others ($M = 1.54$, $SD = 1.06$) than those who engaged in high distancing and low forgiveness ($M = 5.17$, $SD = 1.37$, $M = 3.42$, $SD = 1.82$, and $M = 2.85$, $SD = 1.56$, respectively). In addition, those reporting low distancing and high forgiveness were significantly more satisfied ($M = 6.23$, $SD = .82$) and noted that their family evoked hurt less frequently ($M = 2.15$, $SD = 1.21$) than those who reported low distancing and low forgiveness ($M = 5.50$, $SD = 1.00$ and $M = 3.60$, $SD = 1.65$, respectively). The pattern of findings, in short, generally indicated that variations in forgiveness, rather than variations in relational distancing, were associated with differences in satisfaction, frequency, and proclivity.

Directions for the Future: Questions and Concerns

One of the assumptions guiding this chapter was that people's perceptions of their family environment create a context for, and thus influence, the way individuals interpret and respond to hurtful comments made by members of their family. Because the feelings evoked by a hurtful statement or question are relatively aversive, the state of action readiness typically associated with those feelings involves distancing oneself or disengaging from the context in which the feelings were elicited. Inasmuch as this is the case, people who perceive their family fosters a great deal of hurt may be likely to distance themselves from family members who hurt them. In a similar vein, they may be unlikely to forgive hurtful transgressions made by family members because they see members as part of an environment that often creates emotional pain.

Although, on the surface, this line of reasoning may seem theoretically sound, data from an exploratory study show that the relationships among these variables are more complex than one might initially suspect. Findings associated with the data indicated that, indeed, there was a positive zero-order correlation between people's perceptions of their family environment as *frequently* hurtful and their tendency to distance themselves from a family member who hurt them. There also was a positive link between individuals reporting that their family had a *proclivity* to hurt others and their tendency to engage in relational distancing. However, these associations were not significant when family satisfaction was controlled. Satisfaction, in other words, accounted for much of the relationship between people's perceptions of their family environment as hurtful and their tendency to distance themselves from a family member who hurt them. When individuals' tendencies to forgive family members for a hurtful comment was examined, a different pattern of results emerged. Once again, there was a significant association between people's perceptions of their family environment as hurtful and their tendency to forgive a family member who said something that hurt them. More specifically, respondents' reports of the *frequency* with which family members elicited hurt and the *proclivity* of members to hurt others both were linked to forgiveness. Yet, when satisfaction was controlled, only the association between the perceived *frequency* with which family members elicited hurt and forgiveness was significant.

Separating people's reports of distancing and forgiveness into high and low groups and examining the mean values of each group for (a) family satisfaction, (b) the perceived *frequency* with which hurt was elicited in the family, and (c) the perceived *proclivity* of family members to hurt others shed some light on these findings. Generally, satisfaction was higher, and both frequency and proclivity were lower when forgiveness was high; when forgiveness was low, satisfaction was lower and both frequency and proclivity were higher. By contrast, people's tendency to distance themselves from a family member who hurt them did not have as strong an effect as did forgiveness. The notion that there may be links between various aspects of the family environment and forgiveness, but not distancing, suggests a number of propositions that warrant further investigation. Several of these will be discussed next.

Relational Distancing and Forgiveness Are Distinct. Individuals' tendencies to distance themselves from a family member who hurt them and to forgive that family member are inversely related, but they are not mirror images of a single, underlying tendency. Rather, people can engage in relational distancing with or without forgiving, and they can forgive with or without distancing (Flanigan, 1998). Individuals may opt not to distance themselves from family members for a variety of reasons—many of which may have nothing to do with whether or not they decide to forgive members for transgressions. For instance, people may avoid distancing themselves from a family member who hurt them because they have few alternatives to that family relationship. They may reason that being close to a parent or a sibling who hurt them is a better alternative than "losing" the close relationship altogether. At the same time, they may harbor some ill feelings toward that family member for the hurt he or she elicited. An alternative scenario could occur if individuals decide to set aside their resentment and forgive a family member in order to "preserve peace" in the family. Under such circumstances, people may opt to distance themselves from the person who hurt them—in spite of forgiving him or her—in order to avoid further pain.

Fincham (2000) notes that "forgiveness removes the barrier to relatedness, but other factors (e.g., likelihood of further harm, the harm-doer's reaction to the victim's forgiveness) determine whether a relationship ensues and what specific form the relationship takes" (p. 7). Similar to the exploratory study described here, this claim suggests that the "specific form" of a relationship (how close or distant partners choose to be) and forgiveness function in distinct ways. The factors that encourage distancing, thus, may be quite different than those that promote forgiveness.

Distancing May Be a Less Sensitive Barometer of the Family Environment Than Forgiveness. The findings of the current study imply that people's tendency to distance themselves from a family member who hurt them may be less sensitive to variations in the family environment than their tendency to forgive a family member for the same act. The family environment, in other words, might be one of several factors that influence forgiveness but not distancing. Why might this be the case? One way to address this question is to focus on qualities associated with forgiveness. For instance, it may be that forgiveness is particularly responsive to variations in the family environment. Because forgiveness is intentional (Enright & Coyle, 1998; Fincham, 2000), people may be able to modify their tendency to forgive a family member so that it is consistent with certain qualities of their family. Forgiveness, in other words, may be more controllable than distancing. If the family context is one that is rarely associated with hurt— one in which family members infrequently hurt each other and show dismay when they do—individuals may feel compelled to forgive. They may see a lack of forgiveness as inconsistent with the attitudes and behaviors of their family. As such, family members may socialize each other to be forgiving. By contrast, if the environment is one that typically is hurtful—one in which family members frequently hurt each other and even relish doing so—a lack of forgiveness would be quite consistent with the family's norms. In such families, forgiveness may be seen as a sign of weakness or gullibility. It also is likely that people's perceptions of their family environment affect the way they view members' hurtful communication. Again, if the family context is one rarely associated with hurt, people may view any hurtful behavior that does occur as a fluke or a mistake. Data from the current study and others indicated that people who saw hurtful communication as accidental or unintentional were more likely to forgive family members who hurt them than were those who saw the communication as intentional.

Another way to respond to the question is to focus on the properties associated with relational distancing. Compared to forgiveness, distancing may be somewhat resistant to variations in the larger social environment and more sensitive to variations in individuals and individual relationships. As conceived here, relational distancing is the state of action readiness (Frijda, 1986; Frijda et al., 1989) associated with being hurt by another person. Because distancing is a response to another individual's (hurtful) behavior, qualities associated with that individual, more so than the social context he or she inhabits, may influence the degree to which people opt to engage in relational distancing. Previous studies, for example, show that when people who are hurt perceive the individual who hurt them did so frequently and had a general tendency to hurt others, they were more likely to distance themselves from that individual (e.g., Vangelisti & Young, 2000).

Also, in many cases, the nature of family relationships may make distancing a more difficult response to hurt feelings than forgiveness. Because family relationships have a lengthy history and are difficult to replace, it may be relatively difficult for people to distance themselves from members who hurt them—even when the family environment is one that would seem to incite repeated hurtful episodes. The literature on family violence certainly supports this possibility. Individuals often stay "close" to a family member who physically hurts them, and even make excuses for the violent behavior, because they feel they have few, if any, alternatives to staying in that relationship (Herbert, Silver, & Ellard, 1991).

People May Already Have Distanced Themselves From the Person Who Hurt Them. Although some people may have difficulty distancing themselves from a family member who hurt them, others may not. Indeed, one reason that relational distancing may appear to be less sensitive to variations in the family environment is that some individuals already may have distanced themselves from the source of their pain. Thus, when called on to describe a hurtful interaction and to note how much of a distancing effect that interaction had on their relationship with the person who hurt them, these individuals may report little, if any, distancing. Having already been exposed to a hurtful family environment, they may have become callous and may, as a consequence, show little reaction to hurtful things their family members say.

People who have an avoidant attachment style (see, e.g., Bartholomew & Horowitz, 1991; Hazan & Shaver, 1987) are a case in point. Because individuals who are avoidant feel uncomfortable with intimacy and tend to distrust others, they are likely to enter any interaction ready to protect themselves from emotional pain. They are less likely to be vulnerable to hurt at the outset, so they may be less likely to respond to a hurtful family environment. In support of this line of reasoning, Simpson (1990) found that those who are avoidant, particularly males, noted feeling much less distress than did others after the dissolution of their relationships. In a family setting, these same individuals are likely to protect themselves from being vulnerable to emotional pain. Their tendency to mistrust others may encourage them to stay relatively distant—regardless of whether or not the family environment is one that tends to be hurtful.

The Influence of the Family Environment on Hurtful Interactions Is Complex and Multifaceted. Individuals' attachment style and their tendency to trust each other are just two examples of variables that could affect the influence of the family environment on hurtful interactions. Others include the amount of time family members spend together, the degree of cohesiveness in the family, and the ability of the family to cope with stressors. Indeed, the list of variables that might influence the family context is nearly endless. This long list of variables and their potentially complex associations with the family environment suggests that any influence the family environment has on hurtful interactions is almost necessarily complex and multifaceted. The notion that the family creates a context for interpreting and responding to hurtful interactions, in other words, does not mean that the context has simple, direct effects on family members or their relationships. Instead, the implication is that the context affects, and is affected by, what happens between family members. It creates a background against which complex social interactions between members emerge and are understood.

It also is important to note that ways the family environment might influence people's responses to hurtful interactions may vary over time. The exploratory study described in this chapter took a single snap-shot of the potential association between people's perceptions of their family environment and the way they responded to a hurtful interaction with a family member. Taking another snap-shot at some point in the future or collecting numerous snapshots over an extended period of time might provide a very different view of the relationships observed in the current study.

Kelly and McGrath (1988) describe a variety of ways a circumstance or event, X (e.g., the family environment) can effect an outcome Y (e.g., the tendency of individuals to distance themselves from, or forgive, family members who hurt them). Because the data for the current study were collected at a single point in time, it is tempting to assume that any influence of the family environment on distancing or forgiveness took place "all at once" and was maintained over time. Kelly and McGrath, however, point out several other temporal patterns that could characterize the findings. For instance, the influence of the family context could be immediate and then dissipate over time as family members become callous to hurtful comments they receive. By contrast, it could reflect a linear process that increases over time so that family members become more and more distant (or less and less forgiving). The influence of the family environment also might involve a delayed effect—one that is the cumulative result of numerous hurtful interactions. Or it could be characterized by a cyclical pattern that reflects modulations in distancing and/or forgiveness. It would be interesting for researchers to explore which of these temporal patterns best captures the effect of the family context on distancing or forgiveness—and to examine the circumstances that encourage one pattern over another.

Distancing and Forgiveness May Serve Different Functions. The notion that there may be links between various aspects of the family environment and forgiveness, but not distancing, also suggests that distancing and forgiveness can serve different functions for people who are hurt. Scholars have long theorized about what these functions might be and how they might operate in the context of the family, but systematic, empirical work on this topic is lacking. As a consequence, the functions that have been discussed do not comprise an exhaustive list. For instance, a number of theorists have argued that one of the primary functions of distancing or disengaging onself from the social environment is to avoid an aversive stimulus (Frijda, 1986; Lazarus, 1991; Parkinson, 1997). People who have been hurt by a family member, therefore, decrease their vulnerability to being repeatedly hurt by distancing themselves from the individual who hurt them. Although, conceived in this way, distancing serves as the state of action readiness associated with being hurt, it is possible that distancing serves other secondary functions as well. Hess (2000), for example, argued that people may engage in relational distancing to avoid hurting others. Individuals who have been hurt by a family member may distance themselves from that individual because that is the only way they can refrain from "striking back."

The degree to which these, and other, functions of distancing overlap with those associated with forgiveness is questionable—in part because the functions of forgiveness (like those of distancing) have yet to be delineated. Certainly, one of the major functions of forgiveness is to maintain or repair interpersonal relationships (Fincham, 2000; McCullough, Rachal, Sandage, Worthington, Brown, & Hight, 1998). Researchers and clinicians also have argued more broadly that forgiving may be "positively transforming for self, the injurer, and our communities" (Enright & Coyle, 1998). Forgiveness, thus, appears to function on several levels. It can provide a context for relational reconciliation (Coleman, 1998; Gordon, Baucom, & Snyder, 2000),

TABLE 2.3
Examples of Possible Functions of Relational Distancing and Forgiveness

	Self	*Other*	*Relationship*	*Society*
Distancing	Decrease vulnerability	Protect from retaliation	Avoid conflict	Maintain social structure
Forgiveness	Alleviate resentment	Provide absolution	Allow for reconciliation	Restore peace

serve as a means for alleviating an individual's ongoing anger or hostility (Baumeister, Exline, & Sommer, 1998; Fitzgibbons, 1998), or provide a way to restore harmony to a social group (Couper, 1998). Inasmuch as this is the case, it may be useful for scholars to classify the functions of forgiveness (and perhaps those of distancing) as focusing on the self, the other, the relationship, or the society at large (see, e.g., Table 2.3). Exploring ways to better describe the functions of forgiveness and distancing would allow researchers to compare the two and to see how they operate in situations when hurt feelings are evoked. Studying the functions of distancing and forgiveness as responses to hurt in family relationships not only would provide more information about how hurt is elicited but also would tell us more about how and why the pain evoked by family members' hurtful comments sometimes lingers.

REFERENCES

Bartholomew, K., & Horowitz, L. M. (1991). Attachment styles among young adults: A test of a four-category model. *Journal of Personality and Social Psychology, 61*, 226–244.

Baumeister, R. F., Exline, J. J., & Sommer, K. L. (1998). The victim role, grudge theory, and two dimensions of forgiveness. In E. L. Worthington, Jr. (Ed.), *Dimensions of forgiveness: Psychological research and theological perspectives* (pp. 79–104). Philadelphia: Templeton Foundation.

Booth, A. (1991). *Contemporary families: Looking forward, looking back*. Minneapolis: National Council on Family Relations.

Coleman, P. W. (1998). The process of forgiveness in marriage and the family. In R. D. Enright & J. North (Eds.), *Exploring forgiveness* (pp. 75–94). Madison, WI: The University of Wisconsin Press.

Couper, D. (1998). Forgiveness in the community: Views from an Episcopal priest and former chief of police. In R. D. Enright & J. North (Eds.), *Exploring forgiveness* (pp. 121–130). Madison, WI: The University of Wisconsin Press.

Enright, R. D., & Coyle, C. T. (1998). Researching the process model of forgiveness within psychological interventions. In E. L. Worthington, Jr. (Ed.), *Dimensions of forgiveness: Psychological research and theological perspectives* (pp. 139–161). Philadelphia: Templeton Foundation.

Fincham, F. D. (1985). Attributions in close relationships. In J. Harvey & G. Weary (Eds.), *Attribution: Basic issues and applications* (pp. 203–234). New York: Academic.

Fincham, F. D. (2000). The kiss of the porcupines: From attributing responsibility to forgiving. *Personal Relationships, 7*, 1–23.

Fitzgibbons, R. P. (1998). The cognitive and emotive uses of forgiveness in the treatment of anger. *Psychotherapy, 23,* 629–633.

Flanigan, B. (1998). Forgivers and the unforgivable. In R. D. Enright & J. North (Eds.), *Exploring forgiveness* (pp. 95–105). Madison, WI: The University of Wisconsin Press.

Folkes, V. S. (1982). Communicating the causes of social rejection. *Journal of Experimental Social, Psychology, 18,* 235–252.

Fox, N. A., & Davidson, R. J. (1984). EEG asymmetry and the development of affect. In N. A. Fox & R. J. Davidson (Eds.), *The psychology of affective development.* Hillsdale, NJ: Lawrence Erlbaum Associates.

Frijda, N. H. (1986). *The emotions.* Cambridge, UK: Cambridge University Press.

Frijda, N. H., Kuipers, P., & ter Schure, E. (1989). Relations among emotion, appraisal, and emotional action readiness. *Journal of Personality and Social Psychology, 57,* 212–228.

Galvin, K. M., & Cooper, P. J., (1990, May). *Development of involuntary relationships: The stepparent–stepchild relationship.* Paper presented at the annual meeting of the International Communication Association, Dublin, Ireland.

Gordon, K. C., Baucom, D. H., & Snyder, D. K. (2000). The use of forgiveness in marital therapy. In M. E. McCullough, K. I. Pargament, & C. E. Thorsesen (Eds.), *Forgiveness: Theory, research, and practice* (pp. 203–227). New York: Guilford Press.

Gray, J. A. (1987). *The psychology of fear and stress* (2nd ed.). New York: Cambridge University Press.

Grigg, F., Fletcher, G. J. O., & Fitness, J. (1989). Spontaneous attributions in happy and unhappy dating relationships. *Journal of Social and Personal Relationships, 6,* 61–68.

Hazan, C., & Shaver, P. R. (1987). Romantic love conceptualized as an attachment process. *Journal of Personality and Social Psychology, 59,* 511–524.

Helgeson, V. S., Shaver, P. R., & Dyer, M. (1987). Prototypes of intimacy and distance in same-sex and opposite-sex relationships. *Journal of Social and Personal Relationships, 4,* 195–233.

Herbert, T. B., Silver, R. C., & Ellard, J. H. (1991). Coping with an abusive relationship: I. How and why do women stay? *Journal of Marriage and the Family, 53,* 311–325.

Hess, J. A. (2000). Maintaining nonvoluntary relationships with disliked partners: An investigation into the use of distancing behaviors. *Human Communication Research, 26,* 458–488.

Holtzworth-Munroe, A., & Jacobson, N. S. (1985). Causal attributions of married couples: When do they search for causes? What do they conclude when they do? *Journal of Personality and Social Psychology, 48,* 1398–1412.

Horney, K. (1945). *Our inner conflicts: A constructive theory of neurosis.* New York: W. W. Norton.

Huston, T. L., McHale, S. M., & Crouter, A. C. (1986). When the honeymoon's over: Changes in the marriage relationship over the first year. In R. Gilmour & S. Duck (Eds.), *The emerging field of interpersonal relationships* (pp. 109–132). Hillsdale, NJ: Lawrence Erlbaum Associates.

Kelley, H. H., Berscheid, E., Christensen, A., Harvey, J. H., Huston, T. L., Levinger, G., McClintock, E., Peplau, L. A., & Peterson, D. R. (Eds.). (1983). *Close relationships.* Beverly Hills, CA: Sage.

Kelly, J. R., & McGrath, J. E. (1988). *On time and method.* Newbury Park, CA: Sage.

Kelvin, P. (1977). Predictability, power, and vulnerability in interpersonal attraction. In S. Duck (Ed.), *Theory and practice in interpersonal attraction* (pp. 355–378). New York: Academic.

L'Abate, L. (1977). Intimacy is sharing hurt feelings: A reply to David Mace. *Journal of Marriage and Family Counseling, 3,* 13–16.

Lazarus, R. S. (1991). *Emotion and adaptation.* New York: Oxford University Press.

Leary, M. R., Springer, C., Negel, L., Ansell, E., & Evans, K. (1998). The causes, phenomenology, and consequences of hurt feelings. *Journal of Personality and Social Psychology, 74,* 1225–1237.

Malle, B. F., & Knobe, J. (1997). The folk concept of intentionality. *Journal of Experimental Social Psychology, 33,* 101–121.

McCullough, M. E., Rachal, K. C., Sandage, S. J., Worthington, W. L., Brown, S. W., & Hight, T. L. (1998). Interpersonal forgiving in close relationships: II. Theoretical elaboration and measurement. *Journal of Personality and Social Psychology, 75,* 1586–1603.

McCullough, M. E., Worthington, E. L. Jr., & Rachal, K. C. (1997). Interpersonal forgiving in close relationships. *Journal of Personality and Social Psychology, 73*, 321–336.

Murray, S. L., Holmes, J. G., & Griffin, D. W. (1996). The self-fulfilling nature of positive illusions in romantic relationships: Love is not blind, but prescient. *Journal of Personality and Social Psychology, 71*, 1155–1180.

Oatley, K. (1992). *Best laid schemes: The psychology of emotions.* New York: Cambridge University Press.

Ortony, A., Clore, G. L., & Collins, A. (1988). *The cognitive structure of emotions.* Cambridge, UK: Cambridge University Press.

Parkinson, B. (1997). Untangling the appraisal-emotion connection. *Personality and Social Psychology Review, 1*, 62–79.

Scherer, K. R. (1984). Emotion as a multicomponent process: A model and some cross-cultural data. In P. Shaver (Ed.), *Review of personality and social psychology: Vol. 5. Emotion, Relationships, and health* (pp. 37–63). Beverly Hills, CA: Sage.

Simpson, J. (1990). The influence of attachment styles on romantic relationships. *Journal of Personality and Social Psychology, 59*, 971–980.

Thompson, S. C., Armstrong, W., & Thomas, C. (1998). Illusions of control, underestimations, and accuracy: A control heuristic explanation. *Psychological Bulletin, 123*, 143–161.

Vangelisti, A. L. (1994). Messages that hurt. In W. R. Cupach & B. H. Spitzberg (Eds.), *The darkside of interpersonal communication* (pp. 53–82). Hillsdale, NJ: Lawrence Erlbaum Associates.

Vangelisti, A. L., & Crumley, L. P. (1998). Reactions to messages that hurt: The influence of relational contexts. *Communication Monographs, 65*, 173–196.

Vangelisti, A. L., & Maguire K. (in progress). *The influence of the family environment on people's responses to hurtful messages.* Unpublished manuscript.

Vangelisti, A. L., & Sprague, R. J. (1998). Guilt and hurt: Similarities, distinctions, and conversational strategies. In P. A. Anderson & L. K. Guerrero (Eds.), *Handbook of communication and emotion* (pp. 123–154). San Diego, CA: Academic.

Vangelisti, A. L., & Young, S. L. (2000). When words hurt: The effects of perceived intentionality on interpersonal relationships. *Journal of Social and Personal Relationships, 17*, 393–424.

Weiner, B. (1986). *An attributional theory of motivation and emotion.* New York: Springer-Verlag.

Weiner, B. (1995). *Judgments of responsibility: A foundation for a theory of social conduct.* New York: Guilford.

Weiner, B., Amirkhan, J., Folkes, V. S., & Verrette, J. A. (1987). An attributional analysis of excuse giving: Studies of a naive theory of emotion. *Journal of Personality and Social Psychology, 52*, 316–324.

3

The Application of Attachment Theory to Individual Behavior and Functioning in Close Relationships: Theory, Research, and Practical Applications

Leonard J. Simms
University of Iowa

The attachment theories of Bowlby (1969/1982, 1973) and the research of Ainsworth (Ainsworth, Blehar, Waters, & Wall, 1978) have provided a solid foundation on which a number of researchers have built theories of relating in close relationships. Hazan and Shaver (1987) were the first to suggest that attachment theory provides a basis for understanding individual differences in behavior and feelings in adult romantic relationships. Since that time, the literature has exploded with data seeking to support Hazan and Shaver's (1987) extension of attachment theory to romantic relationships. Much of this data is cross-sectional, but a number of limited, short-term longitudinal studies have also been reported. The initial data have been supportive, but the most convincing studies—namely, prospective long-term longitudinal studies—have yet to be reported.

In this chapter, the basic premises of attachment theory, as Bowlby (1969/1982, 1973, 1980) and Ainsworth et al. (1978) originally envisioned it, are outlined. Next, the extent to which attachment theory has been broadened to include an understanding close relationship processes (Hazan & Shaver, 1987) will be described. Third, cross-sectional and longitudinal data that speak to the temporal stability of attachment style as well as the validity and limitations of Hazan & Shaver's extension are presented. And finally, future directions and applications of the theory to the practice of psychotherapy are discussed. A primary theme of this chapter is that, whereas the preliminary data are promising, long-term longitudinal data are definitely needed that link attachment behavior measured in childhood with adult ro-

mantic relationship outcomes. A second theme is that despite these empirical limitations, attachment theory has provided a sound foundation on
which researchers and practitioners have built an impressive amount of
theoretical work and practical applications.

ATTACHMENT THEORY

According to Bowlby's (1969/1982, 1973, 1980) formulation of attachment
theory, a behavioral system has evolved in humans that has been naturally
selected to maintain proximity between infants and their primary caregivers. The theory posits that infants who perceive their caregivers as responsive and available feel confident to stray from that "secure base" and
explore the environment. Alternatively, when infants perceive their caregivers as insufficiently available or responsive (e.g., as a result of separation or other distress), the behavioral system activates attachment behaviors to restore proximity between the infant and caregiver. Over repeated
interactions, individual differences emerge based on infants' expectations
regarding caregiver responsiveness and dependability. Bowlby (1988b) suggested that these individual differences, once formed, are likely to remain
stable over time but also indicated that attachment patterns are not necessarily static. He theorized that early in life (i.e., during the first 2 or 3 years),
attachment patterns can vary across significant relationships (e.g., with
mother vs. father). With increasing age, however, attachment patterns become less plastic, more resistant to change.

Whereas Bowlby provided the theory and original vision, Ainsworth and
her colleagues (Ainsworth et al., 1978) were the first to empirically test his
theory. To systematically examine attachment behaviors in infants, Ainsworth developed an experimental procedure known as the *strange situation*.
The strange-situation procedure was designed to activate the attachment
behavioral system by exposing infants to low levels of stress. The stress experience was achieved through placement of an infant in a strange room,
the presence of a stranger in the room, and brief separations from mother.
Using this procedure, Ainsworth and her colleagues identified three discrete patterns of attachment between infants and their primary caregivers:
(a) secure, (b) anxious–ambivalent (also sometimes referred to as resistant), and (c) avoidant. Secure attachment is characterized by trust in the
availability, responsiveness, and helpfulness of attachment figures in stressful or frightening situations. Within the strange situation paradigm, securely
attached children play comfortably with toys, react positively to strangers,
and do not stay especially close to mother during the preseparation phase.
When mother is absent, play is reduced and children become visibly distressed. When mother returns, however, children are quickly calmed and
soon resume play (Ainsworth et al., 1978).

Anxious–ambivalent and avoidant attachments are both characterized by lack of trust in attachment figures but can be more finely differentiated. Anxious–ambivalent attachment occurs in infants who are uncertain about the availability and responsiveness of their attachment figures and is associated with overt anxiety and a desire for greater interpersonal closeness. During the strange situation, anxious–ambivalent children are likely to be wary and vigilant during the preseparation phase and to have difficulty using mother as a secure base for exploration. On being reunited with mother, these children simultaneously seek contact with and show anger toward mother and do not return promptly to play (Ainsworth et al., 1978). Avoidant attachment occurs when infants have no confidence that their attachment figures will be available and responsive to their needs in times of stress. This pattern is associated with attachment figure rejection and a preference for interpersonal distance. In the strange situation, avoidant childrens' exploration and play is relatively unaffected by the presence or absence of mother (Ainsworth et al., 1978). On reunion, after the separation phase, these children generally ignore mother. A fourth attachment pattern—known as disorganized attachment—was identified later (Main & Soloman, 1986, 1990) and is characterized by infants who develop no organized strategy for achieving proximity to their caregivers or gaining care or protection.

In a summary of U.S. studies of the three main types of infants, Campos, Barrett, Lamb, Goldsmith, and Stenberg (1983) reported that 62% of their combined sample were securely attached, with 23% and 15% manifesting avoidant and anxious–ambivalent attachments, respectively. In a more recent meta-analysis of strange situation classifications, van IJzendoorn, Goldberg, Kroonenberg, and Frankel (1992) found that secure attachment was the modal classification (55%) across studies, with avoidant, anxious–ambivalent, and disorganized attachments identified in 23%, 8%, and 15% of the subjects, respectively.

ADULT ROMANTIC ATTACHMENT

Hazan and Shaver (1987) proposed that the three main attachment styles identified by Ainsworth et al. (1978)—secure, anxious–ambivalent, and avoidant—also operate in adulthood and color the ways in which adults experience romantic love and behave in romantic relationships. They argued that romantic love can be viewed as "an attachment process (a process of becoming attached) [that is] experienced somewhat differently by different people because of variations in their attachment histories" (p. 511). To measure the adult versions of these constructs, Hazan and Shaver (1987) developed a simple self-report measure of the three adult attachment styles based on the descriptions provided by Ainsworth et al. (1978). This measure consisted of three separate one-paragraph descriptions, each corresponding to one of the original attachment patterns, and participants were asked simply to select the paragraph description that most accurately described their feelings and experiences in close romantic relationships.

Recruiting participants with a "love quiz" that they published in a local newspaper, Hazan and Shaver found that the relative prevalence of the three attachment patterns was similar in adulthood to that identified in infancy: 56% classified themselves as secure, 25% were avoidant, and 19% were anxious–ambivalent. In addition, adults who varied on these attachment patterns differed predictably in the ways they reported experiencing romantic love and in their mental models of self and social relationships more generally. Secure participants rated their primary love relationship as happy, friendly, and trusting; avoidant individuals were more likely to be fearful of intimacy and experience emotional extremes and jealously in their primary love relationship; and anxious–ambivalent participants' primary relationships were characterized by obsession, extreme sexual attraction and jealousy, emotional extremes, and desire of reciprocation and union. Hazan and Shaver also attempted to cross-validate these findings in a sample of college undergraduates, with largely similar results. A number of subsequent empirical studies (reviewed by Shaver & Hazan, 1993) using the same measure have found that the distribution of attachment styles is similar to those identified previously for both infants and adults: approximately 55% of individuals are classified as secure, 25% are avoidant, and 20% are anxious–ambivalent.

More recently, Mickelson, Kessler, and Shaver (1997) examined the relation of sociodemographics and a number of other variables to adult attachment in a large, nationally representative sample of American adults in an effort to replicate previous findings. The distribution of adult attachment styles was similar to that found in prior studies: 59% secure, 25% avoidant, and 11% anxious–ambivalent. In addition, adult attachment was associated with several sociodemographic variables not previously studied. Specifically, being White, female, well-educated, middle-class, married, middle-aged, and from the Midwest were all significantly associated with an increased likelihood of attachment security in adulthood. However, because of the cross-sectional nature of the study, the direction of effect was unclear.

At roughly the same time as Hazan and Shaver (1987), another adult attachment conceptualization emerged that was based on Bowlby's (1973) contention that working models of self and working models of others (i.e., attachment figures) underlie attachment behavior (Bartholomew, 1990; Bartholomew & Horowitz, 1991). Bartholomew (1990) argued that these working models represent two dimensions on which individuals vary and that the two extremes of each dimension (i.e., positive vs. negative model of self and positive vs. negative model of others) could be crossed to form four (as opposed to three) distinct attachment patterns. Bartholomew labeled individuals who reported positive models of both self and others as *secure*, individuals negative on both dimensions as *fearful*, negative–positive individuals as *preoccupied*, and positive–negative individuals as *dismissing*.

To tap each of the four quadrants, Bartholomew and Horowitz (1991) developed a four-category, forced-choice paragraph measure that is structurally similar to Hazan and Shaver's (1987) original three-category measure. Although Bartholomew's terminology differs somewhat from that of Hazan and Shaver (1987), the three-category and four-category measures are related in predictable ways (Brennan, Shaver, & Tobey, 1991). Brennan et al. (1991) reported that individuals who select the secure description from one measure are likely to do the same on the other. In addition, those choosing Bartholomew's preoccupied description are likely to select the anxious–ambivalent description from Hazan and Shaver's instrument, and those who select the fearful description on Bartholomew's measure are likely to also endorse the avoidant paragraph on Hazan and Shaver's measure.

These early forced-choice measures are still quite popular because of their brevity and ease of use but have been criticized by a number of researchers (e.g., Collins & Read, 1990; Levy & Davis, 1988; Simpson, 1990). Two primary concerns have been that (a) the forced-choice format ignores variation within each category that might be interesting or important, and (b) single-item tests are less reliable than multiple-item measures. To that end, a number of researchers have attempted to improve on the original measures by asking for Likert-style ratings of each paragraph description (e.g., Levy & Davis, 1988) and by extracting sentences and phrases from the paragraph descriptions to create multi-item scales (e.g., Collins & Read, 1990; Griffin & Bartholomew, 1994; Simpson, 1990). These adaptations have resulted in more reliable measurement and have fueled a recent proliferation of new self-report, multi-item attachment measures (see Brennan, Clark, & Shaver, 1998 or Crowell, Fraley, & Shaver, 1999 for a review of adult attachment measures).

Brennan et al. (1998) improved our structural understanding of the adult attachment domain by factor analyzing the nonredundant items from all self-report attachment measures in a large sample of 1,086 adults. Consistent with previous work, Brennan et al. found that two primary factors—*anxiety* (e.g., "I worry about being abandoned") and *avoidance* (e.g., "I prefer not to show a partner how I feel deep down")—underlie these adult attachment measures. From these analyses, they constructed the "Experiences in Close Relationships" scale by selecting 18 items to represent each dimension, obtaining reliability coefficients greater than .90 for both scales. Moreover, the content included on these two scales is consistent with and ties together other two-factor models of attachment behavior that have been previously proposed and studied (Bartholomew, 1990; Bartholomew & Horowitz, 1991; Feeney, Noller, & Callan, 1994; Simpson, Rholes, & Nelligan, 1992).

ATTACHMENT STABILITY AND TRAITEDNESS

Attachment styles are thought to be relatively stable characteristics of individuals. In infancy, however, the degree of attachment stability has been found to depend on the stability of social circumstances (e.g., stressful life events, changing family characteristics, and mother–father relationship quality), especially as they affect they quality of the infant–caregiver interaction. In stable settings, high rates of attachment stability have been reported (e.g., Waters, 1978), whereas in unstable settings, attachment stability rates tend to be lower but still significant (e.g., Egeland & Farber, 1984). Continuing into early childhood, a large number of investigators have reported longitudinal links between infant attachment patterns and subsequent relationships with peers during childhood (e.g., Arend, Grove, & Sroufe, 1979; Erickson, Sroufe, & Egeland, 1985; Main, Kaplan, & Cassidy, 1985; Sroufe, 1983; Waters, Wippman, & Sroufe, 1979). In one recent longitudinal study, significant attachment stability was found over the 10-year period following classification at 12 months (Elicker, Englund, & Sroufe, 1992). These findings suggest that attachment patterns evolve to reflect a stable characteristic of the child.

The short-term stability of adult attachment patterns appears to parallel that of infants. The stability of Hazan and Shaver's (1987) three-category and Bartholomew & Horowitz's four-category, forced-choice measures of attachment have been reported to be approximately 70% over intervals ranging from 8 months to 4 years (e.g., Baldwin & Fehr, 1995; Kirkpatrick & Hazan, 1994; Shaver & Brennan, 1992). Test–retest correlations for rating scales and continuous, self-report scales derived from these measures have been moderate in magnitude and have generally indicated greater stability than has been found with the categorical measures (e.g., Collins & Read, 1990; Feeney, Noller, & Callan, 1994; Levy & Davis, 1988). In addition, interview-based measures (e.g., the Adult Attachment Interview [AAI; George, Kaplan, & Main, 1985]) have been shown to be more stable than self-report measures (Scharfe & Bartholomew, 1994). It appears that attachment stability increases as a function of measurement refinement, which suggests that at least some of the instability identified across studies can be attributed to measurement error.

Thus, attachment style appears to be reasonably stable and trait-like, at least over short intervals. To that end, several researchers have examined associations between attachment style and personality variables. Shaver and Brennan (1992) measured attachment style and the "Big Five" personality traits (i.e., neuroticism, extraversion, openness to experience, agreeableness, and conscientiousness) in 242 undergraduates. Attachment self-ratings were related in predictable ways to the Big Five dimensions. Secure attachment was significantly related to extraversion ($r = .32$), agreeableness ($r = .30$), and low neuroticism ($r = -.39$); anxious–ambivalent attachment was associated primarily with neuroticism ($r = .33$); and avoidant attachment was correlated with neuroticism ($r = .23$) and low levels of agreeableness ($r = -.29$) and extraversion ($r = -.23$). Interestingly, Shaver and Brennan also reported that attachment style measures predicted 8-month romantic relationship outcomes better than the Big Five scales and attributed this finding to the greater specificity of attachment measures. Mickelson, Kessler, and Shaver (1997) replicated the relations between attachment style and the neuroticism and extraversion components of the Big Five. Unlike Shaver and Brennan (1992), however, Mickelson et al. (1997) also found that openness to experience was positively related to secure attachment and was negatively related to both avoidant and anxious–ambivalent attachment styles.

Attachment also has been associated with various forms of psychopathology in adults, and a number of theories have emerged to explain the relationship between early childhood attachment experiences and later psychosocial development and functioning (e.g., Dozier, Stovall, & Albus, 1999; Sroufe, 1997; Sroufe, Carlson, Levy, & Egeland, 1999). In general, securely attached individuals tend to exhibit high self-esteem and are rated as well-adjusted by their peers (e.g., Bartholomew & Horowitz, 1991; Brennan & Morris, 1997; Collins & Read, 1990; Feeney & Noller, 1990). Insecure attachments, on the other hand, have been associated with a host of psychological problems and disorders in adults, including depression (e.g., Carnelley, Pietromonaco, & Jaffe, 1994), eating disorders such as bulimia nervosa and anorexia nervosa (e.g., Brennan & Shaver, 1995; Burge et al., 1997), dissociative symptoms (e.g., Carlson, 1998; Ogawa, Sroufe, Weinfield, Carlson, & Egeland, 1997), posttraumatic stress disorder (e.g., Mikulincer, Horesh, Eilati, & Kotler, 1999), borderline personality disorder (e.g., Patrick, Hobson, Castle, & Howard, 1994), and social phobia (e.g., Wenzel, this volume). Moreover, within the sphere of close romantic relationships, insecure attachment has been associated with both partner abuse (e.g., Dutton, Saunders, Starzomski, & Bartholomew, 1994; Kesner & McKenry, 1998) and child abuse (e.g., Moncher, 1996) perpetration. It is important to note, however, that all of these studies measured attachment style concurrently, so determinations regarding direction of effect are difficult to make. Prospective, longitudinal studies linking infant attachment styles to adult psychopathology have yet to be reported.

ATTACHMENT AND RELATIONSHIP QUALITY

Attachment style has been studied in relation to a wide variety of relationship outcome and quality variables, but many of the initial studies linking attachment processes to close relationships have been cross-sectional in nature. Early cross-sectional studies (e.g., Feeney & Noller, 1990; Hazan and Shaver, 1987, 1990; Levy & Davis, 1988; Simpson, 1990) have indicated that securely attached individuals tend to report higher levels of satisfaction, interdependence, trust, intimacy, and commitment in their relationships. In contrast, individuals with avoidant attachment patterns report lower levels of these same attributes, and anxious–ambivalent relationship partners tend to report less satisfaction and more conflict and ambivalence over their relationships. Collins and Read (1990), who included the attachment dimensions of *comfort with closeness* (i.e., secure attachment) and *anxiety over abandonment* (i.e., anxious–ambivalent attachment), reported that these dimensions were differentially related to relationship satisfaction variables as a function of gender. In men, for instance, comfort with closeness was more predictive of relationship satisfaction than was anxiety over abandonment. For women, however, relationship satisfaction was more highly associated with anxiety over abandonment. In addition, a number of studies have converged to indicate that the relationship satisfaction experienced by both partners decreases when the male partner is avoidantly attached or when the female partner is anxiously attached (Collins & Read, 1990; Simpson, 1990; Tucker & Anders, 1999). Thus, gender has been identified as an intriguing moderator in these initial cross-sectional studies.

Numerous cross-sectional studies have examined the relations between attachment style and a host of more specific relationship quality variables. Communication patterns, for example, are influenced by attachment style. Keelan, Dion, and Dion (1998) attempted to explain the link between secure attachment and relationship satisfaction through the communication concept of self-disclosure. Using both self-report and behavioral indices of self-disclosure, Keelan et al. found that securely attached participants disclosed more intimate details to their partners than to strangers, whereas those with insecure attachment styles disclosed similarly across discussants. Some researchers have speculated that communication patterns mediate the link between secure attachment and relationship satisfaction (e.g., Feeney, 1994; Feeney et al., 1994; Keelan et al., 1998), but the results have been mixed. In a study of marital satisfaction, Feeney (1994) found that the connection between relationship satisfaction and secure attachment was mediated by communication patterns for wives only, but other studies (Feeney et al., 1994; Keelan et al., 1998) have failed to replicate this finding, suggesting instead that attachment style and communication patterns exert independent effects on marital satisfaction.

Sexuality is another important aspect of relationship satisfaction that is related to attachment style. Several researchers have found that avoidant individuals tend to hold more permissive views of casual sex than those who are securely or anxiously attached (Brennan & Shaver, 1995; Feeney, Noller, & Patty, 1993; Hazan & Zeifman, 1994). Hazan & Zeifman (1994) also found that secure individuals were more likely than others to be involved in mutually initiated sex and to enjoy physical contact. Anxious–ambivalent attachment has been associated with exhibitionism, domination, bondage, and voyeurism in females, whereas anxious–ambivalent males tend to be more sexually reserved (Feeney et al., 1993; Hazan & Zeifman, 1994).

Attachment style has been linked to differential conflict resolution strategies. Pistole (1989) investigated adult attachment style in relation to conflict resolution and relationship satisfaction among 147 undergraduates. Compared with avoidant and anxious–ambivalent individuals, securely attached participants were more likely to select a mutually focused conflict resolution strategy (i.e., working together to solve a problem). Furthermore, the use of compromise was greater among secure subjects than among anxious–ambivalent subjects, and anxious–ambivalent participants were more likely than avoidant individuals to acquiesce to their partners' wishes. Simpson, Rholes, and Phillips (1996) investigated how attachment style affected individuals' conflict resolution behavior and perceptions of current dating partners. After performing a laboratory conflict resolution task involving a "major problem" in their relationship, anxious–ambivalent individuals perceived their partner and relationship in relatively less positive terms, and men with an avoidant attachment style were rated as less warm and supportive. Beyond verbal conflict resolution behavior, a number of studies have examined attachment style factors that increase the likelihood that conflicts will turn aggressive or physical (Bookwala & Zdaniuk, 1998; Dutton, Saunders, Starzomski, & Bartholomew, 1994; Kesner & McKenry, 1998), finding that individuals with insecure attachments are more prone to relationship aggression than those who are securely attached.

The studies presented thus far in this section have been cross-sectional in nature, and although studies such as these have been and can be informative, prospective and longitudinal studies that examine attachment and relationship functioning over time provide a more continuous picture of relationship functioning and can often help tease apart questions about the direction of causality. In the past few years, a number of longitudinal studies have appeared in the close relationships literature. Kirkpatrick and Hazan (1994) reported a 4-year prospective study of attachment styles and close relationships in 177 adults recruited from the newspaper. In this study, attachment style measured at Time 1 with Hazan and Shaver's (1987) three-category attachment measure was significantly related to a number of relationship variables at Time 2 (4 years later). Individuals who self-rated themselves as securely attached at Time 1 were the most likely at Time 2 to be married and the least likely to be separated or divorced; anxious–ambivalent individuals were the most likely to be searching for a partner at Time 2; and, interestingly, those classified as avoidantly attached at Time 1 were the most likely not to be dating or looking for a romantic partner and were also the most likely to be dating more than one partner at Time 2.

In another longitudinal study, Kirkpatrick and Davis (1994) examined attachment styles and relationship functioning in 354 heterosexual couples in serious dating relationships over a 3-year period. In addition to replicating many of Kirkpatrick and Hazan's (1994) findings, Kirkpatrick and Davis (1994) found that male and female attachment styles were nonrandomly paired. In this sample, no avoidant–avoidant pairs and no anxious–anxious pairs were found. However, their most interesting finding was that the long-term relationship stability associated with different attachment pairings was moderated by gender. The relationships of avoidant men and anxious–ambivalent women—the relationships that received the most negative ratings at Time 1—were *as stable* as those of secure subjects when assessed 3 years later. Conversely, anxious–ambivalent men and avoidant women evidenced the greatest relationship termination rates over time. Kirkpatrick and Davis concluded that the relationships of anxious–ambivalent women, for whom abandonment and relationship loss are central concerns, are more stable due to greater relationship maintenance efforts. The relationships of avoidant men were also surprisingly stabile, which the authors explained by noting that avoidant men were paired only with anxious–ambivalent or secure women. Because both secure and anxious–ambivalent women are thought to have relationship maintenance skills and motivation, they can hold onto their avoidant males if they so choose.

Although these longitudinal results are impressive, longer follow-up intervals are necessary to determine whether the effects of attachment security can be generalized across relationships or are relationship-specific. Klohnen and Bera (1998) recently published a 31-year longitudinal study of adult attachment based on Ravenna Helson's Mills Longitudinal Study sample (Helson, 1967). Attachment patterns of women avoidantly or securely attached at age 52 were studied by examining life outcomes, observer descriptions of behavioral and personality characteristics, and self-reports of working models collected four times between ages 21 and 52. Across adulthood, avoidant compared with secure individuals (a) experienced relationships that were less happy and less stable, (b) were more interpersonally distant, defensive, and vulnerable, (c) reported stable working models characterized by distrustful self-reliance and interpersonal distance, and (d) developed in environments with fewer interpersonal opportunities. Although Klohnen and Bera's data argue convincingly for the stability of attachment style manifestations across adulthood, the study's lack of male participants as well as its focus only on secure and avoidant attachment are clear limitations. Moreover, attachment style was measured only once, at age 52, using the original three-category Hazan and Shaver (1987) measure.

Thus, the cross-sectional and longitudinal data are beginning to paint an interesting picture about the links between attachment style and relationship functioning. Securely attached individuals appear to experience happier relationships, less frequent breakups, and fewer personality concomitants than do those who have formed insecure attachments. However, these data are fraught with a number of limitations. First and foremost, the longitudinal studies that have been conducted thus far (e.g., Kirkpatrick & Davis, 1994; Kirkpatrick & Hazan, 1994; Klohnen & Bera, 1998), albeit informative, have fallen short of the ideal mark. We know quite a bit about the stability of attachment patterns and attachment sequalae in either childhood or adulthood, but not across the entire lifespan. To establish a conclusive link between infant–caregiver attachment (as Bowlby and Ainsworth originally formulated it) and adult romantic attachment (as Hazan and Shaver have outlined), prospective, long-term studies must be conducted that assess attachment style in infancy (using Ainsworth's strange situation paradigm) and follow the participants through childhood, adolescence, and into adulthood. While in adulthood, these participants must then complete multiple adult attachment measures (including interviews, multi-item self-report scales, and collateral reports) and measures of relationship quality and functioning. Such studies have yet to be reported, but the seeds have been planted (e.g., see the prospective work of Sroufe, Carlson, & Shulman, 1993); we must patiently await their fruition.

PSYCHOTHERAPEUTIC APPLICATIONS

Given its relationship focus, attachment theory has been attractive to psychotherapists who wish to better understand and conceptualize interpersonal processes affecting individuals, couples, and families. Bowlby (1977) paved the way for such extensions of attachment theory by proposing a general approach to psychotherapy. According to Bowlby, psychotherapy should help clients examine important interpersonal relationships and understand how these relationships have developed in the context of attachment figure experiences in childhood, adolescence, and adulthood. Bowlby (1988a) further defined the role of the therapist in individual psychotherapy. In particular, he indicated that the attachment-mined therapist's tasks are to (a) provide a secure therapeutic base, (b) explore the client's relationships with significant others, (c) explore the therapist–client relationship, (d) review how current interpersonal functioning may reflect past attachment experiences, and (e) seek to change patterns that may not be appropriate for optimal future functioning.

The theories and data presented previously suggest that certain types of psychotherapy (i.e., therapies that utilize attachment concepts) may helpful for the treatment of individuals and couples with attachment-related problems. Whereas much data have pointed to the trait-like quality of attachment patterns, the link between attachment experiences and later individual and relationship functioning is not deterministic. Kirkpatrick and Hazan (1994), in their 4-year longitudinal study, revealed that changes in relationship status may influence the stability of attachment styles. For example, secure respondents who experienced breakups were less likely to remain secure than those who did not experience breakups, and avoidant respondents who initiated new relationships were less likely to remain avoidant than those who did not. Thus, attachment is not a fixed entity that binds an individual to a static developmental trajectory.

Indeed, a number of promising psychotherapies (e.g., Byng-Hall, 1995; Holmes, 1996; Johnson, 1996; Klerman, Weissman, Rounsaville, & Chevron, 1984) have been developed to help individuals and couples change maladaptive patterns of relating that have their roots in early experience. According to Holmes (1996), evolutionary biology, psychoanalysis, and cognitive science have each offered unique insights into the general practice of psychotherapy, but, until recently, no unifying theory had been proposed to clarify the relations among these schools of thought. To remedy this, Holmes developed an attachment-based psychotherapy in an attempt to integrate these disparate perspectives. According to Holmes' theory, the central goals of psychotherapy are the development of autonomy and intimacy. Autonomy and intimacy are thought to be reciprocally related, and insecure attachments are typically associated with an imbalance between the two. Thus, psychotherapy seeks to restore secure attachment by working toward an appropriate autonomy–intimacy balance. Holmes' psychotherapy also utilizes "attachment narratives," or stories that clients develop and modify to help them make sense of their own particular problems. The therapist works with clients to craft authentic narratives within which their life difficulties can be located and understood. Finally, he proposes a typology of attachment narratives that includes the likely therapeutic trajectory associated with each narrative theme.

Attachment theory has also contributed to our understanding of couples and family psychotherapy. Emotionally Focused Therapy (EFT; Johnson, 1996; Johnson & Sims, 2000) is a model of couples therapy that derives its theory of change and therapeutic goals from an attachment theory perspective. According to EFT, the underlying causes of marital and couple distress are the lack of accessibility and responsiveness of at least one partner and the problematic manner with which relationship partners deal with their individual attachment insecurities. In contrast to other modes of couples therapy that give behavioral techniques primacy (e.g., teaching better communication or negotiating skills), EFT concentrates primarily on the role of emotion in marital and couple distress. Within a short-term framework, EFT strives to move couples away from escalating cycles of attack and defensiveness and toward the formation of a secure bond that can serve as a safe haven and secure base for each partner in times of future conflict or distress. With a model similar to EFT, Byng-Hall (1995) applied attachment principles to the theory and practice of family therapy. In his model, attachment theory serves as a heuristic for understanding the process by which families can change their patterns of functioning from insecure to secure. To that end, family therapy provides a secure base from which individual family members can feel safe to explore new ways of relating with each other. The therapist's role is to establish a safe therapeutic environment, encourage exploration of alternative ways of relating, and maintain his/her availability both within and outside sessions. Empirical support has begun to appear for both EFT (Johnson & Sims, 2000) and Byng-Hall's family therapy (Byng-Hall, 1999), but rigorously controlled clinical trials are needed that compare these attachment-oriented therapies with behaviorally oriented marital therapies that have been more thoroughly tested and supported in the empirical literature.

Of the psychotherapies that have their roots in attachment theory, Interpersonal Psychotherapy (IPT; Klerman et al., 1984) is the best studied. IPT was initially developed to treat symptoms of depression and was based, at least in part, on a foundation laid by attachment theory. According to Klerman et al., "The threat of loss of an important attachment figure creates anxiety and sadness, and frequent threats of such loss may predispose to later depression. Many psychiatric disorders are results of inability to make and keep affectional bonds" (p. 52). Thus, IPT provides a theoretical basis for depression and other psychiatric disorders and provides therapeutic strategies to help therapy clients examine current relationship problems and understand how they evolved from faulty attachment experiences in childhood. In practice, IPT focuses on one of four current problem areas—grief, interpersonal disputes, interpersonal deficits, and role transitions—that can each be conceptualized and understood in the context of attachment theory. Methodologically sound clinical trials have suggested that IPT brings about symptom relief as well as other empirically supported treatments (e.g., Elkin, Shea, Watkins, Imber, et al., 1989). Numerous IPT variations have been developed to treat a myriad of other psychological problems and disorders (Klerman & Weissman, 1993), such as anorexia nervosa (McIntosh, Bulik, McKenzie, Luty, & Jordan, 2000), bulimia nervosa (Fairburn, 1998), dysthymia (Markowitz, 1998), and social phobia (Lipsitz, Markowitz, Cherry, & Fyer, 1999). Thus, attachment theory has informed the process of psychotherapy, and the resultant therapies have begun to gain respect among both researchers and clinicians.

SUMMARY

With its roots in the seminal works of both Bowlby and Ainsworth, attachment theory research and applications have proliferated in recent years. Its application to close relationships and to adult development in general began later, but an impressive body of research has accumulated to suggest that attachment patterns are reasonably stable and exert important influences on individual behavior and functioning within romantic relationships. Claims about cross-relationship stability of attachment style have been controversial. Much of the data have been cross-sectional, and the most definitive studies—namely, prospective longitudinal studies originating in childhood and extending into adulthood—have yet to be reported. Despite these missing research links, attachment theory has served both researchers and clinicians well. A number of attachment-based psychosocial interventions have been developed, and attachment theory research continues to fill the pages of journals of child development, interpersonal relationships, and psychotherapeutic processes.

REFERENCES

Ainsworth, M. D. S., Blehar, M., Waters, E., & Wall, S. (1978). *Patterns of attachment.* Hillsdale, NJ: Lawrence Erlbaum Associates.

Arend, R., Grove, F., & Sroufe, L. A. (1979). Continuity of individual adaptation from infancy to kindergarten: A predictive study of ego resiliency and curiosity in preschoolers. *Child Development, 50,* 950–959.

Baldwin, M. W., & Fehr, B. (1995). On the instability of attachment style ratings. *Personal Relationships, 2,* 247–261.

Bartholomew, K. (1990). Avoidance of intimacy: An attachment perspective. *Journal of Social and Personal Relationships, 7,* 147–178.

Bartholomew, K., & Horowitz, L. M. (1991). Attachment styles among young adults: A test of a four-category model. *Journal of Personality and Social Psychology, 61,* 226–244.

Bookwala, J., & Zdaniuk, B. (1998). Adult attachment styles and aggressive behavior within dating relationships. *Journal of Social & Personal Relationships, 15,* 175–190.

Bowlby, J. (1969/1982). *Attachment and loss: Volume I. Attachment.* New York: Basic Books.

Bowlby, J. (1973). *Attachment and loss: Volume II. Separation: Anxiety and anger.* New York: Basic Books.

Bowlby, J. (1977). The making and breaking of affectional bonds: II. Some principles of psychotherapy. *British Journal of Psychiatry, 130,* 421–431.

Bowlby, J. (1980). *Attachment and loss: Volume III. Loss.* New York: Basic Books.

Bowlby, J. (1988a). *A secure base: Clinical applications of attachment theory.* London: Routledge.

Bowlby, J. (1988b). Developmental psychiatry comes of age. *American Journal of Psychiatry, 145,* 1–10.

Brennan, K. A., Clark, C. L., & Shaver, P. R. (1998). Self-report measurement of adult attachment: An integrative overview. In J. A. Simpson & W. S. Rholes (Eds.), *Attachment theory and close relationships* (pp. 46–76). New York: Guilford.

Brennan, K. A., & Morris, K. A. (1997). Attachment styles, self-esteem, and patterns of seeking feedback from romantic partners. *Personality and Social Psychology Bulletin, 23*, 23–31.

Brennan, K. A., & Shaver, P. R. (1995). Dimensions of adult attachment, affect regulation, and romantic relationship functioning. *Personality and Social Psychology Bulletin, 21*, 267–283.

Brennan, K. A., Shaver, P. R., & Tobey, A. E. (1991). Attachment styles, gender, and parental problem drinking. *Journal of Social and Personal Relationships, 8*, 451–466.

Burge, D., Hammen, C., Davila, J., Daley, S. E., Paley, B., Lindberg, N., Herzberg, D., & Rudolph, K. D. (1997). The relationship between attachment cognitions and psychological adjustment in late adolescent women. *Development and Psychopathology, 9*, 151–167.

Byng-Hall, J. (1995). *Rewriting family scripts: Improvisation and systems change.* New York: Guilford.

Byng-Hall, J. (1999). Family and couple therapy: Toward greater security. In J. Cassidy & P. R. Shaver (Eds.), *Handbook of attachment: Theory, research, and clinical applications* (pp. 625–645). New York: Guilford.

Campos, J. J., Barrett, K. C., Lamb, M. E., Goldsmith, H. H., & Stenberg, C. (1983). Socioemotional development. In M. M. Haith & J. J. Campos (Eds.), *Handbook of child psychology: Vol. 2. Infancy and psychobiology* (pp. 783–915). New York: Wiley.

Carlson, E. A. (1998). A prospective longitudinal study of disorganization/disorientation attachment. *Child Development, 69*, 1107–1128.

Carnelley, K. B., Pietromonaco, P. R., & Jaffe, K. (1994). Depression, working models of others, and relationship functioning. *Journal of Personality and Social Psychology, 66*, 127–140.

Collins, N. L., & Read, S. J. (1990). Adult attachment, working models, and relationships quality in dating couples. *Journal of Personality and Social Psychology, 58*, 644–663.

Crowell, J. A., Fraley, R. C., & Shaver, P. R. (1999). Measurement of individual differences in adolescent and adult attachment. In J. Cassidy & P. R. Shaver (Eds.), *Handbook of attachment: Theory, research, and clinical applications* (pp. 435–465). New York: Guilford.

Dozier, M., Stovall, K. C., & Albus, K. E. (1999). Attachment and psychopathology in adulthood. In J. Cassidy & P. R. Shaver (Eds.), *Handbook of attachment: Theory, research, and clinical applications* (pp. 497–519). New York: Guilford.

Dutton, D. G., Saunders, K., Starzomski, A., & Bartholomew, K. (1994). Intimacy–anger and insecure attachment as precursors of abuse in intimate relationships. *Journal of Applied Social Psychology, 24*, 1367–1386.

Egeland, B., & Farber, E. A. (1984). Infant–mother attachment: Factors related to its development and change over time. *Child Development, 55*, 753–771.

Elicker, J., Englund, M., & Sroufe, L. A. (1992). Predicting peer competence and peer relationships in childhood from early parent–child relationships. In R. Parke & G. Ladd (Eds.), *Family–peer relations: Modes of linkage* (pp. 77–106). Hillsdale, NJ: Lawrence Erlbaum Associates.

Elkin, I., Shea, M. T., Watkins, J. T., Imber, S. D., Sotsky, S. M., Collins, J. F., Glass, D. R., Pilkonis, P. A., Leber, W. R., Docherty, J. P., Fiester, S. J., & Parloff, M. B. (1989). NIMH treatment of depression collaborative research program: General effectiveness of treatments. *Archives of General Psychiatry, 46*, 971–982.

Erickson, M. F., Sroufe, L. A., & Egeland, B. (1985). The relationship between quality of attachment and behavior problems in preschool in a high-risk sample. *Monographs of the Society for Research in Child Development, 50*, 147–166.

Fairburn, C. G. (1998). Interpersonal psychotherapy for bulimia nervosa. In J. C. Markowitz (Ed.), *Interpersonal psychotherapy. Review of psychiatry series* (pp. 99–128). Washington, DC: American Psychiatric Press.

Feeney, J. A. (1994). Attachment, communication patterns, and satisfaction across the life cycle of marriage. *Personal Relationships, 1*, 333–348.

Feeney, J. A., & Noller, P. (1990). Attachment style as a predictor of adult romantic relationships. *Journal of Personality and Social Psychology, 58*, 281–291.

Feeney, J. A., Noller, P., & Callan, V. J. (1994). Attachment style, communication, and satisfaction in the early years of marriage. In K. Bartholomew & D. Perlman (Eds.), *Advances in personal relationships: Vol. 5. Attachment processes in adulthood* (pp. 269–308). London: Jessica Kingsley.

Feeney, J. A., Noller, P., & Patty, J. (1993). Adolescents' interactions with the opposite sex: Influence of attachment style and gender. *Journal of Adolescence, 16,* 169–186.

George, C., Kaplan, N., & Main, M. (1985). *Adult Attachment Interview* (2nd ed.). Unpublished manuscript, University of California at Berkeley.

Griffin, D. W., & Bartholomew, K. (1994). The metaphysics of measurement: The case of adult attachment. In K. Bartholomew & D. Perlman (Eds.), *Advances in personal relationships: Vol. 5. Attachment processes in adulthood* (pp. 17–52). London: Jessica Kingsley.

Hazan, C., & Shaver, P. R. (1987). Romantic love conceptualized as an attachment process. *Journal of Personality and Social Psychology, 52,* 511–524.

Hazan, C., & Shaver, P. R. (1990). Love and work: An attachment-theoretical perspective. *Journal of Personality and Social Psychology, 59,* 270–280.

Hazan, C., & Zeifman, D. (1994). Sex and the psychological tether. In D. Perlman and K. Bartholomew (Eds.), *Advances in personal relationships* (Vol. 5, pp. 151–180). London: Jessica Kingsley.

Helson, R. (1967). Personality characteristics and developmental history of creative college women. *Genetic Psychology Monographs, 76,* 205–256.

Holmes, J. (1996). Attachment, intimacy, autonomy: Using attachment theory in adult psychotherapy. Northvale, NJ: Jason Aronson.

Johnson, S. M. (1996). *The practice of emotionally focused marital therapy. Creating connection.* New York: Brunner/Mazel.

Johnson, S. M., & Sims, A. (2000). Attachment theory: A map for couples therapy. In T. M. Levy (Ed.), *Handbook of attachment interventions* (pp. 169–191). San Diego: Academic Press.

Keelan, J. P. R., Dion, K. K., & Dion, K. L. (1998). Attachment style and relationship satisfaction: Test of a self-disclosure explanation. *Canadian Journal of Behavioural Science, 30,* 24–35.

Kesner, J. E., & McKenry, P. C. (1998). The role of childhood attachment factors in predicting male violence toward female intimates. *Journal of Family Violence, 13,* 417–432.

Kirkpatrick, L. A., & Davis, K. E. (1994). Attachment style, gender, and relationship stability: A longitudinal analysis. *Journal of Personality and Social Psychology, 66,* 502–512.

Kirkpatrick, L. A., & Hazan, C. (1994). Attachment styles and close relationships: A four-year prospective study. *Personal Relationships, 1,* 123–142.

Klerman, G. L., & Weissman, M. M. (1993). *New applications of interpersonal psychotherapy.* Washington, DC: American Psychiatric Press.

Klerman, G. L., Weissman, M. M., Rounsaville, B. J., & Chevron, E. S. (1984). *Interpersonal psychotherapy of depression.* New York: Basic Books.

Klohnen, E. C., & Bera, S. (1998). Behavioral and experiential patterns of avoidantly and securely attached women across adulthood: A 31-year longitudinal perspective. *Journal of Personality and Social Psychology, 74,* 211–223.

Levy, M. B., & Davis, K. E. (1988). Lovestyles and attachment styles compared: Their relations to each other and to various relationship characteristics. *Journal of Social and Personal Relationships, 5,* 439–471.

Lipsitz, J. D., Markowitz, J. C., Cherry, S., & Fyer, A. J. (1999). Open trial of interpersonal psychotherapy for the treatment of social phobia. *American Journal of Psychiatry, 156,* 1814–1816.

Main, M., & Soloman, J. (1986). Discovery of an insecure–disorganized/disoriented attachment pattern. In T. Brazelton & M. Yogman (Eds.), *Affective development in infancy* (pp. 95–124). Norwood, NJ: Ablex.

Main, M., & Soloman, J. (1990). Procedure for identifying infants as disorganized/disoriented during the Ainsworth strange situation. In M. Greenberg, D. Cicchetti, & M. Cummings (Eds.), *Attachment in the preschool years* (pp. 273–310). Chicago: University of Chicago Press.

Main, M., Kaplan, N., & Cassidy, J. (1985). Security in infancy, childhood, and adulthood: A move to the level of representation. *Monographs of the Society for Research in Child Development, 50*, 66–104.

Markowitz, J. C. (1998). *Interpersonal psychotherapy for dysthymia*. Washington, DC: American Psychiatric Press.

McIntosh, V. V., Bulik, C. M., McKenzie, J. M., Luty, S. E., & Jordan, J. (2000). Interpersonal psychotherapy for anorexia nervosa. *International Journal of Eating Disorders, 27*, 125–139.

Mickelson, K. D., Kessler, R. C., & Shaver, P. R. (1997). Adult attachment in a nationally representative sample. *Journal of Personality and Social Psychology, 73*, 1092–1106.

Mikulincer, M., Horesh, N., Eilati, I., & Kotler, M. (1999). The association between adult attachment style and mental health in extreme life-endangering conditions. *Personality & Individual Differences, 27*, 831–842.

Moncher, F. J. (1996). The relationship of maternal adult attachment style and risk of physical child abuse. *Journal of Interpersonal Violence, 11*, 335–350.

Ogawa, J. R., Sroufe, L. A., Weinfield, N. S., Carlson, E. A., & Egeland, B. (1997). Development and the fragmented self: Longitudinal study of dissociative symptomatology in a nonclinical sample. *Development & Psychopathology, 9*, 855–879.

Patrick, M., Hobson, R. P., Castle, D., & Howard, R. (1994). Personality disorder and the mental representation of early social experience. *Development & Psychopathology, 6*, 375–388.

Pistole, M. C. (1989). Attachment in adult romantic relationships: Style of conflict resolution and relationship satisfaction. *Journal of Social & Personal Relationships, 6*, 505–512.

Scharfe, E., & Bartholomew, K. (1994). Reliability and stability of adult attachment patterns. *Personal Relationships, 1*, 23–43.

Shaver, P. R., & Brennan, K. A. (1992). Attachment styles and the "Big Five" personality traits: Their connections with each other and with romantic relationship outcomes. *Personality and Social Psychology Bulletin, 18*, 536–545.

Shaver, P. R., & Hazan, C. (1993). Adult romantic attachment: Theory and evidence. In D. Perlman & W. Jones (Eds.), *Advances in personal relationships* (Vol. 4, pp. 29–70). London: Jessica Kingsley.

Simpson, J. A. (1990). Influence of attachment styles on romantic relationships. *Journal of Personality and Social Psychology, 59*, 971–980.

Simpson, J. A., Rholes, W. S., & Nelligan, J. S. (1992). Support seeking and support giving within couples in an anxiety-provoking situation: The role of attachment styles. *Journal of Personality and Social Psychology, 62*, 434–446.

Simpson, J. A., Rholes, W. S., & Phillips, D. (1996). Conflict in close relationships: An attachment perspective. *Journal of Personality & Social Psychology, 71*, 899–914.

Sroufe, L. A. (1983). Infant–caregiver attachment and patterns of adaptation in preschool: The roots of maladaptation and competence. In M. Perlmutter (Ed.), *Minnesota symposium on child psychology* (Vol. 16, pp. 41–83). Hillsdale, NJ: Lawrence Erlbaum Associates.

Sroufe, L. A. (1997). Psychopathology as an outcome of development. *Development and Psychopathology, 9*, 251–268.

Sroufe, L. A., Carlson, E. A., Levy, A. K., & Egeland, B. (1999). Implications of attachment theory for developmental psychopathology. *Development and Psychopathology, 11*, 1–13.

Sroufe, L. A., Carlson, E., & Shulman, S. (1993). Individuals in relationships: Development from infancy through adolescence. In D. C. Funder, R. D. Parke, C. Tomlinson-Keasey, & K. Widaman (Eds.), *Studying lives though time: Personality and development* (pp. 315–342). Washington, DC: American Psychological Association.

Tucker, J. S., & Anders, S. L. (1999). Attachment style, interpersonal perception accuracy, and relationship satisfaction in dating couples. *Personality & Social Psychology Bulletin, 25*, 403–412.

van IJzendoorn, M. H., Goldberg, S., Kroonenberg, P., & Frankel, O. (1992). The relative effects of maternal and child problems on the quality of attachment: A meta-analysis of attachment in clinical samples. *Child Development, 63*, 840–858.

Waters, E. (1978). The reliability and stability of individual differences in infant–mother attachment. *Child Development, 49*, 483–494.

Waters, E., Wippman, J., & Sroufe, L. A. (1979). Attachment, positive affect, and competence in the peer group: Two studies in construct validation. *Child Development, 50*, 821–829.

4

Couples' and Children's Functioning in Families: Toward a Family Perspective on Relationship Maintenance and Enhancement

E. Mark Cummings
Marybeth Graham
University of Notre Dame

Approaches to the maintenance and enhancement of couple relationships typically focus on the relationship between the couple, treating that relationship as a therapeutic context relatively independent of other family relationships. However, additional relationships in the family may powerfully affect and be affected by the quality and characteristics of the relationship between couples, particularly when couples have children. Moreover, current theory and research supports a family perspective on maintaining and enhancing close relationships, especially when families include children. Accordingly, bases exist for those concerned with practice directions for couples to be informed of the theory and evidence supportive of family perspective, and to take into account, or at least consider, this broader family perspective on couple functioning in their own work.

The effects of children on couples' functioning are rarely considered but are a promising direction for future research and practice toward couple maintenance and enhancement. Exploring "the state of the art" in this regard, this chapter examines themes on a broader family perspective on couple maintenance and enhancement for couples with children. First, a theoretical framework supportive of this perspective is presented in terms of systems theory and applications of systems theory to understanding of couple and family functioning. Second, illustrating the close interrelations between marital, child, and family functioning, research concerned with the effects of marital conflict on children and families is considered. Although a direction of effects from couple conflict to child and family functioning has been emphasized, associations identified reflect directions of causality that go both ways. The implications of this literature for couple functioning are especially evident when the associations are interpreted from a systems perspective. Finally, children's reactions are an important perspective in their own right on the quality of couple functioning from a family perspective. Information about children's reactions may also be a powerful motivation for parents to change their couple interaction styles (i.e., for the sake of the children). A family perspective has implications for practice directions towards the maintenance and enhancement of close relationships in families, including couple relationships. Accordingly, messages for how couples can better handle their differences that can be inferred from the children's perspective on marital conflict are examined from a clinician's perspective. Finally, the chapter closes with a brief consideration of new clinical and research directions toward enhancing couple functioning based on a children's perspective on family functioning.

A CONCEPTUAL FRAMEWORK FOR A FAMILY PERSPECTIVE ON COUPLE RELATIONSHIPS: COUPLE RELATIONSHIPS AFFECT AND ARE AFFECTED BY OTHER FAMILY SYSTEMS

Systems theory provides a conceptual framework for positing that family systems mutually influence each other, including that the couple dyad affects the child, and the child, in turn, affects the couple dyad. General systems theory stresses the interdependence of parts of a system. In addition, systems theory emphasizes (a) wholeness and order, meaning that relationships and connections within the whole add to effects associated with individual parts of a system; and (b) hierarchical interactions, referring to the idea that systems are composed of subsystems that are systems of their own (Sameroff, 1989).

   Developmental researchers along with family therapists have extended the general systems viewpoint to articulate family systems theory, which posits that individual family members and systems are necessarily interrelated and influence one another (Minuchin, 1985). According to this viewpoint, families are relational environments with systems qualities (see Cummings, Davies, & Campbell, 2000, for a comprehensive treatment). Figure 4.1 illustrates some pathways of influence whereby marital relations can be seen to influence children and other family systems, which, in turn, would be expected to affect couple relationships. This figure illustrates that interparental relations directly affect children by exposing children to contexts of the marital relationship, including exposure to marital interactions, and indirectly affect children by influencing parental behaviors in the parent–child relationships. In turn, children are hypothesized to directly affect con-

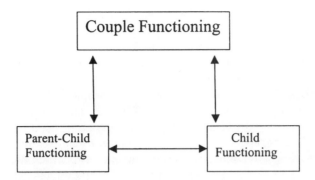

FIG. 4.1. Hypothesized relations between couple and child functioning from a family perspective.

texts of marital interaction by their reactions to the relationship and indirectly influence the couple relationship due to qualities of children's functioning in parent–child relationships. Thus, couple's and children's functioning are hypothesized to exhibit multiple patterns of mutual influence in day-to-day interactions.

Thus, this perspective asserts that patterns of mutual influence characterize relations between couple, parent-, and child-related systems within the family. Accordingly, although this perspective emphasizes viewing families as organized wholes, it also follows from systems theory that the family is appropriately seen as composed of multiple distinct systems, with each exercising influence on the others and on the whole. Accordingly, the actions and emotions of family members are necessarily interdependent, having a reciprocal and continuous influence on other family members, with each individual or dyadic unit inextricably embedded within the larger family system (Cowan, Powell, & Cowan, 1998; Cox & Paley, 1997). Thus, a family systems model advocates against simple linear models of causality or the assumption that one can adequately understand family influences by focusing exclusively on certain individual systems (Emery, Fincham, & Cummings, 1992).

The emphasis in much research on families and children is on the influence of parents, principally the mother, on the children in terms of the parent–child system. A family systems perspective calls attention to the influence of other aspects of family functioning and other family systems on the children. Thus, couple functioning is presumed to affect children's functioning, a proposition that has found considerable support in recent years in family research (Cummings & Davies, 1994). In addition, it is hypothesized that children's emotions and behaviors will affect the couple's emotions and behaviors, a proposition that is much less understood. It follows from this perspective that in order to understand relations between couple functioning and families, it is important to consider not only how marital relations affect others in the family, but also how other family systems affect couple relationships. Thus, multiple units within the family associated with children may be pertinent to an understanding of the maintenance and enhancement of couple relationships (Cox & Paley, 1997; see Fig. 4.1).

However, based solely on the theoretical principles of systems theory, there are endless possibilities for patterns, levels, and directions of influence, with no basis for deciding among the alternatives based solely on systems theory. This perspective does not specify or demonstrate the relative size of effects between family systems, or the extent to which the causal arrows may be stronger in one direction than the other. Thus, the contribution towards a family perspective on couple relationships is a general heuristic for outlining such a perspective, but it remains for family research and other directions in research on close relationships to articulate the specific process models for the role of families in enhancing and maintaining couple relationships.

INTERRELATIONS BETWEEN MARITAL, CHILD, AND PARENT–CHILD RELATIONSHIPS: RESEARCH FOUNDATIONS FOR A FAMILY PERSPECTIVE ON COUPLE RELATIONSHIPS

Research concerned with the maintenance and enhancement of couples' functioning has often focused on interadult relations without considering the children. As we have indicated, effects associated with the children are likely to provide a more advanced explanations of couple functioning based on a family systems perspective. Moreover, substantial literature has developed to indicate that there are significant interrelations between marital, child, and parent–child relationships (Cummings & Davies, 1994; Erel & Burman, 1995; Grych & Fincham, 1990). Although interpretations of data typically stress a direction of effects from couple relations to child or parent–child outcomes, the associations found are appropriately seen as reflecting directions of effects that go both ways (Emery, 1982; see Fig. 4.1). Thus, although the extant research supports effects of the couple relationship on child and parent–child systems, speculations about possible directions of effects that go the other way are justified from a systems perspective.

Marital Conflict as a Context Pertinent to Couples' and Children's Functioning

Couple conflict is a significant interactional context in terms of influence on family systems. From the couples's perspective, marital discord is a principal reason that couples seek counseling (Bradbury & Fincham, 1990). At the same time, conflict is inevitable in relationships and can foster relationship maintenance or enhancement, depending on how conflict is handled (Gottman, 1994). Couple conflict is also a significant predictor of child and parent–child functioning (Davies & Cummings, 1994; Emery, 1982; Grych & Fincham, 1990). From the couples' perspective, children are often an integral part of a couple's desire to maintain and enhance their relationship and build a family. Moreover, the process of building a family may increase couple conflict as it changes the dynamics that previously existed between the couple and creates new challenges in bringing together two individuals, each with histories from their own families of origin (Belsky & Rovine, 1990). At the same time, conflict can be seen as a necessary part of the socialization process in children that teaches them how to negotiate the interpersonal terrain with others in their lives.

COUPLE CONFLICT AND OTHER FAMILY SYSTEMS: TOWARDS ESTABLISHING INTERRELATIONS BETWEEN FAMILY SYSTEMS

Interrelations between marital conflict and other family systems are supported by recent research (Cummings, Davies, & Campbell, 2000; see Fig. 4.1). Next, the evidence for these relations is reviewed briefly.

Couple Conflict and Children's Adjustment

Problems in the marriage predict problems in the children. Marital conflict predicts children's externalizing (e.g., aggression and conduct problems) and internalizing (e.g., anxiety and depression) disorders. Associations have also been reported with children's lower social competence with peers and problems in school (e.g., poor grades, problems in intellectual achievement; Grych & Fincham, 1990). These relations are low to moderate in studies of community samples (Fincham & Osborne, 1993), but effects may be moderate to large when clinical samples are examined (Jouriles, Murphy, & O'Leary, 1989). Adjustment problems in the children increase the challenges, stresses, and difficulties faced by couples in relationship maintenance and enhancement. For example, behavior problems in children increases the likelihood of coercive family processes in the family (Patterson, 1982). However, although problems in couple and child functioning are linked, many questions remain about the extent to which the behavior problems in the children that follow from problems in couple relationships serve to exacerbate further the difficulties of the parents (Emery, 1982).

Couple Conflict and Family Problems

Couple conflict is also associated with other family processes that are linked with children's adjustment. For example, how marital conflict is handled is a factor in children's adjustment before, during, and after divorce (Amato & Keith, 1991; Emery, 1994). Couple conflict has also been identified as a factor in the effects of parental depression on the children. Couple conflict and parental depression are highly associated, indicating the significance of conflict for the maintenance and satisfaction of relationships in families (Whisman, 2000). Marital conflict is a significant predictor of negative outcomes in the children in families with depressed parents, with some longitudinal studies finding that marital conflict is a stronger predictor of adjustment problems than parental depression (Cox, Puckering, Pound, & Mills, 1987). Finally, parental physical abuse of children and interspousal conflict and aggression are linked (Jouriles, Barling, & O'Leary, 1987). In community samples, the co-occurrence rate is estimated at about 6%, but in clinical samples the percentage overlap in published research ranges as high as 100% (Appel & Holden, 1998). Thus, considerable evidence exists for the comorbidity and possible causal interrelations between problems in marital, child, and family functioning.

Direct Effects of Couple Conflict on Children's Functioning

Children's reactions during and following exposure to couple conflict have been well-documented, with behavioral reactions reported in children as young as 6 months of age. Children may be the topics of conflicts or potentially influence couple conflict due to their emotional (e.g., expressions of distress or anger; Cummings, Zahn-Waxler, & Radke-Yarrow, 1981) or social behavior (e.g., increased aggression; Cummings, Iannotti, & Zahn-Waxler, 1985) in reaction to exposure to conflict expressions, either as observers or as members of triadic, or more complex, interactions emerging in response to couple conflict. Children's distress reactions take multiple forms, including motor inhibition and freezing; self-reported anger, sadness, and fear; behavioral responses indicative of anger, distress, and aggression; physiological stress reactions (e.g., heightened blood pressure); and children's efforts to mediate or otherwise ameliorate the parents' disputes. Confidence that couple's interactions are the cause of children's responding is increased by the fact that these effects have been shown in analogue, laboratory and field studies, including instances in which children's reactions to couple conflicts have been compared to responses to other forms of couple interaction (Cummings & Davies, 1994).

Even when the parents are not fully aware of the more subtle of children's emotional reactions, these behaviors, constituting a type of emotional background for couple interactions, may nonetheless affect parents' behaviors towards each other. Consistent with this proposition, recent research suggests that simply the children's presence versus absence during couple conflict has been linked with differences in couple conflicts (Cummings, Goeke-Morey, & Papp, in press). Moreover, their mediation or intervention efforts in marital conflicts influence couple conflicts as children become players in these conflict scenarios (Cummings & Davies, 1994). Children's overt distress and anger expressions may elicit parental responses and interfere with couple communication. Other potentially disruptive behavior by children may occur after the conflict scenarios have ended. For example, exposure to couple conflicts increases the aggressiveness of children in play with other children (Cummings et al., 1985; Cummings, 1987). However, research has focused on children's reactions to couple conflict, so that information about *parental* reactions to children's emotional expressions during couple conflict, and the implications for couple relationship maintenance and enhancement, is scant.

Couples' histories of conflict also affect children's reactions to marital conflicts. Thus, children do not just react to the content of present conflicts but also respond as a function of couples' conflict histories (Cummings, Davies, & Campbell, 2000). Children show more extreme reactions, that is, sensitization, in virtually all domains of responding (e.g., distress and hostility; intervention and mediation in couple conflict; negative cognitions about marital and family relations) in association with more negative marital conflict histories (e.g., Davies, Myers, Cummings, & Heindel, 1999).

In sum, children's responses are more aversive, and more interfering and disruptive, in reaction to couple conflict when couples have more problematic relationship behaviors and histories. Moreover, children's negative reactions to marital conflict have been linked with children's adjustment problems (Davies & Cummings, 1998), which, as we have noted, can only increase the stress on couple relationships. Relatedly, exposure to negative marital conflict styles provides a negative role model for children in terms of their own conflict behavior. Thus, although the evidence is only suggestive at this point, children's behaviors during couple interactions may have the effect typically of increasing couple's problems in the very cases in which couples already have the most difficulty.

Couple Conflict and Parent–Child Relationships

A substantial literature supports relations between marital conflict and negative changes in parenting. To synthesize the information from studies of marital relations and parent–child relations, Erel and Burman (1995) performed a meta-analysis of 68 pertinent studies. The results indicated a moderately large relationship between marital conflict and parenting. Furthermore, significant relations were found between marital conflict and multiple forms of problems in parenting. Thus, parenting problems have been shown to be another pathway of the effects of marital conflict on children (Cummings & Davies, 1994).

For example, the consistency of parenting, the extent to which parenting is hostile or inappropriate, the emotional availability of parents, and other parenting dimensions have been linked with the quality of marital relations. Marital relations are also predictive of the quality of the emotional bond or attachment that forms between parents and children, that is, the emotional security of the attachment between parents and children (Davies & Cummings, 1994). Finally, children's relationships with the parents can also change because of the negative effects on their sense of trust or high regard for parents due to watching the parent behave in mean or hostile way towards their spouse, thus, the impact of marital conflict on parenting may be direct (Owen & Cox, 1997).

One hypothesis for the relations between couple and parent–child functioning is that anger and hostility between the parents spills over into interactions with the child, thereby increasing the likelihood of abuse or alienating interactions between parent and child. For example, relationships marked by the presence of violence or as high frequency of overt conflict have been linked to inconsistent child rearing (Holden & Ritchie, 1991; Webster-Stratton, 1990) and disciplinary behavior (Stoneman, Brody, & Burke, 1989). Another hypothesis is that the parents' preoccupation with their own marital problems causes them to be unresponsive to the children's needs and signals and ineffective, or inconsistent in discipline and other parenting practices. Marital conflict has been associated with increased parental negativity and intrusive control (Belsky, Youngblade, Rovine, & Volling, 1991; Hetherington & Clingempeel, 1992) and low levels of parental warmth and responsiveness (Cox, Owen, Lewis, & Henderson, 1989; Holden & Ritchie, 1991).

However, as Erel and Burman (1995) indicate, it is not yet clear why the relations between couple functioning and parent–child relations are found. Moreover, little is known about how parent–child relationships affect couple relationships. The birth of children increases the stresses on the marriage, but positive effects for couples also undoubtedly ensue from having children. A particular gap in information concerns the pathway between couple functioning, effects on parent–child relationships and, in turn, effects on couple relationships (see Fig. 4.1). From a systems perspective, the literature indicates that effects must go both ways, and that patterns of reciprocal chains of effects are likely to occur, but many questions remains about these patterns of family processes aside from literature on more negative coercive family processes (Patterson, 1982).

It Is How, Not Whether, Couples Engage in Conflict That Matters

However, conflicts in relationships are inevitable, thus, the message of research cannot be to avoid conflicts. Moreover, conflicts can take many forms and couple conflict can be a positive as well as a negative for couple and family functioning (Gottman, 1994). Thus, the implications for couple, child, and family relationships depend on how conflict is handled.

Evidence emerging in recent years indicates that some forms of marital conflict can be regarded as destructive from the child's perspective whereas other forms can be regarded as constructive. Typically, these determinations have been based on children's emotional reactions in response to interparental conflict, and links found between conflict behaviors and children's adjustment. Thus, in this sense, children's reactions have implications for a family perspective on couple relationships.

Cummings (1998) surveyed the evidence for constructive versus destructive conflict based on the children's perspective on couple conflict. The classification of marital conflict as destructive are based on links with children's distress and adjustment problems. The behaviors identified as destructive included interpersonal aggression, aggression with objects, child-blaming conflicts, and the silent treatment. The classification of marital conflict behaviors as constructive was based, again rather loosely, on links with non-negative emotional responses by children to these forms of conflict or a reduction in negative responding to conflict with the introduction of these forms of conflict. A much-replicated finding concerns the highly ameliorative effects of the resolution of conflict, or progress towards resolution, on children's functioning, suggesting one clear direction toward how couples might handle conflicts better for the sake of the children.

The identification of the distinction between constructive and destructive conflict from the children's perspective is vital because it informs couples how to better handle conflicts. Moreover, a likely bonus of handling conflicts better for the sake of the children is that parents will learn how to handle conflicts better for their own sake as well, as the message of findings from the literature on children and marital conflict are largely consistent with the literature on couple conflict resolution from the adults' perspective (Gottman, 1994).

Recent work has further advanced the study of the distinctions between constructive and destructive marital conflict from the children's perspective. A conceptual advance that overcomes theoretical imprecision regarding the bases for this distinction is to define the relative constructiveness of couple conflict in terms of children's emotional reactions to conflict. From the perspective of recent theory (Davies & Cummings, 1994), children's emotional reactions provide an index of the relative constructiveness versus destructiveness of couple conflict from the children's perspective. Interestingly, recent work suggests that even a dichotomy between constructive and destructive conflict may oversimplify matters, and that a more appropriate classification system is to distinguish between constructive, destructive, and productive conflicts (Cummings, Goeke-Morey, & Papp, in press).

For example, based on the results of a recent study from our laboratory, Goeke-Morey (1999) provided evidence for a tripartite classification of marital conflict behaviors, distinguishing between destructive, constructive, and productive conflict behaviors. Destructive interparental conflict behaviors were those that elicited significantly higher rates of negative than positive emotional responses from children. From a theoretical perspective, these behaviors decrease children's emotional security and contribute to children's experiences of stress and anxiety (Davies & Cummings, 1994). Over time, it would be predicted that exposure to these behaviors contribute to patterns of emotional and behavioral dysregulation in the children that undermine their adjustment. Constructive interparental conflict behaviors were defined as those that elicited significantly higher rates of positive than negative emotional responses from the children. From a theoretical perspective, such behaviors exhibited by the parents during conflict would increase children's emotional security, and thus might be expected to enhance children's capacity to regulate their functioning when faced with family stresses. On the other hand, *productive* conflict behaviors (for example, parents' calm discussion of a marital problem) were those for which the comparison of positive and negative emotional responding was nonsignificant and that, moreover, elicited low levels of both positive and negative emotional responses from the children. Interestingly, it may well be that productive conflict behaviors are the most frequently occurring in marital disputes (e.g., calm discussion). In such interactions, the parents communicate about everyday matters of differences of opinion or sources of tension, but the observation of these conflicts by the children has no discernable impact on their own functioning, including their sense of emotional security.

This approach to testing the effects of different forms of interparental communications during disputes provides a theoretical as well as empirical basis for making distinctions between constructive, destructive, and productive conflict. Moreover, the lexicon for couple conflict behaviors is enhanced with the provision of bases for classifying the many forms of couple conflict behaviors from the children's perspective (see review in Cummings, Goeke-Morey, & Papp, in press). The findings from the emerging empirical literature on constructive, destructive, and productive conflict are incorporated into the messages for clinicians that follow. An intriguing issue for future research is to examine how positive forms of conflict behaviors enhance children's functioning and how this more positive functioning in the children might positively impact on couple functioning.

Finally, one caveat for research to date is that most couples participating in marital research are Caucasian, legally married couples who are generally better educated and of a higher socioeconomic status (SES). Some of the conclusions of research to date thus may not apply to other types of families. It is important to assess the same types of constructs in families of differing ethnic status, adoptive families, gay and lesbian families, and families of multiple remarriages.

CLINICAL IMPLICATIONS FOR COUPLE CONFLICT FROM THE CHILDREN'S PERSPECTIVE

Children's reactions to couple conflict provide one guide for couple behavior as children react to conflict between their parents within a larger context of how they interpret the meaning and potential consequences of the conflict for their own well-being. Given that this volume is dedicated to the maintenance and enhancement of close romantic relationships, next we focus on including a consideration of the role of conflict in couple and child functioning when working with couples with children who present for therapy. Having a couple acknowledge the effects of marital conflict from the children's perspective may make it easier for parents who take their children to therapy to accept that their relationship needs to be more closely examined as well. Parents need to realize that not only is their relationship with their child important, but their relationship with each other is closely monitored by their children and potentially affects children's functioning in substantive ways.

BASIC MESSAGES

Conflict and Expressions of Anger Within Families Are Normal

Before elaborating on the effects of conflict between parents on the children, it is important to emphasize at the outset that getting angry is a natural part of being human. Although extreme forms of couple conflict behavior have been shown to be detrimental to the well-being of children, the development of a healthy family life inevitably requires that both parents and children deal with some degree of conflict. Couples interact in a variety of ways; some are quiet and deal with conflict in a reserved manner with little display of emotion, others are loud and boisterous and become visibly upset quickly but then may move on to interactions that are quite positive after working things out within a relatively short period of time. There is no one perfect way to fight. What our research has shown, however, is that there are some guidelines for couples with children to keep in mind as they attempt to work out their differences.

Does It Matter How Couples Get Angry With Each Other?

Numerous studies have documented reactions of anger, sadness, and fear that children show when witness to anger between couples. Conversely, children's happiness and social competency is not about eliminating anger and conflict in their environments altogether, but it is about learning how to maneuver life's daily problems to best resolve interpersonal difficulties to which they are exposed. Marital conflict affects couples in terms of their consistency, discipline, and affirmation of the children. If the primary manner in which couples are channeling their energy is in the undermining of the other's ability to set rules, enforce discipline, or provide a nurturing environment free of criticism, not much may be left over for the positive benefit of the children.

All forms of unresolved anger expressions between couples (verbal, nonverbal, and verbal with some form of physical aggression involved) are perceived as negative events by children and elicit negative emotional responses from children. Just because couples do not yell or talk to each other does not mean that children do not know that couples are angry with one another. Anger involving physical contact, however, is clearly judged to be the most negative form of anger expression and is the most disturbing to children. Children that come from homes with a history of physical aggression or other intense discord between the parents have a tendency to be more distressed and become more involved in their parent's disputes than those children whose parents do not have a history of violence between them. It is important for clinicians to recognize this pattern of children's responding in homes with distressed marriages.

Specific Recommendations

It Is Okay to Get Angry. Normalize angry reactions for couples and let them know that it is okay to be angry with one another and to have differences of opinion.

Do Not Avoid Anger or Conflict. Anger is often not a pleasant emotion, but it is a natural part of being human. Tell couples not to avoid conflict because then neither they nor their children have any way of learning the nuts and bolts of struggling with an issue and coming to some type of agreement. Besides, trying to exist in a family without any conflict is surely attempting the impossible!

Do Not Hold in the Conflict. What is more important is that parents strive to work on their problems openly without holding emotions or thoughts in and expressing themselves nonverbally (silent treatment) as this shuts off all possible avenues of communication and makes coming up with solutions less likely as couples may never actively recognize the problem that needs resolving.

There Are Ways of Handling Conflict That Are Less Disturbing for the Children. Children respond the most positively to verbal ways of dealing with problems. Nonverbal ways may be threatening to many children as there is no explicit recognition of the problem or any active signs that a couple is on their way towards working things out.

Do Not Use Physical Aggression. Stress the importance of not using aggression as a means of expressing frustration or anger during a fight. Help parents to understand that if they feel as if their anger is getting out of control, it is much better to let the other parent know that they need to take a break to cool down but that they will continue to discuss the issue at a later date. Normalize that "time-outs" are not just for children and can be beneficial in helping to separate the immediate emotional reaction from getting in the way of constructive problem solving and resolution. Also inform couples that children view aggression toward objects during interparental conflicts as nearly as distressing as aggression that is directed towards people. Hitting a wall is better than hitting the other person during couple conflict, but is also likely to upset children. Both types of actions indicate to the child that the adult is out of control.

Does It Matter How Things Are Worked Out? Recent studies have shown that unresolved anger (e.g., continuing to fight, the silent treatment) was perceived as a far more negative event by children than resolved anger (e.g., compromise, apology) and induced far greater feelings of anger and distress in children. In fact, resolution of anger seemed to largely ameliorate any negative impact of anger exposure. Moreover, when conflicts are resolved, children appear to care exactly how things are worked out. From the child's point of view, compromise is perceived as a strategy that more completely settles the issues of the conflict when compared with an apology. Children report feeling the need to be involved further in helping work out the issue when just an apology is present. Based on recent findings, we conclude that the process involved in reaching a compromise is more instructive and soothing to children in terms of future expectations about interactions between adults. On the other hand, in several studies that presented children with friendly interactions and interactions that involved anger but that were worked out at the end, children did not distinguish between the two scenarios in terms of their overall level of distress. In other words, resolving an angry conflict was just like a friendly interaction in terms of the impact it had on children at the end.

Attempt to Work Things Out Even if It Is Only a Partial Solution. Research shows that even fights that are partially resolved (e.g., letting the other adult win, changing the topic) are more beneficial in terms of the level of distress reported by children than unresolved fights and anger. If, however, couples intentionally do not deal with conflict in front of their children, being able to provide an explanation to the children later that they were able to work things out has been shown to be beneficial to children. There is also evidence that children understand and benefit from observing nonverbal cues that couples had worked things out "behind closed doors." Finally, children may also benefit from an explanation that things are not worked out but that it is OK, implying either that it is a small matter for the family, or that parents are optimistic that they can work it out.

Just Because the Children Do Not Look Upset, Do Not Assume That They Are Not. Children actually show several different patterns of behavioral responding to couple conflict. There are those who evidence some visible concern; those who are highly distressed and emotionally dysregulated, with a disposition towards displays of anger and aggression; and those who do not show any overt behavioral or emotional reaction. Studies have shown that children who revealed no observable reaction later reported feeling even more angry then those children who showed visible concern about the adults' conflict. More generally, children, particularly as they get older, may learn to mask or limit their expressions of concern, perhaps to avoid involvement in conflict or exacerbating couple's conflicts. However, interviews with the children after exposure to couple conflicts and other types of data suggest that children of all ages are distressed by unresolved couple conflicts.

Risk Factors to Look for With Couples in Conflict

Mood Disorders in Parents. If a serious affective condition that affects one or both parents is present or one or both parents are struggling with alcoholism, it is more likely that children will show difficulty in regulating their emotional reactions to anger within the home and may be observed as intervening more in the disputes of their parents. Similarly, if a child is already experiencing some type of emotional or behavioral difficulty, exposure to anger between parents may contribute to an exacerbation of the already present symptomatology.

History of Physical Abuse in the Family. If children have experienced some type of abuse in the home, they are likely to be more sensitive to any future conflicts between parents and may tend to respond with greater fear than children who have not experienced some type of physical aggression themselves. These children also report heightened fear in situations where conflict is not resolved. It may be that within abusive families, interparent aggression is more closely linked with violence directed toward children. Thus, fear responses exhibited by physically abused children may reflect their experience that conflict and fighting between parents, particularly when it is unresolved, results in a greater tendency toward parental hostility and aggression directed towards them. It may also be that some types of caretaking responses by the children may represent fear-based attempts to calm or soothe angry parents in order to avoid becoming the recipient of parental aggression.

Impending Separation or Divorce. Conflict between couples does not always end when one moves out or the divorce is final. In working with couples who are engaged in a last ditch effort to "save" their marriage by attending counseling, it is important to determine the level of commitment of each toward working on making the marriage work. Recognition that the process of counseling itself is unlikely to bring any immediate relief to couples is an important first step as many couples become quickly disillusioned when the quick-fix to their problems does not materialize in the first several sessions. It may be beneficial to contract with the couples to bring all conflict issues into the sessions with their therapist and attempt to avoid continuing destructive patterns at home in front of the children while they are involved in counseling. In effect, declaring a moratorium on conflict in the home and stressing the importance of counseling as a conflict-management, skill-building time for the couple may reduce the negative effects of conflict on their children. It may also provide a message to the children that their parents are attempting a change toward working through their difficulties. Recent work suggests the promise of programs for educating parents about better ways of handling conflicts (Shifflett & Cummings, 1999).

Inappropriate Mediation Efforts by the Child. Efforts by the child to relieve distress by preventing conflict between the parents, soothing adults who are fighting, and taking sides, may have reinforcement value for the family (i.e., a ready arbiter who becomes involved at the first sign of conflict) but can have severe emotional repercussions for the child that may not always be apparent in the beginning stages of marital discord. Such reactions by the child can also be maladaptive in settings outside the home. An important message for couples is that they should not involve children in their disputes or allow the children to involve themselves, even if doing so may seem advantageous in the short-term.

Presence of Psychopathology in Children

Anger in the home between parents has been shown to lead to more emotional reactions and increased aggression with peers in children; however, increased aggression in children depends on a number of factors including gender, socialization history, and individual characteristics of the child (Cummings & Zahn-Waxler, 1992). It would seem that there is almost an implicit acceptance of the use of aggressive strategies to resolve interpersonal problems that children learn from their parents and are more likely to use in situations with their peers if these children are from homes in which aggressive strategies are used. Exposure to aggression and violence may lead to aggression and violence in children as well as a number of problematic emotional responses, including depression, withdrawal, and severe anxiety. Co-occurring risk factors (e.g., couple discord, depression, poverty, abuse) increase children's risk for adjustment problems. It is important to conduct a thorough intake with any couple that presents for therapy as research has indicated that stronger links with negative outcomes are more typically seen in at-risk populations than in community samples, and detection of the various risk factors better informs the potential for adjustment problems in children.

Buffers and Resilience Factors

A secure relationship with at least one parent in homes where there are high levels of conflict between parents may help buffer children to some extent from the negative impact of familial stresses (see reviews in Emery 1982, 1988). Some patterns of coping with the stress of family discord may be more adaptive developmentally than others and, thus, might be viewed as a resilience factor. For example, children who respond with appropriate concern, without overresponding with aggressiveness or underresponding with denial and covert anger, might constitute one resilience group. A problem here, of course, is that our research suggests that appropriate levels of responding are less likely when there is a history of marital conflict; thus, resilient coping styles may be least likely when they are most needed. Nonetheless, an important message of research is that parents should strive to maintain a good individual relationship with the children despite the level of conflict between the adults (Shifflett & Cummings, 1999).

NEW DIRECTIONS FOR CLINICAL RESEARCH AND PRACTICE

General Recommendations

In the face of evidence of children's social, academic, and interpersonal difficulties, interest in the role of the family in children's development is considerable. As we have noted, if the broader family context is challenged, as is often the case when couples present for therapy, the children will likely be affected. Therapy directed at children and adolescents often has a family component built in; however, the focus is often specifically on parenting and neglects the broader range of ways in which couples interact in the family system. The role of parents in the lives of their children is multidimensional and unequivocally important. There is no claim that conflict and anger between parents or caretakers is the sole reason behind the risk for the development of emotional and behavioral problems in children (Cummings, Davies, & Campbell, 2000), nor that it should be the only focus of couples who present for therapy, merely that its inclusion offers a more complete manner by which to intervene with families who are experiencing problems. At a minimum, one positive implication of research findings for clinical practice is that the communication to parents of the impact of conflict on children may help motivate couples and parents to work more effectively towards resolving their difficulties and in other ways enhancing their relationship as a couple (Shifflett & Cummings, 1999).

Possible Directions for Practice

The following section offers specific practical suggestions for each point of contact with couples with children who are seeking therapy with regard to enacting a family perspective based on research on couples and children's functioning.

Intake and Assessment. Care must be taken up front to describe the intake and assessment process to the parents and explain that there is a great deal of information-gathering for a family perspective on couple functioning that must take place before any treatment can begin. Enlist their support by drawing them into the process and explaining that they are the experts in their own family dynamics, and that your job as clinician is to help uncover the information that they already have and are just having difficulty accessing and putting together. Allow them the opportunity to express any frustrations throughout the process by building this mechanism into the sessions at the outset. Explain that it is normal for parents to want to begin to work to solve the problem immediately as their arrival in therapy is usually prompted by extremely negative and upsetting circumstances at home. The assessment process is a part of the process of optimizing the possibilities for treatment and provides a solid foundation on which to build an informed and accurate conceptualization of the difficulty that they are experiencing.

Given that there is a substantial research foundation on which to base a family perspective on couple functioning, it makes sense to screen for child-related problems in the context of a marital therapy intake and assessment. A complete intake should incorporate questions about the ways that couples handle their problems, frequency of aggressive or violent tactics used in the handling or resolving of problems, and how often the child is believed to be aware of these types of interactions between parents. Understanding the background to which the child is exposed will help provide a more complete picture of the context in which the couple is operating and any subsequent problems they report about their child.

Another matter to keep in mind is that the form of expression of psychopathology in children may change with age. Even if couples report that there are no signs of psychopathology in their children at the outset of their involvement in therapy, it is important to continue to monitor children's status by periodically asking the couple how their children are and any changes that they have noticed. This is significant as certain behaviors and reactions may precede and be systematically related to later-developing psychopathology but may not be explicitly classified as abnormal responses according to standard diagnostic criteria, especially in younger children (Cummings, Davies, & Campbell, 2000).

Treatment Planning. Clinicians are encouraged to view both parents' and children's functioning within the larger context of the family and society. It is especially important to show sensitivity to the difficulty of parenting in the face of adversity (e.g., poverty, unemployment, disability or disease, etc.) and discord and conflict between the parents. It may help to recognize the strain that having children often places on the marriage in terms of increasing rapport and bolstering credibility when making suggestions about changes in parenting practices or conflict management strategies. Include such issues in the discussion about the effects of marital conflict on the children. It may also be useful to discuss such matters as children's attempts to intervene in their parents' fights, withdrawal of unhappily married fathers from their children as well as from their wives, angry parents who subvert each other's discipline, and troubled parents who scapegoat a child as a way of avoiding their own problems (Shifflett & Cummings, 1999). Finally, an effective clinical technique may be to enter into a collaboration with parents, recognizing that no one will know the most effective means of effecting change and that all parties are part of an experimental process to determine which approaches work best for which families with which types of problems.

The information gathered in the intake and assessment process is a rich source for determining relevant issues. Allow the couple to choose the order in which they would like to handle their issues. One way to incorporate a more family-oriented means of ongoing evaluation is to ask the couple to monitor how their child(ren) react(s) to them at home as they continue their involvement in therapy and do the homework exercises that the therapist prescribes. As they begin to notice change in the ways in which they handle conflict, ask them to observe any changes in their children's reactions. Conversely, if they do not notice any changes in the way they handle conflict and instead notice that things are worsening between them, ask them if they notice any negative changes or reactions in their children. Using the children's behavioral and emotional reactions as a barometer for measuring how well or poorly their commitment to change is progressing may make couples more motivated to work together to change any negative conflict management and resolution patterns. This is also a strategy for keeping couples grounded in the reality that their fighting affects those in their family environments and is not just between them.

Research on the Promise of Couple Intervention for Family Functioning

One of the most logical yet difficult steps in clinical research is bridging the gap between what is learned in basic research and what can be applied in basic practice. There is often a gap between what is learned in clinical and developmental research and what is practiced in clinical interventions.

There has been little work done in the area of clinical intervention with couples from a family perspective and its subsequent impact on child adjustment. One study found that an intervention that combined parenting skills training with communication and conflict management skills training yielded better outcomes for both parents and children than standard parenting training alone for children who had been referred for conduct behavior problems (Dadds, Schwartz, & Sanders, 1987; see also Shifflett & Cummings, 1999).

An intriguing recent study suggests that for couples with children, maritally focused psychoeducational programs focused on communication skills and understanding family processes may have advantages over parenting-focused programs. Thus, Cowan, Cowan, and Heming (1999) reported that maritally focused programs for two-parent intact families improved both marital quality and parenting, but parenting-focused programs did not benefit marital quality. Further analyses assessing the direction of effects over time indicated that shifts in marital conflict in the maritally focused intervention group lead to later shifts in parenting quality, whereas shifts in parenting for those in the parenting-focused group were not followed by later improvements in terms of marital conflict (Cowan & Cowan, 1999). Thus, although beneficial effects on children's adaptation (internalizing and externalizing problems; academic achievement) over time (kindergarten to age 10) were found for both couple intervention conditions, the effects of the maritally focused condition on child and family functioning were more pervasive than for the parenting-focused condition. That is, parents participating in a couples group meeting that targeted specific marital and parenting skills were found to show higher levels of improvement in all skills, which were subsequently related to lower levels of behavior problems in their children, than were parents who were part of a control group that did not target marital skills. Thus, these findings suggest the promise of maritally focused interventions as another direction for prevention or intervention programs for couples with children.

These studies point to the fact that relationships within the family are intertwined and changes in one system can have an impact on another system within the family. Moreover, recent work attests to the central role of couple functioning as an influence on multiple family systems.

CONCLUSIONS

Given the high numbers of couples with children who will experience conflicts in their relationship and ultimately present for therapy, a family perspective offers promise towards more effective interventions. Family systems theory, research on couple functioning from a family perspective, and recent clinical research based on couples and children's functioning each support a more wholistic, systems-oriented perspective on treatment that includes consideration of effects on the children. The well-being of couples ultimately is importantly influenced by the well-being of the family. That is, although many questions remain unanswered, couple maintenance and enhancement is surely tied to broader dimensions of child and family functioning. In particular, children are an integral part of any family and intimately experience the conflict that occurs in their homes. Insuring that their presence is accounted for in any therapeutic intervention with their parents or caretakers, even if children are not physically present for therapy sessions, can only serve to advance clinical directions towards improving couples' and children's functioning. In particular, conflict between couples is not just between couples. Conflict is experienced by everyone in the home, including the children, and the effects on multiple family systems may have implications for couple functioning.

ACKNOWLEDGMENTS

We wish to thank Jennifer S. Cummings for her valuable comments on an earlier draft of this chapter. Preparation for this chapter was supported in part by a grant from the National Institute of Child Health and Human Development (HD 36261) to the first author.

REFERENCES

Amato, P. R., & Keith, B. (1991). Consequences of parental divorce for children's well-being: A meta-analysis. *Psychological Bulletin, 110*, 26–46.

Appel, A. E., & Holden, G. W. (1998). The co-occurrence of spouse and physical child abuse: A review and appraisal. *Journal of Family Psychology, 12*, 578–599.

Belsky, J., & Rovine, M. (1990). Patterns of marital change across the transition to parenthood. *Journal of Marriage and the Family, 52*, 5–19.

Belsky, J., Youngblade, L., Rovine, M., & Volling, B. (1991). Patterns of marital change and parent–child interaction. *Journal of Marriage and the Family, 53*, 487–498.

Bradbury, T. N., & Fincham, F. D. (1990). Attributions in marriage: Review and critique. *Psychological Bulletin, 107*, 3–33.

Cowan, P. A., & Cowan, C. P. (1999, August). *What an intervention design reveals about how parents affect their children's academic achievement and social competence.* Paper presented at the Conference Parenting and the Child's World: Multiple Influences on Intellectual and Social–Emotional Development, Bethesda, MD.

Cowan, C. P., Cowan, P. A., & Heming, G. (1999). *Two variations of a preventive intervention for couples: Effects on parents and children.* Unpublished manuscript.

Cowan, P. A., Powell, D., & Cowan, C. P. (1998). Parenting interventions: A family systems perspective. In I. E. Sigel & K. A. Renninger (Eds.), *Handbook of child psychology. Vol. 4. Child psychology in practice* (5th ed., pp. 3–72). New York: Wiley.

Cox, M. J., Owen, M. T., Lewis, J. M., & Henderson, V. K. (1989). Marriage, adult adjustment, and early parenting. *Child Development, 60*, 1015–1024.

Cox, M. J., & Paley, B. (1997). Families as systems. *Annual Review of Psychology, 48*, 243–267.

Cox, A. D., Puckering, C., Pound, A., & Mills, M. (1987). The impact of maternal depression in young children. *Journal of Child Psychology and Psychiatry and Allied Disciplines, 28*, 917–928.

Cummings, E. M. (1987). Coping with background anger in early childhood. *Child Development, 58*, 976–984.

Cummings, E. M. (1998). Children exposed to marital conflict and violence: Conceptual and theoretical directions. In G. Holden, B. Geffner, & E. Jouriles (Eds.), *Children exposed to marital violence: Theory, research, and applied issues* (pp. 55–94). Washington, DC: American Psychological Association.

Cummings, E. M., & Davies, P. T. (1994). *Children and marital conflict: The impact of family dispute and resolution.* New York: Guilford.

Cummings, E. M., Davies, P. T., & Campbell, S. B. (2000). *Developmental psychopathology and family process: Theory, research, and clinical implications.* New York: Guilford.

Cummings, E. M., Goeke-Morey, M. C., & Papp, L. M. (in press). A family-wide model for the role of emotion in family functioning. *Marriage and Family Review.*

Cummings, E. M., Iannotti, R., & Zahn-Waxler, C. (1985). The influence of conflict between adults on the emotions and aggression of young children. *Developmental Psychology, 21*, 495–507.

Cummings, E. M., & Zahn-Waxler, C. (1992). Emotions and the socialization of aggression: Adults' angry behavior and children's arousal and aggression. In A. Fraczek & H. Zumkley (Eds.), *Socialization and aggression* (pp. 61–84). New York and Berlin: Springer-Verlag.

Cummings, E. M., Zahn-Waxler, C., & Radke-Yarrow, M. (1981). Young children's responses to expressions of anger and affection by others in the family. *Child Development, 52,* 1274–1282.

Dadds, M. R., Schwartz, S., & Sanders, M. R. (1987). Marital discord and treatment outcomes in behavioral treatment of child problems. *Journal of Consulting and Clinical Psychology, 55,* 396–403.

Davies, P. T., & Cummings, E. M. (1994). Marital conflict and child adjustment. *Psychological Bulletin, 116,* 387–411.

Davies, P. T., & Cummings, E. M. (1998). Exploring children's emotional security as a mediator of the link between marital relations and child adjustment. *Child Development, 69,* 124–135.

Davies, P. T., Myers, R. L., Cummings, E. M., & Heindel, S. (1999). Adult conflict histories and children's subsequent responses to conflict: An experimental test. *Journal of Family Psychology, 13,* 610–628.

Emery, R. E. (1982). Interparental conflict and the children of discord and divorce. *Psychological Bulletin, 92,* 310–330.

Emery, R. E. (1988). *Marriage, divorce, and children's adjustment.* Newbury Park, CA: Sage.

Emery, R. E. (1994). *Renegotiating family relationships: Divorce, child custody, and mediation.* New York: Guilford.

Emery, R. E., Fincham, F. D., & Cummings, E. M. (1992). Parenting in context: Systemic thinking about parental conflict and its influence on children. *Journal of Consulting and Clinical Psychology, 60,* 909–912.

Erel, O., & Burman, B. (1995). Interrelations of marital relations and parent–child relations: A meta-analytic review. *Psychological Bulletin, 188,* 108–132.

Fincham, F. D., & Osborne, L. N. (1993). Marital conflict and children: Retrospect and prospect. *Clinical Child Psychology, 13,* 75–88.

Goeke-Morey, M. C. (1999). Children and marital conflict: Exploring the distinction between constructive and destructive marital conflict behaviors. (Unpublished dissertation).

Gottman, J. M. (1994). *Why marriages succeed or fail.* New York: Simon & Schuster.

Grych, J. H., & Fincham, F. D. (1990). Marital conflict and children's adjustment: A cognitive–contextual framework. *Psychological Bulletin, 108,* 267–290.

Hetherington, E. M., & Clingempeel, W. G. (1992). Coping with marital transitions: A family systems perspective. *Monographs of the Society for Research in Child Development, 57* (2–3, Serial No. 227).

Holden, G. W., & Ritchie, K. L. (1991). Linking extreme marital discord, child rearing, and child behavior problems: Evidence from battered women. *Child Development, 62,* 311–327.

Jouriles, E. N., Barling, J., & O'Leary, K. D. (1987). Predicting child behavior problems in maritally violent families. *Journal of Abnormal Child Psychology, 15,* 165–173.

Jouriles, E. N., Murphy, C. M., & O'Leary, K. D. (1989). Effects of maternal mood on mother–son interaction patterns. *Journal of Abnormal Child Psychology, 17,* 513–525.

Minuchin, P. (1985). Families and individual development: Provocations from the field of family therapy. *Child Development, 56,* 289–302.

Owen, M. T., & Cox, M. J. (1997). Marital conflict and the development of infant–parent attachment relationships. *Journal of Family Psychology, 11,* 152–164.

Patterson, G. R. (1982). *Coercive family process.* Eugene, OR: Castalia.

Sameroff, A. J. (1989). Commentary: General systems and the regulation of development. In M. R. Gunnar and E. Thelen (Eds.), *Systems and development. The Minnesota symposia on child psychology, Vol. 22* (pp. 219–235). Hillsdale, NJ: Lawrence Erlbaum Associates.

Shifflett, K., & Cummings, E. M. (1999). A program for educating parents about the effects of divorce and conflict on children: An initial evaluation. *Family Relations, 48,* 79–89.

Stoneman, Z., Brody, G. H., & Burke, M. (1989). Marital quality, depression, and inconsistent parenting: Relationship with observed mother–child conflict. *American Journal of Orthopsychiatry, 59*, 105–117.

Webster-Stratton, C. (1990). Long-term follow-up of families with young conduct problem children: From pre-school to grade school. *Journal of Clinical Child Psychology, 19*, 144–149.

Whisman, M. (2000). Marital distress and depression: Findings from community and clinical studies. In S. R. H. Beach (Ed.), *Marital and family processes in depression: A scientific foundation for clinical practice* (pp. 3–24). Washington, DC: American Psychological Association.

5

Relationship Maintenance and Enhancement in Stepfamilies: Clinical Applications

Lawrence H. Ganong
Marilyn Coleman
University of Missouri, Columbia

Shannon Weaver
Texas Tech University

Stepfamilies are common throughout Western, industrialized nations (Cherlin, 1992; Kiernan, 1992). In the United States, an estimated one third of all children will spend some time living with a remarried or cohabiting stepparent before they reach adulthood, and 60% of U.S. women will spend time over their life course in a stepparent household (Bumpass, Raley, & Sweet, 1995). The remarriage divorce rate is about 10% higher than the divorce rate of first marriages (Bumpass, Sweet, & Castro Martin, 1990) and serial cohabiting relationships have become more common. These demographic changes have created increasingly complicated family histories for stepfamilies (Wojtkiewicz, 1994).

The defining characteristic of stepfamilies is that one of the adults is the parent of a child who is not related to the other adult (Ganong & Coleman, 1994). This property, that one adult and a child are related through adoption or birth—and the child has no legal or genetic connection to the other adult in the household—is the crux of most stepfamily dynamics, including relational maintenance and enhancement.

Relationship maintenance has been defined as both a relational state and as the processes involved in maintaining relationships (Canary & Stafford, 1994). What is being maintained has been defined in several ways: as *relational continuity* (i.e., the relationship continues), as *continuity in a stable state* of intimacy or quality, as *relational satisfaction*, and as keeping the relationship in "*good working condition*" and preventing damage (Dindia, 2000).

Relationship enhancement is what is done to achieve a more satisfying relationship; *relational repair* is enhancing the relationship after it has deteriorated. Relational maintenance and enhancement can be either strategic or routine, depending on whether or not the person intended to enhance their relationship. Stepfamily relationships can represent all of these definitions of relationship maintenance and enhancement, even within the same family.

The purpose of this chapter is to examine clinicians' perspectives on relationship maintenance and enhancement in stepfamilies. We identify common problems encountered by stepfamilies and their members, examine barriers to relationship maintenance and enhancement in stepfamilies, and explore clinicians' suggestions for individuals, for relationships, and for entire stepfamily systems. We specifically examine relationship maintenance and enhancement among remarried and cohabiting couples, parents and children, coparents of children from prior relationships, and stepparents and stepchildren.

STEPFAMILY RELATIONSHIP MAINTENANCE AND ENHANCEMENT

A list of skills necessary to maintain and enhance relationships in stepfamilies is familiar to most readers of this book. In fact, most of the clinical advice to stepfamilies, such as *spend time together doing mutually enjoyable activities* and *do things to help the other person*, seem no more than common sense. However, if the requisite maintenance skills are widely known, why then do so many stepfamilies have relationship problems? We can think of four general responses to this question:

1. Stepfamily members lack the skills to maintain relationships.
2. Stepfamily members neglect maintaining their relationships.
3. The relationship partner does not respond to stepfamily members' relational maintenance strategies.
4. Stepfamily members do not know how to use relationship maintenance skills within stepfamily contexts.

Stepfamily Members Lack Relationship Maintenance Skills

Some stepfamily members may not have the necessary skills to maintain and enhance relationships with other family members. For instance, there is evidence that some serial remarriers may have personal problems (e.g., substance abuse, clinical depression) or personality characteristics (e.g., impulsivity, low frustration tolerance) that predispose them to difficulties in maintaining satisfying relationships (Brody, Neubaum, & Forehand, 1988). Although such at-risk individuals probably have some relationship maintenance and enhancement skills or they would not be able to attract and keep partners long enough to remarry, these characteristics may prevent them from engaging effectively in relational maintenance activities over longer periods of time.

For other stepfamily members, it may be that they lack knowledge about how to develop certain types of relationships, rather than a true absence of relationship maintenance skills. In particular, stepparents who have neither had children of their own nor been around children may lack the skills needed to maintain relationships with stepchildren because they know little about children's emotional, psychological, social, cognitive, and physical development, and therefore, do not know what to expect from children at different ages (Keshet, 1989). Consequently, they may not know how to relate to children.

Although some stepfamily members need help developing relationship skills, most probably have the competence to maintain relationships. However, unresolved feelings from prior family experiences, such as anger toward an ex-spouse or guilt about how a loved one was treated, may temporarily constrain them from effectively employing relational maintenance strategies they may have used successfully in the past. Unresolved feelings may serve as barriers to engaging wholeheartedly in developing and nourishing stepfamily relationships (Visher & Visher, 1996).

Clinical Interventions

First, clinicians need to assess whether or not an individual stepfamily member lacks relational maintenance skills, and, if so, why. If the clinician's assessment is that personal problems or unusual personality characteristics prevent an individual from engaging in satisfying relationships, then intensive individual therapy may be necessary before relational therapy or skills training is effective. Referrals to AA or other 12-step programs for substance abusers and individual or group psychotherapy focusing on specific problems also may be necessary. If a clinician is working with a couple who have not yet cohabited or remarried (i.e., premarriage counseling or education), and if the individual's problems are serious enough to warrant intensive therapy, then the clinician may want to encourage the clients to postpone making further plans until these problems are resolved.

If the paucity of relational maintenance and enhancement abilities are due to a lack of knowledge, as in the case of stepparents who are clueless about children's development, then education (e.g., books, adult education courses) designed to address this information gap would be prerequisite to relational skills training. For example, books on child development for lay audiences could be shared with new stepparents (e.g., Leach & Matthews, 1997, for 0–5; Gianneti & Sagarese, 1997, for ages 10–15; Steinberg & Levine, 1997, for ages 10–20).

Stepfamily members who are having problems now but who have demonstrated aptitudes for sustaining relationships in the past may need individual counseling to help them explore unresolved issues that might be hindering their attempts at relational maintenance. In other cases, family counseling or counseling with specific stepfamily dyads might be indicated. For example, some mothers become enmeshed with their children during the single-parent household stage and have trouble resolving the issue of sharing parenting responsibilities with their new spouse. An unwillingness to trust a spouse with the stepchildren is likely to inhibit overall stepfamily functioning and could certainly hinder the development of a strong couple bond. Other parents may be so angry with their children's other parent that they damage their children by placing them in the middle of their conflicts. Individual therapy to resolve distrust and anger might be helpful, but couple therapy or coparent therapy might also be needed before relationships can be stabilized.

Two general relational maintenance skills are fundamental to building and maintaining stepfamily relationships. Therefore, clinicians should teach communication skills and affinity strategies.

Teach Communication Skills. It is vitally important that stepfamily members be able to discuss their expectations for roles and relationships, clearly articulate their wants and needs, and be able to resolve conflicts through discussion. Unclear, indirect, and evasive communication contributes to greater misunderstandings (Morrison & Stollman, 1995). Communication skills that facilitate relationship maintenance in stepfamilies include conflict resolution skills, negotiation skills, and skills in constructively voicing feelings and opinions. New and changing relationships can challenge even the skills of good communicators. For example, stepparents and stepchildren may be unsure about how to talk to each other, former spouses may no longer know how to appropriately communicate, nonresidential parents may be at a loss for ways to interact with their children, and new partners may have no idea of appropriate discourse with their stepchildren's nonresidential parents. Therefore, the development of communication skills should not only involve learning universal strategies, but also explicit ways to communicate to specific family members should be taught.

Because stepfamily members may have very different lifestyles (i.e., values, ideas, ways of doing things), the ability to negotiate is a necessary skill for maintaining and enhancing relationships (Visher & Visher, 1996). For example, a stepparent may strongly believe that children should earn their spending money, yet the parent thinks that they should receive an allowance. It is important for clinicians to facilitate methods of interacting that allow everyone to state their own needs and preferences, to recognize and acknowledge when these differ from those of others, and to create acceptable solutions.

New stepfamily relationships may be tenuous, so the indiscriminate voicing of thoughts and opinions may do more damage than good and should not be encouraged (Papernow, 1995). Therefore, it may be important to coach stepfamily members on how to be assertive, but constructive, in stating what they see as problematic or would like changed. For example, making comments such as, "I have noticed you do not say hello to me when you come home. Saying 'hi' even once in a while would make me feel more comfortable," is more positive than "Why are you so rude? You don't even speak to me when you come in the house."

Teach Affinity Strategies. Spending one-on-one time in relationships builds affinity, is crucial to the maintenance and enhancement of dyadic connections, and often spills over into other relationships (E. B. Visher, 1994). "At times it seems almost magical how much the giving of undivided attention nourishes interpersonal relationships" (Visher & Visher, 1996, p. 126). Clinicians suggest that spending time together in dyads is particularly helpful in the early stages of stepfamily development (Papernow, 1995), but researchers have found that time together is not adequate. *How* the time is spent is critical to both affinity development and affinity maintenance (Ganong, Coleman, Fine, & Martin, 1999). Stepparents who participated in dyadic activities that *the stepchild instigated or particularly enjoyed* had the closest and most satisfying relationships. Stepparents who engaged in dyadic activities that *they wanted to share with the child* or that they thought would be good for the child (e.g., taking a stepson hunting to "make a man" of him) were less successful in building affinity. It also is critical that affinity-building techniques continue over time; when stepparents stopped affinity-maintaining efforts following remarriage, relationships with stepchildren were not as close as when affinity-maintaining strategies were ongoing.

STEPFAMILY MEMBERS NEGLECT MAINTAINING RELATIONSHIPS

Another problem in maintaining stepfamily relationships is when stepfamily members do not use their maintenance skills, allowing relationships that once were close to deteriorate. This occurs most frequently with the adult couple and residential parent–child relationships.

Couple Maintenance and Enhancement

Family therapists contend that a strong couple bond is a primary contributor to stepfamily stability and satisfaction (Burt & Burt, 1996; Papernow, 1993; Visher & Visher, 1996). However, couple bonding in stepfamilies is different than in first-marriage families because couples must concurrently develop relationships with new stepchildren and new extended kin as well as maintain ties with their children's other parent and perhaps nonresidential children. Multiple relationships are difficult for some people to handle. The couple relationship may be neglected because other relationships demand more attention.

Moreover, the presence of children means that adult couples have an audience of interested and powerful third parties all or most of the time. Children may have little motivation to help make the couple relationship strong, and they may view the stepparent as an intruder into their relationship with their parents (Visher & Visher, 1996). In addition, because the parent–child bond is older and generally stronger than the couple relationship, at least early on, parents' loyalties may lie with their children more than with the partner. Children may want the couple to fail because the stepparent may represent to them lost status, power, and time with the parent. Consequently, couple relationships are developed and maintained in the presence of third parties that may be interested in dissolving those bonds. Even if they do not succeed in ending the couple relationship, children can disrupt adults' efforts to maintain a strong relationship and they can divert attention away from the couple relationship. Former partners can also be intrusive and disruptive to couples' relationship maintenance efforts.

Another barrier to the adults' efforts to repair or enhance a deteriorating relationship is their fear of future loss (Coleman & Ganong, 1985). Adults may so desperately want the new couple relationship to succeed that they refrain from honest communication when they have disagreements. Rather than confront and challenge each other when things are not going smoothly, adults who fear another breakup may deny that problems exist. Consequently, problems do not get resolved, leading to feelings of alienation and powerlessness and a deterioration of the relationship (Sager, Brown, Crohn, Engel, Rodstein, & Walker, 1983).

Helping Couples Maintain and Enhance Their Relationship. Clinicians advise remarried couples to strengthen their bond by learning how to create boundaries around their relationship that exclude children, former partners, and other "third parties." One way to do this is to periodically spend time together relaxing, having fun, or talking (Visher & Visher, 1996). In addition to "dates," couples can also spend time together meeting as the "executive committee" of the family, discussing goals, dreams, strategies for resolving problems, and plans for the future. Such meetings allow couples to face children and others as a unit working together for the good of the entire family.

Couples also may need help learning more effective communication and conflict resolution skills (Bray, Berger, Silverblatt, & Hollier, 1987; Farrell &

Markman, 1986). Those individuals who deny couple difficulties because they fear dissolution may need special encouragement to risk sharing concerns they have. Denial is dangerous and should not go unchecked; remarried individuals resort to divorce more quickly than those in first marriages when they are dissatisfied (Booth & Edwards, 1992).

Relationship Maintenance and Enhancement Between Parents and Children

The relationship between residential parent and child in stepfamilies is perhaps the one most neglected by researchers and clinicians (Ganong & Coleman, 1994). Problems ensue in stepfamilies when parents also ignore this significant relationship. Parents sometimes take these bonds for granted, turning their energies more to the couple relationship and to developing ties with stepchildren. Children may experience this as an unwelcome loss of parental attention and time. If children lack the awareness or verbal skills to articulate what they want from their parents, they may respond by misbehaving, by rejecting the stepparent, or by moving to their other parents' residences.

Helping Residential Parents and Children Maintain Their Relationships. Just as with couple relationships, and other relationships, setting aside time for parent and child to be together without others present can help them maintain strong ties. Time alone with a parent is reassuring to a child who may have had the parent's undivided attention prior to remarriage. Parents may underestimate the importance of spending time and paying attention to children alone because they are focused on creating a sense of family (Visher & Visher, 1996). Spending time enhancing specific relationships also helps promote overall family ties and functioning. Ideas for developing and strengthening dyadic relationships in stepfamilies can be found in *Stepping Ahead* (E. B. Visher, 1989).

Children should be helped to assertively ask parents for what they want and need from them (Craven, 1982), rather than threaten to leave or sabotage the time parents spend with new partners. Rituals or routine daily activities that hold special meaning for the parent–child relationship should be continued if at all possible, or new routines and rituals should be established. This seemingly simple directive is difficult for parents to remember, perhaps because ordinary behaviors are not thought of as strategies to maintain or enhance relationships. Consequently, both children and adults probably need to be given specific strategies and scripts for asking for the renewal or instigation of ordinary and "special" opportunities to maintain the parent–child relationship (Papernow, 1993; Visher & Visher, 1996).

The Relationship Partner Does Not Respond to
Stepfamily Members' Relational Maintenance Strategies

Sometimes in stepfamilies, relational maintenance and enhancement behaviors are rejected or the relational partner responds in ways that are designed to increase distance in the relationship. There are a number of reasons why relational maintenance behaviors are not reciprocated: differing timetables for relational development, divergent expectations, variable motivations to maintain relationships, and mourning losses.

Differing Timetables. Stepfamily members may be on different timetables for relationship development. Typically, adults are more eager than children are to build and maintain emotionally close bonds. Stepfamilies with more than one child may find that children vary in their openness to enhancing new relationships, and even the adults may have divergent expectations about the speed at which relationships will develop. It is important that these various timelines are understood and respected by stepfamily members. If they are not, then some individuals' relational building and maintaining behaviors will seem inappropriate or unwelcome to others, and will not be reciprocated. An example of this is when parents push children to bond emotionally with stepparents before the children are ready to do so or at a pace that is uncomfortable for the children. When that happens, children often react by distancing themselves from stepparents and rejecting their overtures (Bray, 1998; Hetherington, 1993).

Divergent Expectations. Divergent relationship expectations also lead to the rejection of maintenance behaviors. Children are not passive participants in the step-relationship formation process (Coleman, Ganong, & Fine, 2000). For example, Russell and Searcy (1997) found that adolescent stepchildren often respond to stepparents in ways that create distance between them. Relationship maintenance, therefore, is bidirectional. Adolescent stepchildren's expectations may be that their parent's new partner has joined the family to be their parent's companion, but not to have a close relationship with them. The stepparent, on the other hand, may expect to become an important person in the stepchildren's lives. If these conflicting expectations are not clarified, and compromises reached, then the stepparent will find that their attempts to get close to the stepchildren are rebuffed because the stepchildren perceive such behaviors to be unnecessary and unwelcome.

Moreover, negative cultural stereotypes about stepfamilies, stepchildren, and stepparents also may adversely affect how stepfamily members see each other and their expectations for each other. For example, stereotypes such as "stepmothers are mean, uncaring, and wicked" make it difficult for stepchildren to be aware of friendly overtures or other positive behaviors of the stepmother that do not fit the stereotype. Positive behaviors are either ignored or they are interpreted as manipulation, bribery, or attempts to usurp emotional bonds between the children and their fathers.

Different Motivations. Various family members have different levels of motivation to develop and maintain close relationships with each other. The adults have the strongest incentive to bond as a couple, and they often do so with considerable success (Ganong & Coleman, 1994). Parents and children generally want to maintain close relationships as well, but this may be less true for other stepfamily relationships. For example, coparents may prefer not to be involved with each other but are forced to by law (i.e., joint custody) or because of a sense of duty to their children. Motivations to maintain stepparent–stepchild relationships may vary—both relationship partners may be highly motivated if they like each other and have a lot in common, motivation may be low for both, or one person may be more motivated than the other. The desire to maintain step-relationships may be due to characteristics of the relational partner (e.g., "I like my stepmother because she is a great person who has helped me a lot.") or out of a sense of responsibility to the parent/partner (e.g., "I am nice to my stepfather because he treats my mother well, and she loves him."). Stepparents and stepchildren that are motivated to develop close ties will engage in more maintenance behaviors, and will respond positively and appropriately to such strategies. Stepparents and stepchildren who are less invested in seeing the relationship last will either reject maintenance strategies, will respond to them less enthusiastically, and will be unlikely to attempt their own affinity-building or -maintaining efforts.

Mourning Losses. A major reason for differing timetables for relational development, divergent expectations, and variable motivations to maintain relationships may be found in the precursors to stepfamily living. Stepfamilies are formed after the dissolution of marriages by death or divorce, or in the case of cohabitation, after the informal severing of ties. These transitions trigger multiple changes for stepfamily members, involving relationships, roles, and even personal and family identities. Some of these changes represent significant losses for stepfamily members (Papernow, 1995). Adults have lost a partner, children may have lost some or all contact with a parent living elsewhere, and families may have moved, with resulting changes in neighborhoods, living arrangements, schools, friendship and support networks, employment, and lifestyles. Not recognizing and dealing with losses and the lingering emotional attachments interferes with the formation of stepfamily relationships (Coale Lewis, 1985; Visher & Visher, 1996). Incomplete mourning of losses prevents people from moving ahead.

It is not unusual for some family members to adapt to changes and to resolve feelings of loss more quickly than others do. Adults often mourn the
end of their marriage and their dream of "living happily ever after" *before*
the divorce takes place. Children, on the other hand, typically begin this
mourning process *after* the parents separate or even *after* the divorce.
Therefore, single parents who initiate new romantic relationships often are
more ready for change than are their children. Parents, happy with their
new partner, may be oblivious to their children's negative reactions to this
new relationship.

When attempts to maintain or enhance a relationship are rejected, the
consequences can be extremely negative for the rejected individuals, the
relationship, and the entire stepfamily. Individuals who are rebuffed feel
badly about themselves and their relational partner, eventually withdraw
from further attempts if repeated efforts fail, and the indirect fallout from
unhappy individuals and distant, perhaps distressed relationships, poisons
other stepfamily relationships. For example, when stepparents' positive
overtures are ignored or actively rebuffed, it is not unusual for them to be
upset with themselves and angry at stepchildren. Parents who observe these
interactions may feel guilty for exposing their loved ones to each other with
such negative results, and if such interactions continue unabated, all stepfamily relationships become strained. Consequently, clinical interventions focus on: helping individuals cope who are rejected, teaching alternative strategies for maintaining and enhancing relationships, and working with
relational partners to increase incentives to reciprocate maintenance behaviors. Prior to these interventions, clinicians may have to help stepfamily
members be aware of reasons why maintenance strategies are not working.

Increasing Awareness

Clinicians may need to help parents see these changes through the eyes of
their children so they can help their children cope with feelings of loss and
perhaps resentment towards a parent who is moving on when the children
are not yet ready for another family change. Bibliotherapy can aid such efforts. Bibliotherapy is a technique that uses short stories and books related
to stepfamilies' experiences to inform and educate both adults and children.
Works may include both fiction and nonfiction, but the quality of these materials should be assessed very carefully before giving them to clients. Guidelines for the use of bibliotherapy with stepfamilies can be found in Coleman
and Ganong (1990). For instance, having adults read novels about stepfamilies written for children and adolescents can help make the adults aware
of how the stepfamily is experienced from the stepchildren's perspective,
because most novels are framed from the young person's point of view
(Coleman & Ganong, 1988).

To facilitate acknowledgement of losses by clients, the Vishers (1996)
suggest helping stepfamily members examine the changes they have expe-

rienced prior to and following formation of the stepfamily. Family members may be only vaguely aware of the magnitude of change they have experienced, both in major areas of family life (e.g., moves, children going back and forth between two households) and in subtle ways (e.g., loss of daily routines). Clients should be allowed ample time to catalog and mourn losses as a result of these transitions.

Moreover, gains should be identified. For instance, after remarriage, household finances may have improved, and individuals may have gained opportunities to learn from new family members (Coleman, Ganong, & Gingrich, 1985). Clinicians can help stepfamily members through the processes of mourning losses and celebrating gains (as well as noting those changes that have mixed effects for all or that have different effects for different family members). Once losses have been mourned, stepfamily members are more likely to be ready to face new challenges.

Helping Individuals Cope

If rejected stepfamily members feel badly about themselves and others, it is unlikely that there will be future attempts to enhance relationships. Therefore, it is important for clinicians to validate feelings that arise, work to reduce feelings of helplessness, and reframe the situation.

Validating Feelings. Knowing that it is normal and acceptable to feel frustrated and upset lessens negative self-perceptions by normalizing emotional reactions to stressful relationships. Validating feelings is particularly important for women in stepfamilies (Visher, Visher, & Pasley, 1997), because women often feel responsible for family functioning (Wood, 1994). For example, mothers may feel especially torn trying to balance and maintain relationships with their new partner and their children (Weaver & Coleman, 1998).

It may be particularly important for clinicians to help clients be aware that ambivalent feelings are common in stepfamilies when relationships are strained. For example, stepparents may feel affection for their stepchildren, but at the same time, they also may feel relieved when the children leave to spend time with their other parent. Ambivalent feelings toward family members are not unique to stepfamilies, but stepfamily members tend to be acutely aware of contrasting feelings, which makes them feel guilty or confused. Clinicians must normalize these ambivalent reactions to stepfamily relationships. In other words, stepfamily members should be assisted in accepting the normality of their ambivalent feelings.

Reducing Feelings of Helplessness. When maintenance efforts are rejected, individuals commonly feel powerless to change the situation. This may be especially true when stepparents encounter the paradoxical situation in which the nicer they act, the more rejecting the stepchildren are (this is a common reaction to feeling torn loyalty between the stepparent and non-residential parent). Feelings of helplessness are important to address because they can lead to withdrawal from the relationship.

Helping stepfamily members understand the dynamics that may be underlying rejections of relationship maintenance efforts may aid in lowering feelings of impotence (Bernstein, 1994). When clinicians facilitate stepfamily members' understandings of the varying perceptions and needs of individual family members, clients begin to understand that their efforts may not be doomed to failure forever. They also realize that their experiences are not deviant or extreme, which improves self-esteem and reduces a sense of incompetence (Visher & Visher, 1996).

Reframing the Situation. Another strategy for coping with rejection of relationship enhancement and maintenance efforts is reframing experiences. Individuals are encouraged to redefine a situation or experience in a more positive and manageable way (Pasley & Dollahite, 1995; Visher & Visher, 1996). For example, Ahrons has reframed divorce as a normative process that results in family reorganization (i.e., the binuclear family, a family system with two households) rather than disintegration (i.e., broken home; Ahrons & Perlmutter, 1982). Reframing is helpful for the adjustment of both adults and children (Pasley & Dollahite, 1995; Quick, McKenry, & Newman, 1994). Intervention strategies that help individuals change the way in which they think about a situation, such as failed attempts at relational maintenance, make the situation seem more manageable. Adolescent stepchildren can be taught, for example, that rather than labeling their stepparents' questions about their activities as intrusive and nosy, they can think of it in other ways: (1) "My stepmom is asking because she cares about me"; (2) "My stepfather needs to be informed about what modern adolescents do for fun"; or (3) "If I tell him what he wants to know, he will like me better and will be more likely to do things for me when I ask." Reframing is a useful technique for many stepfamily relationship issues.

Teaching Alternative Maintenance Strategies

Perhaps a first step in teaching alternative maintenance strategies is to help stepfamily members understand normative experiences of stepfamily development. For instance, helping adults see that children may be moving according to a different timetable than they are, that children might have different levels of motivation to bond than adults do, and that various family members may want differing levels of closeness, gives stepfamily members a frame of reference with which to plan strategies and helps reduce the sense of urgency to integrate the family as rapidly as possible.

Stepchildren often have definite expectations regarding stepparents, and they should be encouraged by clinicians to identify what it is they want and need from their stepparents. If what stepchildren want are stepparents who leave them alone but provide love and support to their parents, then stepparents who want and expect to discipline and instill stepchildren with their values are probably going to be disappointed and frustrated. The worse the match between the stepchildren's and stepparents' wants and expectations, the harder it will be to maintain good relationships. Even very young children who have begged for a "new daddy" or "new mommy" need to be queried about their behavioral expectations for this new parent. Differing expectations, especially if unexpressed, create problems for individuals in remarried families as well as for the clinicians whose help is sought. Until expectations and wants are clarified, it is often recommended that biological parents retain responsibility for most of the parenting, especially discipline (Bernstein, 1994; Kelley, 1992; Visher & Visher, 1988). Clinicians, therefore, should facilitate the development of strategies that maintain discipline as a responsibility of the parent, particularly during the early years in a remarried family (Pasley & Dollahite, 1995).

Clinicians advise stepfamily members to go slowly in developing relationships (J. S. Visher, 1994). Dyadic relationships in stepfamilies develop only at the pace of the person who is less ready, less interested, and less motivated, so it does little good to push for premature intimacy. Sometimes by not trying as hard as they have, stepparents who have been rejected by stepchildren find that their more relaxed attempts are more well received. Stepfamily members who want to be closer to others are advised to not give up their efforts but to continue maintenance behaviors in a low-key manner.

This advice is difficult to follow for assertive individuals with high needs for control. They tend to be insensitive to the reactions of others (Patterson & Beckett, 1995). Therefore, it is important for clinicians to assist stepfamily members in gaining a realistic sense of control by helping them differentiate the aspects of stepfamily life that they can control and those that are beyond their control. Sometimes, simply making stepfamily members aware of how complex their families are and how much they differ from first marriage families is enough to reduce inappropriate and insensitive efforts to control.

Increasing Partner's Reciprocity of Maintenance Behaviors

Just suggesting strategies for stepparents and others to use in forming close relationships may not be enough; working with stepchildren and other relationship partners to increase reciprocity of maintenance behaviors also may be necessary. Anderson and White (1986) found that stepparents' positive involvement with their stepchildren did not differ in functional and dysfunctional stepfamilies, but the level of reciprocity between stepparents and stepchildren did.

It may be necessary to teach stepfamily members how to act in ways that are different from how they feel (Visher & Visher, 1996). Suggesting that stepchildren respond politely, even enthusiastically, to stepparents' attempts to bond with them, even when they do not feel like it, helps by changing the tenor of interactions, reducing conflicts and bad feelings, and takes less energy usually than rejecting such offers. Moreover, behaving towards someone in the stepfamily as if a closer, more positive relationship exists can help bring about a cognitive shift; by acting as if they feel closer than they do, partners' feelings and thoughts often become more positive. Although stepchildren (and others) may initially perceive this to be hypocritical, by appealing to self-interests, stepchildren can be persuaded to give this strategy a try. This is another way that reframing can be used— rather than encouraging adolescents to interact positively with stepparents because they should, clinicians can encourage them to do so because they will then be more likely to get what they want. For example, teaching adolescents the concept of *quid pro quo* (something for something) can provide them with a frame of reference for interacting with stepparents and parents in ways that maximize their gains by giving the adults what they want from them (e.g., "If I am polite to my stepfather when he asks me how my day was, I can avoid a big fight about my attitude, and will not get grounded for talking back").

If stepchildren are using distancing techniques because of loyalty conflicts, clinicians can assure them that it is possible to be close to both a stepfather and a father. Stepchildren also can be helped to think of each adult's "specialties." For instance, a stepfather might become the math homework expert while the father remains the social studies homework expert. Individuals should be helped to accept the notion that affection is not a zero-sum gain; loyalty conflicts are not likely to occur when parents specifically give children permission to like their new stepparents.

Another way to increase reciprocity to a relational partner is to appeal to individuals' obligations to third parties. For instance, stepchildren can be invited to "be nice to your stepdad for your mother, it will make her happy." In a parent education program we help teach, coparents are taught in several ways to put aside self-interests and focus on their children's well-being.

Members Do Not Know How to Apply Relational Maintenance Skills Within Stepfamily Contexts

The most complex explanation for why stepfamily members have problems initiating, maintaining, and enhancing their family relationships, even when they have good relationship maintenance skills, is because they are attempting to base their stepfamily relationships on an inappropriate model of family life, that of the first marriage family. Individuals' cognitive models of family life are related to what they do in their families. That is, their behaviors reflect their beliefs about the right way to be a family (Dallos, 1991). In first marriages, the couple negotiates a joint construction of marital reality as they interact over time, sharing expectations, beliefs (personal and normative), and opinions about what the marriage should be like (Berger & Luckmann, 1966). There are also many social norms to help guide them through the stages of parenthood. Stepfamilies have a more arduous task because they must negotiate the beliefs and expectations of more people, and there are few societal norms to guide them (Cherlin, 1978). Moreover, they may be more likely to contain individuals with generally unrealistic beliefs about family relationships, which may have contributed to problems in the first marriage family. Unfortunately, rather than thinking creatively or adapting beliefs and behaviors to fit the unique attributes of stepfamilies, many attempt to recreate themselves as a first marriage family (Fishman & Hamel, 1981; Ganong & Coleman, 1994; Visher & Visher, 1988), a strategy that usually creates more relationship problems than it solves.

The first-marriage family model *does* work for some stepfamilies, however. For it to succeed, all members of the stepfamily must collude on implementing the model. This requires the willing cooperation of family members outside the household as well as in, because it essentially means that the stepparent in the household replaces the nonresidential parent, who gives up parental rights and responsibilities. If nonresidential parents cooperate by ending contact with their children, the model still only works if the children willingly accept the replacement of their parent by a stepparent. Even the commonly used strategy of formalizing the model via legal adoption does not enhance relationships unless the children are agreeable and fully aware of the consequences (Ganong, Coleman, Fine, & McDaniel, 1998).

Stepfamilies employ the first marriage family model in attempts to reduce stress and anxiety related to stepfamily complexity and because they are unclear how to be a well-functioning stepfamily. However, few individuals are comfortable denying past family histories, and few children are happy cutting off ties with nonresidential parents. For most stepfamilies, employing a first-marriage family model is predicated on a number of erroneous assumptions that exacerbate rather than relieve stress and anxiety (Kaplan & Hennon, 1992; Leslie & Epstein, 1988; McGoldrick & Carter, 1989).

Unrealistic Expectations. Examples of typical erroneous assumptions include: *Stepchildren will accept the stepparent's discipline without question.* Stepparents who move quickly into parental roles may focus on discipline and other parental responsibilities and not realize the necessity of first developing strong emotional bonds with stepchildren that are based on affection and friendship. Stepparents whose idea of parenting is to discipline or establish new rules often encounter resistance from stepchildren and even their spouses (Weaver & Coleman, 1998). *Adjustment to the new family will happen rapidly.* Mills (1984) suggested that clinicians tell stepfamilies that it will take as many years to feel like a family as the age of the child at remarriage. For instance, if the child was 7 when the remarriage occurred, it will be 7 years before the stepfamily feels like a family to its members. Whether Mills believed that or not, his message was intended to slow down stepparents' and parents' efforts to become like a first-marriage family, or maybe even shock them into lowering their expectations for instant togetherness. *Stepparents and stepchildren will quickly feel love and affection for each other.* A first-marriage belief is that children and parents innately and naturally love each other. Perhaps of most importance for relationship maintenance, stepparents who assume that their stepchildren will love them automatically may make little effort to purposefully develop and maintain affinity with them. Researchers have found that strategic affinity-seeking and affinity-maintaining are of critical significance in establishing satisfying stepparent–stepchild relationships (Ganong et al., 1998).

When unrealistic expectations for relationships fail to materialize, individuals may feel angry, betrayed, confused, anxious, dissatisfied, and disillusioned (Burt & Burt, 1996; Kaplan & Hennon, 1992; Leslie & Epstein, 1988). Consequently, in the long run, stepfamily relationships are often harmed. Unfortunately, couples seldom discuss their expectations prior to forming their stepfamilies (Ganong & Coleman, 1989). They also tend not to prepare in other ways that would reduce unrealistic expectations, such as reading about stepfamilies, talking with people living in stepfamilies, or participating in premarriage education or counseling. The lack of preparation, coupled with the absence of stepfamily models, means that adults too often think they will quickly become just like a first-marriage family.

Relationship Maintenance and the First-Marriage Family Model

The entire stepfamily is affected when they try to function as if they were first marriage families, but the relationships between stepparents and stepchildren, coparents, and nonresidential parents and children are most negatively influenced. The latter two relationships are either ignored or actively denied because they are incompatible with the first marriage family model. The stepparent–stepchild relationship, however, is just as profoundly affected.

Stepparents and Stepchildren

Most clinicians consider stepparents attempting to relate to stepchildren as if they were their parents to be problematic (Visher & Visher, 1982). Early in the formation of stepfamilies, using the first marriage family model means that there is a large discrepancy between how stepparents and stepchildren relate to each other and the emotional and interpersonal realities that are characteristic of newer relationships (Coale Lewis, 1985; Goldner, 1982). Such discrepancies require cognitive distortions, denial of individual and familial histories that may differ, and efforts to speed up the normative processes of relational development.

The stepparent and residential parent often end up competing with the nonresidential parent over the child, which is stressful for children. They must either choose one parent over the other or remain torn between conflicting loyalties. Children with loyalties to nonresidential parents may avoid forming close relationships with stepparents for fear of hurting the feelings of their fathers or mothers (Bray, 1995).

Stepmothers. Relational maintenance difficulties in stepparent–stepchild relationships probably depend to some extent on the sex of the stepparent. Stepmothers have more difficulty adjusting to stepfamily roles than stepfathers do (Bernstein, 1989). This is partly due to gender role stereotypes. Women are expected to want to be mothers and to engage in mothering behaviors. Therefore, when a woman marries a man who has children, she is expected to take on the mothering role. Residential stepmothers are more likely than residential stepfathers to try to function like parents, and as a result are often extremely frustrated with their family responsibilities and frequently feel helpless and burned out (Morrison & Thompson-Guppy, 1985). Furthermore, because they are embarrassed by their feelings of frustration and ineptness, they may not seek clinical assistance or if they seek it, it will be for other problems instead.

Stepfathers. Many stepfathers simply assume they will function as fathers to their stepchildren (Visher & Visher, 1982). With little preparation for stepfamily roles, some stepfathers assume that things will naturally fall into place and that their spouse will guide their interactions with stepchildren (Visher & Visher, 1988). In some cases, these stepfathers give little thought to how their roles might differ from that of fathers because they do not expect to be involved with the stepchildren very much. What is the role of the father that stepfathers try to emulate? Stepfathers that see the father role as secondary to that of the mother, and one that is relatively uninvolved with the children, interact little and take a rather passive role in child discipline; these men are less likely to come into conflict with the stepchild (Hetherington & Henderson, 1997) because they basically see fathering as paying the bills. Of course, some stepfathers expect to be the primary disciplinarians, because they see this as an important function of a father's responsibilities. Others see their duty as rescuing their wives from being overwhelmed by their disobedient children. By laying down a strict set of rules and enforcing them, these stepfathers also see themselves as teaching values to their stepchildren. The reaction of wives and children in many of these stepfamilies range from passive resistance and resentment to outright rebellion. Seldom do these approaches result in enhanced relationships.

Clinicians can help stepparents find a unique niche in the stepfamily, and more specifically, in the lives of their stepchildren, instead of attempting to become a substitute for an absent parent. The goal should be a mutually acceptable relationship for the stepparent and each stepchild (Crosbie-Burnett, 1984). However, what is mutually satisfying may differ from family to family and may even differ from stepchild to stepchild within the same family. For example, a stepparent and a very young stepchild may successfully reenact a parent–child relationship in the family, while the relationship between the same stepparent and an older stepchild is maintained as a friendship. To adults it may seem wrong to have variable stepparent–stepchild relationships within the same family, but one size seldom fits all. Relationships need to be tailored to fit the needs of the children.

Coparents

Following the first-marriage family model requires ignoring or eliminating the coparental relationship. This may hurt children, and nonresidential parents seldom welcome being "replaced." Therefore, maintaining and enhancing postdivorce coparental relationships are important. In fact, the relationship quality between coparents has been found to be related to parents' well-being (Masheter, 1991), their children's adjustment (Amato & Keith, 1991; Crosbie-Burnett, 1991), the quality of remarriages (Buehler & Ryan, 1994), residential parent–child relationship quality (Bowman & Ahrons, 1985), and nonresidential parents' involvement with children (Ahrons & Miller, 1993; Whiteside, 1998).

Coparenting is difficult, even under the best of circumstances—there are few norms regarding the maintenance and enhancement of postdivorce coparental relationships (Madden-Derdich & Arditti, 1999), and there is little social support to continue such relationships (Ahrons & Perlmutter, 1982). Instead, societal perceptions are that coparental relationships should be detached or, if they exist at all, negative and hostile.

As an alternative to the first-marriage family model, clinicians could assist stepfamilies in maintaining a working relationship with the coparents of their children. This would include normalizing coparental relationships (Cole & Cole, 1999), aiding coparents in establishing boundaries between households, and assisting them in redefining their relationship from marital to coparental (Madden-Derdich & Arditti, 1999). Stepparents' child-rearing duties also must be clarified when children spend time in both households (Cole & Cole, 1999; Whiteside, 1998).

Clinicians should first focus on helping coparents explore goals for the relationship (Madden-Derdich & Arditti, 1999) and identify appropriate interactions (Ahrons & Perlmutter, 1982). For example, attainable goals for most coparents would be to maintain relationships in which adults *do not* talk negatively about each other to the children and *do* make reasonable accommodations so that both parents can be involved in children's activities such as school functions and sports (Whiteside, 1998). Secondly, explore with coparents what shared parenting involves now and in the future. How will childcare tasks be divided? What needed resources will be provided and by whom? What will visitation involve? How will emergencies, holidays, and special events be handled? Although coparental relationships can take many forms, what is most important is that they support each other's involvement with their children. A final clinical recommendation is to teach conflict resolution strategies (Whiteside, 1998). With concerted effort, coparents can manage cooperative interactions and resolve conflicts over time (Ahrons & Rodgers, 1987).

Nonresidential Parent–Child Relationships

Maintaining and enhancing relationships between nonresidential parents and children is challenging, given that interactions gradually decline after separation or divorce (Stephens, 1996). Although about 25% of children see their nonresidential fathers at least once a week (Seltzer & Brandeth, 1994) approximately 50% lose contact with their fathers over time. Potential barriers to continued involvement include the logistics of arranging contacts, coparental strains, a lack of norms for nonresidential parent–child relationships (Seltzer, 1991), and competition from the stepparent. Although negotiating visits and maintaining relationships with nonresidential children may be difficult, it is stressful for children to not be able to see their nonresidential parents (Lutz, 1983). Clinicians can help facilitate nonresidential father involvement by assuring fathers that the quality of the contact may be more important than frequency or duration of visits (Buchanan, Maccoby, & Dornbusch, 1996) and that being emotionally supportive and providing behavioral guidelines for children facilitates positive child outcomes (Amato & Gilbreath, 1999).

The nonresidential parent–child relationship may change following remarriage of either parent. When fathers remarry, they often assume additional responsibilities; how these are combined with existing obligations to his children may affect the maintenance of nonresidential father–child relationships (Braver, Wolchik, Sandler, & Sheets, 1993). When mothers remarry, nonresidential fathers may experience feelings of helplessness. To deal with such feelings, nonresidential fathers may either attempt to control individuals in the step-household or relinquish any existing power they may have (Visher & Visher, 1996). Neither strategy works well. Therefore, interventions for nonresidential fathers should include fostering ways for them to meet obligations to old and new family members and helping them discover where they can exert influence and how to deal with the situations and experiences that they cannot control.

Provide Education

Many, if not most, stepfamilies need education rather than therapy (Visher & Visher, 1980), and it is important that therapy include an educational component along with the treatment (Browning, 1994). Sometimes simply being aware of stereotyped societal beliefs and that the feelings they are experiencing and the behaviors that they are observing are typical is enough to give them hope and normalize their experiences. The knowledge that stepparents and stepchildren may never truly love each other and that love is certainly unlikely to occur instantly may dispel the guilt many stepparents feel and allow them to develop more realistic expectations for relationships.

Stepfamily members need factual information about how daily life in a stepfamily affects relationship maintenance. Otherwise, stepfamily members may spend time unsuccessfully attempting to achieve the impossible or be at a loss for what to do and expect (Papernow, 1993). In order for clinicians to provide basic information successfully, it is imperative that they educate themselves about common stepfamily tasks, challenges, and experiences (Browning, 1994). A helpful beginning resource is Visher and Visher's (1996) book, *Therapy with Stepfamilies*, which provides a comprehensive list of such tasks.

Moreover, clinicians must be aware of common relationship processes and problems in stepfamilies (Papernow, 1995). It is sometimes difficult for clinicians to know where to start because of the competing demands of the different dyads. For example, for stepparents the establishment of a strong couple bond may be imperative before positive relationships with stepchildren can develop (Visher et al., 1997). Furthermore, relationship maintenance between nonresidential parents and children, and to some extent, nonresidential stepparents and stepchildren, is affected by the relationship between the coparents. If the coparent relationship is hostile, it is very difficult for family members outside of the household to maintain a good relationship with their children or stepchildren. Therefore, in interventions focused on the enhancement and maintenance of relationships in remarried families, the ability to concomitantly consider multiple relationships is crucial. Every intervention is likely to have multiple effects on the various stepfamily dyads.

The utilization of resources, such as bibliotherapy and self-help groups, may be helpful in educating remarried family members about stepfamily dynamics (Browning, 1994; Burt & Burt, 1996). Referrals to educational stepfamily groups and associations, such as local chapters of the Stepfamily Association of America, can also be made (Visher & Visher, 1996).

Papernow (1993) recommends that clinicians make articles, books, and pamphlets available in waiting rooms. Flyers with contact information for groups aimed at stepfamilies can be posted. The importance of providing education to stepfamily members cannot be overstated. Stepfamily adults who had been in therapy identified learning about stepfamilies as one of the most positive aspects of intervention (Visher et al., 1997).

Complexity in and of itself is not a relationship maintenance problem, but challenges arise because stepfamily members do not anticipate the extent of how complicated their family lives will be (Goldner, 1982). For the adults, challenges include maintaining ties with children from previous relationships, continuing to coparent with a former spouse or partner, and developing and maintaining relationships with new partners and perhaps stepchildren. Stepchildren are faced with maintaining ties with nonresidential parents, and perhaps nonresidential siblings, while developing and maintaining relationships with one or more stepparents and stepsiblings. Consequently, they are unprepared or underprepared, they may feel overwhelmed, and they may find it difficult, if not impossible, to rely on "the effortless familiarity that comes from time and physical proximity" (p. 197). Goldner argues that some stepfamilies become stuck in early developmental stages because they cannot manage to form a family and new family relationships while simultaneously maintaining relationships that are further along in the family life cycle (e.g., parent–child relationships). For instance, some individuals have a hard time handling the activity of children moving in and out of the household and having to consult with coparents before activities can be planned. Using genograms has been recommended as a way to help stepfamilies understand the complexity of their families and as a therapeutic tool (Visher & Visher, 1996). Genograms are "family trees," graphic representations of family histories that include relationships, multigenerational and cross-household patterns of interaction, and information about family structure and structural changes over time. Doing genograms with stepfamilies helps clinicians be more aware of their complexity.

Stepfamilies challenge the ways clinicians typically think about families and intervention, and require them to proceed in ways that may seem counterintuitive to them (Browning, 1994). To be successful, clinicians must understand the wide-ranging complexity of stepfamily structures. Clinicians must especially consider the structure of the family, including members who may not live in the client's household (e.g., former spouses and their new partners, nonresidential children and stepchildren, grandparents). Relationships in stepfamilies have the potential to be close and satisfying and clinicians can play major roles in helping stepfamily members achieve relationship goals and enhance the quality of their lives. Samuel Johnson called remarriage "the triumph of hope over experience." Skillful clinicians can help remarried couples and other stepfamily members learn from their experiences and build stable and satisfying lives together.

REFERENCES

Ahrons, C. R., & Miller, R. B. (1993). The effect of the postdivorce relationship on paternal involvement: A longitudinal analysis. *American Journal of Orthopsychiatry, 63*, 441–450.

Ahrons, C. R., & Perlmutter, M. S. (1982). The relationship between former spouses: A fundamental system in the remarriage family. In L. Messinger (Ed.), *Therapy with remarriage families* (pp. 31–46). Rockville, MD: Aspen Systems Corp.

Ahrons, C. R., & Rodgers, R. H. (1987). *Divorced families*. New York: W. W. Norton.

Amato, P., & Gilbreath, J. G. (1999). Nonresident fathers and children's well-being: A meta-analysis. *Journal of Marriage and the Family, 61*, 557–573.

Amato, P. R., & Keith, B. (1991). Parental divorce and the well-being of children: A meta-analysis. *Psychological Bulletin, 110*, 26–46.

Anderson, J. Z., & White, G. D. (1986). An empirical investigation of interaction and relationship patterns in functional and dysfunctional nuclear families and stepfamilies. *Family Process, 25*, 407–422.

Bernstein, A. (1989). Gender and stepfamily life: A review. *Journal of Feminist Family Therapy, 1*, 1–27.

Bernstein, A. (1994). Women in stepfamilies: The fairy godmother, the wicked witch, and Cinderella reconstructed. In M. P. Mirkin (Ed.), *Women in context: Toward a feminist reconstruction of psychotherapy* (pp. 188–213). New York: Guilford.

Berger, P., & Luckmann, T. (1966). *The social construction of reality: An essay in the sociology of knowledge*. New York, NY: Doubleday.

Booth, A., & Edwards, J. N. (1992). Starting over: Why remarriages are more unstable. *Journal of Family Issues, 13*, 179–194.

Bowman, M. E., & Ahrons, C. R. (1985). Impact of legal custody status on fathers' parenting postdivorce. *Journal of Marriage and the Family, 47*, 481–487.

Braver, S., Wolchik, S., Sandler, I., & Sheets, V. (1993). A social exchange model of nonresidential parent involvement. In C. Depner & J. Bray (Eds.), *Nonresidential parenting: New vistas in family living* (pp. 87–108). Newbury Park, CA: Sage.

Bray, J. H. (1995). Children in stepfamilies: Assessment and treatment issues. In D. K. Huntley (Ed.), *Understanding stepfamilies: Implications for assessment and treatment* (pp. 59–72). Alexandria, VA: American Counseling Association.

Bray, J. (1998). *Stepfamilies*. New York: Broadway.

Bray, J. H., Berger, S. H., Silverblatt, A. H., & Hollier, A. (1987). Family process and organization during early remarriage: A preliminary analysis. In J. P. Vincent (Ed.), *Advances in family intervention, assessment, and theory* (pp. 253–279). Greenwich, CT: JAI Press.

Brody, G. H., Neubaum, E., & Forehand, R. (1988). Serial marriage: A heuristic analysis of an emerging family form. *Psychological Bulletin, 103*(2), 211–222.

Browning, S. W. (1994). Treating stepfamilies: Alternatives to traditional family therapy. In K. Pasley & M. Ihinger-Tallman (Eds.), *Stepparenting: Issues in theory, research, and practice* (pp. 175–198). Westport, CT: Greenwood.

Buchanan, C. M., Maccoby, E. E., & Dornbusch, S. M. (1996). *Adolescents after divorce*. Cambridge, MA: Harvard University Press.

Buehler, C., & Ryan, C. (1994). Former-spouse relations and noncustodial father involvement during marital and family transitions: A closer look at remarriage following divorce. In K. Pasley & M. Ihinger-Tallman (Eds.), *Stepparenting: Issues in theory, research, and practice* (pp. 127–150). Westport, CT: Greenwood.

Bumpass, L., Raley, R. K., & Sweet, J. (1995). The changing character of stepfamilies: Implications of cohabitation and nonmarital childbearing. *Demography, 32*, 425–436.

Bumpass, L., Sweet, J., & Castro Martin, T. (1990). Changing patterns of remarriage. *Journal of Marriage and the Family, 52*, 747–756.

Burt, M., & Burt, R. (1996). *Stepfamilies: The step by step model of brief therapy.* New York: Brunner/Mazel.

Canary, D. J., & Stafford, L. (1994). Maintaining relationships through strategic and routine interaction. In D. J. Canary & L. Stafford (Eds.), *Communication and relational maintenance* (pp. 3–22). San Diego, CA: Academic Press.

Cherlin, A. (1978). Remarriage as an incomplete institution. *American Journal of Sociology, 84*(3), 634–650.

Cherlin, A. J. (1992). Marriage, divorce, remarriage. *Social trends in the United States.* Cambridge, MA: Harvard University Press.

Coale Lewis, H. (1985). Family therapy with stepfamilies. *Journal of Strategic and Systemic Therapies, 4*, 13–23.

Cole, C. L., & Cole, A. L. (1999). Boundary ambiguities that bind former spouses together after the children leave home in post-divorce families. *Family Relations, 48*, 271–272.

Coleman, M., & Ganong, L. (1985). Remarriage myths: Implications for the helping professions. *Journal of Counseling & Development, 64*, 116–120.

Coleman, M., & Ganong, L. (1988). Bibliotherapy with stepchildren. Springfield, IL: Charles C Thomas.

Coleman, M., & Ganong, L. (1990). The uses of juvenile fiction and self-help books with stepfamilies. *Journal of Counseling and Development, 68*, 327–331.

Coleman, M., Ganong, L., & Fine, M. (2000). Decade review on remarriage and stepfamilies. *Journal of Marriage and the Family, 62*(4), 1288–1307.

Coleman, M., Ganong, L., & Gingrich, R. (1985). Stepfamily strengths: A review of the popular literature. *Family Relations, 34*, 583–589.

Craven, L. (1982). *Stepfamilies: New patterns of harmony.* New York: Mesner.

Crosbie-Burnett, M. (1984). The centrality of the step relationship: A challenge to family theory and practice. *Family Relations, 33*, 459–464.

Crosbie-Burnett, M. (1991). Impact of joint versus sole custody and quality of co-parental relationship on adjustment of adolescents in remarried families. *Behavioral Sciences and the Law, 9*, 439–449.

Dallos, R. (1991). Family belief systems, therapy and change: A constructional approach. Milton Keynes, UK: Open University Press.

Dindia, K. (2000). Relational maintenance. In C. Hendrick & S. Hendrick (Eds.), *Close relationships: A sourcebook* (pp. 287–300). Thousand Oaks, CA: Sage.

Farrell, J., & Markman, H. (1986). Individual and interpersonal factors in the etiology of marital distress: The example of remarital couples. In R. Gilmour & S. Duck (Eds.), *The emerging field of personal relationships* (pp. 251–263). Hillsdale, NJ: Lawrence Erlbaum Associates.

Fishman, B., & Hamel, B. (1981). From nuclear to stepfamily ideology: A stressful change. *Alternative Lifestyles, 4*, 181–204.

Ganong, L., & Coleman, M. (1989). Preparing for remarriage: Anticipating the issues, seeking solutions. *Family Relations, 38*, 28–33.

Ganong, L., & Coleman, M. (1994). *Remarried family relationships.* Newbury Park, CA: Sage.

Ganong, L., Coleman, M., Fine, M., & Martin, P. (1999). Stepparents' affinity-seeking and affinity-maintaining strategies with stepchildren. *Journal of Family Issues 20*, 299–327.

Ganong, L., Coleman, M., Fine, M., & McDaniel, A. K. (1998). Issues considered in contemplating stepchild adoption. *Family Relations, 47,* 63–71.

Gianetti, C. G., & Sagarese, M. (1997). *The roller coaster years: Raising your child through the maddening yet magical middle school years.* New York: Broadway.

Goldner, V. (1982). Therapy with remarriage families: XII. Remarriage family: Structure, system, future. *Family Therapy Collections, 2,* 187–206.

Hetherington, M. (1993). An overview of the Virginia longitudinal study of divorce and remarriage with a focus on early adolescence. *Journal of Family Psychology, 7,* 39–56.

Hetherington, E. M., & Henderson, S. H. (1997). Fathers in stepfamilies. In M. Lamb (Ed.), *The role of the father in child development* (3rd ed.; pp. 212–226). New York: Wiley.

Kaplan, L., & Hennon, C. B. (1992). Remarriage education: The personal reflections program. *Family Relations, 41,* 127–134.

Kelley, P. (1992). Healthy stepfamily functioning. *Families in Society, 73,* 579–587.

Keshet, J. K. (1989). Gender and biological models of role division in stepmother families. *Journal of Feminist Family Therapy, 1*(4), 29–50.

Kiernan, K. E. (1992). The impact of family disruption in childhood on transitions made in young adult life. *Population Studies, 46,* 213–234.

Leach, P., & Matthews, J. (1997). *Your baby and child: From birth to age five.* New York: Knopf.

Leslie, L. A., & Epstein, N. (1988). Cognitive–behavioral treatment of remarried families. In N. Epstein, S. Schlesinger, & W. Dryden (Eds.), *Cognitive–behavioral therapy with families* (pp. 151–182). New York: Brunner/Mazel.

Lutz, P. (1983). The stepfamily: An adolescent perspective. *Family Relations, 32,* 367–375.

Madden-Derdich, D. A., & Arditti, J. A. (1999). The ties that bind: Attachment between former spouses. *Family Relations, 48,* 243–250.

Masheter, C. (1991). Postdivorce relationships between ex-spouses: The roles of attachment and interpersonal conflict. *Journal of Marriage and the Family, 53,* 103–110.

McGoldrick, M., & Carter, B. (1989). Forming a remarried family. In B. Carter & M. McGoldrick (Eds.), *The changing family life cycle: A framework for family therapy* (2nd ed.; pp. 399–429). New York: Gardner.

Mills, D. M. (1984). A model for stepfamily development. *Family Relations, 33,* 365–372.

Morrison, K., & Stollman, W. (1995). Stepfamily assessment: An integrated model. *Journal of Divorce and Remarriage, 24,* 163–182.

Morrison, K., & Thompson-Guppy, A. (1985). Cinderella's stepmother syndrome. *Canadian Journal of Psychiatry, 30,* 521–529.

Papernow, P. (1993). *Becoming a stepfamily: Patterns of development in remarried families.* San Francisco, CA: Jossey-Bass.

Papernow, P. (1995). What's going on here? Separating (and weaving together) step and clinical issues in remarried families. In D. K. Huntley (Ed.), *Understanding stepfamilies: Implications for assessment and treatment* (pp. 3–24). Alexandria, VA: American Counseling Association.

Pasley, K., & Dollahite, D. C. (1995). The nine Rs of stepparenting adolescents: Research-based recommendations for clinicians. In D. K. Huntley (Ed.), *Understanding stepfamilies: Implications for assessment and treatment* (pp. 87–98). Alexandria, VA: American Counseling Association.

Patterson, B., & Beckett, C. (1995). A re-examination of relational repair and reconciliation: Impact of socio-communicative style on strategy selection. *Communication Research Reports, 12,* 235–240.

Quick, D. S., McKenry, P., & Newman, B. (1994). Stepmothers and their adolescent children: Adjustment to new family roles. In K. Pasley & M. Ihinger-Tallman (Eds.), *Stepparenting: Issues in theory, research, and practice* (pp. 105–126). Westport, CT: Greenwood.

Russell, A., & Searcy, E. (1997). The contribution of affective reactions and relationship qualities to adolescents' reported responses to parents. *Journal of Social & Personal Relationships, 14,* 539–548.

Sager, C. J., Brown, H. S., Crohn, H., Engel, T., Rodstein, E., & Walker, L. (1983). *Treating the remarried family*. New York: Brunner/Mazel.

Seltzer, J. A. (1991). Relationships between fathers and children who live apart: The father's role after separation. *Journal of Marriage and the Family, 53*, 79–101.

Seltzer, J. A., & Brandeth, Y. (1994). What fathers say about involvement with children after separation. *Journal of Family Issues, 15*, 49–77.

Steinberg, L., & Levine, A. (1997). *You and your adolescent: A parent's guide for ages 10–20*. New York: HarperCollins.

Stephens, L. S. (1996). Will Johnny see daddy this week? An empirical test of three theoretical perspectives of postdivorce contact. *Journal of Family Issues, 17*(4), 466–494.

Visher, E. B. (1989). *Stepfamilies stepping ahead: An eight-step program for successful stepfamily living*. Lincoln, NE: Stepfamilies Press.

Visher, E. B. (1994). Lessons from remarriage families. *American Journal of Family Therapy, 22*, 327–336.

Visher, E. B., & Visher, J. S. (1980). *Stepfamilies: Myths and realities*. Secus, NC: Citadel Press.

Visher, E. B., & Visher, J. S. (1982). Stepfamilies in the 1980's. In L. Messinger (Ed.), *Therapy with remarriage families* (pp. 105–119). Rockville, MD: Aspen Systems Corp.

Visher, E. B., & Visher, J. S. (1988). *Old loyalties, old ties*. New York: Brunner/Mazel.

Visher, E. B., & Visher, J. S. (1996). *Therapy with stepfamilies*. New York: Brunner/Mazel.

Visher, E. B., Visher, J., & Pasley, K. (1997). Stepfamily therapy from the client's perspective. In I. Levin & M. Sussman (Eds.), *Stepfamilies: History, research, and policy* (pp. 191–214). New York: Haworth.

Visher, J. S. (1994). Stepfamilies: A work in progress. *The American Journal of Family Therapy, 22*(4), 337–344.

Weaver, S. E., & Coleman, M. (1998, November). *A grounded theory study of women's role construction in stepfamilies*. Paper presentation at the Theory Construction and Research Methodology Workshop at the National Council on Family Relations Annual Conference, Milwaukee, WI.

Whiteside, M. F. (1998). The parental alliance following divorce: An overview. *Journal of Marital and Family Therapy, 24*(1), 3–24.

Wojtkiewicz, R. A. (1994). Parental structure experiences of children: Exposure, transitions, and type at birth. *Population Research & Policy Review, 13*, 141–159.

Wood, J. T. (1994). *Who cares? Women, care, and culture*. Carbondale, IL: Southern Illinois University.

PSYCHOPATHOLOGY AND CLOSE RELATIONSHIPS

6

The Empirical Underpinnings
of Marital Therapy
for Depression

Sammy F. Banawan
Heather A. O'Mahen
Steven R. H. Beach
Melanie H. Jackson
University of Georgia

DEPRESSION IN MARRIAGE

The close relationships of depressed persons are particularly likely to be disrupted, and depressed persons often are acutely aware of the impact of relationship difficulties on their moods. In this chapter, we focus on the link between marital discord and depression because marriage is a relationship that often remains intact despite high levels of dissatisfaction among depressed persons (Whisman, Sheldon, & Goering, 2000). This makes it a potentially valuable point of intervention for therapeutic activity. Accordingly, we begin by highlighting issues concerning direction of causality and specific interpersonal processes that might be particularly consequential in linking marital problems and depression. We then examine an intermediate-level theory that helps to organize much of the theoretical and empirical literature, stress generation theory (Hammen, 1991). Next, we turn to marital therapy for depression, reviewing the literature on efficacy of behavioral marital therapy and similar communication training approaches in the treatment of depression. Finally, we discuss alternative formats for marital therapy with depressed clients that have been proposed and conclude with a brief discussion of potential future directions in the use of marital therapy in the treatment of depression and depressive symptomatology.

Evidence Regarding the Relationship Between Marital Discord and Depression

A strong association between depression and relationship disturbance has been noted in a number of different relationship literatures; however, the reasons provided have varied. Accordingly, it is informative to consider briefly the various explanations that have been provided and the types of associations that have been noted.

The Link Between Relationship Distress and Depression Across Relationship Type

Evidence that depressive symptoms are related to interpersonal distress has been found across a broad range of research designs and assessment strategies. For example, in a review of the marital literature, Whisman (2001) found that, across 17 cross-sectional studies, marital quality was negatively related to both depressive symptomatology and diagnostic depression. In their review of the child depression literature, Cummings and Davies (1994; see also Cummings, Dearth-Pendley, & Smith, 2001) noted that the parenting behavior of depressed persons often is compromised. In their recent review of the postpartum depression literature, Whiffen and Johnson (1998) suggested that lack of social support from close others and social provisions within the marital relationship might be important in understanding the onset of depression postpartum. Likewise, in their review of adolescent depression, Barrera and Li (1996) suggested that support from peers and family members is strongly and negatively related to depressive symptoms. Disturbance in coworker relationships also has been found in the relationships of individuals experiencing depression (Beach, Martin, Blum, & Roman, 1993a). Accordingly, across various stages of the life cycle, in various populations, and with regard to various close relationships, there is a strong inverse relationship between the quality of close relationships and the level of depression. These findings suggest a robust link between depression and relationship difficulties in general (see also Joiner & Coyne, 1999). However, cross-sectional associations appear to be interpreted differently in these literatures. In some literatures, a strong cross-sectional correlation is taken as evidence of the impact of depression on close relationships (e.g., in the parenting and adolescent literatures). In other literatures (e.g., the postpartum literature), a similar cross-sectional relationship might be interpreted as evidence of the impact of disruptions in close relationships on depression. Thus, the presence of a strong cross-sectional association leaves open the question of direction of the effect between interpersonal difficulties and depression.

Can we establish the direction of causal relation between social provisions and level of dysphoria? Can we better explicate the specific causal mechanisms that give rise to the observed covariation between interpersonal disruptions and depressive symptoms? To probe these questions in more detail, we examine recent work on marital problems and depression.

Is There a Causal Relationship Between Marital Problems and Depressive Symptoms in Community Samples?

Possible causal relationships between marital discord and depression include an effect of marital discord on depression, an effect of depression on marital discord, and a bidirectional pattern of causation, as well as possible third variable explanations. To separate these possibilities, a range of causal models has been investigated using structural equation modeling approaches (Beach, Harwood, et al., 1995; Fincham, Beach, Harold, & Osborne, 1997; Kurdek, 1998).

Beach, Harwood, et al. (1995). In a national random probability sample of women working full-time ($N = 577$), Beach, Harwood, et al. (1995) found a significant effect of marital satisfaction on depressive symptomatology 1 year after the initial assessment. Women who endorsed low levels of marital satisfaction showed greater future depressive symptoms. This effect remained even after controlling for the association between marital satisfaction and depression at the initial assessment. Accordingly, the prospective effect of marital satisfaction on depression for women might be generalizable to a broad cross-section of employed women. For men, controlling for initial depressive symptoms reduced the prospective effect of marital satisfaction on depression to nonsignificance.

Fincham, Beach, Harold, and Osborne (1997). Fincham et al. (1997) examined a series of complementary causal models in a sample of 150 newlywed couples. Couples were assessed at two time points separated by an 18-month interval. Replicating earlier work, marital satisfaction and depressive symptomatology were related to each other cross-sectionally. For husbands, there were significant cross-lagged effects from earlier marital satisfaction to later depressive symptomatology and from earlier depressive symptomatology to later marital satisfaction. By contrast, marital satisfaction affected later depressive symptomatology among wives, whereas depressive symptoms did not exert a significant effect on later marital satisfaction. Accordingly, the Fincham et al. study suggests that the flow of causality from marital dissatisfaction to depression might be more pronounced when it is the wife rather than the husband who is depressed.

Kurdek (1998). Kurdek (1998) examined a series of models similar to those examined by Fincham et al. (1997) using a sample of 198 newlywed couples. For both husbands and wives, marital quality and depressive symptoms were related to each other cross-sectionally, and changes in level of depressive symptoms covaried with changes in level of marital quality. In contrast to the Fincham et al. (1997) study, however, longitudinal paths generally were nonsignificant, and patterns did not differ significantly for husbands and wives.

Is There a Causal Relationship Between Marital Problems and Diagnosis of Depression or in Clinical Samples Diagnosed With Depression?

Although more commonly retrospective than prospective, there has also been work within clinical samples directed at the question of direction of causality between marital problems and the diagnostic entity of depression. In particular, work by O'Leary, Risso, and Beach (1990), Burns, Sayers, and Moras (1994); Whisman and Bruce (1999); and Gotlib, Lewinsohn, and Seeley (1998) have addressed the issue directly.

O'Leary, Risso, and Beach (1990). Following up on earlier work by Birtchnell and Kennard (1983), O'Leary, Risso, and Beach (1990) asked a group of depressed, maritally distressed women seeking treatment to make precedence judgments (i.e., whether depression or marital distress preceded the other problem) and attributions about the primary cause of their depression (i.e., whether marital distress or some other factor caused their depression). Results suggested that, on average, these women believed that their marital problems preceded their depression and viewed their marital problems as causing their depression (p. 417).

Burns, Sayers, and Moras (1994). Burns et al. (1994) investigated relationship satisfaction and depression in a sample of 115 patients receiving cognitive therapy for depression. Married patients ($n = 68$) rated their marital relationships, and unmarried patients ($n = 47$) rated their closest intimate relationships. Reciprocal effects between relationship satisfaction and depression were investigated. Burns et al. found no evidence that depression exerted a causal effect on relationship satisfaction. However, they found a significant, albeit weak, effect of relationship satisfaction on depression.

Whisman and Bruce (1999). Whisman and Bruce (1999) examined the effect of marital distress on onset of diagnosable episodes of major depressive disorder (MDE) in a large community sample. Using data from the New Haven Epidemiologic Catchment Area program, they examined new cases of depression in a community sample of married individuals who did not meet criteria for MDE at baseline. Results suggested that risk for onset of MDE at follow-up was related to level of earlier marital distress. Specifically, distressed spouses were 2.7 times more likely to experience onset of MDE than were nondistressed members of the sample. The association between marital distress and risk of MDE remained significant even after controlling for demographic characteristics and history of MDE. No difference was found in the apparent effect of marital distress as a function of either sex or history of MDE.

Gotlib, Lewinsohn, and Seeley (1998). Highlighting the potential for marital problems to follow from earlier episodes of depression, Gotlib et al. (1998) examined the relationship between major depressive disorder in adolescence and later marital status and marital functioning in early adulthood. They found that history of major depressive disorder during adolescence was associated with lower level of marital quality (i.e., greater marital distress) during early adulthood. Furthermore, this association appeared to be specific to history of major depression, as history of nonaffective disorder was not associated with lower marital quality during adulthood.

Whisman, Sheldon, and Goering (2000). Highlighting the potential centrality of the marital relationship in accounting for interpersonal disturbance among depressed married persons, Whisman et al. (2000) examined the specificity of the connection between marital problems and depression as well as several other psychological disorders. Participants were sampled from the adult population of Ontario and were assessed using the Composite International Diagnostic Interview (CIDI). The resulting sample of married persons was 4,933. Whisman et al. (2000) found that even after controlling for the quality of other social relationships, getting along with one's spouse was related to presence of diagnosis of depression. Accordingly, for many depressed persons, interpersonal difficulties may be especially prominent in their most intimate relationships.

Summary

Together, these results replicate and extend the pivotal hypothesis of covariation between marital discord and depression. That is, marital problems both covary with current symptoms of depression and covary over time with symptoms of depression (see also Dehle & Weiss, 1998; Karney, 2001; Ulrich-Jakubowski, Russel, & O'Hara, 1988). However, the results also highlight the difficulty in using longitudinal designs to identify the direction of causality between marital problems and depression, largely because of the difficulty of specifying in advance the correct time course for lags (see Beach et al., 1999 for an extended discussion).

The various patterns observed across samples also suggests that there might be bidirectional effects, that the effects might vary by gender, and that the effect of marital problems on depressive symptoms might occur at shorter lags than those used to date (see Beach, Davey, & Fincham, 1999 for a more extended discussion). These considerations suggest that advances in the longitudinal investigation of the link between marital discord and depression must go hand-in-hand with advances in theory regarding the link between these constructs.

At the same time, recent meta-analysis of the cross-sectional relationship between marital dissatisfaction and depression symptoms suggests it is reliably stronger for women than for men (Whisman, 2001). In addition, marital discord appears to be a better predictor of longitudinal change in depression symptoms for women than for men. This suggests that sex differences must also continue to be a focus of theoretical attention.

DEPRESSION AND PROBLEMS IN CLOSE RELATIONSHIPS: POSSIBLE MEDIATORS OF CAUSAL EFFECTS

Longitudinal research makes salient the possible bidirectional nature of the link between marital problems and depression. In this section, we examine coercion, psychological abuse, and lack of support as potential causal mediators for effects of marital processes on depression. We also consider communication, reassurance seeking, negative feedback seeking, and poor role performance as potential causal mediators for the effects of depression on marital processes. We discuss the stress generation model (Hammen, 1991) as an integrative framework that might help organize many of the bidirectional effects observed between marital problems and depression (for an extension to premarital romantic relationships, see Davila, 2001).

Problem-Solving Deficits and Coercive Processes

Marital difficulties often are traced to difficulties in problem solving (Markman, Stanley, & Blumberg, 1994). At the same time, negative behavior displayed during problem-solving discussions is a robust cross-sectional correlate of marital satisfaction (Weiss & Heyman, 1997), suggesting that poor marital problem solving is a potential source of stress generation in marriage. However, Christian, O'Leary, and Vivian (1994) found that, among discordant couples, depression was associated with poorer self-reported problem-solving skills in both husbands and wives. Confirming these self-reported deficits is a literature on the communication problems of depressed persons. Much of the research on problem-solving communication difficulties in depression has been influenced by the coercion model (Biglan, Lewin, & Hops, 1990; Hops, Biglan, Sherman, Arthur, Friedman, & Osteen, 1987). This model identifies depressive behavior (i.e., self-derogation, physical and psychological complaints, displays of depressed affect) as a functional, albeit coercive, set of behaviors that are most likely to be reinforced when there is a high level of negative verbal behavior in the home environment. It has been found that partners react to depressive behavior differently from how they react to critical or aggressive behavior, both emotionally (Biglan, Rothlind, Hops, & Sherman, 1989) and behaviorally (Hops et al., 1987; Nelson & Beach, 1990; Schmaling & Jacobson, 1990). In particular, partners are much less likely to respond to depressive behavior with verbal aggression than they are to reciprocate verbal aggression (Beach, Brooks, Nelson, & Bakeman, 1993; Katz, Jones, & Beach, 2000).

Expressed Emotion, Psychological Abuse, and Humiliation

Depressed individuals also might be particularly responsive to various forms of criticism from close others. For example, Vaughn and Leff (1976) found that depressed people were particularly vulnerable to family tension and to hostile statements made by family members. Schless, Schwartz, Goetz, and Mendels (1974) also demonstrated that this vulnerability to marital and family-related stresses persisted in depressed persons even after recovery. Hooley, Orley, and Teasdale (1986) expanded these findings when they reported that the level of "expressed emotion" predicted relapse of depression. As they noted, expressed emotion is an index whereby implied criticism of the target individual figures prominently. Likewise, Mundt, Fiedler, Ernst, and Backenstrass (1996) found that long chains of negative marital interaction predicted relapse for a subgroup of endogenously depressed patients.

This research is supplemented by earlier observational work that reported that spouses of depressed partners seldom agreed with their partners, offered help in an ambivalent manner, and often evaluated their depressed partners negatively (Hautzinger, Linden, & Hoffman, 1982). The sum of these results suggests that depressed persons both are differentially sensitive to negative emotion and appear to have an increased frequency of conflictual interactions with their partners.

These findings hold particular meaning for women in physically abusive relationships. Women in these relationships often report that psychological abuse has more negative effects than does physical abuse (Arias, 1995; Folingstad, Rutledge, Berg, Hause, & Polek, 1990). One mediator of the effect

of physical violence on depression, then, might be the level of verbal humiliation, overcontrol, and criticism expressed by the partner (i.e., psychological abuse) that often is a concomitant of physical violence.

Several studies have examined the possibility that humiliation may be
particularly powerful in producing or triggering a depressive episode. In a
study of community wives by Brown, Harris, and Hepworth (1995), humiliation events including discovery of infidelity, husband-initiated divorce, and
marked violence by the husband were found to be more likely to precipitate a depressive episode than were nonhumiliating events (e.g., divorce
not due to husband's infidelity). Following up on these findings, Christian-
Herman, O'Leary, and Avery-Leaf (2001) examined incidence of major depressive episodes in a sample of community wives free of prior episodes of
depression. They found an incidence rate of 38% within 4 weeks following
the negative marital event. Subsequent research by Cano and O'Leary (in
press) has shown that humiliating events in marriage increase the occurrence of major depressive episodes beyond the effect of marital discord
alone, suggesting that discrete, humiliating events in marital relationships
may have a powerful impact on the occurrence of depressive episodes
among married women.

Loss of Support

Perceived support often is a better predictor of individual reactions to
stressors than is received support. In fact, received support often is unrelated to various psychological symptoms (Barrera, 1986) and does not show
stress-buffering effects (Cohen & Wills, 1985). In a provocative analysis of this
finding, Lakey and Lutz (1996) suggested that this pattern might result from
the interaction of support behavior with a range of individual characteristics
and expectations. Specifically, they hypothesized that different people might
feel most supported by different sets of behaviors. Lakey, McCabe, Fisicario,
and Drew (1996) had participants rate an array of possible support providers
on general level of perceived support. Data from three samples indicated
that characteristics of both the supporters and the perceivers influenced ratings of supportiveness. However, in each study, the Perceiver × Supporter interaction accounted for the greatest amount of variance in support judgments. They concluded that "supportiveness is in the eye of the beholder"
(Lakey & Lutz, 1996, p. 451). Their findings suggest that any attempt to prescribe a universally applicable set of supportive behaviors should be likely to
fail because different individuals could vary widely in their perceptions of the
supportiveness of the prescribed behaviors. These findings have additional
implications for the literature linking support to depression (Cutrona, 1986;
Jackson, 1992), suggesting that consideration of the idiographic nature of
perceived support may well inform this link.

Summary

The three models discussed in this section help to concretize the types of interpersonal processes that can generate depression and the way in which depression can generate interpersonal disturbance. In so doing, they underscore the reciprocal impact of these processes on both relationship satisfaction and individual mental health. It is useful to note that these interpersonal processes share certain properties. In particular, coercive processes, psychological abuse, and perceived low supportiveness of the partner all reflect situations in which the partner is engaging in behavior that can damage the person's sense of competence and/or the person's sense of felt security. Each of the three models also suggests mechanisms that could unfold over relatively short time periods. Indeed, one might reasonably hypothesize very fast effects of psychological abuse or humiliation on depression, moderately fast effects of a coercive environment, and a somewhat slower time frame for low perceived partner supportiveness to exert its effect. Accordingly, these considerations highlight the potential complexity of examining lagged effects of interpersonal processes on depression.

STRESS GENERATION THEORY AS AN INTEGRATIVE FRAMEWORK

Hammen's (1991) stress generation theory expands on the three models described previously by positing that depressed individuals can generate stress in their environments, particularly in their interpersonal environments, in a variety of ways. The increased level of stress to which depressed persons are exposed, in turn, exacerbates their depressive symptomatology. Hammen's model suggests that, in addition to the effect of marital dissatisfaction and various other stresses on later depressive symptoms, depressive symptoms should lead to a variety of marital difficulties and should increase marital stress (and perhaps dissatisfaction). The theory is supported by evidence that depressed persons often are seen as a burden (Coyne, Kahn, & Gotlib, 1987; Coyne, Kessler, Tal, Turnbull, Wortman, & Greden, 1987), that spouses might be silently upset with depressed partners (Biglan, Rothlind, Hops, & Sherman, 1989), and that spouses might be ambivalent about the causes of their partners' impairment (Coyne & Benazon, 2001). In a direct test of stress generation theory, Hammen (1991) compared unipolar depressed women to bipolar, medically ill, and control group women over 1-year time period. She found that unipolar depressed patients experienced more total stressful life events during this time period than did controls and that stressful interpersonal events were the most elevated among the unipolar depressed group.

Stress Generation and Communication

Davila, Bradbury, Cohan, and Tochluk (1997) extended the stress generation paradigm by examining the effects of depression on behaviors emitted
during a supportive interaction and the subsequent effect on the individual's depression. Elaborating previous findings that depressed persons are
less effective at providing and eliciting support (Rook, Pietromonaco, &
Lewis, 1994), Davila et al. (1997) found that wives with greater levels of depressive symptomatology showed more negative (but not less positive)
support behaviors and expectations. In keeping with Hammen's (1991) theory, negative support behaviors mediated the effect of prior depressive
symptoms on later marital stress. Marital stress, in turn, predicted more depressive symptoms.

Stress Generation and Reassurance Seeking

Reassurance-seeking behaviors represent another potential category of
stress generators in relationships. Particularly when conjoined with depression and negative feedback seeking, reassurance-seeking behavior is associated with negative reactions by close others (Joiner, Alfano, & Metalsky,
1993; Katz & Beach, 1997; Katz, Beach, & Anderson, 1996). Coyne's interactional theory of depression suggests that, in the context of depression, demands for reassurance and support from the partner can contribute to partner rejection (Coyne, 1976; Coyne, Kahn, & Gotlib, 1987). Supporting the
theory, significant associations between reassurance seeking and depression have been found (Joiner et al., 1993; Joiner & Metalsky, 1995; Katz &
Beach, 1997). Expanding on Coyne's theory, Joiner and Metalsky (1995) proposed that both reassurance seeking and negative feedback seeking can be
important in accounting for the negative impact of depression on others.
That is, depressed persons search both for negative feedback consistent
with their self-views and for reassurance, creating confusing and increasingly intense interpersonal demands. Thus, the three-way interaction of depression, reassurance seeking, and negative feedback seeking should predict rejection by others. Extending and replicating the Joiner and Metalsky
theory in the realm of romantic relationships (Joiner & Metalsky, 1995; see
also Joiner et al., 1993), Katz and Beach (1997) found that men were significantly more likely to report relationship dissatisfaction when their partners
reported elevated depressive symptoms in conjunction with elevated levels
of reassurance seeking and negative feedback seeking.

Stress Generation and Poor Role Performance

Failure to perform well in various roles (e.g., work, family) also could be associated with stress generation. A study by Wells, Stewart, Hays, Burnam,
Rogers, Daniels, Berry, Greenfield, and Ware (1989) provided evidence that

depressed persons report more difficulties in role performance. They found that persons with significant, but subclinical, depressive symptoms exhibited substantially poorer performance at work and at home compared to persons with a variety of other ailments. Replicating and extending these results, a study of 495 adults by Beach, Martin, Blum, and Roman (1993b) found that role functioning was related to level of depressive symptoms. Furthermore, decreased functioning was reported both by the depressed persons and by the spouses or others close to the depressed persons. Accordingly, role performance decrements are reported by both self and others and can constitute an important source for the generation of stress in marriage and continuing vulnerability to future episodes of depression.

The decrement in role performance that stems from a depressive episode and the resulting negative reactions from close others also might lead depressed persons to reorganize their lives so that they have fewer performance demands (Coyne & Calarco, 1995). Such changes also have the potential to constrict both opportunities for social interaction and opportunities for self-enhancement. Hence, role decrements might survive the depressive episode and leave the previously depressed person with substantially impoverished social and coping resources (cf. Coyne & Benazon, 2001; Joiner, 2000). If this is the case, then it could contribute to a higher risk of relapse.

Summary

The stress generation framework highlights the way in which several problematic behavior patterns might come to supplant more adaptive, problem-focused coping behavior as a result of dysphoria or a depressive episode. In so doing, it emphasizes specific mechanisms through which relationship functioning may be disrupted. Depressed persons might be more likely to both expect and provide negative support behavior and also might be more likely to direct negative behavior toward partners in the context of problem solving. Because support and problem solving represent two important areas of marital functioning, difficulties in these areas could easily accumulate over time to create misunderstandings and unnecessary disagreements. Likewise, poor role performance might not immediately affect partner satisfaction or relationship quality but could exert a cumulative effect over time. As these examples suggest, in contrast to the rapid effect of marital dissatisfaction on depression, one might anticipate that a longer time course would be required to capture the impact of depression on marital satisfaction. As with the effect of marital discord on depression, however, this expectation could vary substantially depending on the particular effect examined, with the effects of poor communication or problem solving appearing before the effects of poor role performance. Accordingly, there might be substantial complexity in determining the optimal lag to capture the effect of depression on marital discord or vice versa. Not only might there not be a single lag time that best captures the reciprocal influences of marital discord and depression on each other, there might not be a single lag time that best captures all the effects going in a single direction.

INDIVIDUAL DIFFERENCES AND BIDIRECTIONAL EFFECTS OF DEPRESSION

There is strong potential for some type of individual difference analysis to contribute to our understanding of the bidirectional effects of depression and marital processes. Accordingly, we consider, for illustrative purposes, two robust individual difference variables that might modify the action or time course of depressogenic or stress-generating processes (for additional discussion of individual differences see Davila, 2001; Joiner, 2000).

Can Individual Differences Contribute to This Model?

Recently, theorists from several perspectives have suggested the potential importance of an interrelated set of individual difference variables as potential moderators of the relationship between marital processes and depression. In particular, shyness, neuroticism, dependency, perfectionism, and insecure attachment styles have been advanced as potentially contributing to our understanding of the bidirectional connection between marriage and depression. Although space limitations preclude thorough coverage of all these developments, we can point to relevant discussions and highlight the common themes.

Joiner (2000) hypothesizes that shyness may serve to increase vulnerability for loneliness, rendering shyness a risk factor for depression. At the same time, shyness may focus the negative interpersonal effects of depression on a smaller available social network, intensifying the negative effects of depression on close relationships. Because it may increase the magnitude of reactions, neuroticism may have similar effects as shyness on intensifying the connection between marital discord and depression. Supporting this conjecture, neuroticism is related to lower marital satisfaction (Karney & Bradbury, 1997) and was shown to intensify the effect of marital satisfaction on change in depression among wives and intensify the effect of depression on change in marital satisfaction among husbands (Karney, 2001). In keeping with current views of personality disorder, Davila (2001) divides neuroticism into dependency symptoms and obsessive–compulsive symptoms. Dependency symptoms include submissiveness, reliance on others for self-esteem, and fears of abandonment. The obsessive–compulsive symptoms include perfectionism, rigidity, and mistrust of other's abilities. As she notes, these clusters of characteristics could work in different ways to increase vulnerability to the depressogenic effects of stress in romantic relationships or to increase the relationship disturbance produced by depressive symptoms.

Viewing attachment style as a proxy for individual differences in dependency and interpersonal trust suggests that persons who enter marriage with either an avoidant or preoccupied attachment style might be at increased risk of depression in response to marital discord. Preoccupied individuals display a negative view of self but a positive view of others' abilities to help. However, avoidant individuals display a negative view of both self and others' ability to help (Bartholemew & Horowitz, 1991). Indeed, avoidantly attached persons appear to be at particularly increased risk of clinical depression (Carnelley, Pietromonaco, & Jaffe, 1994), but both avoidant and preoccupied individuals are at risk for dysphoria (Carnelley et al., 1994; Cole-Detke & Kobak, 1996; Roberts, Gotlib, & Kassel, 1996).

Summary. As these various potential moderators suggest, a compelling case can be made that some individuals are either more disposed to depression or are especially likely to have negative experiences in romantic relationships, and to have these experiences interwoven with depressive symptoms. In particular, some individuals may find themselves especially vulnerable to challenges to their sense of competence or their sense of felt relationship security. Because these areas are closely connected with the experience of depression, such vulnerabilities or difficulty in recovering from challenges in these areas should be related to depression (cf. Beck, 1983; Blatt & Zuroff, 1992). Thus, attention to individual differences underscores variables that impact the person's ability to maintain satisfactory relationship functioning, which, in turn, may lead to depression and subsequent decrements in relationship satisfaction.

Are Gender Differences Important?

Because women are about twice as likely as men to experience clinical depression (Weissman, 1987), it is important to remain alert for possible gender differences in the relationship between marital discord and depression. However, existing cross-sectional data reveal only modest gender differences in the magnitude of the cross-sectional relationship between marital discord and depression (Whisman, 2001). This is somewhat surprising given that there are several reasons to expect more robust gender differences in the discord–depression association. For example, women are more likely to take on the role of maintaining the relationship and, therefore, might have a sense of increased responsibility both for their relationships and for the status of their relationships (Bar Tal & Frieze, 1977; Lerner, 1987). This sense of responsibility, coupled with women's preferential use of emotion-focused coping, might lead women to blame themselves for marital problems, consequently placing them at greater risk of depression (Nolen-Hoeksema, 1987). As a result, one might hypothesize a relatively stronger effect of marital discord on depressive symptomatology for women than for men (Fincham et al., 1997).

Conversely, the male gender role is more consistent with activity and displays of anger and retaliation (Kuebli & Fivush, 1992). Thus, men might be less likely to take responsibility for marital discord and more likely to minimize the seriousness of partner concerns. Likewise, the greater tendency by men to withdraw from problem discussions, a tendency that may be exacerbated by feelings of depression, also is consistent with a relatively stronger effect of depression on later marital satisfaction for men than for women. Accordingly, one might anticipate stronger stress generation effects for men. These gender differences in the "impact" of various individual difference variables, such as coping (for women) and withdrawal (for men), highlight the potential complexity of attempting to model longitudinal effects.

In view of this complexity, it is not surprising that the longitudinal data reviewed earlier only weakly support the presence of gender differences in magnitude or direction of effects. Accordingly, hypotheses regarding gender differences should be viewed as speculative at present. It seems likely that identifying such differences, if they exist, will require attention to better specification of the lag over which effects might operate and clarification of the specific processes influenced by gender.

Clinical Implications

Current empirical support for reciprocal effects between depression and relationship satisfaction, although far from complete, is sufficient to provide important support for the use of marital therapy in treating depression (see Cordova & Gee, 2001; O'Leary & Cano, 2001, for comprehensive reviews). In addition, several well randomized trials of marital therapy have been conducted to test the potential efficacy of marital therapy in the treatment of depression.

Foley, Rounsaville, Weissman, Sholomaskas, and Chevron (1989). In this study, 18 depressed outpatients were randomly assigned to either individual interpersonal psychotherapy (IPT) or a newly developed couple format version of IPT. This latter intervention was structured to include a focus on conjoint communication training, making it similar to behavioral marital therapy (BMT). This study included depressed husbands ($n = 5$) as well as wives (n = 13) but did not examine whether gender of the patient influenced response to treatment. Foley et al. (1989) found that participants in both treatments exhibited a significant reduction in depressive symptoms. However, they found no differential improvement on measures of depressive symptomatology between the two groups. Both interventions also produced equal enhancement of general interpersonal functioning. However, participants receiving couple IPT reported marginally higher marital satisfaction scores on the Locke–Wallace Short Marital Adjustment Test and scored significantly higher on one subscale of the DAS at session 16. Thus, compared to individual therapy, marital therapy proved as effective in reducing depressive symptomatology and somewhat more effective in enhancing the marital relationship.

Jacobson, Dobson, Fruzzetti, Schmaling, and Salusky (1991). Jacobson et al. (1991) randomly assigned 60 married women who had been diagnosed depressed to either BMT, individual cognitive therapy (CT), or a treatment combining BMT and CT. Couples were not selected for the presence of marital discord. In the half of the sample that reported some marital discord, BMT was as effective as CT in reducing depression. Further, only BMT resulted in significant improvement in marital adjustment for couples reporting some marital dissatisfaction. Supporting the Foley et al. (1989) results, these findings suggest that marital therapy may be as effective as an individual approach in relieving a depressive episode when provided to discordant–depressed couples. In these cases, marital therapy also may have the added benefit of enhancing marital functioning.

Beach and O'Leary (1992). Beach and O'Leary randomly assigned 45 couples in which the wife was depressed to one of three conditions: conjoint BMT, individual cognitive therapy (CT), or a 15-week waiting list condition. To be included in the study, both partners had to score in the discordant range of the Dyadic Adjustment Scale (DAS) and present clinically as discordant. BMT and CT both were equally effective in reducing depressive symptoms, and both were clearly superior to the wait-list control group. However, only BMT improved the marital relationship. Posttherapy, BMT produced a statistically significant (i.e., 20-point) increase in DAS scores compared to pretherapy. In contrast, wives in the CT and wait-list groups showed little change (−2 and 1 scale points for cognitive and wait-list groups, respectively). Replicating and extending the results of the Foley et al. (1989) and the Jacobson et al. (1991) studies, marital therapy was found to be as effective as an individual approach in relieving a depressive episode and more effective in enhancing marital functioning. In addition, marital therapy was found to be significantly better than wait-list.

Emanuels-Zuurveen and Emmelkamp (1996). In this study, 27 depressed outpatients were randomly assigned to either individual cognitive–behavioral therapy or communication-focused marital therapy. As in Foley et al. (1989), the sample for this study included both depressed husbands (n = 13) as well as depressed wives (n = 14). Participants in both treatments exhibited a significant reduction in depressive symptom, and there was no differential improvement between the two groups. In contrast, there was a significant, differential effect of treatment on marital outcomes, with the marital therapy condition producing substantially greater gains in marital satisfaction. In addition, there was a significant reduction in the depressed patient's criticism of the nondepressed partner only among those receiving marital therapy. Thus, this investigation replicated the pattern obtained in each of the three earlier studies, showing an equivalent outcome when the dependent variable was depressive symptoms and a better outcome in marital therapy than in individual therapy when the dependent variable was marital functioning.

Mediation. Two studies indicate that the effect of marital therapy on depression is mediated by changes in marital adjustment. Beach and O'Leary (1992) found that posttherapy marital satisfaction fully accounted for the effect of marital therapy on depression. Likewise, Jacobson et al. (1991) found that change in marital adjustment and depression covaried for depressed individuals who received marital therapy, but not for those who received cognitive therapy. Therefore, it appears that marital therapy may reduce level of depressive symptomatology primarily by enhancing the marital environment, whereas cognitive therapy appears to work through a different mechanism of change (i.e., cognitive change, see Whisman, 1993). Further research is needed to identify specific behavioral changes that contribute to this mediation (cf. Jacobson et al., 1993).

Predicting Who Will Do Better in Marital Therapy for Depression

The outcome research indicates that marital interventions are probably efficacious treatments for depression. However, information regarding differential response to treatment may highlight potential prescriptive indicators and so influence decisions about which treatment to use for which clients. Several attempts have been made to examine this issue.

Marital Problems Versus Cognitive Errors. Beach and O'Leary (1992) investigated pretherapy marital environment and pretherapy cognitive style as two potential predictors of treatment outcome. A better pretreatment marital environment predicted less depressive symptomatology at posttreatment among wives receiving cognitive therapy. Furthermore, among wives in the cognitive therapy condition, more pretreatment cognitive errors predicted better marital functioning at posttreatment. However, neither factor predicted outcome among wives in the marital therapy condition.

Perceived Etiology. O'Leary, Risso, and Beach (1990) attempted to predict differential response to treatment from temporal order of problem onset. Women entering the treatment protocol were asked which problem came first, marital discord or depression. The correlation between temporal order ratings and residualized gains in marital satisfaction was significant in the cognitive therapy condition but nonsignificant in the marital therapy condition. Depressed patients who reported that their marital problems preceded their depression had poor marital outcomes if they were assigned to cognitive therapy but positive marital outcomes if they were assigned to marital therapy. Conversely, for depressed patients who reported that depression preceded their marital problems, marital outcomes were equally positive in both conditions.

In an examination of the relationship between clients' reasons for depression and their responses to treatment it was found that clients who viewed relationship factors as strongly related to their depression were less likely to respond well to cognitive therapy. These clients completed less homework, viewed therapy as less helpful, and showed less improvement in level of depressive symptomatology. This work is in keeping with the assumption that therapy is most effective when there is a match between patient expectations and the treatment model (Whisman, 1993).

Other Approaches and Other Points of Intervention

These studies point to the utility of marital therapy in treating depression, particularly when the couple is discordant. In addition, they suggest that marital therapy with discordant and depressed clients may have its effect by relieving their marital distress. However, it is clear that this initial round of outcome work examining behavioral marital therapy for depression might not fully capture the power of marital interventions for depression. As we continue to develop more powerful models of the reciprocal relationship between marital problems and depression, we are likely to find additional points of clinical intervention and to substantially enhance the effectiveness of marital interventions for depression. It seems likely that advances guided by the stress generation model and an integration of the stress generation model with an individual difference perspective will produce a variety of new suggestions for clinical technique (e.g., Beach, Fincham, & Katz, 1998). If this is the case, then there will be substantial development and improvement in the use of marital treatments for depression during the coming decade. Already, several well-developed alternative approaches to marital therapy have been proposed.

Integrative Couple Therapy (Cordova & Gee, 2001). One approach that has been described at some length is Integrative Couple Therapy (ICT; Cordova and Gee, in press). These authors highlight the potential for ICT to benefit nondistressed couples in which one partner is depressed. In particular, they note that ICT is designed to help partners unite around a problem that confronts them. By making one partner's depression this problem, ICT may make the depression an opportunity for closeness and intimacy rather than a threat to the relationship. In their discussion of ICT for depression, these authors also discuss fostering a sense of "we-ness" and of collaboration against the depression. At the same time, they discuss fostering each partner's ability to respond flexibly in situations in which the depression might lead to relationship strains or ultimately to increased depression. In this way, Cordova and Gee (2001) may be seen as proposing an approach that is responsive to much of the "stress-generation" literature.

Emotion-Focused Marital Therapy (Johnson & Whiffen, 1999). Another approach to marital therapy that has been explicitly proposed as fitting well with the needs of depressed and discordant couples is emotion-focused therapy (EFT). This approach is derived from an attachment perspective and so highlights the potential continuity between family of origin issues and the current marital relationship. EFT emphasizes insecure bonds in which healthy attachment needs cannot be met (Johnson & Greenberg, 1995). Therapy focuses on helping partners explore and communicate emotional experience in order to foster a new view of self and of partner. EFT also has been designated as an efficacious and possibly specific intervention for marital discord (Baucom, Shoam, Mueser, Daiuto, & Stickle, 1998). Accordingly, its potential to serve as an intervention for depressed and discordant couples deserves close examination.

Self-Regulation Couples Therapy (SRCT; Halford, 1998). Reasoning that clients have the most control over their own behavior, Halford and colleagues proposed to focus therapy on individual, self-directed change by each of the partners. In the context of ongoing relationship problems, this results in encouraging each partner to change their own behavior, cognitions, and affect to enhance their personal satisfaction with the relationship. One potential advantage of the SRCT approach in the context of marital discord and depression is that much more time is spent on helping partners identify their goals and find ways to help them feel that they are moving toward these personal goals. Accordingly, this approach has the potential to directly counteract the avoidance that is so characteristic of depressed partners and allow them to experience the positive affective consequences of moving toward well-defined goals. One potential advantage of SRCT for many discordant and depressed women is that it calls for individual tailoring to meet the circumstances and goals of each participant. Demonstrating the flexibility of the approach, it was adapted to assist wives who were married to heavy drinkers, most of whom would not participate in any form of conjoint marital therapy. In this context, the approach was successfully adapted to focus on reducing the wives' sense of burden and distress rather than on increasing their marital satisfaction. Because the literature suggests that many depressed wives may be in equally untenable situations, such flexibility is an attractive feature.

CONCLUSIONS

This chapter has suggested that stress generation theory can organize many of the bidirectional effects between marital processes and depression and might stimulate researchers to refine the questions being asked. We also suggest that three types of problem behaviors are of particular importance in accounting for the impact of marital discord on depression: coercive processes, psychological abuse, and erosion of support. Likewise, three problem behaviors are of particular importance in accounting for the impact of depression on marital discord: communication, reassurance seeking, and negative feedback seeking, and decreased role performance. Attention to each of these behaviors might prove useful in developing more comprehensive explanatory models. Superior models, in turn, will help to guide better investigations of longitudinal effects and so provide improved tests of causal hypotheses. Such investigations are, in turn, likely to suggest more powerful forms of intervention for depression and better ways in which to help ameliorate the negative impact of depression on close relationships.

As we continue to derive potential targets of intervention from the basic literature, it is also instructive to note that BMT has proven relatively successful as a treatment for co-occurring marital discord and depression. In addition, it appears that BMT works by relieving marital distress, suggesting that its mechanism of action is consistent with that hypothesized. However, several newer forms of marital therapy await investigation, and each appears to provide a promising new line of investigation in the pursuit of more powerful interventions for this troubling constellation of problems.

REFERENCES

Arias, I. (1995, October). *The impact of psychological abuse on battered women*. Invited paper presented at the National Violence Prevention Conference of the Centers for Disease Control and Prevention, Des Moines, IA.

Barrera, M. (1986). Distinctions between social support concepts, measures, and models. *American Journal of Community Psychology, 14*, 413–455.

Barrera, M., & Li, S. A. (1996). The relation of family support to adolescent's psychological distress and behavior problems. In G. R. Pierce, B. R. Sarason, & I. G. Sarason (Eds.), *Handbook of social support and the family* (pp. 313–343). New York: Plenum.

Bar Tal, D., & Frieze, I. H. (1977). Achievement motivation for males and females as a determinant of attributions for success and failure. *Sex Roles, 3*, 301–314.

Bartholomew, K., & Horowitz, L. M. (1991). Attachment styles among young adults: A test of a four-category model. *Journal of Personality and Social Psychology, 61*, 226–244.

Baucom, D. H., Shoam, V., Mueser, K. T., Daiuto, A., & Stickle, T. R. (1998). Empirically supported couple and family interventions for marital distress and adult mental health problems. *Journal of Consulting and Clinical Psychology, 66*, 53–88.

Beach, S. R. H., Brooks, A. E., Nelson, G. M., & Bakeman, R. (1993, November). *The relationship between aggressive and depressive behavior revisited.* Paper presented to the 27th annual convention of the Association for the Advancement of Behavior Therapy, Atlanta, GA.

Beach, S. R. H., Fincham, F. D., & Katz, J. (1998). Marital therapy in the treatment of depression: Toward a third generation of therapy and research. *Clinical Psychology Review, 18*, 635–661.

Beach, S. R. H., Harwood, E. M., Horan, P. M., Katz, J., Blum, T. C., Martin, J. K., & Roman, P. M. (1995, November). *Marital effects on depression: Measuring the longitudinal relationship.* Paper presented at the 29th Annual Convention of the Association for the Advancement of Behavior Therapy, Washington, DC.

Beach, S. R. H., Martin, J. K., Blum, T. C., & Roman, P. M. (1993a). Subclinical depression and role fulfillment in domestic settings: Spurious relationships, imagined problems, or real effects? *Journal of Psychopathology and Behavioral Assessment, 15*, 113–128.

Beach, S. R. H., Martin, J. K., Blum, T. C., & Roman, P. M. (1993b). Effects of marital and co-worker relationships on negative affect: Testing the central role of marriage. *American Journal of Family Therapy, 21*, 312–322.

Beach, S. R. H., & O'Leary, K. D. (1992). Treating depression in the context of marital discord: Outcome and predictors of response for marital therapy versus cognitive therapy. *Behavior Therapy, 23*, 507–258.

Beck, A. T. (1983). Cognitive therapy of depression: New perspectives. In P. J. Clayton & J. E. Barrett (Eds.), *Treatment of depression: Old controversies and new approaches* (pp. 265–290). New York: Raven Press.

Biglan, A., Lewin, L., & Hops, H. (1990). A contextual approach to the problem of aversive practices in families. In G. R. Patterson (Ed.), *Depression and aggression in family interaction* (pp. 103–129). Mahwah, NJ: Lawrence Erlbaum Associates.

Biglan, A., Rothlind, J., Hops, H., & Sherman, L. (1989). Impact of distressed and aggressive behavior. *Journal of Abnormal Psychology, 98*, 218–228.

Blatt, S. J., & Zuroff, D. C. (1992). Interpersonal relatedness and self-definition: Two prototypes for depression. *Clinical Psychology Review, 12*, 527–562.

Brown, G. W., Harris, T. O., & Hepworth, C. (1995). Loss, humiliation, and entrapment among women developing depression: A patient and non-patient comparison. *Psychological Medicine, 25*, 7–21.

Burns, D. D., Sayers, S. L., & Moras, K. (1994). Intimate relationships and depression: Is there a causal connection? *Journal of Consulting and Clinical Psychology, 62*, 1033–1043.

Cano, A., & O'Leary, K. D. (in press). Extramarital affairs precipitate major depressive episodes and symptoms of non-specific depression and anxiety. *Journal of Consulting and Clinical Psychology.*

Carnelley, K. B., Pietromonaco, P. R., & Jaffe, K. (1994). Depression, working models of others, and relationship functioning. *Journal of Personality and Social Psychology, 66*, 127–140.

Christian, J. L., O'Leary, K. D., & Vivian, D. (1994). Depressive symptomatology in maritally discordant women and men: The role of individual and relationship variables. *Journal of Family Psychology, 8*, 32–42.

Christian-Herman, J. L., O'Leary, K. D., & Avery-Leaf (in press). The impact of severe negative events in marriage on depression. *Journal of Social and Clinical Psychology, 20*, 24–40.

Cohen, S., & Wills, T. (1985). Stress, social support and the buffering hypothesis. *Psychological Bulletin, 116*, 457–475.

Cole-Detke, H., & Kobak, R. (1996). Attachment processes in eating disorder and depression. *Journal of Consulting and Clinical Psychology, 64*, 282–290.

Cordova, J., & Gee, C. B. (2001). Couple therapy for depression: Using healthy relationships to treat depression. In S. R. H. Beach (Ed.), *Marital and family processes in depression: A scientific foundation for intervention* (pp. 185–203). Washington, DC: American Psychological Association.

Coyne, J. C. (1976). Depression and the response of others. *Journal of Abnormal Psychology, 85*, 186–193.

Coyne, J. C., & Benazon, N. R. (2001). Not agent blue: Effects of marital functioning on depression and implications for treatment. In S. R. H. Beach (Ed.), *Marital and family processes in depression* (pp. 25–43). Washington, DC: American Psychological Association.

Coyne, J. C., & Calarco, M. M. (1995). Effects of the experience of depression: Application of focus group and survey methodologies. *Psychiatry: Interpersonal and Biological Processes, 58*, 149–163.

Coyne, J. C., Kahn, J., & Gotlib, I. H. (1987). Depression. In T. Jacob (Ed.), *Family interaction and psychopathology* (pp. 509–533). New York: Plenum.

Coyne, J. C., Kessler, R. C., Tal, M., Turnbull, J., Wortman, C. B., & Greden, J. F. (1987). Living with a depressed person. *Journal of Consulting and Clinical Psychology, 55*, 347–352.

Cummings, E., & Davies, P. T. (1994). *Children and marital conflict: The impact of family dispute resolution*. New York: Guilford.

Cummings, E. M., Dearth-Pendley, G., & Smith, D. A. (2001). Parental depression and family functioning: Towards a process-oriented model of children's adjustment. In S. R. H. Beach (Ed.), *Marital and family processes in depression* (pp. 89–110). Washington, DC: American Psychological Association.

Cutrona, C. E. (1986). Behavioral manifestations of social support: A microanalytic investigation. *Journal of Personality and Social Psychology, 51*, 201–208.

Davila, J. (2001). Paths to unhappiness: The overlapping courses of depression and romantic dysfunction. In S. R. H. Beach (Ed.), *Marital and family processes in depression* (pp. 71–87). Washington, DC: American Psychological Association.

Davila, J., Bradbury, T. N., Cohan, C. L., & Tochluk, S. (1997). Marital functioning and depressive symptoms: Evidence for a stress generation model. *Journal of Personality and Social Psychology, 73*, 849–861.

Dehle, C., & Weiss, R. (1998). Sex differences in prospective associations between marital quality and depressed mood. *Journal of Marriage and the Family, 60*, 1002–1011.

Emanuals-Zuurveen, L., & Emmelkamp, P. M. G. (1996). Individual behavioral–cognitive therapy v. marital therapy for depression in maritally distressed couples. *British Journal of Psychiatry, 169*, 181–188.

Fincham, F. D., Beach, S. R. H., Harold, G. T., & Osborne, L. N. (1997). Marital satisfaction and depression: Longitudinal relationships for husbands and wives. *Psychological Science, 3*, 351–357.

Foley, S. H., Rounsaville, B. J., Weissman, M. M., Sholomaskas, D., & Chevron, E. (1989). Individual versus conjoint interpersonal psychotherapy for depressed patients with marital disputes. *International Journal of Family Psychiatry, 10*, 29–42.

Folingstad, D. R., Rutledge, L. L., Berg, B. J., Hause, E. S., & Polek, D. S. (1990). The role of emotional abuse in physically abusive relationships. *Journal of Family Violence, 5*, 107–120.

Gotlib, I. H., Lewinsohn, P. M., & Seeley, J. R. (1998). Consequences of depression during adolescence: Marital status and marital functioning in early adulthood. *Journal of Abnormal Psychology, 107*, 686–690.

Halford, W. K. (1998). The ongoing evolution of behavioral couples therapy: Retrospect and prospect. *Clinical Psychology Review, 18*, 613–633.

Hammen, C. L. (1991). The generation of stress in the course of unipolar depression. *Journal of Abnormal Psychology, 100*, 555–561.

Hautzinger, M., Linden, M., & Hoffman, N. (1982). Distressed couples with and without a depressed partner: An analysis of their verbal interaction. *Journal of Behaviour Therapy and Experimental Psychology, 13*, 307–314.

Hooley, J. M., Orley, J., & Teasdale, J. D. (1986). Levels of expressed emotion and relapse in depressed patients. *British Journal of Psychiatry, 148*, 642–647.

Hops, H., Biglan, A., Sherman, L., Arthur, J., Friedman, L., & Osteen, V. (1987). Home observation of family interactions of depressed women. *Journal of Consulting and Clinical Psychology, 55*, 341–346.

Jacobson, N. S., Dobson, K., Fruzzetti, A. E., Schmaling, K. B., & Salusky, S. (1991). Marital therapy as a treatment for depression. *Journal of Consulting and Clinical Psychology, 59*, 547–557.

Jackson, P. B. (1992). Specifying the buffering hypothesis: Support, strain, and depression. *Social Psychology Quarterly, 55*, 363–378.

Johnson, S. M., & Greenberg, L. S. (1995). The emotionally focused approaches to problems in adult attachment. In N. S. Jacobson & A. S. Gurman (Eds.), *Clinical handbook of couple therapy* (pp. 121–141). New York: Guilford.

Joiner, T. E. (2000). Depression's vicious scree: Self-propagating and erosive processes in depression chronicity. *Clinical Psychology: Science and Practice, 7*, 203–218.

Joiner, T. E., & Coyne, J. C. (1999). *The interactional nature of depression.* Washington DC: American Psychological Association.

Joiner, T. E., Jr., Alfano, M. S., & Metalsky, G. I. (1993). Caught in the crossfire: Depression, self-consistency, self-enhancement, and the response of others. *Journal of Social and Clinical Psychology, 20*, 179–193.

Joiner, T. E., Jr., & Metalsky, G. I. (1995). A prospective test of an integrative interpersonal theory of depression: A naturalistic study of college roommates. *Journal of Personality and Social Psychology, 69*, 778–788.

Karney, B. R. (2001). Depressive symptoms and marital satisfaction in the early years of marriage: Narrowing the gap between theory and research. In S. R. H. Beach (Ed.), *Marital and family processes in depression* (pp. 45–68). Washington, DC: American Psychological Association.

Karney, B. R., & Bradbury, T. N. (1997). Neuroticism, marital interaction, and the trajectory of marital satisfaction. *Journal of Personality and Social Psychology, 72*, 1075–1092.

Katz, J., & Beach, S. R. H. (1997). Romance in the crossfire: When do women's depressive symptoms predict partner relationship dissatisfaction? *Journal of Social and Clinical Psychology, 16*, 243–258.

Katz, J., Beach, S. R. H., & Anderson, P. (1996). Self-enhancement versus self-verification: Does spousal support always help? *Cognitive Therapy and Research, 20*, 345–360.

Katz, J., Jones, D. J., & Beach, S. R. H. (2000). Distress and aggression during dating conflict: A test of the coercion hypothesis. *Personal Relationships, 7*, 391–402.

Kuebli, J., & Fivush, R. (1992). Gender differences in parent–child conversations about past events. *Sex Roles, 27*, 683–698.

Kurdek, L. A. (1998). The nature of predictors of the trajectory of change in marital quality over the first 4 years of marriage for first-married husbands and wives. *Journal of Family Psychology, 12*, 494–510.

Lakey, B., & Lutz, C. J. (1996). Social support and preventive and therapeutic interventions. In G. R. Pierce, B. R. Sarason, & I. G. Sarason (Eds.), *Handbook of social support and the family* (pp. 435–465). New York: Plenum.

Lakey, B., McCabe, K. M., Fisicario, S. A., & Drew, J. B. (1996). Environmental and perceived determinants of support perceptions: Three generalizability studies. *Journal of Personality and Social Psychology, 70*, 1270–1280.

Lerner, H. G. (1987). Female depression: Self-sacrifice and self-betrayal in relationships. In R. Formanek & A. Guiran (Eds.), *Women and depression: A lifespan perspective* (pp. 200–221). New York: Springer.

Markman, H., Stanley, S., & Blumberg, S. I. (1994). *Fighting for your marriage*. San Francisco: Jossey-Bass.

Mundt, C., Fiedler, P., Ernst, S., & Bakenstrass, M. (1996). Expressed emotion and marital interaction in endogenous depressives. In C. Mundt, M. J. Goldstein, K. Hahlweg, & P. Fiedler (Eds.), *Interpersonal factors in the origin and course of affective disorders* (pp. 240–256). London: Gaskell Academic.

Nelson, G. M., & Beach, S. R. H. (1990). Sequential interaction in depression: Effects of depressive behavior on spousal aggression. *Behavior Therapy, 12*, 167–182.

Nolen-Hoeksema, S. (1987). Sex differences in unipolar depression: Evidence and theory. *Psychological Bulletin, 101*, 259–282.

O'Leary, K. D., & Cano, A. (2001). Marital discord and partner abuse: Correlates and causes of depression. In S. R. H. Beach (Ed.), *Marital and family processes in depression* (pp. 163–182). Washington, DC: American Psychological Association.

O'Leary, K. D., Risso L. P., & Beach, S. R. H. (1990). Attributions about the marital discord/depression link and therapy outcome. *Behavior Therapy, 21*, 413–422.

Roberts, J. E., Gotlib, I. H., & Kassel, J. D. (1996). Adult attachment security and symptoms of depression: The mediating roles of dysfunctional attitudes and low self-esteem. *Journal of Personality and Social Psychology, 70*, 310–320.

Rook, K. S., Pietromonaco, P. R., & Lewis, M. A. (1994). When are dysphoric individuals distressing to others and vice versa? Effects of friendship, similarity, and interaction task. *Journal of Personality and Social Psychology, 67*, 548–559.

Schless, A. P., Schwartz, L., Goetz, C., & Mendels, J. (1974). How depressives view the significance of life events. *British Journal of Psychiatry, 125*, 406–410.

Schmaling, K. B., & Jacobson, N. S. (1990). Marital interaction and depression. *Journal of Abnormal Psychology, 99*, 229–236.

Ulrich-Jakubowski, D., Russel, D. W., & O'Hara, M. W. (1988). Marital adjustment difficulties: Cause or consequence of depressive symptomatology? *Journal of Social and Clinical Psychology, 7*, 312–318.

Vaughn, C. E., & Leff, J. P. (1976). The influence of family and social factors on the course of psychiatric illness: A comparison of schizophrenic and depressed neurotic patients. *British Journal of Psychiatry, 129*, 125–137.

Weiss, R. L., & Heyman, R. E. (1997). A clinical research overview of couple interactions. In W. K. Halford & H. J. Markman (Eds.), *Clinical handbook of marriage and couples intervention* (pp. 13–41). London: Wiley.

Weissman, M. M. (1987). Advances in psychiatric epidemiology: Rates and risks for major depression. *American Journal of Public Health, 77*, 445–451.

Wells, K. B., Stewart, A., Hays, R. D., Burnam, M. A., Rogers, W., Daniels, M., Berry, S., Greenfield, S., & Ware, J. (1989). The functioning and well being of depressed patients: Results from the Medical Outcomes Study. *Journal of the American Medical Association, 262*, 914–919.

Whiffen, V. E., & Johnson, S. M. (1998). An attachment theory framework for the treatment of childbearing depression. *Clinical Psychology: Science and Practice, 5*, 478–493.

Whisman, M. A. (1993). Mediators and moderators of change in cognitive therapy of depression. *Psychological Bulletin, 114*, 248–265.

Whisman, M. A. (2001). Depression and marital distress: Findings from clinical and community studies. In S. R. H. Beach (Ed.), *Marital and family processes in depression* (pp. 3–24). Washington, DC: American Psychological Association.

Whisman, M. A., & Bruce, M. I. (1999). Marital distress and incidence of major depressive episode in a community sample. *Journal of Abnormal Psychology, 108*, 674–678.

Whisman, M. A., Sheldon, C. T., & Goering, P. (2000). Psychiatric disorders and dissatisfaction with social relationships: Does type of relationship matter? *Journal of Abnormal Psychology, 109*, 803–808.

7

The Effects of Postpartum Depression on Close Relationships

Karin E. Larsen
Michael W. O'Hara
University of Iowa

Approximately 13% of childbearing women experience nonpsychotic postpartum depression (O'Hara & Swain, 1996). Postpartum depression is distinct from postpartum blues and postpartum psychosis as the former is less severe and more common with prevalence rates ranging from 26% to 85%, while the latter is quite severe and uncommon with a prevalence rate of about 0.2% (O'Hara, 1991). Postpartum blues is a mild dysphoria occurring within the first week postpartum and lasting from a few hours to several days. On the other end of the range of postpartum mood disturbance is postpartum psychosis, usually involving hallucinations or delusions and requiring hospitalization. This chapter focuses on postpartum depression, the mood disorder that clinicians are most likely to encounter in postpartum women who are self-referred or physician-referred for outpatient treatment.

The *Diagnostic and Statistical Manual of Mental Disorders*, 4th edition (*DSM–IV*; American Psychiatric Association, 1994) categorizes postpartum depression as a major depressive episode with postpartum onset (i.e., within 4 weeks postpartum). However, researchers tend to define postpartum depression more broadly to include women experiencing high levels of depressive symptomatology in the first few months postpartum and beyond (O'Hara, 1995). Whether the onset of emotional disturbance occurs during pregnancy, in the first month postpartum, or later, clinicians are likely to encounter women experiencing mood difficulties related to transitions in childcare, marital relationships, and general psychosocial functioning well into the first year postpartum. These women may present with guilt and frustration related to their interactions with their infants. Although they are likely to believe that other mothers are easily accommodating the needs of their infants, postpartum depressed women often find childcare quite stressful and their infants demanding and difficult. Evidence suggests that these infants may indeed be different from the infants of nondepressed mothers (Gelfand & Teti, 1990). Furthermore, when a depressed mother interacts with her infant, both mother and infant are likely to display behavioral and affective disturbances not found in nondepressed dyads (Field, 1992).

Depressed women tend to experience difficulties in their relationships with their partners as well. When compared with nondepressed postpartum women, depressed women are apt to describe their partners as less positive, caring, and helpful (Boyce, Hickie, & Parker, 1991; Schweitzer, Logan, & Strassberg, 1992). Accordingly, postpartum depressed women may report dissatisfaction with their partner relationship. Thus, clinicians may find that women depressed in the postpartum period feel disappointed in their partners' contribution to their emotional well-being and complain about their partners' lack of involvement in household and childcare duties. Partners of postpartum depressed women are likely to be experiencing adjustment difficulties as well (Zelkowitz & Milet, 1996). Maternal distress and paternal distress may compound family dysfunction and contribute to infant behavioral problems, which may persist into later childhood.

Although social support from friends and family may help to buffer the difficulties women experience relating to their infants and partners, research suggests this is probably not the case for postpartum depressed women (Cutrona, 1984). Instead, some evidence suggests that difficulties in women's parental relationships stemming from childhood and/or developing in adulthood may contribute to women's risk for postpartum depression. This chapter does not provide clinicians with a step-by-step approach to treating postpartum depression but reviews the specific difficulties postpartum depressed women experience as these difficulties affect women's close relationships. Empirical evidence provides the foundation for discussions linking postpartum depression to disturbances in women's relationships with their infants, partners, and parents.

THE MOTHER–INFANT RELATIONSHIP

Depressed mothers and their infants display disturbances during dyadic interactions (Field, 1992). Additionally, child cognitive (Cogill, Caplan, Alexandra, Robson, & Kumar, 1986; Goodman & Brumley, 1990; Whiffen & Gotlib, 1989) and behavioral difficulties (Gelfand & Teti, 1990; Murray, 1992; Whiffen

& Gotlib, 1989; Wrate, Rooney, Thomas, & Cox, 1985) have been associated with postpartum depression. This section focuses on the association between disturbances in the mother–infant relationship and associated deficits in the child's psychosocial and behavioral functioning. These infant deficits have been identified when mothers with high levels of depressive symptomatology and those scoring low on these symptoms have been observed interacting with their infants.

Cohn and Tronick (1983) were the first researchers to use a face-to-face paradigm to explore the links between depression and the mother–infant relationship. These researchers asked mothers to sit face-to-face with their infants while simulating depression (i.e., assuming a "still face"). When mothers presented a still face, infants became more negative—displayed higher proportions of protest, wary, and brief positive (facial expression brightens only briefly and is attenuated) behaviors—than when mothers interacted normally with their infants. The effects of the still-face episode on infants lingered even after mothers returned to their natural demeanor.

Later studies recruited depressed mothers so women did not have to simulate depressed expressions; rather, depressed women were instructed to interact naturally with their infants. Using paradigms incorporating play and other face-to-face dyadic activities, researchers have conducted observational assessments of the relation between maternal depression levels and infant behavior. Researchers comparing depressed mother–infant dyads and nondepressed dyads found mothers diagnosed with a depressive disorder in the first year postpartum were less skillful in play with their infants, and their infants were less likely to smile and vocalize while playing with their mothers (Stein, Gath, Bucher, Bond, Day, & Cooper, 1991). In general, observations of the interactions between depressed mothers and their infants have demonstrated that infants of symptomatic mothers are likely to engage in negative behavior states and/or display fewer positive behaviors (Cohn, Campbell, Matias, & Hopkins, 1990; Field, 1984, 1995). Such findings have prompted at least one researcher to label infants of depressed mothers as "depressed" themselves because their affect, as evidenced by behaviors and facial expressions, reflected their mothers' behaviors (Field, 1986). However, standardized approaches to diagnosing depression in infants have not been established.

Explanations for the general association between mothers' and infants' behavior may shed light on the negative, dyadic interactions that occur when mothers are depressed in the postpartum period. The phenomenon of shared affectivity states in mother–infant dyads does not occur only when mothers are depressed. Studies investigating interactions between mothers and infants have found "matching" or contingent emotional expression within these dyads (Cohn & Elmore, 1988; Field, Healy, Goldstein, & Guthertz, 1990; Izard, Fantauzzo, Castle, Haynes, Rayias, & Putnam, 1995;

Termine & Izard, 1988). Mothers may initiate response-contingent sequences with their infants such that the mother's behavior influences the child's affective expression (Cohn & Tronick, 1987). This possibility may explain why depressed mother–infant dyads display less positive interaction than their nondepressed counterparts: Infants merely respond contingently to their depressed mother's affect. Whether the infant's "depressed" affect is the result of the child mimicking its depressed mother, the mother inducing negative mood in the infant (Termine & Izard, 1988), or the infant experiencing depression is unclear.

Some evidence indicates that infant emotional and behavioral disturbances apparent during episodes of maternal postpartum depression do not persist after maternal depression remits. Instead, maternal depression levels at the time of infant assessment may account for most of the effects of maternal depression on the child. Longitudinal follow-up studies of infants exposed to postpartum depression provide data suggesting the long-term effects of postpartum depression on child behavior is minimal. For example, as part of a larger study conducted by Gotlib, Whiffen, Wallace, and Mount (1991), mothers were asked to rate the behavior of their 2- to 3-year-old children (Carro, Grant, Gotlib, & Compas, 1993). These researchers found that concurrent maternal depression levels accounted for children's behavioral problems (internalizing and externalizing), and maternal depression levels at 1 month postpartum did not explain additional differences in children's difficulties. A 4-year follow-up study of children who were exposed to maternal depression as infants found no direct relationship between postpartum depression and child behavior problems (Philips & O'Hara, 1991). These studies and others suggest that infant behavioral disturbances occurring during dyadic interactions may not linger following the resolution of maternal depression (Caplan, Cogill, Alexandra, Robson, Katz, & Kumar, 1989; Wrate et al., 1985). However, women who experience postpartum depression are at a greater risk for future episodes of depression than women who have no history of depression (Cooper & Murray, 1995). Thus, the effects of postpartum depression on children may be mediated by the effects of subsequent maternal depressions to which the child is repeatedly exposed. That is, an episode of postpartum depression may increase the probability that a mother experiences future depressions, which in turn may have a negative effect on her child (Philips & O'Hara, 1991).

In contrast to findings suggesting postpartum depression does not have long-term effects on child behavior, some studies have found residual effects of postpartum depression on the children of recovered mothers (Ghodsian, Zajicek, & Wolkind, 1984; Uddenberg & Engelsson, 1978). Stein et al. (1991) compared 19-month-old children of women who had been diagnosed with postpartum depression with children of matched control mothers who had not become depressed. Children's ability to share positive affect while playing with their mothers remained significantly lower in children of recovered mothers, suggesting that dyadic disturbances developed during maternal depression persisted. Because the preponderance of evidence suggests that maternal depression does have a negative effect on child behavior at later stages of development, a critical period may exist when maternal depression has a significant impact on later child outcome.

One longitudinal study provides evidence for a critical window or a sensitive period early in development when maternal depression predicts later child behavior difficulties. When children of depressed mothers completed periodic behavioral assessment up to 42 months of age, significant relations between maternal depression level and child behavior problems were not found until the child was 27 months old (Ghodsian et al., 1984). Furthermore, when current levels of depression were controlled, only maternal depression severity at 14 months significantly predicted child behavior problems at 42 months. Importantly, maternal depression before 14 months or after 14 months did not relate significantly to child behavior at 42 months when other relevant variables were controlled. These findings suggest maternal depression at 14 months may have lasting effects on child behavior, but replication of this study and a longer follow-up period is needed for a better understanding of the long-term effects of maternal depression on the child. Undoubtedly, the relationship between timing and duration of maternal depression and child outcome is a complex one.

Infants of depressed mothers are at risk for experiencing attachment difficulties in addition to disturbances in affect (Cummings & Davies, 1994; Gelfand & Teti, 1990; Murray, 1992). The formation of secure emotional attachments to a primary caregiver is a critical task of infancy (Thompson, 1997). The quality of child attachment may be associated with the duration of maternal depression. For example, Teti, Gelfand, Messinger, and Isabella (1995) found that infants whose mothers were more severely depressed for a longer duration were more likely to display disorganized and disoriented attachment behaviors characterized by confused and fearful behavior or difficulty accessing their mothers. Although Murray found duration of maternal depression and infant attachment were not related, she found a significant relation between a diagnosis of postpartum depression and insecure infant attachment at 18 months postpartum. Infants who develop attachment difficulties may continue to experience social and emotional difficulties in later childhood (Sroufe, 1983; Thompson, 1997, pp. 58–65).

Trained observers have described children of depressed mothers as less positive, more negative, and less securely attached than the children of nondepressed mothers. Maternal reports of children are similar to those made by observers: Depressed mothers' child ratings are more negative than nondepressed mothers' ratings (Cummings & Davies, 1994; Downey & Coyne, 1990; Gelfand & Teti, 1990; Whiffen, 1988). Furthermore, when compared to nondepressed postpartum mothers, depressed mothers tend to feel less attached to their infants. For example, when Milgrom and McCloud (1996) followed women from 3 months through 12 months postpartum, postpartum-depressed mothers continued to describe themselves as less emotionally attached to their children than nondepressed mothers, even though their depression levels decreased over this period. Moreover, depressed mothers described their infants as less reinforcing, less acceptable, and more demanding. Not surprisingly, the depressed women experienced higher levels of parenting stress over the follow-up period while nondepressed mothers' parenting stress lessened over time.

Childcare stress may have a significant independent influence on mothers' attachment to their infants. Cutrona (1984) conducted a longitudinal study of depression levels, stress levels, and social support from pregnancy into the postpartum period. Because participants were first-time mothers, measures of childcare stress were collected in the postpartum period only. After accounting for mothers' antenatal attachment (the security and attachment they experienced in interpersonal relationships with adults) and levels of depressive symptomatology, Cutrona found childcare stress levels reported at 2 weeks postpartum predicted mothers' attachment to their 1-year-old child. This result suggests that childcare stress and maternal depression may exert independent effects on maternal attachment. In sum, when mothers experience heightened levels of depression in the postpartum period, they tend to feel less emotionally attached to their infants and to report more childcare stress.

Some researchers have used the term *depressive distortion* to explain the association between maternal depression and elevations in maternal reports of child behavior difficulties. The "depressive distortion hypothesis" suggests that depressed individuals have a tendency to evaluate their situation or, in this case, their child negatively (Richters, 1992; Richters & Pellegrini, 1989). When comparing infants of depressed and nondepressed mothers, Field, Morrow, and Adelstein (1993) videotaped mother–infant dyads engaged in face-to-face interactions. They asked observers as well as mothers to rate infants' positive and negative behavior states while watching these tapes. Although both observers and symptomatic mothers rated their infants as more frequently negative and less frequently positive than the infants of nonsymptomatic mothers, symptomatic mothers rated their infants even more negatively and less positively than the observers rated them. Thus, depressed mothers' infant ratings may be considered negatively exaggerated rather than false.

Whether mothers or trained observers rate infant behavior during dyadic interactions, most studies indicate that infants of postpartum-depressed mothers display more negative behaviors (e.g., gaze aversion, fussiness, negative behavior states) than infants of nondepressed mothers. The cause of infants' negative behavior displays during interactions with their depressed mothers is unknown. If infants are merely reflecting their depressed mothers' affect, then resolution of maternal depression should resolve dyadic disturbances and child behavioral disturbances. However, if relational disturbances persist after maternal depression remits, as some studies suggest, mother–child attachment may be affected. Accordingly, these children may be at risk for behavioral, emotional, and social problems and may have difficulties forming other close relationships (Thompson, 1997). Researchers have not yet established clear links between children's exposure to postpartum depression, disturbances in mother–infant relations, and children's ability to form close relationships with their mothers and other caregivers. Because children's attachment security has been associated with their ability to form relationships when they reach adolescence and adulthood (Thompson, 1997), disturbances in mother–infant relations that occur during postpartum depression may have long-term consequences for both the dyad and the child's general social development.

THE PARTNER RELATIONSHIP

Evidence strongly suggests that maternal depression and poor marital[1] relationships covary (Gotlib & Hooley, 1988). Some studies indicate that relationship difficulties precede postpartum depression (Braverman & Roux, 1978; Dimitrovsky, Perez-Hirshberg, & Itskowitz, 1987; Gotlib et al., 1991; Kumar & Robson, 1984; O'Hara, 1986; Robinson, Olmsted, & Garner, 1989; Watson, Elliot, Rugg, & Brough, 1984; Whiffen, 1988). However, other studies suggest that marital distress during pregnancy does not increase risk for postpartum depression (Blair, Gilmore, Playfair, Tisdall, & O'Shea, 1970; O'Hara, Rehm, & Campbell, 1983). Several prospective studies indicate that decreases in women's marital satisfaction from the antenatal period up to 9 months into the postpartum period are associated with higher postpartum levels of depressive symptomatology (Hock, Schirtzinger, Lutz, & Widaman, 1995; O'Hara et al., 1983; O'Hara, Rehm, & Campbell, 1982). Although the link between antenatal marital satisfaction and postpartum depression is unclear, evidence strongly indicates postpartum-depressed women experience significant marital dissatisfaction following childbirth (Campbell, Cohn, Flanagan, Popper, & Meyers, 1992; Cox, Connor, & Kendell, 1982; Martin, 1977; O'Hara et al., 1983; Paykel, Emms, Fletcher, & Rassaby, 1980). Furthermore, when fathers' assessment of the couple's relationship has been solicited, paternal ratings suggest that partners of depressed women are

---

[1]"Marital" as used here refers to married couples as well as couples who are unmarried but in long-term committed relationships.

also dissatisfied with their relationships (Milgrom & McCloud, 1996; Zelkowitz & Milet, 1996). The passage of time does not seem to remedy the marital relationship for postpartum-depressed women. A longitudinal study comparing a matched sample of postpartum and nonpostpartum women found that depressed women who were not postpartum, reported improved marital adjustment over a 9-week period while postpartum-depressed women did not report similar improvements in the first 9 weeks postpartum (O'Hara, Zekoski, Philipps, & Wright, 1990). Thus, the association between a poor marital relationship and depression may be more enduring in the postpartum period than it is at other times in married women's lives.

One aspect of the marital relationship that appears to be especially sensitive to women's mood disturbance in the postpartum period is sexual satisfaction. A longitudinal study found enjoyment of sexual intercourse decreased more for women experiencing postpartum depression than it did for women experiencing depression at other times (O'Hara et al., 1990). A comparison of depressed and nondepressed postpartum women found frequency of sexual intercourse was significantly lower at 3 months postpartum for depressed participants (Kumar & Robson, 1984). Recent studies including postpartum women and their spouses found that index couples, those in which the woman was experiencing postpartum depression, reported significantly less satisfaction with their marriage and less marital intimacy than control couples (Milgrom & McCloud, 1996; Zelkowitz & Milet, 1996).

In general, studies of postpartum women have found sexual satisfaction decreases in the postpartum period. Reasons for this change may be related to decreases in sexual desire/interest and activity/frequency, as well as increases in sexual problems (e.g., dyspareunia; Barrett, Pendry, Peacock, Victor, Thakar, & Manyonda, 1999; Von Sydow, 1999). Changes in the sexual relationship may be greater for couples experiencing their first postpartum period (Adams, 1988; Kumar, Brant, & Robson, 1981). A prenatal program designed to decrease potential negative effects of childbirth on the marital relationship was offered to first-time parents in a Canadian community (Kermeen, 1995). Accordingly, the intervention program provided couples with information on antenatal and postpartum emotional issues couples may encounter. When compared to couples that completed the intervention program, couples who attended the standard prenatal class reported less satisfaction with the sexual aspects of their relationships at 2 months postpartum. Thus, for women experiencing postpartum depression, sexual satisfaction may be negatively impacted by decreases in intercourse frequency and desire common in the postpartum period, as well as decreases in sexual enjoyment and marital intimacy associated with depression.

In addition to sexual dissatisfaction, depressed postpartum women have identified areas of emotional dissatisfaction in their marital relationships. Specifically, they have reported deficits in their partners' expressions of care and encouragement. Australian researchers screened pregnant women for depression, and those who were nondepressed were followed up to 6 months postpartum (Boyce, Hickie, & Parker, 1991). During their second trimesters, women rated their partners on measures of "caring" (providing consideration and affection) and "control" (being domineering and critical). At 1 month postpartum, risk for depression was higher for women who had described their partners as less caring and more controlling. Risk for depression at 3 months postpartum increased only for women who characterized their partners as controlling in the antenatal period. By 6 months postpartum, no partner characteristics were related to women's risk for depression. Thus, Boyce et al. found that men's antenatal emotional sensitivity towards their partners was more highly associated with women's risk for depression in the early postpartum than in the late postpartum period.

Another study investigating links between partner characteristic and women's depression levels included three groups of women up to 12 months postpartum: women currently depressed, women recovered from an episode of postpartum depression, and women asymptomatic in the postpartum period (Schweitzer et al., 1992). After controlling for current depression levels, results indicated that depressed and recovered women characterized their partners as less caring and more controlling than did asymptomatic women. Because the depressed and recovered-depressed groups provided similar descriptions of their partners, women's recovery did not appear to be related to their partners' sensitivity towards them. The authors provided no information on group differences in average time since delivery. If recovered women were further out from delivery than the women who were still depressed, Schweitzer et al.'s findings corroborate the findings from the Australian study. That is, as they progress through the postpartum period, women's depression levels become less related to their partners' sensitivity and supportive attitudes.

In addition to collecting women's assessments of their partners, researchers have interviewed men to investigate links between men's characteristics and women's diagnostic status. One such study, included partners of pregnant women who met criteria for a previous affective disorder and partners of pregnant women who had no psychiatric history (Marks, Wieck, Checkley, & Kumar, 1996). Based on individual antenatal interviews with men, researchers rated them on their expressed positive and critical feelings toward their pregnant partners. The husbands of women who relapsed in the postpartum period made significantly fewer positive comments about them during individual antenatal interviews. Strangely, the relapse rate was highest for women whose husbands were observed to be "not positive" and "not critical" of their partners. Perhaps these men had emotionally and/or cognitively withdrawn from their wives and therefore did not criticize them or use emotionally expressive language when discussing them. If the "neither critical nor positive" husbands also used this disengaged manner in dealing with their wives, their wives may have experienced a lack of spousal support and care. In sum, several studies have identified a link between men's care and support of their spouses and women's levels of depression in the postpartum period.

Men's sex role attitudes have also been associated with their spouses' depressive symptomatology following childbirth. In a sample of first-time parents, researchers found that men who believed they should have greater power in decision making and division of labor issues than their wives were married to women who reported higher levels of postpartum depressive symptomatology than those whose husbands had more equitable beliefs (Hock et al., 1995). When O'Hara et al. (1983) compared women diagnosed with postpartum depression to their nondepressed counterparts, we found that depressed women perceived their spouses to be less able providers of social support. Based on these two studies and the previously discussed research linking men's care and control to women's risk for depression (Boyce et al., 1991; Schweitzer et al., 1992), clinicians should expect postpartum-depressed women to report deficiencies in their partner and overall dissatisfaction with their marital relationship. Moreover, while symptomatic women would have their partners be more supportive and caring, their spouses may be more invested in making family decisions and exerting control in the relationship. This mismatch in partner desires could explain the relatively poor marital adjustment of depressed couples when compared with the adjustment of nondepressed dyads.

Many researchers have investigated the hypothesis that deficiencies in men's support and care for their partner influences women's adjustment in the postpartum period. However, these studies have largely failed to examine the role women's depression may have on men. Evidence suggests that fathers' psychological adjustment in the postpartum period may be influenced by stresses in the marital relationship. That is, maternal adjustment and functioning may impact paternal adjustment and vice versa. Ballard, Davis, Cullen, Mohan, and Dean (1994) found that men with postpartum-depressed partners were more likely to experience depression in the postpartum period than men whose partners did not meet depression criteria. British researchers found that men whose partners were depressed experienced significant emotional difficulties (Harvey & McGrath, 1988). Specifically, spouses of index women admitted to a psychiatric Mother and Baby Unit had significantly higher levels of psychopathology (anxiety and mood disorders) than husbands whose wives were not diagnosed with psychiatric disorders in the puerperium. Moreover, 17 of the 40 index men (42%) were diagnosed with a psychiatric disorder, and of those 17, only one man's episode began before the pregnancy. Unfortunately, the authors did not report maternal diagnostic classification so it is unclear how many men had depressed partners. Despite this limitation, their findings suggest that men whose partners experience postpartum psychiatric disorders are likely to encounter psychological difficulties of their own.

A later study compared husbands of index women diagnosed with postpartum mood or anxiety disorders to a control group of men whose wives did not have these disorders (Zelkowitz & Milet, 1996). Index husbands were at almost twice the risk for postpartum psychiatric disorders than were husbands of nondisordered-postpartum women (odds ratio = 1.83). Importantly, men whose wives were diagnosed with a psychiatric disorder in the postpartum period were no more likely to have a postpartum psychiatric disorder than men whose wives were well. However, men whose wives had a psychiatric disorder in the postpartum period were at greater risk for onset of a psychiatric disorder in the same period. Even index fathers who did not meet criteria for a psychiatric diagnosis reported significantly higher stress, anxiety, and somatization symptoms than control fathers reported. Index fathers also reported lower marital satisfaction and more negative changes in their families since the postpartum period began. These findings are consistent with other studies reporting that approximately 13% to 15% of fathers experience elevated levels of depressive symptomatology in the postpartum period (Fawcett & York, 1986; Raskin, Richman, & Gaines, 1990). Some researchers have found support for the concurrent onset of psychopathology in couples where the woman meets criteria for a postpartum psychiatric diagnosis (Lovestone & Kumar, 1993; Zelkowitz & Milet, 1996). Thus, factors related to the antenatal and/or postpartum periods may be associated with the emotional difficulties partners of depressed women experience.

In addition to experiencing higher symptom levels and poorer adjustment than husbands of nonpostpartum-depressed women, index husbands have reported lower levels of social support than control spouses. Harvey and McGrath (1988) found that husbands of depressed women perceived less supportive benefit from confiding in their spouses, less emotional support from their social networks (outside of work), and less support from their extended families. At the same time, these index men experienced higher levels of overall marital stress and stress from extended family relationships. Based on the postpartum-depression literature, it is difficult if not impossible to determine whether maternal depression and the associated psychosocial impairments cause partners to feel less supported, be less supportive, and become dissatisfied and depressed; or whether men's impairments cause postpartum women to become depressed and feel unsupported. Possibly the satisfaction and support each partner expresses in the relationship influences the other member in an interactional manner (Coyne, 1976; Downey & Coyne, 1990). Within an interactional model, a depressed individual's interactions with a close other elicits a reaction from the other, for example, avoidance or lack of support. However, the interactional influence need not begin with one partner's depression. The negative interaction could originate from marital disagreement or perceived lack of support and culminate in depression.

Consistent with an interactional model, a father's difficulty making the transition from the antenatal to the postpartum period may interact with a mother's perceived lack of support and elicit maternal depression. However, when investigating men's influence on their partners' postpartum-depression levels, researchers have focused on antenatal *or* postpartum variables and have largely neglected to look at the role transitional factors might play. That is, the changes men experience from the antenatal to postpartum period have rarely been directly evaluated as predictors of maternal depression. One study that included fathers' antenatal and postpartum relationship ratings found that changes in these ratings did not predict maternal depression ratings at 9 months postpartum (Hock et al., 1995). The regression of 9-month maternal depression levels on fathers' and mothers' adjustment and relationship ratings revealed men's antenatal ratings accounted for trivial amount of variance (2.1%) in maternal depression levels. The effects of the *change* in men's marital ratings, appeared to explain no additional variance in women's postpartum-depression levels. Importantly, fathers' marital ratings were entered in the sixth block of predictor variables. The nonsignificant finding is to be expected given that fathers' postpartum marital ratings were highly related to many of the variables already present in the equation. For example, paternal and maternal postpartum marital satisfaction ratings were significantly correlated ($r = .53, p < .001$).

Findings from another study are consistent with the hypothesis: Fathers' ability to smoothly shift from the antenatal to the postpartum period may significantly affect mothers' postpartum adjustment. This longitudinal study found that husbands' depressive symptoms at 1 month postpartum predicted women's symptom levels at 2 to 3 years postpartum (Carro et al., 1993). However, the converse was not true. That is, women's depressive symptomatology in the early postpartum period did not predict husband's symptomatology at the 2- to 3-year follow-up. Because no information about fathers' functioning in the antenatal period was collected, fathers' ease of transition to the postpartum period and how their transitional experiences might affect their partners' adjustment could not be addressed.

Women's mood may be affected by disturbances in their partners' early postpartum mood, and this effect may linger. Whether fathers' difficulties making the transition to the postpartum period initiate or maintain maternal depression is an open question. The evidence presented here suggests men's postpartum mood may be determined by their own antenatal mood and may be influenced by other factors soon thereafter. Perhaps fathers adjust to the new baby more quickly than mothers. Because mothers tend to do most of the childcare, those whose depression levels elevate in the early postpartum period may feel more stressed and overwhelmed for longer periods of time than fathers who are symptomatic in the early postpartum period. If fathers' adjustment in the early postpartum period has a significant influence on mothers' mood and this influence is long lasting, then providing interventions and support for at-risk fathers before or immediately after delivery may be important for both mothers and fathers.

Determining what event or which partner "caused" the depression may ultimately be impossible. Instead, researchers' and clinicians' time may be better spent investigating the ways partners influence each other in the postpartum period. Interactional influences may explain index couples' reports of relatively low marital consensus and affection. Moreover, outside variables may interact with relationship adjustment resulting in impairment of one or both individuals in the dyad. For example, the burden of stressful life events on a woman already experiencing relationship problems was found to increase her risk for postpartum depression (Paykel et al., 1980).

With the baby's arrival, new dyadic relationships form with their own interactional influences. Postpartum depression may affect the infant as it influences both parents' perceptions, behaviors, and moods (Downey & Coyne, 1990). Using a interactional model to understand maternal depression, clinicians can appreciate how parental functioning might influence disordered parents' perceptions of their children and their behavior towards their children—especially if either parent believes their own or their spouse's difficulties are related to their child's birth. Furthermore, parents' behaviors may elicit negative or disturbed behavior from their infants. To the extent that interactions between members of a family system produce effects upon other family members, a systems approach may prove effective for treating postpartum depression.

Accordingly, systems approaches have been recommended for the treatment of postpartum depressed women (Clark, Fedderly, & Keller, 1991; Gruen, 1993; Kraus & Redman, 1986; Olson, Cutler, & Legault, 1991). Although few empirical studies to test these hypotheses have been reported, some research findings are consistent with a systems approach to postpartum depression. First, mothers with postpartum depression and their spouses tend to perceive themselves, their infants, and their marital relationships more negatively than control couples (Goodman & Brumley, 1990; Gotlib & Whiffen, 1989). One longitudinal study found that even when maternal depression levels decreased, depressed dyads continued to view these members of their family system more negatively than couples who did not experience postpartum depression (Milgrom & McCloud, 1996). Second, mothers' quality of play with their infants have been linked to mothers' social problems, marital difficulties, and depression levels (Downey & Coyne,

1990). Stein et al. (1991) found that elevations in these variables predicted decreases in depressed mothers' attempts to maintain their infants' interest in play, and deficits in their infants' positive engagement (e.g., smiling at mother, showing mother toy) during play. Third, the quality of the marital relationship or father's adjustment may affect the infant by affecting the mother. For example, Stein et al. reported that antenatal or concurrent maternal depression levels were not related to observers' ratings of maternal warmth (mothers' endearments to and physical contact with their children); however, social and marital difficulties *were* related to maternal warmth. Based on a longitudinal study, Carro et al. (1993) concluded that father's depression levels at 1 month postpartum predicted maternal depression levels at 2- to 3-years postpartum, which in turn predicted toddler behavior problems. Thus, the psychosocial difficulties associated with postpartum depression may exert direct as well as indirect effects on various members of the family system.

In sum, these findings suggest impairment in depressed women's dyadic functioning with their partners and infants as well as adjustment difficulties in their partners. As discussed previously, women's behavior and displays of affect towards their infants are related to their infants' behavior and functioning. Because most studies have not included fathers, no discussion of how maternal postpartum depression affects fathers' interactions with their infants is possible at this time. To gain an understanding of how postpartum depression affects and is affected by family members, studies must include maternal and paternal reports, as well as observational assessments including episodes of mother–infant interaction and episodes of father–infant interactions.

THE PARENTAL RELATIONSHIP

Her family's history of psychopathology may relate to a woman's risk for postpartum depression (Campbell et al., 1992; Nilsson & Almgren, 1970; O'Hara, Neunaber, & Zekoski, 1984; Watson et al., 1984; for opposing findings, see Kumar & Robson, 1984; O'Hara, Schlechte, Lewis, & Varner, 1991). Reasons for the link between family history of psychopathology and postpartum depression are likely to include a genetic component as well as an environmental one. This section focuses on the environmental links between women's relationships with their parents and her risk for postpartum depression. Research suggests that women's reports of childhood parental loss, parental separation, or parental conflict are not related to a diagnosis of postpartum depression (Paykel et al., 1980; Watson et al., 1984). However, a recent study incorporating a large sample of pregnant women found links between their ratings of parental care during childhood and postpartum depression (Gotlib et al., 1991). Pregnant women who described their early parental relationships as less caring were more likely to experience a postpartum depressive episode. These studies suggest that women's perceptions of early parental care may be related to postpartum depression, yet early parental loss and separation may not.

Although attachment research suggests that loss of an attachment object, such as a parent, will have consequences for the child's future relationships, the aforementioned findings indicate that such a loss may not predict adult maternal depression in the postpartum period. Perhaps parental loss did not destroy these women's childhood attachment organizations because they had other caregivers who provided them with a secure attachment base. However, the significant relationship between parental care and postpartum depression suggests a link between women's childhood attachment organization and their mood disturbance following childbirth. If these women's parents were present but did not provide sufficient emotional care for them, they may not have formed secure attachments in childhood. On becoming the parent of an infant, these women may have worried that, like their parents, they would be inadequate caregivers for their children. Indeed, studies of postpartum depression have linked parenting stress to levels of depressive symptomatology (see the partner relationship and the mother–infant relationship sections in this chapter). Not surprisingly, some researchers have recommended that postpartum depression be understood with an attachment framework (Whiffen & Johnson, 1998).

Accordingly at least one group intervention for postpartum depression has included a session during which women discuss their own experiences of being mothered and how this experience has influenced their current relationships with their infants (Clark et al., 1991). Because this group included several components including partner and infant participation, it is unclear what specific effect the mothering discussion had on the women's functioning and adjustment. An empirically supported individual treatment for depression, Interpersonal Psychotherapy (IPT), is based on the premise that disturbances in an individual's early attachments contribute to later depression (Klerman, Weissman, Rounsaville, & Chevron, 1984). Evidence suggests that IPT may be an effective treatment for women experiencing depression during the puerperium (O'Hara, Stuart, Gorman, & Wenzel, 2000; Spinelli, 1997; Stuart & O'Hara, 1995). Subsequent research may shed light on the associations between women's experiences of being parented, their current relational difficulties, and their emotional health in the postpartum period.

Women's adult relationships with their parents may predict their emotional difficulties in the postpartum period. Several studies have found associations between poor mother–daughter relationships and postpartum depression (Kumar & Robson, 1984; Nilsson & Almgren, 1970; Uddenberg,

1974), although not all studies have found support for this link (Dimitrovsky et al., 1987). Because those studying postpartum depression have rarely asked women for historical information regarding their relationships with their mothers, it is unclear if the quality of current relationships was influenced by the maternal care these women experienced during childhood. If difficulties in adult daughter–mother relationships mediate the link between early attachment disturbances and adult postpartum depression, then new mothers' attachment organization may be a related to their risk for postpartum depression. Whether or not the difficulties in the current mother–daughter relationships stemmed from earlier problems, these studies suggest that postpartum-depressed women tend to experience difficulties relating to at least one of their parents.

CONCLUSIONS

Exploring relationship difficulties throughout a woman's social network is crucial for those treating postpartum-depressed women. Whether or not difficulties between mother and partner precede delivery, mother–father as well as mother–infant dyadic relationships are compromised during episodes of postpartum depression. We know that emotional attachment suffers and the tone of interactions becomes more negative in mother–infant dyads during postpartum depression. Infant behavioral disturbances may continue into toddlerhood and beyond. Postpartum depressed women as well as their partners may be dissatisfied with the emotional support expressed in their relationship. These women are also likely to report a lack of instrumental support from their partners. In addition, postpartum-depressed mothers are likely to report a lack of instrumental support from their partners. Thus, the marital relationship is likely to be unsatisfying for the depressed woman and her partner, and this dissatisfaction may linger after the depression remits. Although it is unclear how long the negative effects of postpartum depression continue to reverberate in the lives of mother, father, and child, postpartum depression most certainly has adverse effects on the depressed woman and those in close relationships with her.

REFERENCES

Adams, W. J. (1988). Sexuality and happiness ratings of husbands and wives in relation to first and second pregnancies. *Journal of Family Psychology, 2,* 67–81.

American Psychiatric Association. (1994). *Diagnostic and statistical manual of mental disorders* (4th ed.). Washington, DC: Author.

Ballard, C. G., Davis, R., Cullen, P., Mohan, & Dean, R. N. C. (1994). Prevalence of postnatal psychiatric morbidity in mothers and fathers. *British Journal of Psychiatry, 164,* 782–788.

Barrett, G., Pendry, E., Peacock, J., Victor, C., Thakar, R., & Manyonda, I. (1999). Women's sexuality after childbirth: A pilot study. *Archives of Sexual Behavior, 28*, 179–191.

Blair, R. A., Gilmore, J. S., Playfair, H. R., Tisdall, M. W., & O'Shea, M. W. (1970). Puerperal depression: A study of predictive factors. *Journal of the Royal College of General Practitioners, 19*, 22–25.

Boyce, P., Hickie, I., & Parker, G. (1991). Parents, partners or personality? Risk factors for postnatal depression. *Journal of Affective Disorders, 21*, 245–255.

Braverman, J., & Roux, J. F. (1978). Screening for the patient at risk for postpartum depression. *Obstetrics and Gynecology, 52*, 731–736.

Campbell, S. B., Cohn, J. F., Flanagan, C., Popper, S., & Meyers, T. (1992). Course and correlates of postpartum depression during the transition to parenthood. *Development and Psychopathology, 4*, 29–47.

Caplan, H. L., Cogill, S. R., Alexandra, H., Robson, K. M., Katz, R., & Kumar, R. (1989). Maternal depression and the emotional development of the child. *British Journal of Psychiatry, 154*, 818–822.

Carro, M. G., Grant, K. E., Gotlib, I. H., & Compas, B. E. (1993). Postpartum depression and child development: An investigation of mothers and fathers as sources of risk and resilience. *Development and Psychopathology, 5*, 567–579.

Clark, R., Fedderly, S. A., & Keller, A. (1991). *Therapeutic mother–infant groups for postpartum depression: Process and outcome.* Paper presented at the National Center for Clinical Infant Programs Seventh Biennial National Training Institute, Washington, DC.

Cogill, S. R., Caplan, H. L., Alexandra, H., Robson, K. M., & Kumar, R. (1986). Impact of maternal postnatal depression on cognitive development of young children. *British Medical Journal, 292*, 1165–1167.

Cohn, J. F., Campbell, S. B., Matias, R., & Hopkins, J. (1990). Face-to-face interactions of postpartum depressed and nondepressed mother–infant pairs at two months. *Developmental Psychology, 26*, 15–23.

Cohn, J. F., & Elmore, M. (1988). Effect of contingent changes in mothers' affective expression on the organization of behavior in three-month-old infants. *Infant Behavior and Development, 11*, 493–505.

Cohn, J. F., & Tronick, E. Z. (1983). Three-month-old infants' reaction to simulated maternal depression. *Child Development, 54*, 185–193.

Cohn, J., & Tronick, E. (1987). Mother–infant interaction: The sequence of dyadic states at 3, 6, and 9 months. *Child Development, 54*, 185–193.

Cooper, P. J., & Murray, L. (1995). Course and recurrence of postnatal depression: Evidence for the specificity of the diagnostic concept. *British Journal of Psychiatry, 166*, 191–195.

Cox, J. L., Connor, Y., & Kendell, R. E. (1982). Prospective study of the psychiatric disorders of childbirth. *British Journal of Psychiatry, 140*, 111–117.

Coyne, J. C. (1976). Toward an interactional description of depression. *Psychiatry, 39*, 28–40.

Cummings, E. M., & Davies, P. T. (1994). Maternal depression and child development. *Journal of Child Psychology and Psychiatry, 35*, 73–112.

Cutrona, C. E. (1984). Social support and stress in the transition to parenthood. *Journal of Abnormal Psychology, 93*, 378–390.

Dimitrovsky, L., Perez-Hirshberg, M., & Itskowitz, R. (1987). Depression during and following pregnancy: Quality of family relationships. *Journal of Psychology, 121*, 213–218.

Downey, G., & Coyne, J. C. (1990). Children of depressed parents: An integrative review. *Psychological Bulletin, 108*, 50–76.

Fawcett, J., & York, R. (1986). Spouses' physical and psychological symptoms during pregnancy and the postpartum. *Nursing Research, 35*, 144–148.

Field, T. (1984). Early interactions between infants and their postpartum depressed mothers. *Infant Behavior and Development, 7*, 517–522.

Field, T. (1986). Models for reactive and chronic depression in infancy. In T. Field & E. Z. Tronick (Eds.), Maternal depression and child development (*New Directions for Child Development*, No. 34, pp. 47–60). San Francisco: Jossey-Bass.

Field, T. (1992). Infants of depressed mothers. *Development and Psychopathology, 4*, 49–66.

Field, T. (1995). Presidential address: Infants of depressed mothers. *Infant and Behavior Development, 18*, 1–13.

Field, T., Healy, B., Goldstein, S., & Guthertz, M. (1990). Behavior–state matching and synchrony in mother–infant interactions of nondepressed versus depressed dyads. *Developmental Psychology, 26*, 7–14.

Field, T., Morrow, C., & Adelstein, D. (1993). Depressed mothers' perceptions of infant behavior. *Infant Behavior and Development, 16*, 99–108.

Gelfand, D. M., & Teti, D. M. (1990). The effects of maternal depression on children. *Clinical Psychology Review, 10*, 329–353.

Ghodsian, M., Zajicek, E., & Wolkind, S. (1984). A longitudinal study of maternal depression and child behavior problems. *Journal of Child Psychology and Psychiatry and Allied Disciplines, 25*, 91–109.

Goodman, S. H., & Brumley, H. E. (1990). Schizophrenic and depressed mothers: Relationship deficits in parenting. *Developmental Psychology, 26*, 31–39.

Gordon, R. E., & Gordon, K. K. (1960). Social factors in the prevention of postpartum emotional problems. *Obstetrics and Gynecology, 15*, 433–438.

Gotlib, I. H., & Hooley, J. M. (1988). Depression and marital distress: Current status and future directions. In S. Duck, D. F. Hay, et al. (Eds.), *Handbook of personal relationships: Theory, research and interventions* (pp. 543–570). Chichester, England UK: Wiley.

Gotlib, I. H., & Whiffen, V. E. (1989). Depression and marital functioning: An examination of specificity and gender. *Journal of Abnormal Psychology, 98*, 22–30.

Gotlib, I. H., Whiffen, V. E., Wallace, P. M., & Mount, J. H. (1991). Prospective investigation of postpartum depression: Factors involved in onset and recovery. *Journal of Abnormal Psychology, 100*, 122–132.

Gruen, D. S. (1993). A group psychotherapy approach to postpartum depression. *International Journal of Group Psychotherapy, 43*, 191–203.

Harvey, I., & McGrath, G. (1988). Psychiatric morbidity in spouses of women admitted to a mother and baby unit. *British Journal of Psychiatry, 152*, 506–510.

Hock, E., Schirtzinger, M. B., Lutz, W. J., & Widaman, K. (1995). Maternal depressive symptomatology over the transition to parenthood: Assessing the influence of marital satisfaction and marital sex role traditionalism. *Journal of Family Psychology, 1*, 79–88.

Izard, C. E., Fantauzzo, C. A., Castle, J. M., Haynes, O. M., Rayias, M. F., & Putnam, P. H. (1995). The ontogeny and significance of infants' facial expressions in the first 9 months of life. *Developmental Psychology, 31*, 997–1013.

Kermeen, P. (1995). Improving postpartum marital relationships. *Psychological Reports, 76*, 831–834.

Klerman, G. L., Weissman, M. M., Rounsaville, B. J., & Chevron, E. S. (1984). *Interpersonal psychotherapy of depression*. New York: Basic Books.

Kraus, M. A., & Redman, E. S. (1986). Postpartum depression: An interactional view. *Journal of Marital and Family Therapy, 12*, 63–74.

Kumar, R., & Robson, K. M. (1984). A prospective study of emotional disorders in childbearing women. *British Journal of Psychiatry, 144*, 35–47.

Kumar, R., Brant, H. J., & Robson, K. M. (1981). Childbearing and maternal sexuality: A prospective survey of 119 primiparae. *Journal of Psychosomatic Research, 25*, 373–383.

Lovestone, S., & Kumar, R. (1993). Postnatal psychiatric illness: The impact on partners. *British Journal of Psychiatry, 163*, 210–216.

Marks, M., Wieck, A., Checkley, S., & Kumar, C. (1996). How does marriage protect women with histories of affective disorders from post-partum relapse? *British Journal of Medical Psychology, 69,* 329–342.

Martin, M. E. (1977). A maternity hospital study of psychiatric illness associated with childbirth. *Irish Journal of Medical Science, 146,* 239–244.

Milgrom, J., & McCloud, P. (1996). Parenting stress and postnatal depression. *Stress Medicine, 12,* 177–186.

Murray, L. (1992). The impact of postnatal depression on infant development. *Journal of Child Psychology and Psychiatry, 33,* 543–561.

Nilsson, A., & Almgren, P. E. (1970). Para-natal emotional adjustment: A prospective investigation of 165 women, Part II. *Acta Psychiatrica Scandinavica, Supplementum 220,* 62–141.

O'Hara, M. W. (1986). Social support, life events, and depression during pregnancy and the puerperium. *Archives of General Psychiatry, 43,* 569–573.

O'Hara, M. W. (1991). Postpartum mental disorders. In J. J. Sciarra (Ed.), *Gynecology and obstetrics* (Vol. 6). Philadelphia: Harper & Row.

O'Hara, M. W. (1995). *Postpartum depression: Causes and consequences.* New York: Springer-Verlag.

O'Hara, M. W., Neunaber, D. J., & Zekoski, E. M. (1984). A prospective study of postpartum depression: Prevalence, course, and predictive factors. *Journal of Abnormal Psychology, 93,* 158–171.

O'Hara, M. W., Rehm, L. P., & Campbell, S. B. (1982). Predicting depressive symptomatology: Cognitive–behavioral models and postpartum depression. *Journal of Abnormal Psychology, 91,* 457–461.

O'Hara, M. W., Rehm, L. P., & Campbell, S. B. (1983). Postpartum depression: A role for social network and life stress variables. *Journal of Nervous and Mental Disease, 171,* 336–341.

O'Hara, M. W., Schlechte, J. A., Lewis, D. A., & Varner, M. W. (1991). A controlled prospective study of postpartum mood disorders: Psychological, environmental, and hormonal variables. *Journal of Abnormal Psychology, 100,* 63–73.

O'Hara, M. W., Stuart, S., Gorman, L., & Wenzel, A. (2000). Efficacy of interpersonal psychotherapy for postpartum depression. *Archives of General Psychiatry, 57,* 1039–1045.

O'Hara, M. W., & Swain, A. M. (1996). Rates and risk of postpartum depression—A meta-analysis. *International Review of Psychiatry, 8,* 37–54.

O'Hara, M. W., Zekoski, E. M., Philipps, L. H., & Wright, E. J. (1990). A controlled prospective study of postpartum mood disorders: Comparison of childbearing and nonchildbearing women. *Journal of Abnormal Psychology, 99,* 3–15.

Olson, M. R., Cutler, L. A., & Legault, F. (1991). Bittersweet: A postpartum depression support group. *Canadian Journal of Public Health, 82,* 135–136.

Paykel, E. S., Emms, E. M., Fletcher, J., & Rassaby, E. S. (1980). Life events and social support in puerperal depression. *British Journal of Psychiatry, 136,* 339–346.

Philips, L. H. C., & O'Hara, M. W. (1991). Prospective study of postpartum depression: 4½-year follow-up of women and children. *Journal of Abnormal Psychology, 100,* 151–155.

Raskin, V. D., Richman, J. A., & Gaines, C. (1990). Patterns in depressive symptoms in expectant and new parents. *American Journal of Psychiatry, 147,* 658–660.

Richters, J. E. (1992). Depressed mothers as informants about their children: A critical review of the evidence for distortion. *Psychological Bulletin, 112,* 485–499.

Richters, J. E., & Pellegrini, D. (1989). Depressed mothers' judgments about their children: An examination of the depression–distortion hypothesis. *Child Development, 60,* 1068–1075.

Robinson, G. E., Olmsted, M. P., & Garner, D. M. (1989). Predictors of postpartum adjustment. *Acta Psychiatrica Scandinavica, 80,* 561–565.

Schweitzer, R. D., Logan, G. P., & Strassberg, D. (1992). The relationship between marital intimacy and postnatal depression. *Australian Journal of Marriage & Family, 13,* 19–23.

Spinelli, M. G. (1997). Interpersonal psychotherapy for depressed antepartum women: A pilot study. *American Journal of Psychiatry, 154,* 1028–1030.

Sroufe, L. A. (1983). Infant–caregiver attachment and patterns of adaptation in preschool: The roots of maladaptation and competence. In M. Perlmutter (Ed.), *Minnesota symposium in child psychology* (Vol. 16, pp. 41–81). Hillsdale, NJ: Lawrence Erlbaum Associates.

Stein, A., Gath, D. H., Bucher, J., Bond, A., Day, A., & Cooper, P. J. (1991). The relationship between post-natal depression and mother–child interaction. *British Journal of Psychiatry, 158,* 46–52.

Stuart, S., & O'Hara, M. W. (1995). Interpersonal psychotherapy for postpartum depression: A treatment program. *Journal of Psychotherapy Practice and Research, 4,* 18–29.

Termine, N. T., & Izard, C. E. (1988). Infants' responses to their mothers' expressions of joy and sadness. *Developmental Psychology, 24,* 223–229.

Teti, D. M., Gelfand, D. M., Messinger, D. S., & Isabella, R. (1995). Maternal depression and the quality of early attachment: An examination of infants, preschoolers, and their mothers. *Developmental Psychology, 31,* 364–376.

Thompson, R. A. (1997). Early sociopersonality development. In W. Damon & E. Eisenberg (Eds.), *Handbook of child psychology: Vol. 3. Social, emotional, and personality development* (5th ed., pp. 25–104). New York: Wiley.

Uddenberg, N. (1974). Reproductive adaptation in mother and daughter. A study of personality development and adaptation to motherhood. *Acta Psychiatrica Scandinavica, Supplementum 254.*

Uddenberg, N., & Engeisson, I. (1978). Prognosis of postpartum mental disturbance: A prospective study of primiparous women and their 4-year-old children. *Acta Psychiatrica Scandinavica, 58,* 201–212.

Von Sydow, K. (1999). Sexuality during pregnancy and after childbirth: A metacontent analysis of 59 studies. *Journal of Psychosomatic Research, 47,* 27–49.

Watson, J. P., Elliott, S. A., Rugg, A. J., & Brough, D. I. (1984). Psychiatric disorder in pregnancy and the first postnatal year. *British Journal of Psychiatry, 144,* 453–462.

Whiffen, V. (1988). Vulnerability to postpartum depression: A prospective multivariate study. *Journal of Abnormal Psychology, 97,* 467–474.

Whiffen, V. E., & Gotlib, I. H. (1989). Infants of postpartum depressed mothers: Temperament and cognitive status. *Journal of Abnormal Psychology, 98,* 274–279.

Whiffen, V. E., & Johnson, S. M. (1998). An attachment theory framework for the treatment of childbearing depression. *Clinical Psychology–Science & Practice, 5,* 478–493.

Wrate, R. M., Rooney, A. C., Thomas, P. F., & Cox, J. L. (1985). Postnatal depression and child development: A three-year follow-up study. *British Journal of Psychiatry, 146,* 622–627.

Zelkowitz, P., & Milet, T. H. (1996). Postpartum psychiatric disorders: Their relationship to psychological adjustment and marital satisfaction in the spouses. *Journal of Abnormal Psychology, 105,* 281–285.

Anxiety Disorders and Relationships: Implications for Etiology, Functionality, and Treatment

Lydia C. Jackson
Amy Wenzel
University of North Dakota

Whereas another chapter in this volume presents an empirical study aimed at conceptualizing the nature of close relationships in individuals with social phobia, this chapter explores the reciprocal interaction between relationship difficulties and disabilities associated with a number of other anxiety disorders. To date, much of the literature concerning anxiety disorders and their impact on interpersonal functioning pertains to individuals with panic disorder with agoraphobia. In fact, reviews that describe relational interventions for individuals with anxiety disorders almost exclusively focus on this condition (e.g., Craske & Zoellner, 1995; Hafner, 1988). In addition to examining theory and treatment pertaining to relationship functioning in agoraphobic individuals, we also consider these issues in research examining obsessive–compulsive disorder (OCD) and posttraumatic stress disorder (PTSD). Regardless of the specific diagnosis, we argue that clinicians should consider the manner in which interpersonal relationships contribute to the maintenance of anxiety and the manner in which interpersonal relationships are negatively impacted by anxiety.

This chapter is organized according to the following structure. First, theories conceptualizing the development and maintenance of anxiety within a relational context are presented. In addition, functional difficulties related to the manifestation of agoraphobia, OCD, and PTSD are discussed. Next, models for treating agoraphobia and PTSD from a couple therapy approach are provided. Finally, couple and family treatment outcome literatures for agoraphobia, OCD, and PTSD are reviewed. Throughout this chapter, the terms "couple" and "marital" are employed interchangeably in accordance with the usage cited by authors.

ETIOLOGY, MAINTENANCE, AND FUNCTIONALITY

There is some evidence that a number of individuals with anxiety disorders are in distressed relationships (e.g., Hand, Lamontange, & Marks, 1974). Although etiological theories of anxiety stemming from cognitive behavioral models (e.g., Barlow, 1988) have received the most attention and empirical support, it has also been suggested that interpersonal functioning serves as both as a precipitating and maintenance factor in some anxiety disorders, particularly agoraphobia. Specifically, interpersonal, psychodynamic, and attachment models provide a relational mechanism for the development and maintenance of anxiety disorders. According to these models, maladaptive interpersonal styles predispose individuals to develop an anxiety disorder. In contrast, other research has examined marital and family difficulties that result from one individual's anxiety disorder. This research considers the manner in which anxiety disorders create the context for relationship distress to develop where it did not exist before the onset of the disorder. Literature associated with both of these perspectives is reviewed below.

Predisposing and Maintenance Factors

Interpersonal Model of Complex Agoraphobia. "Complex agoraphobia" is an anxiety disorder characterized by pervasive fearfulness that renders an individual incapable of independent functioning (Goldstein & Chambless, 1978). Individuals with complex agoraphobia experience marked social anxiety and conflicts between the desire to become autonomous and the "need" to remain in a familiar and secure environment. This syndrome may be associated with secondary gains such as attention from significant others. Moreover, attempts at autonomy may be met with punishment or negative reinforcement by the spouse or partner, which reinforces dependency. Through this type of interactional pattern, agoraphobics and their partners may become mutually dependent on disordered behavior (Jacobson, Holtzworth-Munroe, & Schmaling, 1989). Carter and Schultz (1998) provided an illustration of this phenomenon, whereby increased independence of the agoraphobic patient leads to the partner's dissatisfaction. For example, patients with agoraphobia may become particularly adept at household duties. As the patient's symptomatology improves, s/he spends less time at home, and the partner is forced to take on additional chores. Such a role transition often results in dissatisfaction and conflict in the marital relationship.

Craske and Zoellner (1995) posited that this model accounts for the onset of agoraphobia, as agoraphobic symptoms develop when the person attempts to break free of a problematic relationship but does not have the skills to do so. We view this model predominately as one of maintenance, in that symptoms of agoraphobia are prolonged by the mutual reinforcement that the condition provides. Specifically, this model puts forth that the partner of an individual with agoraphobia benefits from the client's symptomatology. Because of this benefit, s/he is not particularly supportive of the agoraphobic patient in changing his or her behavior. Conversely, the agoraphobic patient benefits because s/he is not challenged to engage in the uncomfortable process of changing his or her pathological behavior. It is speculated that when these well-established roles change, perhaps through the mechanism of psychotherapy, that relationship distress occurs (although empirical research generally has not supported this notion; see Craske & Zoellner, 1995 for a full discussion). Thus, this model provides a mechanism for relationship maintenance, although clinicians clearly would not suggest that this sort of arrangement contributes to the enhancement of relationships.

Psychodynamic Models. According to the psychodynamic approach, particular parenting styles may serve as catalysts for the expression of panic if patients with panic disorder were not taught strategies for developing a personal sense of control over emotionality in times of stress as children (Ballenger, 1989). It is normal for children to rely on their parents for assistance in dealing with stress and conflict. As children age, they begin to develop the skills to differentiate from their parents and handle sources of stress on their own. If children do not develop such skills, they will continue to rely on their parents to guide them through these difficult times. It is not difficult to imagine how this dependence gets transferred to a significant other when the child becomes involved romantically as an adult.

In his discussion of psychodynamic approaches to anxiety disorders, Ballenger (1989) also reviewed the maintenance of anxiety from an object relations perspective. Specifically, he indicated that normal child development involves a healthy internalized object representation of the mother. This internal representation soothes the individual in times of stress, and later in life a significant other may assume this role, especially in situations that elicit panic symptomatology. The safe person allows the patient to avoid or decrease the severity of a panic attack because the anxious individual views him or her as a safety signal. From the perspective of this model, the significant other assumes the role of the internalized object relation of the mother.

The psychodynamic model, then, provides an account of the etiology of anxiety disorders in which the anxious individual has not learned appropriate coping skills to deal with stress and instead relies on a significant other for a sense of control over his or her environment. From this perspective, anxiety disorders are maintained to the degree that the significant other assumes the caretaker role without negative consequences to the anxious individual.

Attachment Models

According to Sable (1997), "psychopathology is conceived as an impairment in the capacity to make and maintain close affectional bonds and is manifest in a variety of clinical syndromes" (p. 286). Bowlby (1973) suggested that the attachment system developed as a mechanism to maintain proximity to individuals who provide security, warmth, and protection. In times of stress or perceived danger, the attachment system is activated, and individuals seek the comfort of individuals who have provided protection in the past. Although attachment theory originally was developed to provide a mechanism to account for the nature of the bond between an infant and its mother, the past 15 years has witnessed an abundance of work illustrating the manner in which early attachment styles are played out in adult relationships (cf. Hazan & Shaver, 1987).

Psychopathology, according to this model, results from disruptions in early attachment experiences, primarily those with the mother. Instances in which the child felt unsafe, experienced a traumatic event, or failed to have his or her needs met contribute significantly to an internalized working model of relationships as unstable, inconsistent, and unsatisfying. Individuals with these working relational models often experience symptoms of anxiety and depression and have difficulty forming mutually satisfying relationships as adults. Sable (1997) suggested that individuals with anxiety disorders, particularly agoraphobia, are often characterized by an anxious–ambivalent attachment style. Individuals with this style "are uncertain that they can count on affectional figures and feel they must stay close to, and keep vigil on, persons or places that represent safety and protection" (p. 290). Moreover, they often present as being dependent and demanding because they fear being abandoned by significant others. Preliminary research demonstrated that individuals with social phobia indeed were more likely to be characterized by this attachment style than nonanxious individuals (Wenzel, this volume). However, this notion has not been investigated empirically in samples of individuals with other anxiety disorders.

From an attachment perspective, disrupted relations between infants and their primary caretakers accounts for the etiology of anxiety disorders. These children form a mental representation of close relationships as being unstable and disappointing. As adults, these individuals demonstrate a great deal of anxiety about relationships, desperately wanting to be in a stable relationship but also driving their partners away by their insecure behavior. Anxiety disorders are maintained to the extent that this representational model of close relationships remains unchallenged.

Functional Difficulties

Agoraphobia. There is inconsistent evidence for the notion that the relationships of individuals with agoraphobia are distressed. For example, Hand et al. (1974) reported that two thirds of their agoraphobic patients reported an unsatisfactory marriage. In contrast, Arrindell and Emmelkamp (1986) found that individuals with agoraphobia were assessed as having only slightly more maladjusted relationships than nonanxious individuals, and their relationships were more well-adjusted than individuals in relationships categorized as distressed or psychiatric controls. Social-role theorists have proposed that agoraphobic women are vulnerable to anxiety symptomatology because they are predisposed to play passive, dependent roles in their relationships (Hafner, 1986). It is likely that these individuals, who bear a strong resemblance to Goldstein and Chambless' description of complex agoraphobia, would have greater difficulties in their marital relationships as a result of relationship dissatisfaction, skills deficits, and role restriction. Indeed, Carter & Schultz (1998) suggested that agoraphobics with dependent personality characteristics are the most likely subgroup of patients with this disorder to manifest relationship difficulties. Thus, although there is some evidence that the close relationships of at least a subset of individuals with agoraphobia are distressed, no research exists that examines particular areas of dysfunction and disability that account for relationship dissatisfaction.

Obsessive–Compulsive Disorder. As we saw with agoraphobia, there is little research that examines relationship dysfunction that arises as a result of an individual's OCD symptomatology. Foa (1979) suggested that family relationships often play a large role in the maintenance of obsessive–compulsive symptoms. Although Emmelkamp and de Lange (1983) did not find that patients with OCD were in particularly distressed relationships, Emmelkamp, de Haan, and Hoogduin (1990) reported that over half of their patients with OCD scored in the distressed range on the Maudsley Marital Questionnaire. Thus, there is some evidence that OCD is related to relationship distress.

A recent study provided some evidence that the clinical expression of OCD is influenced by sociocultural factors related to gender. Matsunaga and his colleagues sought to clarify the effect of gender on clinical features in a Japanese sample of patients with OCD. They found that males with OCD had a higher likelihood of never being married or being assessed as having major impairments in social or occupational functioning compared to men without OCD. Moreover, females were more likely to involve other persons (such as parents, siblings, or husbands) in their OCD symptoms by forcing them to offer reassurance or to perform ritualistic behaviors. Although generalization to other cultural settings remains to be demonstrated, these differential manifestations of OCD have important implications for relationship functioning (Matsunaga, Kiriike, Matusi, Miyata, Iwasaki, Fujimoto, Kasai, & Kojima, 2000). Specifically, these data suggest that obsessive–compulsive men tend to avoid close relationships entirely, and obsessive–compulsive women tend to draw partners and family members into their world.

Posttraumatic Stress Disorder. Unlike the literature on functional difficulties associated with agoraphobia and OCD, there has been considerable discourse on the effects of PTSD on close romantic and family relationships. It is apparent that distressed relationships constitute an important aspect of the clinical presentation in PTSD symptomatology. Johnson and Williams-Keeler (1998) described such relationships as being similar to other distressed couples. They characterized individuals suffering from a trauma as becoming "stuck in constricted, self-reinforcing relationship cycles, such as pursue/withdraw and attack/defend, that make positive emotional engagement almost impossible" (p. 26). These authors also indicated that the aftereffects of trauma can prime, intensify, and exacerbate marital distress. Specifically, negative affect may be more intense, and potentially soothing activities, such as confiding and lovemaking, may instead become a source of threat or retraumatization.

Riggs, Byrne, Weathers, and Litz (1998) reviewed literature suggesting that combat veterans with PTSD may be at risk for significant relationship problems, are less satisfied with their intimate relationships, and have relationships that are less cohesive, less expressive, more conflictual, and more violent than the relationships of veterans without PTSD. These authors reported that PTSD symptoms such as emotional numbing, irritability, and decreased concentration may adversely affect couples' functioning. However, Riggs et al. cautioned that there is little empirical data to support these hypotheses and that most studies that have addressed these relationships have used broad or unstandardized measures of functioning (e.g., divorce rates, satisfaction), or relied only on the veteran's reports.

In an effort to improve on these methodological shortcomings, they explored these factors by assessing the relationship quality of male Vietnam veterans and their female partners using standard measures of relationship distress. They found that over 70% of veterans with PTSD and their partners endorsed clinically significant levels of relationship distress compared to 30% of veterans without PTSD and their partners. Specific relationship prob-

lems included a sense of anxiety concerning intimacy and a positive correlation between the degree of emotional numbing and the degree of relationship distress. From these results, Riggs et al. concluded that these couples
may benefit from treatment including communication and problem-solving
skills.

Drawing on sociological concepts of the family life cycle and Haley's
(1973) six stages of family life, Scaturo and Hayman (1992) discussed the effects of PTSD upon the family life of traumatized individuals. Specifically,
the authors examined relationship dysfunction in (a) courtship and mate
selection; (b) marriage; (c) childbirth and childrearing; (d) marriage at
midlife; (e) children leaving home; and (f) retirement and late life. The
courtship process, which occurs in late adolescence and early adulthood, is
typically the time period in which individuals serve in the military during
wartime. There are two clinical presentations of distressed relationships
that present during the courtship process. Partners of individuals who experience a traumatic event and are subsequently diagnosed with PTSD often face dealing with a "different person" (p. 275), and therapy during these
circumstances is aimed at helping the couple integrate the experience and
its aftermath into their relationship. In contrast, in cases where the individual with PTSD experienced the event prior to mate selection, his or her
partner may take on a helping or therapeutic role in the relationship that
may or may not be adaptive. In reference to the second stage of Haley's
model, marriage, Scaturo and Hayman indicated that expectations that a
man provide for his family in addition to dealing with PTSD symptomatology could create a great deal of stress for male combat veterans. Couple
interventions at this stage are particularly useful at helping the spouse to
understand the relation between the trauma experienced by the veteran
and associated stress.

When a couple is faced with childrearing, they must accept parental responsibilities and adjust to a greater degree of complexity in their intimate
relationships. Scaturo and Hayman (1992) indicated that, "There is no area
of family life in which the emotional numbing of PTSD as a psychological defense against traumatic recollections is felt more acutely than in the struggle to bond and remain attached to one's own children" (p. 279). "Secondary traumatization" has been coined as a term to describe the symptomatic
behavior seen in children of veterans with PTSD that results from marital
conflict, separation, and divorce (Rosenheck & Nathan, 1985). Couple or
family therapy in this case should provide preventative interventions directed toward the emotional well-being of the children of individuals with
PTSD. In addition, family members may find it quite difficult to understand
the anguish incurred by the reexperiencing of the traumatic event and
other PTSD-related symptoms. Clinicians seeking to work with such individuals should be sensitive to these issues, assisting the family in reacting to

their loved one's experiences while at the same time helping the veteran in dealing with the PTSD symptoms.

Moreover, there is evidence that the effects of PTSD on close, familial relationships continue well beyond the first few years after the traumatic event. During midlife, veterans with PTSD may experience a diminished sense of respect and effectiveness from their spouses and/or children. This is often related to a perceived failure to achieve vocationally, which often results from interference due to PTSD symptomatology. Family therapy implemented at this stage might assist the veteran and his family in redefining aspects of their lives, including the combat experience as well as areas such as work and family life. When their children leave home, veterans with PTSD may report an increased sense of separation anxiety and abandonment. Further, they may direct anger and resentment toward their children for re-exposing them to emotions similar to those they experienced during the trauma. In this case, family therapy would target communication between the veteran with PTSD and his or her children. Finally, veterans with PTSD may present with acute generalized anxiety, worry, and depression during retirement and late life when the loss of certain responsibilities has a major impact on both the patient and his or her spouse. Oftentimes, they have distracted themselves from re-experiencing symptoms by directing their attention to work, and once they retire, they endure a flooding of unwanted memories. Scaturo and Hayman (1992) posited that these symptoms often reflect underlying existential concerns and that one way for veterans with PTSD to "make peace with the world" (p. 285) is to facilitate a manner in which to pass their knowledge down to younger generations.

COUPLE INTERVENTIONS IN THE TREATMENT OF INDIVIDUALS WITH ANXIETY DISORDERS

According to Baucom, Shoham, Mueser, Daiuto, and Stickle (1998), there is considerable variation in the strategies used and targets of intervention involved in couple or family therapy for individual disorders. In their review of couple and family therapy for anxiety disorders, Baucom et al. classified these treatments into three broad types. Partner-assisted or family-assisted interventions (PFAIs) utilize the partner or family as a surrogate therapist or coach in treating the identified patient. Most PFAIs are developed from a cognitive–behavioral framework, in which the patient has specific assignments outside of the treatment session that at least partially involve the partner or family member. In "pure" PFAIs, the marital or family relationships are used to support the treatment plan, but these relationships are not a focus of the intervention. Such interventions do not consider directly the manner in which interpersonal, psychodynamic, or attachment processes may have contributed to the development or maintenance of the disorder.

A second method of incorporating a partner or family in the therapeutic process is through the use of a disorder-specific couple or family intervention. A disorder-specific partner or family intervention focuses on the manner in which a couple or family interacts in situations related to the disorder, perhaps maintaining or exacerbating the disorder. These interventions target the couple's or family's relationships, but the targets for interventions are limited to relational variables that directly influence either the disorder or its treatment. In these interventions, interpersonal factors that maintain anxiety disorders are of primary importance.

Finally, general couple or family therapy is the third method by which patients may be treated for their individual adult disorders. Such therapy stems from the belief that the functioning of the couple or family contributes to the development or maintenance of individual symptoms. Specific symptoms of psychopathology are not addressed in these particular models; rather, relationship distress is the primary target of treatment. It is important to note that, although each of these three types of interventions is described as a separate category of treatment, often they do not appear in pure form. Instead, most of the therapeutic strategies contain a mixture of the prior methods. The following is a description of two comprehensive couple's approaches to treating anxiety disorders.

Couple Therapy and Agoraphobia:
A Step-by-Step Approach

Craske and Zoellner (1995) described the following couple's approach based on standardized intervention research protocols developed at the University of Albany Center for Stress Anxiety Disorders. The standard cognitive behavioral strategies for treating anxiety, including exposure, relaxation training, and breathing retraining are integrated into this comprehensive treatment. This treatment protocol may be conducted in both individual and group treatment formats and utilizes the partner as a coach who assists the agoraphobic client in much the same way as would a therapist. This approach represents a partner-assisted intervention that includes a disorder-specific component that also allows for consideration of the manner in which the relationship culture contributes to the anxiety disorder. Specifically, Craske and Zoellner suggested that spousal involvement enhances therapeutic outcome by facilitating recovery through enhanced generalization and increased skill practice. In addition, this approach to treatment may address the relationship difficulties that have contributed or might contribute to the maintenance of anxiety symptomatology. The treatment follows a 12-session format, with the first 8 sessions conducted weekly and the last 4 sessions conducted biweekly. Both the spouse and client attend all sessions. Craske and Zoellner's step-by-step protocol for couple therapy includes education, coping strategies, communication surrounding exposure tasks, in vivo practice, and specific communication training.

Education. The chief purpose of this phase is to provide education about the nature of anxiety to both the client and the spouse. The spouse is encouraged to be an active participant in therapy and provide his or her viewpoint of the client's behavior and the manner in which their relationship has been affected. Importantly, the manner in which the agoraphobic problems have impacted on the couple's daily activities are discussed, and factors that might be reinforcing the agoraphobic behavior are identified. In this format, both the client and spouse are able to express their concerns about the anxiety problem as well as collaboratively agree on goals for treatment. Craske and Zoellner suggested that incorporating the spouse in this aspect of therapy is important, as it may reduce the amount of negative attributions directed at the client for his or her behavior and instead promote an environment ripe for support and understanding.

Coping Strategies. In this phase, both the client and spouse are taught a variety of cognitive and somatic anxiety management skills. Negative automatic thoughts pertaining to the catastrophic effects of panic and an inability to cope are identified, and skills to challenge these self-statements are considered. The couple engages in role-plays that allow the patient to practicing using cognitive restructuring skills in feared situations. Further, somatic coping strategies, such as relaxation and breathing exercises, are taught. Also during this phase, the therapist helps the couple to explore the manner in which the spouse might be reinforcing the agoraphobic problem, and s/he is taught to support the client by encouraging the use of coping skills rather than providing increased attention and sympathy. The therapist encourages the spouse to be supportive and patient and provides realistic expectations for the client's progress.

Communication Surrounding Exposure Tasks. According to Craske and Zoellner, care must be taken to prepare the couple for in vivo exposure tasks to alleviate any embarrassment or awkwardness. One way to prepare for this daunting task is to assist couples in developing effective communication skills specifically about agoraphobic distress and behavior. Therapists often suggest that clients and their spouses use an 8-point rating scale (0 indicating no distress; 8 indicating maximal distress) to communicate with each other the level of distress the client is feeling. During this time, any concerns the client might have about his or her partner being domineering or unsupportive are addressed and described as understandable as they gain the skills to communicate effectively about these issues. Role-playing is a useful technique to reinforce these skills.

In Vivo Practice. Similar to individual psychotherapy for agoraphobia, a graduated hierarchy of feared situations is developed. Unlike individual therapy, the spouse works collaboratively with the client to develop this list. In this phase of therapy, the spouse serves as a coach to facilitate exposure exercises and encourage the use of coping strategies to address fear and avoidance. Exposure exercises begin around the fifth session of this protocol and continue for the remainder of the 12 sessions. The therapist specifies that each item on the hierarchy should be practiced at least three times before the subsequent session. The spouse should accompany the client on at least one occasion, and the client should complete the task alone on at least one other occasion. This important caveat discourages the client's dependence on the spouse as a safety signal, such that the client learns that he or she is capable of performing the task on his or her own. In vivo exposure exercises are discussed in each session, and the therapist offers corrective feedback.

Specific Communication Training. In the second half of the treatment protocol, a problem-solving approach to communication skills is introduced. Craske and Zoellner noted that specific communication training not only enhances the effectiveness of in vivo exposure, but it also reduces relationship conflict. One part of specific communication training is communication education. Terms such as "intent," "impact," and "cognitive filters" are defined. The therapist works with the couple to develop a list, or hierarchy, of problems they encounter either because they never seem to get resolved or because they tend to escalate into arguments (e.g., going to a party to which the phobic partner refuses to go). This hierarchy, in contrast with the hierarchy utilized for the in vivo exposure component, is used for the applied practice of communication skills that are taught in subsequent sessions.

Next, the concept of "summarizing self-syndrome" is introduced. This communication flaw is a restating of one's own position without listening to the other person, a pattern that often escalates into frustration and a feeling of disrespect by one's partner. Craske and Zoellner described several indicators of this type of communication style. *Drifting off beam* is the sense that the other person does not see one's own point of view, illustrated by moving into other problem areas when trying to resolve a specific issue. *Mind reading* is jumping to the conclusion that one knows what one's partner is thinking. *Kitchen sinking* is bringing in other issues when discussing a specific area of conflict. *Yes butting* is finding flaws in the speaker's point of view. *Cross-complaining* is each partner stating a complaint in response to a complaint. A *standoff* occurs when both partners hold fast to their respec-

tive positions without compromise. In addition to teaching the couple problem-solving skills for ending the summarizing self-syndrome, the therapist
teaches *leveling* techniques, which involve stating one's own thoughts and
feelings without blame or insult. The couple is taught ways of being supportive and understanding while at the same time being honest about their
feelings. Another communication skill, *editing*, is achieved through stating
what can be done instead of what cannot be done, expressing appreciation
for each other's actions, and empathy, which is described as thinking of
how the other person is feeling. Finally, *problem solving* is a component described as gaining the skills to approach issues as a team. This technique
involves brainstorming potential courses of action, evaluating and selecting
the most appropriate courses of action, and instituting the chosen course.

Emotionally Focused Family Therapy (EFT)

Emotionally focused marital therapy (EFT) is a short-term therapy focusing
on reprocessing the emotional responses that organize attachment behaviors that takes place over the course of 12 to 20 sessions (Johnson, 1996).
Johnson and Williams-Keeler (1998) indicated that EFT is particularly useful
in treating individuals with PTSD because it "helps partners to reprocess
their emotional responses to each other and thereby change their interaction patterns to foster more secure attachment" (p. 28). Thus, they characterized EFT as consisting of two tasks: accessing and reprocessing affect;
and shaping new interactions. EFT therapists use experiential techniques
such as empathic reflection and validation as well as systemic techniques
such as identifying patterns of interpersonal interactions. According to the
typology of conjoint approaches for individual disorders put forth by Baucom et al. (1998), EFT is primarily a general couple intervention with components that relate dysfunctional aspects of the relationship to the maintenance of PTSD symptomatology. EFT is comprised of nine steps that
coincide with McCann and Pearlman's (1990) three stages of trauma treatment, including stabilization; rebuilding of the self and relationship capacities; and integration.

   Stabilization.   In this stage of therapy, the therapist assists the couple in
identifying maladaptive patterns of interaction. Problematic interactions,
such as fits of rage, are reframed as a response to the traumatic event
rather than attributable to stable characteristics of the patient or malicious
intentions. The therapist assists the individual with PTSD in communicating
aspects of the trauma to the partner in ways that are more likely to elicit
understanding and support. In addition, the therapist allows the partner to
express his or her views of how the trauma has affected the relationship.

Using an attachment model, the therapist encourages the patient to view his or her partner as a secure figure that can provide a great deal of assistance in coping with the aftermath of the trauma. Thus, in addition to providing some education about the psychological effects of a traumatic event, the therapist creates an environment characterized by empathy and alliance between the patient and his or her partner.

Building Self and Relational Capacities. According to Johnson and Williams-Keeler (1998), the therapist's task at this stage in therapy is to encourage coping skills that will nurture the relationship instead of interfere with it (e.g., withdrawal). The therapist assists the couple in integrating negative affect into the relationship rather than merely tolerating it. Specific processes that occur in this stage of therapy are "reprocessing negative affect, creating new, trusting interactions, and redefining the sense of self" (p. 32). The therapist may use reflection and validation to diffuse negative affect that escalates to an uncomfortable level. In addition, the therapist assists the patient in identifying his or her fears, which usually arise from an insecure attachment style. By addressing the fear in a safe environment, Johnson and Williams-Keeler suggest that the patient will attain a sense of mastery over aspects of the trauma, which in turn should have a positive impact on relationship functioning. Throughout this process, the partner is encouraged to accept these fears and respond to them with empathy rather than frustration or hurt.

Integration. In this final phase of EFT, the therapist assists the patient in integrating new aspects of a sense of self into his or her identity as well as helping the couple to integrate new ways of interacting into their relationship culture. The couple anticipates problematic issues associated with the trauma (e.g., anniversaries) and brainstorms ways to cope with them together.

COUPLE THERAPY AND ANXIETY DISORDERS: TREATMENT OUTCOME LITERATURE

The literature examining conjoint approaches to treating anxiety disorders is relatively scant. Most treatment outcome studies to date have evaluated PFAIs for agoraphobia and OCD. Although there is much discourse about couple and family treatments for PTSD, most of this literature is limited to case studies or treatment recommendations made in the absence of controlled outcome studies.

Agoraphobia

Various studies have shown that partner-assisted exposure (PAE), an exam-
ple of a PFAI, is equivalent to nonassisted exposure therapy (e.g., Cobb,
Mathews, Childs-Clarke, & Blowers, 1984; Emmelkamp, Van Dyck, Bitter,
Heins, Onstein, & Eisen, 1992), group exposure therapy (Hand, Angenendt,
Fischer, & Wilke, 1986), and friend-assisted exposure (Oatley & Hodgson,
1987) in the treatment of agoraphobia. However, PAE was reported to be superior to partner-assisted problem solving (Jannoun, Munby, Catalan, &
Gelder, 1980). Moreover, Barlow, O'Brien, and Last (1984) compared couple
cognitive behavior therapy (CBT) with individual CBT for agoraphobia and
found a distinct advantage for the couple intervention. Cerny, Barlow,
Craske, and Himaldi (1987) reported that these gains were maintained at a 2-
year follow-up assessment. From these studies, it may be concluded PAE
works as least as well as other forms of exposure. In addition, there is some
evidence that PAE has a positive effect on relationship distress as well as
agoraphobic symptoms; marital therapy alone, in contrast, improves relationship distress but has no effect on agoraphobia symptoms (Cobb et al.,
1984). Furthermore, individual treatment for agoraphobia does not affect relationship satisfaction ratings (Himaldi, Cerny, Barlow, Cohen, & O'Brien,
1986). Craske and Zoellner also pointed out that the attrition rates for
agoraphobic clients in PAE consistently are well below rates in individual
therapy or medication trials.

Arnow, Taylor, Agras, and Telch (1985) expanded on the PAE treatment
approach by adding a communication skills training component that focused on constructive speaking, empathic listening, and conflict resolution.
This methodology is similar to that described by Craske and Zoellner
(1995). In this study, couples receiving PAE along with eight sessions of
communication training were compared with couples receiving the same
exposure therapy along with eight sessions of couple relaxation training.
Patients in the exposure plus communication training group had significantly lower subjective anxiety and more unaccompanied excursions than
the exposure plus relaxation couples. These results indicate that teaching
couples to discuss and solve problems surrounding how they handle
agoraphobic symptoms can improve the effectiveness of exposure. Craske,
Burton, and Barlow (1989) provided evidence supportive this conclusion
with their finding that a measure of communication, but not relationship
satisfaction, predicted anxiety during exposure exercises.

Chernen and Friedman (1993) evaluated the treatment of personality disordered agoraphobic patients with both individual and marital therapy.
They proposed that agoraphobic patients with comorbid personality disorders may be less responsive to individual behavior therapy than agoraphobic patients without comorbid personality disorders because of their
ambivalence about independent functioning and their difficulties in inter-

personal relationships. Standard behavioral marital therapy (BMT; Jacobson & Margolin, 1979) and exposure techniques were employed to treat four dually diagnosed individuals. Specifically, patients participated in 10 sessions of individual exposure therapy followed by 10 sessions of BMT. Using a multiple replication, time-series design, the authors found that BMT was a useful adjunct to individual therapy for personality disordered agoraphobic individuals with distressed marriages but may be detrimental to improvement for such individuals who deny marital dysfunctions on self-report scales and clinical interviews. The authors emphasized the need for comprehensive assessment to determine whether couple therapy is a useful intervention for individuals with comorbid agoraphobia and personality disorders.

Therapeutic Mechanisms. Craske and Zoellner (1995) evaluated several therapeutic mechanisms that may be responsible for the efficacy of marital therapy for agoraphobia. Their hypotheses were as follows—Couple therapy: creates a more supportive environment, thereby reducing stress that exacerbates anxiety; (2) removes factors that reinforce dependency; (3) enhances communication skills; and (4) enhances the quality of in vivo exposure exercises. At present, the mechanism that accounts for the efficacy of couple's therapy in treating agoraphobic distress is unclear. There is no direct evidence for any of these hypotheses, and there is only indirect evidence for the first and third hypothesis. It is likely that standard components used in both individual and conjoint approaches to treatment (e.g., exposure, cognitive restructuring) reduce symptoms of anxiety. The benefit of couple's therapy for individuals with agoraphobia may be twofold: (1) it addresses relationship distress that is being experienced concurrently with anxiety symptomatology; and (2) involvement of the partner may ensure success by motivating the patient and providing a safe context for the patient to attempt exposure exercises that would otherwise be intolerable.

Obsessive–Compulsive Disorder

A handful of studies have compared outpatient treatments consisting of in vivo exposure and response prevention with or without the involvement of the patient's partner—the latter deemed partner-assisted exposure (PAE)—and traditional forms of couple therapy. In a comparison of PAE and BMT, Cobb, McDonald, Marks, and Stern (1980) found that PAE improved both OCD symptoms and relationship distress, whereas BMT improved the relationship but not the symptoms of psychopathology. Emmelkamp and de Lange (1983) found that PAE produced significantly better results at posttest than treatment without the involvement of the partner on subjective and therapist-rated measures of anxiety. On the other hand, Emmelkamp, de Haan, & Hoodguin (1990) found no differences between PAE and individual exposure. Together, these studies suggest that the inclusion of the partner during exposure procedures is at least as beneficial as implementing them without the partner.

Family-assisted exposure involves having one family member participate in the role of cotherapist by being present during homework practices, participating in response prevention, supervising relaxation therapy, and supporting the patient when he/she was depressed or anxious. Using this approach, family-assisted treatment has been found to be more effective than treatment without a family member (parents, spouses, or children) on subjective measures of anxiety, depression, obsessions, and adjustment to family interaction and occupational functioning (Mehta, 1990). Furthermore, the superiority of the family-assisted version was maintained at 1-month follow-up. It should be noted that one important difference between the family-assisted exposure treatment and the PAE studies was that family members were instructed to provide emotional support to the patients in the Mehta study, whereas in the Emmelkamp studies partners were instructed to withhold support. Baucom et al. (1998) concluded that this difference may illustrate that the specific role the "cotherapist" is asked to play contributes more to treatment outcome than which family member assists the patient.

Posttraumatic Stress Disorder

Due to the heterogeneous nature of the etiology of PTSD, a number of couple and family interventions for the disorder have been described in the literature. Although much of the PTSD literature pertains to combat veterans (e.g., Scaturo & Hayman, 1992), models of couple therapy for women who have experienced abortion (e.g., Bagarozzi, 1994), sexual abuse, and even spousal abuse have been described. Emotional numbing is a particularly important target for therapeutic interventions dealing with combat veterans; however, other problematic symptoms, such as avoidance behavior, appear to be quite relevant in treating abuse victims. Schlee, Heyman, and O'Leary (1998) compared psychoeducational group couple therapy for spouse abuse in women with and without PTSD. They described two different formats for these groups. In one of these groups, women with PTSD and their partners attended sessions together and gained skills targeting the cessation of violence, anger management, and communication. In the other format, women with PTSD and their partners attended separate groups. The males' group worked on issues of violence cessation, power and control, whereas the women's group worked on violence cessation, assertiveness, and self-esteem issues. Schlee et al. concluded that women with PTSD are appropriate candidates for group spousal therapy, providing that two important caveats are met. First, a careful assessment of avoidance symptomatology is necessary, as high avoidance may indicate risk for attrition. Second, the authors indicated that the severity of the husband's abuse must be assessed, emphasizing that the victim's safety should be of the utmost concern. Certainly, severe spousal abuse signifies that important relationship impairments beyond the scope of this chapter may exist.

CONCLUDING REMARKS AND FUTURE DIRECTIONS

In many instances, anxiety disorder symptomatology has negative effects on the maintenance and enhancement of close relationships. Specifically, a relationship culture may develop where anxiety symptomatology is reinforced, making it unlikely that the anxious individual or his or her partner will be motivated to change. In addition, relationship conflict may result when the individual with an anxiety disorder avoids participating in activities that are pleasurable to his or her partner. Although there is some research demonstrating that one partner's anxiety symptomatology is related to relationship dissatisfaction, we know little about the particular areas of dysfunction that contribute to this state. We encourage anxiety researchers to examine particular aspects of close relationships in anxiety disorders, such as participation in shared activities, intimacy, relationship attributions, and communication patterns. Moreover, little is known about the effects of an individual's anxiety disorder on the nonanxious partner. Future research, perhaps similar to that investigating the effects of depression on spousal functioning (i.e., Coyne, 2000) is beginning to address this issue.

Perhaps most important to the practicing clinician is determining the extent to which relationship difficulties impact on patients presenting with an anxiety disorder, and subsequently, whether to implement a couple or an individual intervention. Hafner (1988) indicated that the severity of the disorder is a useful preliminary guide to the applicability of conjoint therapy. Specifically, he asserted that as an individual's anxiety disorder is more severe and persisting, it is more likely that couple or family therapy will be necessary for successful treatment. In addition, couple therapy is indicated when there is a clear link between an individual's anxiety disorder and interpersonal processes. The work of Chernen and Friedman (1993) suggests that anxious individuals with comorbid personality disorders, presumably reflecting maladaptive interpersonal processes, might be particularly good candidates for couple therapy to treat their anxiety disorder. Moreover, Barlow, O'Brien, Last, and Holden (1983) reported that agoraphobic symptoms improve in individuals who are in distressed relationships only when the partner is included in therapy. Johnson and Williams-Keeler (1998) suggested that EFT may be especially indicated when trauma has disrupted a secure attachment style or when traumatic experiences of interpersonal violence significantly affect the patient's ability to sustain close relationships. Even in patients where couple therapy may not be indicated (such as nonmarried individuals), therapists may wish to incorporate strategies aimed at improving interpersonal functioning to maximize long-term therapeutic efficacy.

It is also interesting that there are no known accounts examining the nature of close relationships in individuals with social phobia. Craske and Zoellner (1995) and Hafner (1988) argued that social phobia (and specific phobias) are less pervasive disorders than panic disorder with agoraphobia, PTSD, and OCD; hence, they felt that couple therapy was less important in these disorders. However, by its very nature, one would expect that individuals with social phobia would experience significant relationship distress because of the social skills deficits and cognitive distortions that have been known to co-occur with this disorder. From our clinical experience, spouses of individuals with social phobia who present for couple therapy are exasperated about the difficulties they have in maintaining open lines of communication with their social-phobic partner (e.g., "like pulling teeth"). We argue not only that social phobia is an anxiety disorder that is accompanied by disturbances in close relationships, but that, in fact, this disorder may be associated with some unique relationship difficulties that are not associated with the other anxiety disorders discussed in this chapter. To address this issue, empirical research must be conducted into the nature of close relationships in individuals with a variety of anxiety disorders, including social phobia.

We must highlight two limitations of this literature. A number of investigations conducted in the 1980s examined the efficacy of PFAIs in the treatment of agoraphobia and OCD. However, very few studies have evaluated the efficacy of couple interventions that target the manner in which the relationship maintains or exacerbates symptoms of anxiety or other standard couple interventions. We believe that a comparison of these three approaches to therapy will help to elucidate the mechanism by which interpersonal functioning is related to anxiety symptomatology. In addition, the generalizability of this research reviewed in this chapter is questionnable. To date, much of this research has been conducted using Caucasian, married female patients with anxiety disorders (Carter & Schultz, 1998). Future research must be sensitive to recruit individuals with demographic characteristics that are representative of the general population. Moreover, it must demonstrate that results generalize to individuals who are in committed relationships but are not married.

Finally, we end our chapter on an optimistic note. Most of the literature reviewed in this chapter describes the nature of or treatments for relationship distress in individuals with anxiety disorders and their partners. The manner in which relationships are enhanced in these couples is rarely considered. However, clinically, we have encountered a number of individuals being treated for an anxiety disorder who describe their spouse or partner as a significant source of strength and support. Many of these individuals regard their partner as being understanding of their condition but also challenging of them to continue treatment and overcome their anxiety. It is important for future research to consider this subset of anxious individuals and their partners who make their relationships work in spite of a sometime debilitating condition. We suspect that researchers who investigate relationship distress in individuals with psychopathology will gain insight into relationship enhancement strategies from these individuals.

REFERENCES

Arnow, B. A., Taylor, C. B., Agras, W. S., & Telch, J. J. (1985). Enhancing agoraphobia treatment outcome by changing couple communication patterns. *Behavior Therapy, 16*, 452–467.

Arrindell, W. A., & Emmelkamp, P. M. G. (1986). Marital adjustment, intimacy, and needs in female agoraphobics and their partners: A controlled study. *British Journal of Psychiatry, 149*, 592–602.

Bagarozzi, D. A. (1994). Identification, assessment and treatment of women suffering from post traumatic stress after abortion. *Journal of Family Psychotherapy, 5*, 25–54.

Ballenger, J. C. (1989). Toward an integrated model of panic disorder. *American Journal of Orthopsychiatry, 59*, 284–293.

Barlow, D. H. (1988). *Anxiety and its disorders: The nature and treatment of anxiety and panic.* New York: Guilford.

Barlow, D. H., O'Brien, G. T., & Last, C. G. (1984). Couples treatment of agoraphobia. *Behavior Therapy, 15*, 41–58.

Barlow, D. H., O'Brien, G. T., & Last, C. G., & Holden, A. E. (1983). Couples treatment of agoraphobia: Initial outcome. In K. D. Craig & R. J. McMahon (Eds.), *Advances in clinical behavior therapy* (pp. 99–126). New York: Brunner/Mazel.

Baucom, D. H., Shoham, V., Mueser, K. T., Daiuto, A. D., & Stickle, T. R. (1998). Empirically supported couple and family interventions for marital distress and adult mental health problems. *Journal of Consulting and Clinical Psychology, 66*, 53–88.

Bowlby, J. (1973). *Separation.* New York: Basic.

Carter, M. M., & Schultz, K. M. (1998). Panic disorder with agoraphobia: Its impact on patients and their significant others. In J. Carlson & L. Sperry (Eds.), *The disordered couple* (pp. 29–56). Bristol, PA: Brunner/Mazel, Inc.

Cerny, J. A., Barlow, D. H., Craske, M. G., & Himaldi, W. G. (1987). Couples treatment of agoraphobia: A two-year follow-up. *Behavior Therapy, 18*, 401–415.

Chernen, L., & Friedman, S. (1993). Treating the personality disordered agoraphobic patient with individual and marital therapy: A multiple replication study. *Journal of Anxiety Disorders, 7*, 163–177.

Cobb, J. P., Mathews, A. M., Childs-Clarke, A., & Blowers, C. M. (1984). The spouse as co-therapist in the treatment of agoraphobia. *British Journal of Psychiatry, 144*, 282–287.

Cobb, J., McDonald, R., Marks, I., & Stern, R. (1980). Marital versus exposure therapy: Psychological treatments of co-existing marital and phobic–obsessive problems. *Behavior Analysis and Modification, 4*, 3–16.

Coyne, J. C. (2000). Living with a depressed spouse. *Journal of Family Psychology, 14*, 70–79.

Craske, M. G., Burton, T., & Barlow, D. H. (1989). Relationships among measures of communication, marital satisfaction and exposure during couples treatment of agoraphobia. *Behaviour Research and Therapy, 27*, 131–140.

Craske, M. G., & Zoellner, L. A. (1995). Anxiety disorders: The role of marital therapy. In N. S. Jacobson & A. S. Gurman (Eds.), *Clinical handbook of couple therapy* (pp. 394–410). New York: Guilford.

Emmelkamp, P. M. G., de Hann, E., & Hoodguin, C. A. L. (1990). Marital adjustment and obsessive–compulsive disorder. *British Journal of Psychiatry, 156*, 55–60.

Emmelkamp, P. M. G., & de Lange, I. (1983). Spouse involvement in the treatment of obsessive–compulsive patients. *Behavioral Research and Therapy, 21*, 341–346.

Emmelkamp, P. M. G., van Dyck, R., Bitter, M., Heins, R., Onstein, E. J., & Eisen, B. (1992). Spouse-aided therapy with agoraphobics. *British Journal of Psychiatry, 160*, 51–56.

Foa, E. B. (1979). Failure in treating obsessive compulsives. *Behaviour Research and Therapy, 17*, 169–176.

Goldstein, A. J., & Chambless, D. L. (1978). A reanalysis of agoraphobia. *Behavior Therapy, 9*, 47–59.

Hafner, R. J. (1986). *Marriage and mental illness*. New York: Guilford.

Hafner, R. J. (1988). Marital and family therapy. In C. G. Last & M. Hersen (Eds.), *Handbook of anxiety disorders* (pp. 386–400). New York: Pergamon.

Haley, J. (1973). *Uncommon therapy: The psychiatric techniques of Milton H. Erickson, M.D.* New York: W. W. Norton.

Hand, I., Angenendt, J., Fischer, M., & Wilke, C. (1986). Exposure in vivo with panic management for agoraphobia: Treatment rationale and long-term outcome. In I. Hand & H.-U. Wittchen (Eds.), *Panic and phobias: Empirical evidence of theoretical models and long-term effects of behavioral treatments* (pp. 104–127). Berlin: Springer-Verlag.

Hand, I., Lamontagne, Y., & Marks, I. M. (1974). Group exposure (flooding) in vivo for agoraphobics. *British Journal of Psychiatry, 124*, 588–602.

Hazan, C., & Shaver, P. (1987). Romantic love conceptualized as an attachment process. *Journal of Personality and Social Psychology, 52*, 511–524.

Himaldi, W. A., Cerny, J. A., Barlow, D. H., Cohen, S., & O'Brien, G. T. (1986). The relationship of marital adjustment to agoraphobia treatment outcome. *Behaviour Research and Therapy, 24*, 107–115.

Jacobson, N. S., Holtzworth-Munroe, A., & Schmaling, K. B. (1989). Marital therapy and spouse involvement in the treatment of depression, agoraphobia, and alcoholism. *Journal of Consulting and Clinical Psychology, 57* (1), 5–10.

Jacobson, N. S., & Margolin, G. (1979). *Marital therapy: Strategies based on social learning and behavior exchange principles*. New York: Brunner/Mazel.

Jannoun, L., Munby, M., Catalan, J., & Gelder, M. (1980). A home-based program for agoraphobia. Replication and controlled evaluation. *Behavior Therapy, 11*, 294–305.

Johnson, S. M. (1996). *The practice of emotionally focused marital therapy: Creating connection*. New York: Brunner/Maze.

Johnson, S. M., & Williams-Keeler, L. (1998). Creating healing relationships for couples dealing with trauma: The use of emotionally focused marital therapy. *Journal of Marital and Family Therapy, 24*, 25–40.

Matsunaga, H., Kiriike, N., Matsui, T., Miyata, A., Iwasaki, Y., Fujimoto, K., Kasai, S., & Kojima, M. (2000). Gender differences in social and interpersonal features and personality disorders among Japanese patients with obsessive–compulsive disorder. *Comprehensive Psychiatry, 41*(4), 266–272.

McCann, I. L., & Pearlman, L. A. (1990). *Psychological trauma and the adult survivor*. New York: Brunner/Mazel.

Mehta, M. (1990). A comparative study of family-based and patient-based behavioral management in obsessive–compulsive disorder. *British Journal of Psychiatry, 157,* 133–135.

Oatley, K., & Hodgson, D. (1987). Influence of husbands on the outcome of their agoraphobic wives' therapy. *British Journal of Psychiatry, 150,* 380–386.

Riggs, D. S., Byrne, C. A., Weathers, F. W., & Litz, B. T. (1998). The quality of the intimate relationships of male Vietnam veterans: Problems associated with posttraumatic stress disorder. *Journal of Traumatic Stress, 11,* 87–101.

Rosenheck, R., & Nathan, P. (1985). Secondary traumatization in children of Vietnam veterans. *Hospital Community Psychiatry, 36,* 538–539.

Sable, P. (1997). Disorders of adult attachment. *Psychotherapy, 34,* 286–296.

Scaturo, D. J., & Hayman, P. M. (1992). The impact of combat trauma across the family life cycle: Clinical considerations. *Journal of Traumatic Stress, 5,* 273–288.

Schlee, K. A., Heyman, R. E., & O'Leary, K. D. (1998). Group treatment for spouse abuse: Are women with PTSD appropriate participants? *Journal of Family Violence, 13,* 1–20.

9

Characteristics of Close Relationships in Individuals With Social Phobia: A Preliminary Comparison With Nonanxious Individuals

Amy Wenzel
University of North Dakota

Social phobia is an anxiety disorder characterized by excessive fears of negative evaluation and embarrassment. Individuals with social phobia experience discomfort in the context of interpersonal interactions, which often leads to avoidance of social and interactional situations. The National Comorbidity Survey recently estimated that 13% of the population suffer from this condition at some point in their life (Magee, Eaton, Wittchen, McGonagle, & Kessler, 1996). Because social phobia is one of the most prevalent disorders in the *Diagnostic and Statistical Manual of Mental Disorders-Fourth Edition* (DSM-IV; American Psychiatric Association, 1994), it is likely that clinicians frequently will be faced with socially anxious patients who are experiencing interactional fears and the adverse consequences of those fears. Unfortunately, few studies have investigated the long-term effects of social phobia on social functioning, and no known studies have examined characteristics of close, romantic relationships in social phobia. Identifying specific problematic aspects of the close relationships of individuals with social phobia is the first step toward designing interventions to ameliorate relationship distress in these individuals and their partners.

Two relatively recent studies have acknowledged that the romantic relationships of individuals with social phobia are impaired. Schneier and his colleagues (Schneier et al., 1994) examined functional impairment in 32 individuals with social phobia, 12 of whom were diagnosed with comorbid psychopathology including major depression, dysthymia, psychoactive substance abuse, and other anxiety disorders. They reported the outcomes of two measures of interest—the Disability Profile, and the Liebowitz Self-Rated Disability Scale. The Disability Profile is a clinician rating that assesses current (i.e., past 2 weeks) and most severe lifetime impairment in a number of domains, including marriage/dating, on a 5-point Likert-type scale (0 = *no impairment*; 4 = *severe impairment*). The Liebowitz Disability Scale is quite similar to the Disability Profile, with the exceptions that it is a self-report instrument rather than a clinician-rated measure and it uses a 4-point Likert-type scale (0 = *not limited*; 3 = *severely limited*) rather than a 5-point scale. Results indicated that the patients with social phobia were mildly impaired in the area of romantic relationships at the time of the assessment (Disability Profile = 1.8; Liebowitz Disability Scale = 1.5). Moreover, they were characterized by moderate impairment at the time of their worst functioning (Disability Profile = 2.6; Liebowitz Disability Scale = 2.1). These scores were significantly higher than those for nonanxious control individuals.

Wittchen and Beloch (1996) also administered the Liebowitz Disability Scale on a sample of 65 individuals with social phobia and 65 nonanxious control individuals. Unlike the study described previously, the individuals with social phobia in this study were required to be free of comorbid psychopathology. These "pure" social phobics were characterized by mild impairment in their partner relationship at the time of the assessment (Liebowitz Disability Scale = 0.9) and mild to moderate impairment during their worst episode of the phobia (Liebowitz Disability Scale = 1.6). Although these values appear to be relatively small, it must be acknowledged that partner relationship was one of the two areas of functioning that received the most severe disability ratings. Wittchen and Beloch suggested that individuals in their social phobia sample experienced the highest degree of severity in early adulthood and had learned to cope with their impairments over time.

Some studies have related aspects of relationship functioning to social anxiety in samples of individuals who are socially anxious or shy but not diagnosed with social phobia. Bruch, Kaflowitz, and Pearl (1988) found that social anxiety (but not social skill knowledge) accounted for 39% of the variance in self-reported loneliness. Solano and Koester (1989) reported that social anxiety and social skills deficits contribute to loneliness in an additive manner, although they acknowledged that the effect size for social anxiety was twice that of social skills. In a study examining the manner in which attributional style was related to self-reported anxiety in an in vivo conversation, Bruch and Pearl (1995) demonstrated that male undergraduates who attributed the outcomes of heterosexual interactions to controllable (vs. uncontrollable) causes reported less social anxiety during a conversation with an attractive female. Although none of these studies ·examined the maintenance and enhancement of close, romantic relationships, their results suggest that social anxiety is related to relationship interference.

In contrast to the paucity of research on social phobia and close relationships, previous studies have yielded robust findings suggesting that depression negatively affects romantic relationships (see O'Mahen, Beach, & Banawan, 2001, for a comprehensive review). Compared with nondepressed individuals, depressed individuals tend to make more negative attributions for their spouses' behavior, are less skilled interpersonally, and participate in fewer shared activities. Moreover, it has been shown that couples therapy with depressed individuals and their spouses not only reduces depressive symptomatology, but it also increases relationship satisfaction (e.g., Beach & O'Leary, 1992). Because anxiety disorders share many features with depression and are associated with adverse effects on interpersonal functioning (e.g., DiNardo & Barlow, 1990), it is likely that anxiety disorders, like depression, negatively affect romantic relationships. Recent work suggests that social phobia is an anxiety disorder that is particularly linked with depression because socially anxious individuals are characterized by low levels of positive affectivity such as depressed individuals (Mineka, Clark, & Watson, 1998). That is, both depressed and social phobic individuals lack enthusiasm, energy, and a general positive engagement with their environment. It is not difficult to imagine that these qualities would impede the maintenance and enhancement of close relationships.

The present study is a preliminary attempt to examine the nature of close, romantic relationships in individuals with social phobia and characterize the manner in which they are different than the close relationships of nonanxious individuals. Social phobic participants were receiving treatment for their disorder at an outpatient psychiatry clinic, and nonanxious control participants were required to be free of psychopathology. All participants completed a number of measures assessing aspects of close, long-term relationships including satisfaction, trust, intimacy, attributions, and relationship strength. In addition, the self-report inventory corresponding to Harvey and Omarzu's (1997, 1999) minding theory was administered to examine specifically whether individuals with social phobia were less adept than nonanxious control individuals at maintaining the cognitive style necessary to manage close relationships.

METHOD

Participants

Participants were seven individuals diagnosed with DSM-IV (American Psychiatric Association, 1994) social phobia and seven nonanxious controls matched for age and gender. Participants with social phobia were recruited from the outpatient psychiatry clinic of the University of Wisconsin Medical School by their primary clinician. Nonanxious control individuals were identified through flyers targeting employees that were posted in the department. All participants were required to be in a romantic relationship of at least 6 months' duration. Inclusion criteria for social phobic participants included a primary diagnosis of social phobia and the absence of bipolar disorder, psychosis, and alcohol or substance abuse or dependence. Inclusion criteria were the same for nonanxious participants, with the exception that they were required to be free of symptoms associated with any anxiety or mood disorder that required treatment. Participants had a mean age of 40.0 years, 86% were female, 93% were Caucasian, and 71% were married. Participants were in their relationships for an average of 8.5 years. These demographic variables did not differ between groups. However, participants with social phobia had significantly fewer years of education than nonanxious control participants (t [12] = –5.61; p < .001). Participants completed the following measures of psychopathology and relationship functioning.

Measures of Psychopathology

Attributional Style Questionnaire (ASQ; Peterson, Semmel, von Baeyer, Abramson, Metalsky, & Seligman, 1982). The ASQ is a self-report measure in which participants are presented with 6 positive, one-sentence scenarios (e.g., You meet a friend who compliments you on your appearance) and six negative scenarios (e.g., You give an important talk in front of a group and the audience reacts negatively). Participants write down one major cause for the situation, and they rate on a 1–7 likert-type scale (a) the extent to which they attribute the cause to an internal (vs. external) locus of control; (b) the extent to which they feel the cause is stable (vs. transient); (c) the extent to which they feel the cause affects other areas of their life, or is global (vs. situational); and (d) how important the situation would be if it happened to them. Higher scores are indicative of increasing internality, stability, and globality. Composite scores for positive and negative situations are obtained by summing the appropriate internal, stable, and global ratings. Peterson et al. obtained coefficient alphas of .75 and .72 for the positive and negative composites, respectively. Previous research suggests that depressed individuals tend to attribute positive events to external, transient, and situational causes, whereas nondepressed individuals tend to attribute positive events to internal, stable, and global causes. Conversely, depressed individuals tend to attribute negative events to internal, stable, and global causes, whereas nondepressed individuals tend to attribute negative events to external, transient, and situational causes. The coefficient αs obtained on the full sample in the present study were .67 and .69 for positive and negative composites, respectively.

Beck Anxiety Inventory (BAI; Beck & Steer, 1993). The BAI is a 21-item, self-report inventory that describes the frequency of symptoms associated with somatic anxiety in the past week. Participants rate the frequency in which they experienced these items on a 0–3 scale (0 = *not at all*; 3 = *severely*). Higher scores are indicative of more severe levels of anxiety. Beck and Steer reported a coefficient α of .94 for patients diagnosed with DSM-III-R anxiety disorders. It is considered primarily a measure of panic-like anxiety rather than of generalized anxiety (Cox, Cohen, Direnfeld, & Swinson, 1996). The coefficient α obtained on the full sample in the present study was .96.

Beck Depression Inventory (BDI; Beck, Ward, Mendelsohn, Mock, & Erbaugh, 1961).

The BDI is a 21-item, self-report inventory in which participants choose one of four ratings on a 0–3 scale to describe their experiences associated with depressive symptomatology over the past week. Higher scores are indicative of more severe levels of depression. Beck et al. reported a split-half reliability of .93. This is a standard measure to assess depressive symptomatology in the literature (see Beck, Steer, & Garbin, 1988 for a comprehensive review of psychometric properties in clinical populations). It must be acknowledged, however, that individuals with anxiety disorders absent of major depression often have elevated scores on this measure (Rudd & Rajab, 1995). The coefficient α obtained on the full sample in the present study was .96.

Penn State Worry Questionnaire (PSWQ; Meyer, Miller, Metzger, & Borkovec, 1990).

The PSWQ is a 16-item, self-report inventory that assesses the worry component of generalized anxiety. Participants rate items about their worry on a 0–4 Likert-type scale (0 = *not at all typical*; 4 = *very typical*). Appropriate items are reversed scored, and all items are summed to obtain a total score. Higher scores are indicative of a greater amount of self-reported worry. Meyer et al. reported a coefficient α of .93. The coefficient α obtained on the full sample in the present study was .90.

Social Interaction Anxiety Scale (SIAS; Mattick & Clarke, 1998).

The SIAS is a 20-item, self-report inventory measuring anxiety and nervousness experienced in meeting or talking with other people. Participants rate their anxiety on a 0–4 Likert-type scale (0 = *not at all*; 4 = *extremely*). Higher scores are indicative of more severe levels of social interaction anxiety. Mattick and Clarke reported a coefficient α of .93 obtained on a sample of 243 individuals diagnosed with social phobia. The coefficient α obtained on the full sample in the present study was .98.

Social Phobia Scale (SPS; Mattick & Clarke, 1998).

The SPS is a 20-item, self-report inventory measuring anxiety and fear about being observed or watched by others when engaging in particular activities. In a similar manner as the SIAS, participants rate their anxiety on a 0–4 Likert-type scale (0 = *not at all*; 4 = *extremely*), and higher scores are indicative of more severe levels of social interaction anxiety. Mattick and Clarke obtained a coefficient α of .89 on their sample of 243 individuals diagnosed with social phobia. In addition, they found that the SPS correlates significantly with the SIAS (r = .72; p < .001). The coefficient α obtained on the full sample in the present study was .97.

State-Trait Anxiety Inventory-State and Trait Versions (STAI-S, STAI-T; Spielberger, Gorsuch, & Lushene, 1970). The STAI-S and STAI-T are both 20-item, self-report inventories that measure an individual's amount of general state-like and trait-like anxiety. On both instruments, participants rate the frequency in which they experience the items on a 1–4 scale (1 = *almost never*; 4 = *almost always*). Scores are obtained by reversing appropriate items and adding the ratings. Scores range from 20–80, and higher scores are indicative of greater state or trait anxiety. Spielberger et al. reported a median α coefficient of .90 for the STAI-S and a mean test–retest reliability over a 1-month period of .74 for the STAI-T. The coefficient αs obtained on the full sample in the present study were .96 and .97 for the STAI-S and STAI-T, respectively.

Relationship Measures

Dyadic Adjustment Scale (DAS; Spanier, 1976). The DAS is a 32-item, self-report inventory that measures the extent to which individuals report disagreements with their partners and are satisfied with their relationship. Specifically, individuals rate the extent to which they disagree about different areas of their relationship (e.g., religious matters), experience relationship distress (e.g., think about divorce), engage in activities together (e.g., laugh together), and regard their relationship in general (from extremely unhappy to perfect). This measure yields four scales—consensus, satisfaction, affectional expression, and cohesion—which are summed to obtain a total score of relationship functioning. Higher scores are indicative of more adaptive relationship functioning. Previous research has identified a total score of 97 to be a cutoff between distressed and nondistressed couples (Jacobson, Folette, Revenstorf, Baucom, Hahlweg, & Margolin, 1984). Scores from 70–90 indicate moderate distress or dissatisfaction, and scores below 70 indicate severe distress or dissatisfaction (John Wimberly, personal communication, December, 1999). Spanier (1976) reported a coefficient α of .96 for the total score on this measure. The coefficient α for the total score obtained on the full sample in the present study was .91.

Dyadic Trust Scale (DTS; Larzelere & Huston, 1980). The DTS is an 8-item, self-report inventory measuring the extent to which individuals trust that their partner will treat them in a benevolent, fair, and honest manner. Individuals rate the items on a 1–7 Likert-type scale (1 = *strongly disagree*; 7 = *strongly agree*). Scores are obtained by reversing the appropriate items and adding the ratings. Larzelere and Huston reported a coefficient α of .93 on a sample of dating and married couples. However, the coefficient α obtained on the full sample in the present study was .46. Because of this low reliability coefficient, results for this measure will not be considered further.

Minding Questionnaire (MQ; Omarzu, Whalen, & Harvey, 2001). The MQ is an 18-item, self-report inventory in which individuals rate aspects of their relationship on a 1–6 Likert-type scale (1 = *strongly agree*; 6 = *strongly disagree*). It was constructed to measure three of the five components of Harvey and Omarzu's (1997, 1999) minding theory of relationships, knowledge, acceptance, and relationship-enhancing attributions. Higher scores are indicative of more adaptive relationship functioning. The coefficient αs obtained in the present study were .79, –.11, and .78 for the knowledge, acceptance, and attribution scales, respectively. Because the α was so low for the acceptance scale, results in this domain will not be considered further.

Personal Assessment of Intimacy in Relationships (PAIR; Schaefer & Olson, 1981). The PAIR is a 36-item, self-report inventory measuring the extent to which individuals experience intimacy with their partners in five domains: emotional, social, sexual, intellectual, and recreational. Items are rated on a 5-point Likert-type scale, and items for each of the five scales are summed. Schaefer and Olson reported coefficient αs for these scales that ranged from .70–.75 on a sample of 192 married couples. The coefficient αs obtained on the full sample in the present study were .80, .87, .89, .56, .78, and .81 for the emotional, social, sexual, intellectual, recreational, and conventionality scales, respectively. Results for the intellectual intimacy scale on this measure will not be considered further because of the low reliability obtained in this study.

Relationship Attribution Measure (RAM; Fincham & Bradbury, 1992). In a similar manner as the ASQ, the RAM is a self-report measure in which individuals are presented with eight negative relationship scenarios (e.g., Your partner criticizes something you say). Individuals subsequently rate a number of statements on a 1–6 scale Likert-type scale (1 = *strongly disagree*; 6 = *strongly agree*). Three of the statements assess causal attributions and reflect the specific dimensions of locus (i.e., the extent to which the cause rests in the partner), stability (i.e., the extent to which the cause is not likely to change), and globality (i.e., the extent to which the cause affects other areas of the relationship). In addition, three statements assess responsibility–blame attributions and reflect the specific dimensions of intentionality (i.e., the extent to which the partner intends the act), motivation (i.e., the extent to which the partner is motivated by selfish [vs. unselfish] concerns), and blame (i.e., the extent to which the partner deserves blame for the action). From these dimensions, causal and responsibility composites are formed by summing the items in these two domains. Fincham and Bradbury reported coefficient αs of .86 and .89 for husbands' and wives' responses on the causal composite and .89 and .93 for husbands' and wives' responses on the responsibility composite. The coefficient αs obtained on the full sample in the present study were .81 and .94 for the causal and responsibility composites, respectively.

Relationship Closeness Inventory-Strength Scale (RCI-S; Berscheid, Snyder, & Omoto, 1989). The RCI-S is a 34-item, self-report scale in which individuals rate the extent to which their partner influences their behavior, decisions, and goals on a 1–7 Likert-type scale (1 = *strongly disagree*; 7 = *strongly agree*). Appropriate items are reverse-scored, and the items are summed to obtain a total score. Berscheid and her colleagues reported a coefficient alpha of .90 for this scale as applied to romantic, family, and friend relationships. The test–retest reliability over a 3–5 week time period was .81. The coefficient alpha obtained on the full sample in the present study was .85.

Relationship Questionnaire (RQ; Bartholomew & Horowitz, 1991). The RQ is a 4-item, self-report inventory in which individuals are presented with four brief paragraphs describing secure, fearful, preoccupied, and dismissing attachment styles and are instructed to rate the extent to which they resemble each style on a 1–7 Likert-type scale (1 = *not at all like me*; 7 = *very much like me*).

RESULTS

Table 9.1 presents participants' scores on the measures of psychopathology. As expected, individuals in the social phobia group scored significantly higher than individuals in the nonanxious control group on all self-report inventories assessing anxiety and depression. Thus, the social phobia sample was characterized by more severe levels of social anxiety, somatic anxiety, state and trait anxiety, worry, and depressive symptomatology than the nonanxious control sample. Although the mean BDI score for the social phobia sample was in a range suggesting mild but clinically significant depressive symptomatology, individuals with social phobia did not score significantly different than nonanxious control individuals on either scale of the ASQ. It is speculated that the depressive symptomatology of

TABLE 9.1
Measures of Psychopathology

	Social Phobia Group (n = 7)		Nonanxious Control Group (n = 7)		t	p
Attributional Style Questionnaire						
Positive Composite	74.4	(9.1)	83.7	(12.7)	−1.57	ns
Negative Composite	81.3	(15.1)	70.8	(6.1)	1.71	ns
Beck Anxiety Inventory	18.4	(15.8)	4.0	(2.9)	2.37	.035
Beck Depression Inventory	19.7	(15.1)	3.6	(3.3)	2.77	.017
Penn State Worry Questionnaire	47.0	(8.7)	32.4	(8.9)	3.11	.009
Social Interaction Anxiety Scale	48.9	(24.6)	15.1	(9.1)	3.42	.005
Social Phobia Scale	38.4	(18.1)	6.9	(5.1)	4.43	.001
State Trait Anxiety Inventory-State	49.6	(15.9)	31.7	(4.5)	2.86	.014
State Trait Anxiety Inventory-Trait	55.1	(13.6)	30.4	(5.7)	4.45	.001

Note. Values in parentheses are standard deviations.

the social phobia sample was not severe enough to influence their attributional style.

Table 9.2 displays results for all relationship measures that achieved adequate reliability. There were no significant differences between groups on the DAS, indicating that both groups were experiencing similar levels of marital distress and satisfaction. The mean scores for both groups fell in the healthy range suggested by Jacobson et al. (1984). Two individuals in

TABLE 9.2
Relationship Measures

	Social Phobia Group (n = 7)		Nonanxious Control Group (n = 7)		t	p
Dyadic Adjustment Scale	104.9	(12.5)	116.7	(16.2)	−1.54	ns
Minding Questionnaire						
Attribution	27.7	(4.0)	27.1	(5.4)	0.23	ns
Knowledge	27.6	(4.8)	27.6	(6.8)	0.00	ns
Personal Assessment of Intimacy in Relationships						
Emotional	19.7	(4.2)	26.6	(4.6)	−2.95	.012
Social	15.4	(5.9)	25.0	(4.4)	−3.42	.005
Sexual	19.4	(7.5)	24.7	(4.2)	−1.61	ns
Recreational	24.3	(3.1)	27.0	(4.1)	−1.40	ns
Relationship Attribution Measure						
Causal Composite	86.7	(3.07)	74.1	(12.2)	2.20	.049
Responsibility Composite	80.1	(13.7)	58.9	(23.4)	2.08	.060
Relationship Closeness Inventory—Strength	124.4	(31.0)	131.9	(21.1)	−0.52	ns

Note. Values in parentheses are standard deviations.

the social phobia group had DAS total scores below 97 (84, 89), and one individual in the nonanxious control group reported a total score of 84. Similarly, there were no differences between groups on either reliable scale of the MQ or the RCI-strength. Thus, it appears that individuals in both the social phobia and nonanxious control groups had close, satisfying relationships with their partners.

Of the four reliable PAIR scales measuring dimensions of intimacy, two revealed significant differences between groups. Specifically, the nonanxious control group scored higher on the emotional intimacy scale than the social phobia group. According to Schaefer and Olson (1981), emotional intimacy reflects a "closeness of feelings" (p. 50). Items on this scale describe feelings of being neglected by one's partner, feeling lonely and distant from one's partner, and feeling as if one's partner listens well and is understanding. In addition, the nonanxious control group scored higher than the social phobia group on the social intimacy scale. Schaefer and Olson described social intimacy as "the experience of having common friends and similarities in social networks" (p. 50). Items on this scale refer to spending time with other couples and having friends in common with one's partner. The social phobia group and the nonanxious control group did not differ in their scores on scales measuring sexual and recreational intimacy.

Although the social phobia group did not report a general maladaptive attributional style (as measured by the ASQ), they scored significantly higher than the nonanxious control group on the causal composite of the RAM. This difference suggests that individuals with social phobia are more likely than nonanxious control individuals to attribute the cause of a negative relationship event to the type of person their spouses are, to view the cause as unlikely to change, and to regard the cause as affecting other areas of their relationship. In addition, there was a trend for individuals with social phobia to score higher than nonanxious individuals on the responsibility–blame composite. This difference between groups indicates that individuals with social phobia are more likely than nonanxious control individuals to believe their partner's behavior was purposeful and motivated by selfish concerns and to place blame on their partner.

Finally, Table 9.3 presents scores on the single items reflecting secure, fearful, preoccupied, and dismissing adult attachment styles from the RQ. There were several notable differences between the social phobia and nonanxious control groups. First, individuals with social phobia indicated that the description of the secure attachment style described them to a lesser extent than the nonanxious control individuals. Their mean score of 3.0 suggests that they disagreed slightly with being comfortable becoming emotionally close to others, depending on others, and having others depend on them. In addition, individuals with social phobia scored higher than nonanxious control individuals on the item describing a fearful attach-

TABLE 9.3
Attachment Styles

	Social Phobia Group (n = 7)		Nonanxious Control Group (n = 7)		t	p
Secure	3.0	(1.7)	5.5	(1.4)	−2.98	.011
Fearful	4.9	(2.0)	2.8	(1.2)	2.38	.035
Preoccupied	4.1	(1.6)	2.0	(1.2)	2.91	.013
Dismissing	3.4	(2.8)	3.1	(2.2)	0.21	ns

Note. Attachment styles measured by the *Relationship Questionnaire* (Bartholomew & Horowitz, 1991). Values in parentheses are standard deviations.

ment style. Their mean score of 4.9 suggests that they agreed moderately with the description of being uncomfortable getting close to others, having difficulty trusting others, and worrying if they allow themselves to be too close to others. Finally, individuals with social phobia scored higher than nonanxious control individuals on the item describing a preoccupied attachment style. Their mean score of 4.1 suggests that they agreed slightly with the description of experiencing others as being reluctant to get close to them and worrying about others not valuing them as much as they value others. There were no differences between groups on the item describing a dismissing attachment style.

DISCUSSION

Results from the present study revealed both adaptive and maladaptive aspects of the close relationships of individuals with social phobia. Specifically, the social phobia sample reported a similar level of relationship functioning, satisfaction, and strength as the nonanxious control sample. Moreover, there were no differences between groups on the two reliable scales of the MQ, a measure included to specifically assess the cognitive style needed to maintain and enhance close relationships. However, individuals with social phobia reported a lower level of emotional and social intimacy than nonanxious control individuals. The group differences on social intimacy are not surprising given that this scale measures social interaction, which is a core fear of most individuals diagnosed with social phobia. There were also group differences on the causal composite and a trend toward significance on the responsibility composite of the RAM. These findings suggest that the relationship attributional style of individuals with social phobia is more negative and blaming of their partners.

An exciting finding that emerged from this study is that individuals with social phobia have substantially different adult attachment styles than nonanxious individuals. Specifically, individuals with social phobia were less likely than nonanxious control individuals to agree with a description of a secure attachment style and more likely to agree with descriptions of fearful and preoccupied attachment styles. Bartholomew and Horowitz (1991) reported that individuals classified as secure receive high ratings on warmth and level of involvement in romantic relationships. Individuals classified as fearful rate particularly low on self-disclosure, intimacy, level of romantic involvement, reliance on others, and use of a secure base when upset. Individuals classified as preoccupied are rated high on elaboration and self-disclosure, representing a tendency to disclose inappropriately. Further, they are rated high on emotional expressiveness, frequency of crying, reliance on others, use of others as a secure base, crying in the presence of others, level of romantic involvement, and caregiving. Thus, having a fearful or preoccupied attachment style appears to predispose one to develop potentially significant psychiatric sequelae. It is intriguing that the social phobia group scored in the direction of both fearful and preoccupied attachment styles given that these styles are characterized by opposite poles of some of the same traits (e.g., level of romantic involvement). Although the small sample size in the present study precludes fine-grained analyses of these data, it would be useful for future research to examine whether social phobia is comprised of a heterogeneous group of individuals characterized by either fearful or preoccupied attachment styles.

Recent research has related adult attachment styles to personality and psychopathology. For example, Murphy and Bates (1997) found that individuals who endorse fearful and preoccupied attachment styles were more likely to report depressive symptomatology. Further, they related the autonomous (i.e., self-critical) subtype of depression with the fearful attachment style and the sociotropic (i.e., dependent) type of depression with the preoccupied attachment style. Roberts, Gotlieb, and Kassel (1996) indicated that insecure attachment is related to dysfunctional attitudes, which in turn serve as a predisposing factor to low self-esteem, which in turn is associated with depressive symptomatology. In a study relevant to social anxiety, Duggan and Brennan (1994) reported that individuals classified as preoccupied and fearful scored higher on a self-reported measure of shyness than individuals classified as secure or dismissing. In all, evidence is quickly mounting that individuals who experience depressive and anxious symptomatology are more likely to be characterized by an insecure attachment style. As Roberts and his colleagues did for depressive symptomatology, it would be useful for future research to outline the mechanism by which insecure attachment causes and/or exacerbates symptoms of social anxiety. Moreover, the incremental validity of assessing attachment style in addition to standard depression and anxiety interviews and self-report measures must be demonstrated.

As researchers continue to identify the specific aspects of close, romantic relationships that are maladaptive in individuals with social phobia, it is likely that these problems can be addressed successfully in psychotherapy. There is some existing evidence that psychotherapy for socially anxious individuals indeed benefits romantic relationships. Alden and Capreol (1993) found that skills training had a positive effect on intimate relationships of individuals with avoidant personality disorder, who are conceptually similar to individuals with social phobia (Holt, Heimberg, & Hope, 1992). Based on preliminary results from the present study, it is speculated that cognitive restructuring might address social phobics' negative attributional tendencies. Further, social skills and other behavioral approaches might address their self-reported deficits in social intimacy. However, the lack of emotional intimacy and insecure attachment style are likely to require longer term, innovative interventions to achieve substantial change. It is likely that a combination of acceptance and some of the change strategies listed before, similar to that proposed by Jacobson and Christensen (1996), will be optimal in addressing these areas of relationship dysfunction in individuals with social phobia.

Several limitations of the present study must be acknowledged. First, small sample sizes were used because data collection in this area of research is still ongoing. In addition, some of the individuals with social phobia were also diagnosed with comorbid depression. Another interpretation of results from the present study is that areas of self-reported relationship dysfunction emerged due to depression rather than social anxiety. Although it would be useful to examine the nature of romantic relationships in individuals with "pure" social phobia, in reality up to 99% of individuals with social phobia have at least one comorbid psychiatric disorder, and up to 70% of them with major depression (Wenzel & Holt, in press). Thus, there is danger that a study examining social phobia in the absence of comorbid psychopathology would not generalize to most individuals diagnosed with this disorder. Perhaps a more useful study would be to investigate the additive (or multiplicative) effects of depression and social anxiety on relationship dysfunction. A third limitation of the present study is that it relied solely on self-report measures of relationship functioning and satisfaction. A logical extension to this study would be to conduct observational analyses of the specific manner in which individuals with social phobia interact with their partners on various tasks, such as discussing a problem in their relationship. Finally, this study is limited in that only individuals already in romantic relationships were included, which might exclude the social phobic individuals who experience the most severe amount of relationship dysfunction and would benefit the greatest from an intervention targeting this area.

In all, preliminary results from this study examining the nature of close, romantic relationships in individuals with social phobia suggest that: (1) socially anxious individuals generally have close, satisfying relationships with their partners; (2) areas of relationship dysfunction in these individuals include a negative relationship attributional style and a deficit in emotional and social intimacy; and (3) socially anxious individuals are characterized by an insecure attachment style. Cognitive and behavioral approaches to the treatment of social phobia are well-established (Heimberg, 1989). This research suggests that the interpersonal and affective components might be important to address, at least in the domain of romantic relationships.

REFERENCES

Alden, L. E., & Capreol, M. J. (1993). Avoidant personality disorder: Interpersonal problems as predictors of treatment response. *Behavior Therapy, 24*, 357–376.

American Psychiatric Association (1994). *Diagnostic and statistical manual of mental disorders, 4th edition.* Washington, DC: Author.

Bartholomew, K., & Horowitz, L. M. (1991). Attachment styles among young adults: A test of a four-category model. *Journal of Personality and Social Psychology, 61*, 226–244.

Beach, S. R. H., & O'Leary, K. D. (1992). Treating depression in the context of marital discord: Outcomes and predictors of response for marital therapy versus cognitive therapy. *Behavior Therapy, 23*, 507–528.

Beck, A. T., & Steer, R. A. (1993). *Beck Anxiety Inventory manual.* San Antonio: The Psychological Corporation.

Beck, A. T., Steer, R. A., & Garbin, M. G. (1988). Psychometric properties of the Beck Depression Inventory: Twenty-five years of evaluation. *Clinical Psychology Review, 8*, 77–100.

Beck, A., Ward, C., Mendelsohn, M., Mock, J., & Erbaugh, J. (1961). An inventory for measuring depression. *Archives of General Psychiatry, 4*, 561–571.

Berscheid, E., Snyder, M., & Omoto, A. M. (1989). The Relationship Closeness Inventory: Assessing the closeness of interpersonal relationships. *Journal of Personality and Social Psychology, 57*, 792–807.

Bruch, M. A., Kaflowitz, N. G., & Pearl, L. (1988). Mediated and nonmediated relationships of personality components to loneliness. *Journal of Social and Clinical Psychology, 6*, 346–355.

Bruch, M. A., & Pearl, L. (1995). Attributional style and symptoms of shyness in a heterosexual interaction. *Cognitive Therapy and Research, 19*, 91–107.

Cox, B. J., Cohen, E., Direnfeld, D. M., & Swinson, R. P. (1996). Reply to Steer and Beck: Panic disorder, generalized anxiety disorder, and quantitative versus qualitative differences in anxiety assessment. *Behaviour Research and Therapy, 34*, 959–961.

DiNardo, P. A., & Barlow, D. H. (1990). Syndrome and symptom co-occurrence in the anxiety disorders. In J. D. Maser & C. R. Cloninger (Eds.), *Comorbidity of mood and anxiety disorders* (pp. 205–230). Washington, DC: American Psychiatric Press.

Duggan, E. S., & Brennan, K. A. (1994). Social avoidance and its relation to Bartholomew's adult attachment typology. *Journal of Social and Personal Relationships, 11*, 147–153.

Fincham, F. D., & Bradbury, T. N. (1992). Assessing attributions in marriage: The Relationship Attribution Measure. *Journal of Personality and Social Psychology, 62*, 457–468.

Harvey, J. H., & Omarzu, J. (1997). Minding the close relationship. *Personality and Social Psychology Review, 1*, 223–239.

Harvey, J. H., & Omarzu, J. (1999). *Minding the close relationship: A theory of relationship enhancement.* New York: Cambridge University Press.

Heimberg, R. G. (1989). Cognitive and behavioral treatments for social phobia: A critical analysis. *Clinical Psychology Review, 9*, 107–128.

Holt, C. S., Heimberg, R. G., & Hope, D. A. (1992). Avoidant personality disorder and the generalized subtype of social phobia. *Journal of Abnormal Psychology, 101*, 318–325.

Jacobson, N. J., & Christensen, A. (1996). *Integrative couple therapy: Promoting acceptance and change.* New York: W. W. Norton.

Jacobson, N. S., Folette, W. C., Revenstorf, D., Baucom, D. H., Hahlweg, K., & Margolin, G. (1984). Variability in outcome and clinical significance of behavioral marital therapy: A reanalysis of outcome data. *Journal of Consulting and Clinical Psychology, 52*, 497–504.

Larzelere, R. E., & Huston, T. L. (1980). The Dyadic Trust Scale: Toward understanding interpersonal trust in close relationships. *Journal of Marriage and the Family, 42*, 595–604.

Magee, W. J., Eaton, W. W., Wittchen, H. U., McGonagle, K. A., & Kessler, R. C. (1996). Agoraphobia, simple phobia, and social phobia in the National Comorbidity Survey. *Archives of General Psychiatry, 53*, 159–168.

Mattick, R. P., & Clarke, J. (1998). Development and validation of measures of social scrutiny fear and social interaction anxiety. *Behaviour Research and Therapy, 36*, 455–470.

Meyer, T. J., Miller, M. J., Metzger, R. L., Borkovec, T. D. (1990). Development and validation of the Penn State Worry Questionnaire. *Behaviour Research and Therapy, 28*, 487–495.

Mineka, S., Clark, L. A., & Watson, D. (1998). Comorbidity of anxiety and unipolar mood disorders. *Annual Review of Psychology, 49*, 377–412.

Murphy, B., & Bates, G. W. (1997). Adult attachment style and vulnerability to depression. *Personality and Individual Differences, 22*, 835–844.

O'Mahen, H. A., Beach, S. R. H., & Banawan, S. (2001). Depression in marriage. In J. H. Harvey & A. Wenzel (Eds.), *Close relationships: Maintenance and enhancement* (pp. 299–319). Mahwah, NJ: Lawrence Erlbaum Associates.

Omarzu, J., Whalen, J., & Harvey, J. H. (2001). How well do you mind your relationship? A preliminary scale to test the minding theory of relating. In J. H. Harvey & A. Wenzel (Eds.), *Close relationships: Maintenance and enhancement* (pp. 345–356). Mahwah, NJ: Lawrence Erlbaum Associates.

Peterson, C., Semmel, A., von Baeyer, C., Abramson, L. Y., Metalsky, G., & Seligman, M. E. P. (1982). The Attributional Style Questionnaire. *Cognitive Therapy and Research, 6*, 287–300.

Roberts, J. E., Gotlieb, I., & Kassel, J. D. (1996). Adult attachment security and symptoms of depression: The mediating roles of dysfunctional attitudes and low self-esteem. *Journal of Personality and Social Psychology, 70*, 310–320.

Rudd, M. D., & Rajab, M. H. (1995). Specificity of the Beck Depression Inventory and the confounding role of comorbid disorders in a clinical sample. *Cognitive Therapy and Research, 19*, 51–68.

Schaefer, M. T., & Olson, D. H. (1981). Assessing intimacy: The Pair Inventory. *Journal of Marital and Family Therapy, 7*, 47–60.

Schneier, F. R., Heckelman, L. R., Garfinkel, R., Campeas, R., Fallon, B. A., Gitow, A., Street, L., Del Bene, D., & Liebowitz, M. R. (1994). Functional impairment in social phobia. *Journal of Clinical Psychiatry, 55*, 322–331.

Solano, C. H., & Koester, N. H. (1989). Loneliness and communication problems: Subjective anxiety or objective skills? *Personality and Social Psychology Bulletin, 15*, 126–133.

Spanier, G. B. (1976). Measuring dyadic adjustment: New scales for assessing the quality of marriage and similar dyads. *Journal of Marriage and the Family, 38*, 15–28.

Spielberger, C. D., Gorsuch, R. L., & Lushene, R. E. (1970). *Manual for the State-Trait Anxiety Inventory.* Palo Alto, CA: Consulting Psychologists Press.

Wenzel, A., & Holt, C. S. (in press). Relation to clinical syndromes in adulthood. In S. G. Hofmann & P. M. DiBartolo (Eds.), *Social phobia and social anxiety: An integrative approach.* New York: Allyn & Bacon.

Wittchen, H. U., & Beloch, E. (1996). The impact of social phobia on quality of life. *International Clinical Psychopharmacology, 11(suppl 3)*, 15–23.

10

When One Marital Partner
Is an Alcoholic

Sara L. Dolan
Peter E. Nathan
University of Iowa

Many people believe substance abuse has a negative impact on the abuser's interpersonal relationships. Any perusal of local Alcoholics Anonymous meetings would yield many men and women who believe their marriages ended because of their (or their spouse's) substance abuse. Indeed, substance abuse is often cited as a reason for divorce in failed marriages (Halford & Osgarby, 1993). Data from eight nations between 1950 and 1972 showed that alcohol consumption is positively correlated with divorce rate (Lester, 1997).

A study by Lester (1997) revealed a number of alcohol-related reasons for marital dissatisfaction and the eventual dissolution of marriages. Among those reasons are intrapersonal factors such as cognitive dysfunction, which may affect communication skills with the spouse, and trait aggression, as well as interpersonal factors such as marital communication, stigma management, and sexual dysfunction. Support for these results comes from other research that points to the quality of marital communication as the most important factor in the happiness of partners (Floyd, Markman, Kelly, Blumberg, & Stanley, 1995) and the most frequent presenting problem in couples therapy (Coche, 1995).

Before these intra- and interpersonal factors can be considered, it is important to note that both partners in an alcoholic marriage are often heavy drinkers. One large community study suggested that the lifetime risk for alcohol dependence for a husband of an alcoholic wife is 3.56 times greater and 1.36 times greater for heavy drinking than for men married to non-alcoholics. In contrast, wives of alcoholic husbands were 4.73 times more likely to meet criteria for alcohol dependence and 1.63 times more likely to meet criteria for heavy drinking than spouses of nonalcoholic husbands. In this study, couples in which neither spouse reported heavy drinking reported greater overall marital satisfaction than couples in which one or both spouses were heavy drinkers (McLeod, 1993).

INTRAPERSONAL FACTORS IN ALCOHOLIC MARRIAGES

One of the many reasons for the dissolution of a marriage in which one partner is an alcoholic is the substantial communication problems that alcoholics experience. These problems may be related to the aggression and violence discussed later, in that a female may be afraid to communicate honestly with her alcoholic, potentially violent spouse, but there is another possible reason for the communication deficits. It has been demonstrated repeatedly that many alcoholics suffer from cognitive deficits (e.g., Delin & Lee, 1992; Fals-Stewart, Schafer, Lucente, Rustine, & Brown, 1994; Grant, 1987). Specifically, many alcoholics, especially males, suffer from memory problems that may affect their communication skills in a variety of ways. For example, he may simply forget that his wife asked him to take out the garbage. For the wife who does not know that her husband suffers from memory loss, this forgetting could be seen as a refusal to comply with her request, causing a potential marital problem.

Another intrapersonal factor negatively influencing marriages are the attributions alcoholics make about their behavior. In a landmark study, Senchak and Leonard (1994) examined attributions couples make for their marital violence as a function of aggression severity and husbands' alcohol use. Subjects were from a community sample of husbands and wives who reported at least one episode of serious physical aggression during the first year of their marriage. Results indicated that husbands' attributions were influenced by both severity of aggression and alcohol use. Specifically, alcoholic husbands tended to accept responsibility for severe aggression, yet nonalcoholic husbands often blamed their wives for severe aggression. Alcoholic husbands blamed the aggression on their heavy drinking, and nonalcoholic husbands, lacking a factor external to their marriage to which to attribute their aggression, blamed their wives. In contrast, wives' attributions were influenced mainly by severity; wives tended to blame their husbands' behavior for the aggression more than their own. These findings have been confirmed in other retrospective (e.g., Heyman, O'Leary, & Jouriles, 1995) and prospective (Leonard & Senchak, 1996) studies.

Gender differences also affect the marital functioning of alcoholics. Results from two studies suggest that when the alcoholic partner is male, marital functioning is poorer than when the alcoholic spouse is female (Noel, McCrady, Stout, & Fisher-Nelson, 1991; Perodeau & Kohn, 1989). Specifically, males tend to have become alcoholic before they marry, and females more often begin abusing alcohol after they marry. Moreover, alcoholic men tend to externalize the reasons for their drinking, where alcoholic women tend to accept responsibility for their drinking and the effect it has on their marriage.

INTERPERSONAL FACTORS

Interpersonal factors may also play a role in the relationships of alcoholics. For example, interpersonal antecedents to alcohol consumption have been frequently found to involve the alcoholic's spouse (e.g., having a quarrel with the spouse). Furthermore, interpersonal stressors (vs. other types of stressors) preceded relapse 100% of the time (Hore, 1971).

Drinking has a number of direct consequences on the alcoholic's interpersonal relationships, including his or her family members, especially children. Social learning theory has suggested that children of alcoholics see drinking being modeled, and this may be a cause for the increased likelihood that an alcoholic's offspring could develop a drinking problem (Nathan, Skinstad, & Dolan, in press). Children are also affected by growing up with an alcoholic parent, in that these families display less interdependence than "dry" families (Steinglass, 1979). Families with an alcoholic parent tend to interact less frequently because the alcoholic parent is not available, emotionally, and sometimes even physically or financially, to the children. As a consequence, children in these families may not learn the skills that are necessary to work in a group environment because they did not grow up learning how to depend on others or how to be dependable to others.

Alcohol intoxication reliably induces physical aggression in some individuals (Nathan, 1993), both in the laboratory and in the real world. Giancola and Zeichner (1995) found that alcohol consumption increases aggression, measured by the number and intensity of electric shocks given to a research confederate, in men, but not women, in the laboratory. In this study, aggressive personality traits, degree of subjective intoxication, and blood alcohol concentration all significantly predicted this physical aggression. Outside of the lab, alcohol has been associated with violent crimes in adults (see Zhang, Wieczorek, & Welte, 1997 for a review) and aggression in adolescents (Moss & Kirisci, 1995).

It is thought that alcohol disinhibits behavior, and it becomes more difficult to control one's behavior while intoxicated, causing interpersonal aggression, both verbal and physical. There is evidence of increased incidence of domestic violence in alcoholic couples (Kaufman Kantor & Strauss,

1987). Four times as many married men who are alcoholics versus non-alcoholics have been physically violent toward their wives (O'Farrell & Murphy, 1995). In fact, extensive data have shown that more than half the female partners of alcoholic men have been physically assaulted in the previous year (Livingston, 1986).

The partner of an alcoholic may feel a responsibility to maintain a public image that hides the alcoholism. In that vein, a study was conducted that examined how wives manage the stigma that may result from having an alcoholic husband (Weinberg & Vogler, 1990). Results of this study indicated that wives began by concealing their husbands' drinking; their behavior then shifted to managing the tension that resulted when interacting with friends and family. This, however, tended to result in hostility and anger toward the alcoholic husband, which affected marital satisfaction. In this study, these wives chose to join support groups such as Alanon. Further evidence showed that habitual drinking outside the home was correlated with decreased marital satisfaction for spouses (Dunn, Jacob, Hummon, & Seilhamer, 1987).

Another interpersonal consequence of alcohol use is impaired sexual functioning in the marriage. Sexual dysfunction can arise from the physiologic effects of alcoholism or from social factors, such as attitudes of the partners when the alcoholic partner is drunk. Wiseman (1985) studied physiological changes versus social factors as reasons for erotic decline in marriages with an alcoholic partner. She found that sexual dysfunction in these types of marriages was more often the result of social factors than physical dysfunction. Furthermore, O'Farrell and his colleagues (O'Farrell & Choquette, 1991) compared a group of couples with alcoholic husbands with two groups of couples without alcohol-related problems (one group had marital conflict, the other was normal) on a range of sexual satisfaction variables. The alcoholic and marital conflict groups both reported lower sexual satisfaction than the normal group. They reported less frequent intercourse, more change desired in intercourse frequency, and greater disagreement about sex.

COMMUNICATION IN ALCOHOLIC MARRIAGES

As mentioned previously, communication in alcoholic marriages can be impaired, partially because of memory deficits experienced by many alcoholics. Another reason for impaired communication, however, is the pattern of communication between partners. Perhaps the most telling data come from studies of dominance in alcoholic marriages. Frankenstein et al. (Frankenstein, Nathan, Hay, Sullivan, & Cocco, 1985) studied eight couples with an alcoholic spouse (6 male, 2 female) and examined self-report and behavioral measures of submissiveness or dominance in marital communication. Submissiveness and dominance were defined as the level of influence each partner had during an interaction task. The dominant partner tended to speak longer than the submissive partner, they held eye contact with their partner for shorter duration, they asked more questions, and they interrupted their partner more often than the submissive partner. They found that alcoholics often perceive themselves as submissive but, on behavioral measures, are actually dominant. They concluded from these findings that alcohol may serve to reduce the discrepancy between alcoholics' perceptions and actual behavior in terms of dominance versus submissiveness. The same group also studied how alcohol consumption also affects problem solving and positivity during marital interactions (Frankenstein, Hay, & Nathan, 1985). They found that alcoholics were more negative and passive during marital interaction than their nonalcoholic spouses.

Another line of research focuses on comparing marital interactions and marital satisfaction among alcoholic couples, couples with a depressed or otherwise distressed partner and nonalcoholic couples. Results from this work suggest that, compared to other distressed couples, alcoholics display more affective behavior during a marital interaction, especially negative affect, when consuming alcohol versus interacting while sober (e.g., Jacob & Krahn, 1988). This study supported an earlier study that found that length of sobriety was consistently negatively correlated with the number of negative statements, disagreements, and aggressive behaviors emitted by the alcoholic spouse (Roberts, Floyd, O'Farrell, & Cutter, 1985).

TYPOLOGIES

There have clearly been inconsistencies in the literature regarding marital outcomes in alcoholic relationships. Some researchers, for example, have suggested that certain methodological considerations have been overlooked in this literature. These methodological inconsistencies have created confusion about the results of some studies. For example, some studies indicate that alcohol consumption can, in some situations, facilitate marital functioning (e.g., Jacob, Dunn, & Leonard, 1983; Steinglass, Davis, & Berenson, 1977). Some research has shown that alcohol increases self-disclosure (Miller, Ingham, Plant, & Miller, 1977) and helping behavior (Steele, Critchlow, & Liu, 1985), both positive influences on marital functioning. Because this is contrary to what would be expected in marriages with an alcoholic spouse, new data analysis techniques were developed.

Jacob and Leonard (1988) hypothesized that consumption patterns may determine how the nonalcoholic spouse reacts during marital conflict, and as discussed next, this hypothesis was supported. This work led to examining the role that alcoholism typologies play in marital outcomes.

Many subgroups of alcoholics have been proposed over the years, the most widely recognized being Cloninger's Type I and Type II distinction (Cloninger, 1987; Cloninger, Sigvardsson, & Bohman, 1996). Epstein and McCrady, building on this distinction (Type I alcoholics have earlier onset of drinking problems, a higher genetic loading for alcoholism, and an antisocial history; Type II alcoholics have the opposite of those characteristics), have studied differences in marital functioning as a function of age of onset of alcoholism (Epstein, McCrady, & Hirsch, 1997). An early-onset couple is one with a partner who began experiencing problems with alcohol at an early age, usually in late adolescence or early adulthood. A late-onset couple, on the other hand, is a couple in which the alcoholic partner began having alcohol-related problems later, usually in adulthood. Following couples for 17 weeks to 1 year after entry into a treatment outcome study, they found that at baseline, early-onset couples reported marital instability and the females reported more distress than those in later-onset couples. As treatment progressed, however, early-onset couples reported higher daily marital satisfaction than late-onset couples. Finally, they examined the predictors of marital satisfaction for males and females in each subtype. For female partners of early-onset husbands, marital satisfaction was most associated with their own psychological distress, unrelated to their husband's drinking. Partners of late-onset alcoholic husbands reported that their marital satisfaction was most associated with their husband's perceptual accuracy of their needs. For the alcoholic husbands, however, the pattern was reversed; marital adjustment of the early-onset alcoholics had the strongest association with the accuracy of their wife's perception of their needs. Further, the psychological distress of late-onset alcoholics was the strongest predictor of their marital satisfaction. The authors of the study speculated that females married to early-onset husbands were already aware of their partner's drinking because he had most likely started drinking before they got married. Because of this, these women discounted its effects on their relationship satisfaction; instead, their preexisting psychological distress, unrelated to their partner's drinking, accounted for marital dissatisfaction. An alternative explanation is that early-onset couples may be less attuned to emotional matters and may, in turn, be less aware of marital dissatisfaction. The authors failed to provide a comment on why the pattern was reversed for males. This pattern of attributions for marital satisfaction may be related to gender differences in coping styles or differences in coping styles between alcoholics and their sober spouses. This difference also may be due to the severity of the alcoholism. For example, early-onset alcoholics may have a more externalizing coping style, and late-onset alcoholics may be internalizers.

Jacob and Leonard (1988) also studied heterogeneity among alcoholic couples. Their research suggested that alcohol problems may differentially affect couples, depending on the drinking pattern and location. They found that women's marital satisfaction was positively correlated with their husband's alcohol consumption for wives of steady drinkers, but negatively correlated with marital satisfaction for wives of episodic (binge) drinkers. Further, they found that an explanation for this may lie in the fact that binge drinkers have greater levels of psychopathology, more negative consequences from their drinking, and more psychopathic behavior. Finally, binge drinkers typically drank outside the home, but steady drinkers drank primarily in the home. Roberts and Leonard (1998) confirmed the ability to distinguish alcoholics based on alcohol consumption. Studying natural typologies of drinking partnerships and their relation to marital functioning, they found that high level of alcohol consumption in a relationship was not consistently related to marital dissatisfaction; in fact, they found a more complicated relation between these variables, mediated by the nonalcoholic spouse's drinking quantity and frequency, percentage of drinking done in each other's presence, and percentage of drinking done in the home. They found five different types of drinking partnerships: compatible, light, infrequent drinking out of the home; discrepant, separate husband and wife drinking, with the husband drinking heavily; light, infrequent drinking together in the home; heavy, but relatively infrequent drinking out of the home; and light, but frequent drinking together in the home. These partnership types were significantly related to marital satisfaction in both husbands and wives. Husbands in types 1, 2, and 5, all light-drinking groups, reported uniformly higher marital satisfaction than husbands who drank more heavily. Wives whose husbands drank heavily reported high depression scores than wives with lighter-drinking husbands. These results suggest that clinicians need to pay attention to the alcohol consumption and patterns of consumption, including drinking context, of both partners, as both of these variables are related to marital satisfaction.

AGGRESSION AND VIOLENCE

Researchers have also studied factors that distinguish alcoholics in relationships with more positive outcomes from those with more negative outcomes. It has been found that alcoholics who are violent in their marriages and those who are not differ in some important ways. For example, violent alcoholics are more likely to have antisocial histories than nonviolent alcoholics (Murphy & O'Farrell, 1996). Also, consumption style differentiates violent from nonviolent alcoholics. Binge-drinking alcoholics have been found to be more violent than those who drink more steadily (Murphy & O'Farrell, 1994). Maritally violent alcoholics also have less confidence in their abilities to weather interpersonal conflicts without drinking (Murphy

& O'Farrell, 1994) than couples with a nonviolent spouse. This may relate to the display of higher levels of hostile and defensive communications and to prolong marital conflict compared to nonviolent alcoholics, because alcoholics are much less likely to exit arguments (Murphy & O'Farrell, 1997).

TREATMENT

At the beginning of this chapter, we outlined a number of problems that couples with an alcoholic partner encounter. The remainder of the chapter focuses on treatment for these problems. Treatment goals for these clients should include both a reduction in or elimination of alcohol intake and an increase in marital satisfaction. Specifically, clinicians should design treatment goals that target areas discussed previously, including increased quality of marital communication, increased sexual satisfaction, and whatever else the client(s) choose to address in therapy. Before treatment begins, however, clinicians should assess the risks for aggression and violence in the relationship and take precautions to protect the couple if they are at risk.

There is empirical evidence for the efficacy of several individual psychotherapeutic interventions for substance abuse. A large, multisite, randomized clinical trial illustrated the efficacy of three such interventions (Project MATCH Research Group, 1997), including Motivational Enhancement Therapy (Miller, Zweben, DiClemente, & Rychtarik, 1992), Cognitive Behavioral Coping Skills (Kadden et al., 1992), and Twelve-Step Facilitation (Nowinski, Baker, & Carroll, 1992). Each of these three types of psychotherapy is an empirically supported, manualized treatment for alcoholism.

Motivational Enhancement Therapy (Miller et al., 1992) is a nondirective treatment based on the Stages of Change model (Prochaska & DiClemente, 1983). This model posits four stages that an alcoholic passes through as s/he decides to become abstinent, and each stage has a mental process associated with it. To succeed in this type of treatment, clients must have high motivation to progress through the stages of change; consequently, the treatment goals are to increase motivation to change, to strengthen commitment to change, and to learn follow-through strategies.

Cognitive-Behavioral Coping Skills Treatment (Kadden et al., 1992) has skill mastery as its treatment goal. Patients who are successfully treated with this type of therapy become better at identifying internal and external high-risk situations. That is, patients who benefit from this treatment learn to first identify internal and external cues for drinking (e.g., depression or being at a bar, respectively), and they develop and employ appropriate alternative behaviors to drinking.

Twelve-Step Facilitation Therapy (Nowinski et al., 1992) was designed to teach patients how to better benefit from participation in Alcoholics Anonymous (AA). The treatment goals in this therapy are cognitive, emotional, behavioral, social, and spiritual growth. Patients work on the principles of AA: acceptance of their alcoholism, surrendering to a higher power, and acknowledgment of the efficacy of AA.

The treatment trial lasted for 12 weeks, and patients were monitored for 1 year following the conclusion of their participation in the treatment. Results indicated that all three treatments worked equally well: Drinking was reduced from an average of 15 to 17 drinks per day at baseline to an average of 3 drinks per day at 1-year follow-up.

There is also recent evidence for the efficacy of an individual psychotherapeutic intervention for the partners of heavy drinkers. Pressures to Change is a treatment designed to help the nondrinking partner encourage a decrease in drinking by the alcoholic partner. This is a 5-to-6 session, highly standardized, manualized treatment that involves a hierarchy of strategies to be employed by the nondrinking spouse with the goal of applying pressure on the alcoholic spouse to reduce consumption or to seek treatment. The following is a brief description of the five levels in the hierarchy:

The pressure at Level 1 consists of applying pressure to change without conflict by simply presenting the alcoholic partner with information about how people change addictive behavior.

At Level 2, the alcoholic's drinking is functionally analyzed, and the drinker is provided with alternative activities to drinking that still provide some of the positive reinforcement that alcohol provides.

Level 3 incorporates the nondrinking spouse by examining both partners' responses to the alcoholic's use of alcohol and any consequences that arise from alcohol use. Both partners are taught to effectively use reinforcers to promote change in the alcoholic's behavior.

Level 4 consists of both partners agreeing to a contract that specifies consequences for alcohol consumption during the high-risk situations identified at Level 2.

Level 5 involves persons outside the relationship dyad to apply pressure for the alcoholic to change. This usually takes the form of a confrontation of the alcoholic by family members and close friends.

A trial comparing this intervention with Alanon and a no-treatment control group indicated that the participants in the Pressures to Change condition reported more marital satisfaction along with decreased alcohol use by their partners after 17 weeks (Barber & Gilbertson, 1996). Before this treatment can be considered efficacious, however, it must be compared with other treatments with documented efficacy and effectiveness.

Historically, however, this population has been very difficult to work with on an individual basis, causing some psychologists to attempt to find different methods for treating their substance abuse. Substance abusers can often be hostile and resistant to change. In 1976, Steinglass suggested that involving the family in the client's treatment may bring about longer-lasting changes in drinking behavior (Steinglass, 1976). A review paper followed, which outlined such a comprehensive treatment approach (Shapiro, 1977). It suggested a number of therapeutic strategies that are still relevant today. For example, because of the lack of effective communication that is typical in marriages with an alcoholic spouse, the therapist may be placed in the role of "referee," with each spouse trying to "woo" the therapist to his or her side. Shapiro warns against taking this role, as well as the role of "expert," in which the client portrays him or herself as helpless. In this situation, the client gives the responsibility for the outcome of the treatment to the therapist, rather than taking it on him or herself. Instead, Shapiro suggests taking on the role of "facilitator" of the therapeutic interaction between spouses. He also suggests that therapists should be aware of signs of depression in the alcoholic, including hypersensitivity to rejection, marked dependency, low self-esteem, and low tolerance for frustration. Further, therapists should take avoid negative criticism or a judgmental attitude, and adopt a matter-of-fact attitude with these clients. In family therapy for alcoholism, it is important to refrain from trying to "change" that drinking pattern of the alcoholic. Alternatively, therapists should attempt to pay careful attention to all aspects of the drinker's life, including work, interests, aspirations, and interpersonal relationships. Counselors should also attempt to provide an in-session model for positive family interactions relating to the alcoholic's problems by making an effort to identify what happened between family members before, during, and subsequent to a drinking episode. If this is done in a manner that does not promote defensiveness in the alcoholic, this technique can be quite helpful (Shapiro, 1977).

There is a large and more recent literature that suggests that treatment of alcoholism that involves the nonalcoholic spouse can be very successful. For example, Bowers and Al-Redha (1990) compared individual and group treatments with alcoholics. The group treatments included many couples in which one spouse was an alcoholic. They found that while the two modes of treatment did not produce different outcomes at termination, at 1-year follow-up, the conjointly treated group reported both significantly less alcohol consumption and better marital adjustment than participants in the individual condition. A 1995 meta-analysis supported the efficacy of family treatment for alcoholism (Edwards & Steinglass, 1995), and further evidence comes from a 1998 review by Epstein and McCrady, which examined Behavioral Couples Treatment of alcohol use disorders. The manualized, cognitive-behavioral Alcohol Behavior Couples Treatment (ABCT) incorporates elements of behavioral self-control and skills training to facilitate abstinence and better spouse coping with drinking-related situations, and contingency management procedures, communication, and problem-solving training to improve relationship functioning. A number of empirical studies have tested its efficacy and found ABCT to be quite efficacious and effective (e.g., McCrady, Stout, Noel, Abrams, & Fisher-Nelson, 1991). Compared to pre-treatment, couples typically report higher levels of marital satisfaction as well as decreased negative interactions after taking part in ABCT. Behavioral Marital Therapy, ABCT's parent treatment, has also been found to decrease violence and aggression both in the alcoholic individual, and between spouses in an alcoholic marriage (O'Farrell & Choquette, 1991).

Recently, a well-controlled follow-up study (Maisto, McKay, & O'Farrell, 1998) was conducted to examine the relationship between abstinence during the first year of marriage and drinking and marital problems in couples enrolled in an ABCT trial. At 30 months posttreatment, the alcoholic men reported a sustained decrease in drinking and better marital functioning, compared to a control group. These results suggest that enrolling couples in ABCT early in the marriage may prevent future marital problems.

CONCLUSIONS

This chapter reviewed the role of alcohol in the maintenance of an alcoholic marriage. In general, it appears that alcohol has deleterious effects on marital satisfaction and survival although, in certain types of alcoholics, alcohol plays an adaptive role in the marriage. It appears that some spouses of early-onset alcoholics are able to function well in spite of their spouse's alcohol use; in some cases, it even appears that alcohol may indeed have a stabilizing effect on their marriages. Perhaps this is because these spouses formed a relationship with the alcoholic while they were drinking. They have a richer understanding of the course of the relationship and especially how alcohol will affect it. Partners of late-onset alcoholics, however, consistently report lower marital satisfaction. This could be because they began their relationship before alcohol was an integral part of the alcoholic's life. Alcohol does not have a stabilizing effect on these relationships because neither spouse had experience with it before they were married. Marital satisfaction may be decreased in these relationships because the necessary coping skills are not in place for dealing with alcohol. Fortunately, there is evidence for an efficacious and effective approach to treatment that includes the nonalcoholic spouse as an integral part of the therapy (ABCT). It is also important to note that this approach is fruitful not only because it produces better drinking and marital satisfaction outcomes but also because it appears that involving the nonalcoholic spouse in treatment keeps the alcoholic in treatment. This is probably because there is more pressure for him/her to attend treatment sessions (Epstein, McCrady, Miller, & Steinberg, 1994).

Limitations

Clearly, there are limitations to the research on how alcohol affects marital satisfaction. First, as with most studies of substance abusers, there are very few representative samples of alcoholics in these studies (Epstein et al., 1997). There are few discussions of subject recruitment, especially in the older studies. It is appropriate, however, to assume that the alcoholics were recruited from treatment samples. It is well known that alcoholics seeking treatment are very different from those who do not seek treatment: They are generally less dependent on alcohol, more motivated, and they have fewer comorbid psychiatric disorders (Nathan et al., in press), meaning, presumably, that they are healthier than some alcoholics who do not voluntarily seek treatment. This could mean that results from research on these alcoholics could be misleading.

It is well known that the presence of comorbid disorders in substance abusers is associated with poorer treatment outcomes. This is often because some clinicians are unfamiliar with the unique problems of comorbidity in a substance abusing population; a patient could meet criteria for multiple psychiatric disorders because the co-occurring conditions could be a cause of the substance abuse or an effect of heavy use of alcohol or drugs. For example, a patient who seeks treatment for substance abuse or dependence may also be depressed. If this patient's drug of abuse was alcohol or painkillers, she or he may be depressed because these drugs are central nervous system depressants that produce psychological and physiological effects similar to those seen in major depressive disorder. Conversely, a patient may have major depressive disorder as a primary diagnosis, and she or he may use alcohol or other drugs in an effort to self-medicate (i.e., dull the feelings of depression). These two patients have entirely different psychopathologies and require entirely different treatments. The first patient, for example, would benefit more from treatment of the substance dependence, and the depression should remit as s/he remains abstinent and the physiological effects of the alcohol or other sedative abate. The second patient, however, needs treatment for depression, with the expectation that the substance abuse will remit as the depression lifts. The same problem exists when anxiety is the comorbid psychiatric condition: The effects of some stimulants mimic the symptoms found in patients with anxiety disorders. Because of this potential uncertainty regarding the cause–effect relationship of the co-occurring disorders, it is always important to perform a thorough diagnostic evaluation of patients presenting with substance abuse or dependence because as can be seen, the diagnosis determines the type of treatment that should be provided.

Also, there are few discussions of the diagnosis of alcoholism in these subjects. There have been many disagreements over the years regarding what symptoms are diagnostic of alcohol dependence. It is also important to consider whether these alcoholics were dependent only on alcohol, or whether they were also dependent on other drugs, as are most substance abusers. Finally, many substance abusers have high levels of comorbidity with other psychological disorders, especially depression, anxiety, and personality disorders (Nathan et al., in press). The presence of any one of these conditions would have a significant impact on the interpersonal relationships of the alcoholic, independent of alcohol use.

Some researchers are cognizant of these issues; this awareness of methodological shortcomings in the literature is a factor in their interest in subtyping alcoholics. Future research in the area of alcohol and close relationships should follow from work similar to theirs, and treatments that address these research limitations should be examined more carefully.

REFERENCES

Barber, J. G., & Gilbertson, R. (1996). An experimental study of brief unilateral intervention for the partners of heavy drinkers. *Research on Social Work Practice, 6*, 325–336.

Bowers, T. G., & Al-Redha, M. R. (1990). A comparison of outcome with group/marital and standard/individual therapies with alcoholics. *Journal of Studies on Alcohol, 51*, 301–309.

Cloninger, C. R. (1987). Neurogenetic adaptive mechanisms in alcoholism. *Science, 23*, 410–415.

Cloninger, C. R., Sigvardsson, S., & Bohman, M. (1996). Type I and Type II alcoholism: An update. *Alcohol Health and Research World, 20*, 18–23.

Coche, J. (1995). Group therapy with couples. In N. S. Jacobsen & A. S. Gurman (Eds.), *Clinical handbook of couple therapy* (pp.). New York: Guilford Press.

Delin, C. B., & Lee, T. H. (1992). Drinking and the brain: Current evidence. *Alcohol & Alcoholism, 27*, 117–126.

Dunn, N. J., Jacob, T., Hummon, N., & Seilhamer, R. (1987). Marital stability in alcoholic-spouse relationships as a function of drinking pattern and location. *Journal of Abnormal Psychology, 96*, 99–107.

Edwards, M. E., & Steinglass, P. (1995). Family therapy outcomes for alcoholism. *Journal of Marital and Family Therapy, 21*, 475–509.

Epstein, E. E., & McCrady, B. S. (1998). Behavioral and couples treatment if alcohol and drug use disorders: Current status and innovations. *Clinical Psychology Review, 18*, 689–711.

Epstein, E. E., McCrady, B. S., & Hirsch, L. S. (1997). Marital functioning in early versus late-onset alcoholic couples. *Alcoholism: Clinical and Experimental Research, 21*, 547–556.

Epstein, E. E., McCrady, B. S., Miller, K. J., & Steinberg, M. (1994). Attrition from conjoint alcoholism treatment: Do dropouts differ from completers? *Journal of Substance Abuse, 6*, 249–265.

Fals-Stewart, W., Schafer, J., Lucente, S., Rustine, T., & Brown, L. (1994). Neurobehavioral consequences of prolonged alcohol and substance abuse: A review of findings and treatment implications. *Clinical Psychology Review, 14*, 755–788.

Floyd, F., Markman, H., Kelly, S., Blumberg, S., & Stanley, S. (1995). Preventative intervention and relationship enhancement. In N. S. Jacobsen & A. S. Gurman (Eds.), *Clinical handbook of couple therapy* (pp.). New York: Guilford Press.

Frankenstein, W., Hay, W. M., & Nathan, P. E. (1985). Effects of intoxication on alcoholics' marital communication and problem solving. *Journal of Studies on Alcohol, 46*, 1–6.

Frankenstein, W., Nathan, P. E., Hay, W. M., Sullivan, R. F., & Cocco, K. (1985). Asymmetry of influence in alcoholics' marital communication: Alcohol's effects on interaction dominance. *Journal of Marital and Family Therapy, 11*, 399–410.

Giancola, P. R., & Zeichner, A. (1995). Alcohol-related aggression in males and females: Effects of blood alcohol concentration, subjective intoxication, personality, and provocation. *Alcoholism: Clinical and Experimental Research, 19*, 130–134.

Grant, I. (1987). Alcohol and the brain: Neuropsychological correlates. *Journal of Consulting and Clinical Psychology, 55*, 310–324.

Halford, W. K., & Osgarby, S. M. (1993). Alcohol abuse in clients presenting with marital problems. *Journal of Family Psychology, 6*, 245–254.

Heyman, R. E., O'Leary, K. D., & Jouriles, E. N. (1995). Alcohol and aggressive personality styles: Potentiators of serious physical aggression against wives? *Journal of Family Psychology, 9*, 44–57.

Hore, B. D. (1971). Life events and alcoholic relapse. *British Journal of Addiction, 66*, 83–88.

Jacob, T., Dunn, N. J., & Leonard, K. E. (1983). Patterns of alcohol abuse and family stability. *Alcoholism: Clinical and Experimental Research, 7*, 382–385.

Jacob, T., & Krahn, G. L. (1988). Marital interactions of alcoholic couples: comparison with depressed and nondistressed couples. *Journal of Consulting and Clinical Psychology, 56*, 73–79.

Jacob, T., & Leonard, K. (1988). Alcoholic-spouse interaction as a function alcoholism subtype and alcohol consumption interaction. *Journal of Abnormal Psychology, 97*, 231–237.

Kadden, R., Carroll, K., Donovan, D., Cooney, N., Monti, P., Abrams, D., Litt, M., & Hester, R. (1992). Cognitive-behavioral coping skills therapy manual: A clinical research guide for therapists treating individuals with alcohol abuse and dependence (Mattson, M. E., ed.). National Institute on Alcohol Abuse and Alcoholism. Project MATCH Monograph Series, Vol. 2 [DHHS publication no. (ADM) 92-1894]. Washington, DC.

Kaufman Kantor, G., & Strauss, M. A. (1987). The "drunken bum" theory of wife beating. *Social Problems, 34*, 213–230.

Leonard, K. E., & Senchak, M. (1996). Prospective prediction of husband marital aggression within newlywed couples. *Journal of Abnormal Psychology, 105*, 369–380.

Lester, D. (1997). Effect of alcohol consumption on marriage and divorce at the national level. *Journal of Divorce and Remarriage, 27*, 159–161.

Livingston, L. R. (1986). Measuring domestic violence in an alcoholic population. *Journal of Sociology and Social Welfare, 13*, 934–951.

Maisto, S. A., McKay, J. R., & O'Farrell, T. J. (1998). Twelve-month abstinence from alcohol and long-term drinking and marital outcomes in men with severe alcohol problems. *Journal of Studies on Alcohol, 59*, 591–598.

McCrady, B. S., Stout, R., Noel, N., Abrams, D., & Fisher-Nelson, H. (1991). Effectiveness of three types of spouse-involved behavioral alcoholism treatment. *British Journal of Addiction, 86*, 1415–1424.

McLeod, J. D. (1993). Spouse concordance for alcohol dependence and heavy drinking: Evidence from a community sample. *Alcoholism: Clinical and Experimental Research, 17*, 1146–1155.

Miller, P. M., Ingham, J. G., Plant, M. A., & Miller, T. (1977). Alcohol consumption and self-disclosure. *British Journal of Addiction, 72*, 296–300.

Miller, W. R., Zweben, A., DiClemente, C. C., & Rychtarik, R. G. (1992). Motivational enhancement therapy manual: A clinical research guide for therapists treating individuals with alcohol abuse and dependence (Mattson, M. E., ed.). National Institute on Alcohol Abuse and Alcoholism. Project MATCH Monograph Series, Vol. 3 [DHHS publication no. (ADM) 92-1895]. Washington, DC.

Moss, H. B., & Kirisci, L. (1995). Aggressivity in adolescent substance abusers: Relationship with conduct disorder. *Alcoholism: Clinical and Experimental Research, 19*, 642–646.

Murphy, C. M., & O'Farrell, T. J. (1994). Factors associated with marital aggression in male alcoholics. *Journal of Family Psychology, 8*, 321–335.

Murphy, C. M., & O'Farrell, T. J. (1996). Marital violence among alcoholics. *Current Directions in Psychological Science, 5,* 183–186.

Murphy, C. M., & O'Farrell, T. J. (1997). Couple communication patterns of maritally aggressive and nonaggressive male alcoholics. *Journal of Studies on Alcohol, 58,* 83–90.

Nathan, P. E. (1993). Alcoholism: Psychopathology, etiology, and treatment. In P. B. Sutker & H. E. Adams (Eds.), *Comprehensive handbook of psychopathology* (2nd ed.; pp. 451–476). New York: Plenum.

Nathan, P. E., Skinstad, A. H., & Dolan, S. L. (in press). The alcohol-related disorders: Psychopathology, diagnosis, etiology, and treatment. In P. B. Sutker & H. E. Adams (Eds.), *Comprehensive handbook of psychopathology* (3rd ed.). New York: Plenum.

Noel, N. E., McCrady, B. S., Stout, R. J., & Fisher-Nelson, H. (1991). Gender differences in marital functioning of male and female alcoholics. *Family Dynamics of Addiction Quarterly, 1,* 31–38.

Nowinski, J., Baker, S., & Carroll, K. (1992). Twelve step facilitation therapy manual: A clinical research guide for therapists treating individuals with alcohol abuse and dependence (Mattson, M. E., ed.). National Institute on Alcohol Abuse and Alcoholism. Project MATCH Monograph Series, Vol. 1 [DHHS publication no. (ADM) 92-1893]. Washington, DC.

O'Farrell, T. J., & Choquette, K. (1991). Marital violence in the year before and after spouse-involved alcoholism treatment. *Family Dynamics of Addiction Quarterly, 1,* 32–40.

O'Farrell, T. J., & Murphy, C. M. (1995). Marital violence before and after alcoholism treatment. *Journal of Consulting and Clinical Psychology, 63,* 256–262.

Perodeau, G. M., & Kohn, P. M. (1989). Sex differences in the marital functioning of treated alcoholics. *Drug and Alcohol Dependence, 23,* 1–11.

Prochaska, J. O., & DiClemente, C. C. (1983). Stages and processes of self-change of smoking: Toward an integrative model of change. *Journal of Consulting and Clinical Psychology, 51,* 390–395.

Project MATCH Research Group (1997). Matching alcoholism treatments to client heterogeneity: Project MATCH posttreatment drinking outcomes. *Journal of Studies on Alcohol, 58,* 7–29.

Roberts, M. C. F., Floyd, F. J., O'Farrell, T. J., & Cutter, H. S. G. (1985). Marital interactions and the duration of alcoholic husbands' sobriety. *American Journal of Drug and Alcohol Abuse, 11,* 303–313.

Roberts, L. J., & Leonard, K. E. (1998). An empirical typology of drinking partnerships and their relationship to marital functioning and drinking consequences. *Journal of Marriage and the Family, 60,* 515–526.

Senchak, M., & Leonard, K. E. (1994). Attributions for episodes of marital aggression: The effects of aggression severity and alcohol use. *Journal of Family Violence, 9,* 371–381.

Shapiro, R. J. (1977). A family therapy approach to alcoholism. *Journal of Marriage and Family Counseling, 3,* 71–78.

Steele, C. M., Critchlow, B., & Liu, T. J. (1985). Alcohol and social behavior: II. The helpful drunkard. *Journal of Personality and Social Psychology, 48,* 35–46.

Steinglass, P. (1976). Experimenting with family treatment approaches to alcoholism. *Family Process, 15,* 97–123.

Steinglass, P. (1979). The alcoholic family in the interaction laboratory. *Journal of Nervous and Mental Disease, 167,* 428–436.

Steinglass, P., Davis, D., & Berenson, D. (1977). Observations of conjointly hospitalized alcoholic couples during sobriety and intoxication: Implications for theory and therapy. *Journal of Family Process, 16,* 137–146.

Weinberg, T. S., & Vogler, C. C. (1990). Wives of alcoholics: Stigma management and adjustments to husband-wife interactions. *Deviant Behavior, 11,* 331–343.

Wiseman, J. P. (1985). Alcohol, eroticism and sexual performance: A social interactionist perspective. *Journal of Drug Issues, 15,* 291–308.

Zhang, L., Wieczorek, W. F., & Welte, J. W. (1997). The nexus between alcohol and violent crime. *Alcoholism: Clinical and Experimental Research, 21,* 1264–1271.

PREVENTION AND INTERVENTION

11

The Role of Clinicians in the Prevention of Marital Distress and Divorce

Natalie D. Monarch
Scott G. Hartman
Sarah W. Whitton
Howard J. Markman
University of Denver

Almost every American marries at some point in their lifetime. Yet, almost half of the 2.4 million marriages taking place every year end in divorce (DeVita, 1996). Furthermore, a large number of couples remain married but dissatisfied (Markman & Hahlweg, 1993). Research conducted over the past two decades has shown that marital conflict and divorce put both adults and children at greater risk for detrimental mental, physical, and emotional consequences (Amato & Keith, 1991; Emery, 1982). Divorce is also associated with economic consequences including lower socioeconomic status for divorced women and losses in work productivity for both men and women (Forthofer, Markman, Cox, Stanley, & Kessler, 1996; Stroup & Pollock, 1994).

Clearly, divorce has a negative impact on our society. Over the past few decades, researchers and clinicians have attempted to understand and combat this destructive pattern. Having been trained as Boulder model psychologists, we have backgrounds in both marital research and in clinical work with couples. Thus, in writing this chapter, we have combined our knowledge of state-of-the-art marital research with an overview of successful couples interventions to provide clinicians with new insight into the field of preventing marital distress and divorce. More specifically, this chapter provides clinicians with: information regarding the effectiveness of marital therapy, an overview of the historical move toward divorce prevention, a review of prevention theory and application, and insight into the dissemination and marketing of divorce prevention programs.

233

HISTORICAL APPROACHES IN MARITAL INTERVENTION

Traditionally, marital therapy has been viewed as the best available means for addressing the epidemic of marital distress. In fact, over the last 30 years, dozens of marital therapy programs have been developed to treat relationship dissatisfaction. However, financial barriers and the perceived social stigma associated with marital therapy have contributed to a relatively low percentage of distressed couples actually seeking help for their relationships. Of the couples who do seek therapy, a majority are already severely distressed by the time they begin treatment (Doherty, 1986; Van Widenfelt, Markman, Guerney, Behrens, & Hosman, 1997). Furthermore, although marital therapists are able to achieve success comparable to other forms of intervention, they are typically not able to move distressed couples into the nondistressed or happy range—even with the best of efforts (i.e., treatment protocols or counseling efforts; Halford, 1998). In fact, approximately half of couples who do take part in marital therapy revert to previous levels of dissatisfaction (Jacobson & Addis, 1993; Kaiser, Hahlweg, Fehm-Wolfsdorf, & Groth, 1998). Given the inadequacies of marital therapy, we believe that the field of marital research should increasingly focus on the role of prevention in lessening the number of distressed and divorcing couples.

A MOVE TOWARD PREVENTING DIVORCE

The theory underlying this proposed move toward prevention of dissatisfaction and divorce, as opposed to the treatment of current marital distress, is based on a number of factors. First, because couples involved in divorce prevention programs are typically quite satisfied with their relationships, they are often more open to changing and compromising. In this respect, divorce prevention is more easily administered than is the treatment of severe marital dysfunction (Coie, Watt, West, Hawkins, Asarnow, Markman, Ramey, Shure, & Long, 1993). Secondly, the time and energy invested in participating in preventative programs is less costly than the social, emotional, and financial burdens associated with marital distress and divorce (Silliman, Stanley, Coffin, Markman, & Jordan, in press; Van Widenfelt, Markman, Guerney, Behrens, & Hosman, 1997). Lastly, unlike marital therapy, clinicians conducting divorce prevention workshops are able to provide help for a large number of couples at once (Fincham & Beach, 1999). The development of existing divorce prevention programs has been based in large part on basic prevention theory.

OVERVIEW OF DIVORCE PREVENTION THEORY

The field of prevention science identifies three broad types of prevention programs: universal, selected, and targeted (Hartman, Whitton, Markman, & Stanley, in press). Applied to prevention with couples, universal prevention programs are open to all couples in a defined population, which is usually delineated by developmental stage (e.g., couples planning marriage, preparing to have their first child, etc.). Selected programs are designed for couples who are at higher risk for problems, such as couples with at least one partner who experienced parental divorce, aggression, or alcoholism. Targeted programs are aimed at couples who are already showing signs of distress (e.g., first time, low-level aggression). In the rest of this chapter, we focus on universal and selected programs. In contrast with targeted programs, which are essentially early treatment programs, universal and selected programs are designed to maintain satisfaction in happy couples by addressing the very factors that both protect and threaten marriages.

Important Factors Related to Marriage and Divorce

General prevention theory suggests two key strategies for preventing negative outcomes: raising protective factors and lowering risk factors (e.g., Coie et al., 1993). In the area of marital and couples interventions, this means raising or strengthening factors that increase the chance that couples will remain satisfied and stable over time, while lowering factors associated with higher risk for marital distress and divorce. Basic research has indicated a number of factors that protect couples' relationships. These include friendship between spouses (e.g., Markman, Stanley, & Blumberg, 1994), interpersonal support (e.g., Pasch & Bradbury, 1998), participation of spouses in joint leisure activities (e.g., Blood & Wolfe, 1960; Hartman, Stanley, & Markman, 2000), teamwork (e.g., Cordova, 2000), mutual dedication (Stanley & Markman, 1992), developing a couple identity (Stanley & Markman, 1992; Monarch, Stanley, & Markman, 2000), and healthy giving, or sacrifice, for one another (Van Lange, Rusbult, Drigotas, Arriaga, Witcher, & Cox, 1997; Whitton, Stanley, & Markman, 2000).

According to prevention theory, efforts should also be made to address known risk factors for divorce and marital distress. These include, but are not limited to, dysfunctional relationship beliefs (e.g., Baucom & Epstein, 1990; Fincham & Bradbury; 1989), parental divorce (Glenn & Kramer, 1987), religious dissimilarity (Heaton & Pratt, 1990; Maneker & Rankin, 1993), marrying after having known each other for a short time (Kurdek, 1993), premarital cohabitation (Bumpass, Martin, & Sweet, 1991; Thomson & Colella, 1992), low or differing levels of education (Bumpass et al., 1991), and young age at marriage (Booth & Edwards, 1985; Bumpass et al., 1991). One particularly potent risk factor linked with increased chance of marital failure is the presence of negative communication patterns (e.g., Clements, Stanley, & Markman, 1998; Gottman, 1994; Karney & Bradbury, 1997; Markman et al., 1994). A number of specific types of negative interactions have been shown to increase the risk of divorce, including negativity in communication (Markman, 1981), withdrawal and invalidation (Markman & Hahlweg, 1993), defensiveness (Gottman & Krokoff, 1989), higher ratio of hostility to warmth (Matthews, Wickrama, & Conger, 1996), difficulties in problem solving (Fowers, Montel, & Olson, 1996), and physiological arousal prior to problem-solving discussions (Levenson & Gottman, 1985). As Matthews and colleagues (1996) summarized, "The weight of the evidence, then, suggests that the quality of marital interactions, whether warm and supportive or hostile and negative, relates to risk for marital distress and even dissolution of the relationship" (p. 643). Thus, addressing the quality of the interactions between the partners may be a particularly important component of divorce prevention. Although research has demonstrated a large number of important protective and risk factors associated with marital outcomes, the development of prevention programs must be based on those factors most amenable to change.

Which Factors Should Divorce Prevention Programs Address?

Many of the protective and risk factors listed are not within the control of couples at the time of premarital intervention (e.g., family history of divorce or violence, differing religions, personality characteristics). These factors are labeled as static, because they are unlikely to change through any intervention. However, there are also numerous factors influencing marital well-being that are amenable to change, or are dynamic in nature. Importantly, some of the more strongly predictive factors of divorce are dynamic, including the very potent risk factors associated with communication patterns. We believe it is important for prevention programs to focus on dimensions that are both predictive of relationship outcome and dynamic. Research suggests that preventive interventions focusing on enhancing dynamic protective factors as well as on teaching skills to help couples avoid dynamic risk factors for relationship distress will result in the greatest success (Coie et al., 1993; Fincham & Beach, 1999). These goals of divorce prevention programs can be reached through a variety of formats.

FORMATS OF DIVORCE AND DISTRESS PREVENTION PROGRAMS

As previously mentioned, the term "divorce prevention" involves raising protective factors and lowering risk factors. Many prevention programs focus on raising couples' awareness about the various pitfalls they may encounter during their union. Other programs contain a strong element focused on facilitating the development of goals for the marriage congruent with traditional notions of marital commitment. Silliman and Schumm (1999) delineate three main program formats, typically given in group settings, within which these types of education may occur: topic instruction, structured assessment/discussion, and skill training.

Topic Instruction Approach

Topic instruction refers to the dissemination of divorce prevention information in the form of lectures, films, or structured workbooks. Typically, topic instruction covers issues such as communication styles, commitment, and expectations regarding finances and children. Researchers have found that couples value learning more about both partners' views on these types of issues (Lyster, Russell, & Hiebert, 1995). Furthermore, in another study (Williams, Riley, Risch, & Van Dyke, 1999), couples reported that "lectures by presenters" were a valuable component of their marriage preparation experience. In the same study, another mode of topic instruction—videos—had a relatively lower rating of helpfulness, while "discussion time with partner" clearly appeared as the most useful aspect of the experience. These findings support the general opinion of marriage educators that although incorporating lectures and videos about the typical challenges that partners face in marriage may be effective, exclusive reliance on topic instruction may be inadequate. Rather, marriage educators suggest the use of interactive methods, either through structured assessment and discussion or skills training, over the use of such topic instruction or lecture format (Fournier & Olson, 1986, as cited in Silliman & Schumm, 1999). Of course, incorporating topic instruction into one of these interactive formats may also be effective.

Assessment and Discussion Approach

The structured assessment and discussion approach involves the use of inventories to both identify needs of the couples/individuals and to stimulate discussion between the couple(s) and the counselor regarding potential problem areas and goal development. This program format has both advantages and disadvantages. One of the reasons for its popularity might be the low cost associated with the format. Although counselors do incur a cost for ordering the materials, the extent of training required in order to administer and then discuss the inventories is minimal. Therefore, clinicians conserve time and energy while stimulating a good degree of interest and participation in their clients. In fact, one sample of marriage education participants rated discussion time with their partner, as well as use of couple inventories, as the most helpful components of their education experience (Williams et al., 1999). Furthermore, the structured assessment and discussion format enables counselors to educate a large number of couples at once.

An excellent inventory overview by Larson, Holman, Klein, Busby, Stahmann, and Peterson (1995) identifies five well-developed and tested self-report questionnaires that family and marital counselors may use with couples including: FOCCUS (Facilitating Open Couple Communication, Understanding, and Study; Markey, Micheletto, & Becker, 1985), CDEM (Cleveland Diocese Evaluation for Marriage; Bechtold & Rebol, 1988), PREP-M (PREParation for Marriage Questionnaire; Holman, Busby, & Larson, 1989), PREPARE (PREmarital Personal and Relationship Evaluation; Olson, Fournier, & Druckman, 1986), and PMIP (Premarital Inventory Profile; Burnett & Sayers, 1988). Larson and colleagues (1995) claim that these couple inventories meet important criteria that ensure their utility, including adequate reliability and validity, ease of administration, and interpretability. Among the five instruments identified, Larson and colleagues (1995) make further comparisons and recommendations for use that clinicians should note. For example, they rate PREPARE, FOCCUS, and the PMIP as the most appealing "because of their strong psychometric properties, fewer number of test items, comprehensive coverage of premarital factors, and support materials (e.g., instructor's manual and couple's guide)" (p. 251). All five inventories are designed to gather information regarding background and contextual factors (e.g., family of origin and sociocultural factors), individual traits and behaviors (e.g., emotional and physical health), and couple interactional processes (e.g., degree of value and attitude similarity). Depending on the length and interpretability of particular inventories, counselors might choose to administer them immediately prior to discussion or have couples complete them in advance and be ready to discuss their "findings" upon arriving at the workshop.

Clearly, there are advantages to incorporating assessment and discussion into prevention programs; however, concerns have been raised about sole reliance on this format (e.g., Renick, Blumberg, & Markman, 1992). Although topic instruction and structured assessment are important components of prevention efforts, research by Renick and colleagues (1992) has suggested that increasing couples' awareness about the pitfalls of marriage and potentially distressing differences between partners, without providing couples the skills to deal with such issues, may be frustrating for marriage education participants. Furthermore, although some marriage educators acknowledge the importance of revealing any likelihood of long-term incompatibility (see Russo, 1997), they see differences between partners as inevitable but also surmountable. According to this philosophy, what is important is how couples handle their differences, which suggests the importance of training couples in skills to deal with their differences and conflicts.

Skills Training Approach

Researchers in the field of divorce prevention (e.g., Gottman, 1994; Notarius & Markman, 1993) have emphasized the vital importance of teaching couples skills that can be used to manage differences, disagreements, and conflict that are certain to arise in marriage. Because communication is key in managing conflict, several programs based in the behavioral and social learning perspectives emphasize the importance of using effective communication skills to resolve differences. A primary component of these programs is training couples in effective communication strategies. Because several of these programs are described in detail later in the chapter, we will not discuss the specifics of skills training here. Prevention programs designed to equip couples with the necessary skills to manage marital conflict have demonstrated their long-term effectiveness within empirical research (e.g., Prevention and Relationship Enhancement Program (PREP); Markman, Renick, Floyd, Stanley, & Clements, 1993; Relationship Enhancement (RE); Guerney, 1977). In essence, this research has shown that skills training has been quite effective in reducing conflict and preventing future distress when incorporated within a preventative format. Thus, it is clear that providing couples with the skills they need to deal with differences between them ought to be a primary aspect of divorce prevention programs.

In sum, among the choices of divorce prevention program formats available, marriage educators and researchers have recognized the effectiveness, and ubiquity, of both topic instruction and structured assessment for use with engaged or newlywed couples. Facilitating awareness of both individual and couple needs is a valuable by-product of these approaches. Furthermore, an interpersonal skills training component appears to be especially conducive to promoting positive marital outcomes. Prevention programs using these formats seem to instill confidence in couples regarding their communication and problem-solving skills, while also enhancing couples' connection and commitment. Overall, programs incorporating the skills-training approach appear to be more effective than those that do not (Sayers, Cohn, & Heavey, 1998).

REVIEW OF EMPIRICALLY EVALUATED DIVORCE PREVENTION PROGRAMS

A multitude of divorce prevention programs exist. However, there is a scarcity of research addressing the effectiveness of most of these programs. After reviewing the published evaluation studies of marriage preparation programs in 1981, Bagarozzi and Rauen (1981) concluded that the majority of existing prevention programs were weak along a number of dimensions.

They found that most programs used an approach that was not based in theory or research, were loosely designed, and did not have specific goals for the intervention. In a more recent review of available marriage preparation programs, researchers (Sayers et al., 1998) noted some progress in the empirical evaluation of these programs' effectiveness. However, these authors also stated that there are "numerous relationship interventions that are conducted extensively, particularly those offered by religious institutions, and many that are marketed commercially with little or no systematic evaluation" (p. 739). As clinicians, we believe it is important to point out that we cannot be sure of the long-term effectiveness of these community interventions unless they are systematically reviewed and evaluated. More specifically, as Boulder-model psychologists, we believe that the most clinically effective treatments are developed using both state-of-the-art empirical research and sound scientific program evaluations.

Universal or selected prevention programs for couples place varying emphasis on the techniques of assessment and awareness of self and partner, enhancing knowledge for decision making, and interpersonal skill development (Silliman, et al., in press). Although the majority of prevention programs are neither based on the best available empirical research nor systematically reviewed, there are a number that are, including Relationship Enhancement (Guerney, 1977), Couples Communication, originally called the Minnesota Couples Communication Project (Miller, Nunally, & Wackman, 1976), Prevention and Relationship Enhancement Program (e.g., Markman et al., 1994), Compassionate and Accepting Relationships through Empathy program (Rogge, Cobb, Bradbury, Lawrence, & Johnson, 2000), Premartial and Education and Training Sequence (Bagarozzi & Bagarozzi, 1982; Bagarozzi, Bagarozzi, Anderson, & Pollane, 1984), and Mutual Problem Solving (Ridley & Nelson, 1984). In the following pages we have summarized a selection of empirically based, divorce prevention programs. Given that programs with a strong skill development component have been found to be relatively more effective than programs that lack this component (Sayers et al., 1998), all of the programs reviewed here have a strong skills based emphasis. The empirically reviewed programs covered in the rest of this chapter include: Relationship Enhancement (RE; Guerney, 1977), which focuses on empathy building and communication skills; Couple Communication (CC; Miller et al., 1976), which is a communication skills training program, including self- and other-awareness exercises; the Prevention and Relationship Enhancement Program (PREP; Markman et al., 1994), which has a main focus on communication skills while addressing the enhancement of some protective factors as well; and the Compassionate and Accepting Relationships through Empathy program (CARE; Rogge et al., 2000), which combines a main emphasis on protective factors with a component on conflict resolution skills.

Relationship Enhancement (RE)

Overview and Rationale. Relationship Enhancement (RE; Guerney, 1977) is one of the most extensively evaluated skills training programs for couples. Originally, the aim of RE was to enhance all intimate relationships, including those between friends and all family members; it was not specifically designed for premarital couples. However, many studies have evaluated RE's effectiveness as a marital preparation program. The primary goal of RE is the teaching of specific interpersonal behavioral skills, not helping the couple solve specific relationship problems. That is, through psychoeducation and the provision of skills (adaptive behaviors), RE aims to prevent the development of distress and help couples find methods of dealing with possible issues rather than curing existent distress (Guerney, 1977). The underlying theoretical rationale of RE is based on a Rogerian communication model, combining an emphasis on expression of empathic acceptance with instruction in behavioral skills that improve communication. Specifically, Guerney (1977) suggests that having empathic acceptance, understanding that one's own view is subjective, and having the ability to express messages to the partner in behavioral terms will increase the couple's ability to resolve conflict and relationship issues.

Format and Skills. The format of RE is very flexible. In the interest of teaching attitudes and behavioral skills that help partners relate to one another in an emotionally and functionally satisfying manner, providers of RE first explain the reasoning behind teaching the skills, then demonstrate the skills, and finally coach the couples as they practice the skills (Guerney, 1977). Three basic sets of behavioral communication skills are taught.

- Expressive Mode of Communication
  First, individuals are taught how to clearly express emotions and thoughts in a manner unlikely to evoke hostility or defensiveness in their partner.
- Empathic Responding
  Second, individuals are instructed in how to convey acceptance of the partner's messages as well as identify with her or his feelings and thoughts. This type of responding is described as involving the depth, intensity, and the enhancing classic qualities of a Rogerian therapist, and thus implies more than mere reflective listening.
- Mode Shifting
  The third set of skills taught involves moving from the role of expresser to that of empathic listener in a way that maximizes mutual understanding, satisfaction, problem solving, and conflict resolution. Sometimes, couples are also taught a fourth set of skills, in which they serve as facilitators for helping other couples learn the RE skills.

Empirical Evidence Regarding Effectiveness. Evaluations of RE have found gains in communication skills, disclosure, and empathy for RE participants over those participating in control groups (Avery, Ridley, Leslie, & Milholland, 1980; Heitland, 1986). However, other studies have shown a lack of sustained gains in disclosure and in problem-solving skills (Ridley & Bain, 1983). Couples' reports indicated increases in trust, warmth, and genuineness following participation in RE (Ridley, Jorgensen, Morgan, & Avery, 1982). In a meta-analysis of research evaluating several marital programs, Giblin, Sprenkle, and Sheehan (1985) found RE to exert stronger average effect sizes across outcome variables, including relational skills, relationship satisfaction, and personality variables, than Couples Communication.

Couples Communication (CC)

Overview and Rationale. Originally called the Minnesota Couples Communication Project, Couples Communication (CC) is another well-researched intervention program. CC is grounded in systems theory, communication theory, and family development theory (Miller et al., 1976). There are two main goals of the program: to help couples develop a greater understanding of their interaction patterns and "rules" of communication, including increasing their ability to accurately perceive and reflect upon the dynamics of their communication, and to enhance communication skills, by increasing the ability to change current interaction rules and patterns that are ineffective and by augmenting the couples' capacity for direct, clear, and open communication about the relationship.

Format and Skills. The developers of CC view the group as an important social context (Miller et al., 1976). Thus, the program is typically given to groups of five to seven couples. Presumed benefits of the group context include the availability of feedback from other couples, exposure to different interaction styles, and the opportunity to model other's communication styles. Most often, CC is a 12-hour program delivered in four weekly 3-hour sessions. CC uses brief didactic presentations, role playing, and homework exercises to accomplish its goals. Each of the four group sessions emphasizes one of four key frameworks presented to couples during the course of the program. These frameworks include: the Awareness Wheel, the Shared Meaning Process, the Communication Styles Framework, and the I Count/ I Count You framework.

- *Awareness Wheel*
  This is a framework for understanding the information that is available to the self about the self, which is used for two purposes: (1) to increase self-understanding and organization of self-knowledge and (2) to guide the choice of what information about the self to disclose to the partner.

First, couples are instructed on the different sources of information about the self; information can come from sensing, doing, thinking, feeling, or wanting. Next, specific skills regarding how to make statements about each of the personal sources of self-information are introduced. Additionally, students are taught to "speak for the self," or to take responsibility for the information that they present about the self.

• *Shared Meaning Process*

This describes a framework in which information exchange between partners can become more accurate, ensuring that the message sent by one partner equals the message received by the other. This process involves three steps: (1) the sender stating an initial message in a short, direct, and clear form, (2) the receiver then restating the message received, and (3) the sender confirming or clarifying the accuracy of this restatement.

• *Communication Styles Framework*

This section is presented to couples to help them identify the different available communication styles by which to express their messages as well as the type of impact these styles tend to have on significant others. According to this framework, there are four styles, each described by where it falls on two dimensions: affective–cognitive, whether the communication emphasizes feeling or thinking, and disclosure–receptivity, whether the communication involves high disclosure–receptivity, or low disclosure–nonreceptivity. Couples are taught the most about Style IV, which is characterized by an emphasis on feelings and high disclosure–receptivity, because it is often unused by couples and can be a particularly effective way of communicating.

• *I Count/ I Count You Framework*

The I Count/ I Count You Framework is similar to the "I'm OK, You're OK" perspective developed by transactional analysts (Harris, 1967). Couples are taught to use the communication skills learned earlier in the CC program to express that they value and respect both the partner and the self. Furthermore, CC emphasizes each partner's responsibility in enhancing his or her own self-esteem as well as the partner's self esteem.

Empirical Evidence Regarding Effectiveness. In a meta-analysis of 16 studies evaluating the effectiveness of CC, Butler & Wampler (1999) found generally positive outcomes for those participating in the program. CC had a large effect on couples' observed communication skills, and a smaller but significant effect on couples' self-report of communication skills. However, gains in communication tended to deteriorate over time. Furthermore, although CC had a large effect on couples' relationship satisfaction immediately following participation, the effect size declined to moderate by follow-up.

Prevention and Relationship Enhancement Program (PREP)

Overview and Rationale. One of the most extensively researched primary prevention programs is PREP, the Prevention and Relationship Enhancement Program (Markman et al., 1994). PREP is an empirically based preventive intervention program designed to help couples who are planning marriage to gain skills to prevent future distress in their relationships. Consistent with prevention theory, PREP has two key goals: (1) to reduce the risk factors associated with marital distress and (2) to raise the protective factors associated with marital satisfaction. Given the empirical evidence suggesting that poor communication, negative reciprocity, decline in positivity, and deficits in conflict management are risk factors for marital distress (as discussed previously), PREP offers in-depth skills training in communication and conflict resolution skills. Furthermore, PREP has a secondary focus on raising the protective factors of commitment, fun, and friendship.

Format and Skills. PREP is a short-term educational program that can be presented in a series of one to six sessions with the entire program lasting between 6 and 16 hours. PREP is typically presented in a group format that consists of lectures, videotapes depicting skills used in conflict management, and group discussions. Throughout the program, partners have opportunities to engage in discussions and to practice the skills they are learning.

- *Speaker–Listener Technique*

The speaker–listener technique, designed to facilitate couple communication, is a main focus of PREP. When using the speaker–listener technique to discuss an issue, one partner is designated as the speaker and the other as the listener. The speaker has the floor and her or his job is to discuss an issue from her or his own point of view. The listener's job is to listen to the speaker, without interrupting, and then to paraphrase the speaker's words. This continues until the speaker feels that she/he has been heard. The floor is then switched and the listener takes on the role of the speaker and vice versa. Use of the speaker–listener technique slows down escalation in heated discussions, allowing both partners to hear and validate each other's point of view. This validation is thought to be essential for healthy communication.

- *Ground Rules*

In addition to the speaker–listener technique, couples are taught to establish ground rules for communication in their relationships to help prevent conflict discussions from becoming destructive. Some of the ground rules include speaking from one's own perspective, rather than assuming what one's partner is thinking, and discussing each partner's feelings about an issue before trying to solve it. One particularly important ground rule that many couples choose to establish is that either partner can use a "time out" when discussions get too heated. This ground rule enables couples to temporarily end a conflict if it is becoming too escalated.

- *Protective Factors*

PREP also addresses the enhancement of protective factors by exploring expectations, commitment, and the protection of fun, friendship, and sensuality. By expressing and evaluating their expectations regarding marriage, couples will be better able to develop a long-term vision of their relationship. Additionally, this assessment and refinement of current expectations is designed to prevent future conflict around issues such as core beliefs and values. PREP also suggests a number of strategies couples can use to think about the role commitment plays in their relationship. Couples are encouraged to put energy into enhancing their own relationships rather than engaging in destructive monitoring of alternative partners. Furthermore, the component on commitment stresses the importance of having a long-term view of their relationship and talking regularly about the vision they have of their future together. The necessity for prioritizing the relationship is also discussed within the commitment component. Additional components on friendship, sensuality, and fun are included in PREP as a means of further enhancing the protective factors in couples' relationships. Presentations emphasize the importance of protecting the time that is set aside for these positive experiences from conflict and other destructive interactions. By investing in and protecting their positive investment in their relationship, couples are taught that they will be better able to constructively handle conflict when it does arise.

Empirical Evidence Regarding Effectiveness. Research shows that couples using the skills taught in PREP workshops report greater satisfaction with conflict discussions, greater relationship satisfaction, and lower levels of conflict escalation. Studies have also shown that PREP is effective in lowering problem intensity, in helping couples to engage in less negative communication patterns, and in lowering negative escalation as much as 4 years after participation in the program (Markman et al., 1993).

Compassionate and Accepting Relationships Through Empathy (CARE)

Overview and Rationale. Although programs have been advancing the range of couple processes targeted, with increased emphasis being placed on dimensions such as friendship and forgiveness (e.g., PREP; Markman et al.,

1994), researchers have highlighted the need to develop additional empiri-cally based interventions that place greater attention on the enhancement of protective factors in couples relationships (Fincham & Beach, 1999; L'Abate, 1990; Sayers et al., 1998). The effectiveness of one such intervention, the Com-passionate and Accepting Relationships through Empathy program (CARE; Rogge et al., 2000), is currently being evaluated. The development of the CARE program (Rogge et al., 2000) has been, in part, based on this research. Al-though the CARE program touches on the reduction of risk factors, its main focus is on strengthening protective factors. The CARE program seeks to en-hance marriages and improve marital outcomes by encouraging and promot-ing development of the nurturing, compassionate behaviors that couples al-ready naturally exhibit to some degree. In essence, the CARE program combines an abbreviated component on conflict resolution skills with numer-ous exercises intended to enhance partners' prosocial behaviors including acceptance, support, friendship, empathy, and forgiveness. The core focus of the program is on empathy, and the program strives to teach couples a set of skills that will enhance their ability to handle both external and internal stressors to their marriages in constructive and compassionate ways.

Format and Skills. Empathy is defined as "an affective state that stems from the apprehension of another's emotional state or condition, and that is congruent with it" (Eisenberg & Miller, 1987, p. 91), and is viewed as the essential ingredient for satisfying, enduring marriage. The CARE program aims to promote greater levels of empathy in three main areas.

- *Empathy Through Social Support*
  In response to the daily stresses of life, the CARE programs suggests that empathy is reflected in social support, which is defined as respon-siveness to another's needs and which involves acts that communicate caring, that validate the partner's worth, feelings, or actions, and that help the partner cope with life's problems (Cutrona, 1996). Conse-quently, CARE teaches couples a set of skills to help them handle the daily stresses of life as a team, supporting each other instead of letting those stresses erode their friendship.

- *Empathy Through Acceptance*
  When conflict arises within a relationship, the CARE program suggests that empathy is reflected in acceptance, defined as the capacity to expe-rience some offensive, unacceptable, or blameworthy action by the part-ner as understandable and tolerable, if not necessarily desirable, or even as something worthy of appreciation (see Christensen, Jacobson, & Bab-cock, 1995). Thus, CARE teaches couples skills to approach conflict with empathy, focusing on understanding and accepting one another instead of trying to change or attack one another.

• *Empathy Through Forgiveness*

When feelings are hurt and trust is betrayed, CARE suggests that empathy is reflected in forgiveness, which is defined here as "the set of motivational changes whereby one becomes (a) decreasingly motivated to retaliate against an offending relationship partner, (b) decreasingly motivated to maintain estrangement from the offender, and (c) increasingly motivated by conciliation and goodwill for the offender, despite the offender's hurtful actions" (McCullough, Worthington, & Rachal, 1997, p. 322). CARE operationalizes forgiveness in a set of skills that challenge couples to work as a team to repair their relationships and rebuild trust by having couples focus on understanding one another instead of attacking or punishing one another.

Empirical Evidence Regarding Effectiveness. Research is currently being conducted to evaluate the effectiveness of the CARE program.

DISSEMINATING AND MARKETING PREVENTION PROGRAMS

Hopefully, we have thus far familiarized clinicians with some of the general methods of premarital intervention currently available in the field, as well as with some of the specific, more well-researched programs. But, what about making use of this information? How do interested clinicians disseminate their services to those in need of them? Our next objective is to present an overview of the research on the dissemination and marketing of divorce prevention programs. Although this research is very much in its nascent stage of development, we believe there are some contributions in this area that can aid in making prevention of marital distress a widespread reality.

Dissemination Within Religious Institutions

As the development of divorce prevention programs advances, the issue of how to disseminate these programs becomes increasingly important. Currently, the main forum for marital education in the United States is religious settings. The large majority of couples still choose to get married through a church or religious institution. In 1988, roughly 69% of couples were married through a church or religious institution (Stanley, Markman, St. Peters, & Leber, 1995). Thus, the majority of premarital intervention occurs in these settings, either because couples seeking such preparation find it convenient and accessible to obtain it there, or because such preparation is a mandatory prerequisite to marriage according to certain religious traditions. For example, it is a well-known fact that many Protestant pastors and virtually all Catholic priests require such preparation before they will perform a marriage ceremony (Stanley et al., 1995).

Community Dissemination

Because premarital education is often mandatory, or at least strongly recommended, in many religious settings, clergy have some degree of leverage in stimulating interest in their marriage preparation efforts. However, it should be noted that religious settings are not the only vehicle for the delivery of these services. Given the rising concern over divorce and domestic violence rates, marriage preparation programs are proliferating in number (Silliman & Schumm, 1999) and are often administered in other therapeutic settings such as community mental health settings, the private practices of mental health counselors, and academic institutions such as high schools and universities. Clinicians and counselors operating in these other settings, however, face the more challenging task of marketing their programs to couples in the community at large. How can these clinicians make their programs attractive enough to couples they have never even seen? This introduces the issue of how to best market divorce prevention programs.

Marketing Divorce Prevention Programs

Although numerous divorce and distress prevention programs exist, few couples actually participate in these workshops (Stanley & Markman, 1998). Given the multitude of couples in distress, it is essential to enlist the use of marketing strategies designed to disseminate these programs to couples most in need. A helpful framework for conceptualizing marketing is provided by Pribilovics (1985) and is applied specifically to marriage education by Morris, Cooper, and Gross (1999). This framework consists of the "five Ps of the marketing mix": Product, Price, People, Place, and Promotion. Price and place will not be addressed here. Presumably, like any consumer, couples engaging in premarital counseling not only want to receive adequate services for their money but also desire aesthetically pleasing and comfortable settings in which to receive these services (for a more thorough consideration of these factors, see Morris et al., 1999). However, the three other "Ps"—Product, People, and Promotion—are discussed here.

Tailoring Programs for Couples—Product. Examining the product being offered in divorce prevention is essential when marketing to couples. According to Pribilovics (1985), product refers to the goods, service, or program designed to offer value to the consumer and satisfy their needs. Unfortunately, the impression that many clinicians have of manualized protocols for prevention and treatment is that of rigidly prescribed suggestions for couples in which the clinician has little, if any, latitude in how he or she administers the protocol (for a discussion of this issue, see Addis, Wade, & Hatgis, 1999). It is hoped that, after reading this chapter, clinicians in the field of divorce prevention will feel a comfortable flexibility in how they might choose to intervene with couples. From our perspective, the leaders of divorce prevention workshops need to be open and creative in how they work with couples, while of course maintaining an adequate degree of standardization in their work. This section examines a number of areas related to the marketing of the programs themselves. Researchers have identified four factors influencing salience of materials presented to couples—attractiveness, readability, relevance, and cultural sensitivity (Hughes, 1994). Although the issues of attractiveness and readability are mostly self-explanatory, the factors of relevance and cultural sensitivity of materials stand out as particularly significant to marketing. Thus, this section reviews the factors of relevance and cultural sensitivity, along with product timing and duration.

—Addressing Relevance in the Product

- *Marital Status.* In order for prevention program materials to be relevant to participants, it is important to consider their marital status, as couples may be premarital, married, or not considering marriage. Components that cater to couples who are just beginning marriage might differ from those directed toward more advanced relationships. For example, asking couples to consider their expectations for their future together (e.g., regarding children, financial status, etc.) might be especially captivating for premarital couples. However, when working with older, married couples, discussions surrounding the empty-nest syndrome might be more relevant.

- *Religion.* Clinicians should be aware of the role religion plays in couples' lives in order to determine how much emphasis to place on religious issues. If the majority of participating couples are religious, spending time discussing the importance of religion and spirituality to marriage would definitely be warranted. Of course, roughly 85% of adults in the United States cite religion as playing an important role in their lives (Spilka, Hood, & Gorsuch, 1985), so some attention to this content area might be worthwhile in any case. Religious matters should certainly be touched on when discussing couples' expectations for their relationship. When intervening with those couples for whom religion is a major facet of their marriage, addressing this topic will be particularly relevant—in one sample of mostly Catholic participants, couples rated "deepening one's relationship with God" as one of the most valuable elements in marriage preparation they had undertaken (Williams et al., 1999).

—Addressing Cultural Sensitivity in the Product

Cultural sensitivity is important to consider when developing products that are designed to reach community-wide couple audiences (i.e., cutting across ethnic and religious barriers). While sexist or racist bias is certainly ill-advised even in more specifically tailored efforts, a particular effort at "diversifying" materials in broad-based primary prevention programs should be made. One concrete way to incorporate cultural sensitivity into a program is through the actual materials through which clinicians channel their message. For example, in PREP (Markman et al., 1994), overheads of cartoons are intermittently used by the leaders to supplement the lecture topics. These cartoons display husbands and wives of various ethnic identifications and religious backgrounds. Another obvious way to address this issue is to have leaders of different ethnicities conducting the workshops. Last, clinicians may choose to openly invite couples to discuss their unique cultural and religious backgrounds; this tactic both validates the diversity present in a workshop and makes the content of the program specifically relevant for each couple attending.

—Addressing the Timing and Duration of the Product

Two other factors that influence the marketing of the product in question are timing of the training and duration of the training. Regarding timing of training, researchers (e.g., Russell & Lyster, 1992) report that in the context of marriage preparation, couples less than two months away from marriage took fewer risks in talking about salient issues in their relationship when compared to couples who were either farther away from their wedding date or already married (as cited in Silliman & Schumm, 1999). Some researchers specify that attending preparation programs 4 to 12 months prior to the wedding date will maximize learning of the material (Center for Marriage and the Family, 1995; Olson, 1983, as cited in Silliman & Schumm, 1999). In addition, booster sessions—review sessions given after the divorce prevention training and wedding date—have been shown to strengthen interpersonal skills among couples (Renick et al., 1992).

Regarding duration of training, Silliman and Schumm (1999) suggest that couples are not as receptive to extremely long training programs. However, they also report that workshops that are too short will not be deemed as credible or comprehensive by couples in the community. Silliman and Schumn (1999) state that to impart skills training to couples might reasonably be expected to take more than 4 to 6 hours—the length of many clergy-led, church-based divorce prevention efforts (Jones & Stahmann, 1994). In fact, research-based programs last, on the average, from 10 to 30 hours. Clinicians should be aware that some programs are divided into sections, which allows practitioners to modify some components while still offering couples fundamental interpersonal skills training. Such compartmentalization may allow clinicians and practitioners to tailor programs for the particular couples with whom they are working. Furthermore, researchers (Halford, Osbargy, & Kelly, 1998) have found that shortened versions of research-based programs, 5 to 6 hours, are quite effective, if not equally as effective as longer programs. Clearly, a balance needs to be struck between quality of program content and swiftness of delivery.

Couples' Satisfaction With Prevention Program Leaders—People. A vital aspect of satisfaction with divorce prevention programs is related to the program leaders. Corey and Corey (1992) have emphasized five perceptions that individuals project or transfer onto their group leader(s): the Expert, the Authority Figure, the Friend, the Superperson, and the Lover. In a study measuring the influence of various marketing factors on couple satisfaction with marriage preparation, Morris and colleagues (1999) developed a 23-item questionnaire to measure these five perceptions of group leaders, as well as a sixth—Competence (Arcus & Thomas, 1993). Within their results, they found that clients' perceptions of the leaders' competence was strongly correlated with their satisfaction with the training experience. In fact, some clients have even gone so far as to say that the leader of the workshop is "the program itself" (Arcus & Thomas, 1993) and that program success and leader success are intimately related (as cited in Morris et al., 1999). In this light, the selection of group leaders as well as the quality of the training provided for them appear paramount.

Researchers (Corey & Corey, 1992) have recommended that leaders publicize or make known their qualifications or educational level to influence their relationship with their clients. One study (Wilkins, 1999) analyzed the effectiveness of more elaborate self-disclosure on the part of the workshop leader and found a positive and significant relationship between this self-disclosure and the degree of working alliance between the couples and their leader. Self-disclosure in this context refers to the degree to which trainers brought in examples from their own lives (i.e., relationships, friends in relationships, etc.) in order to reinforce the principles taught in the program. In all likelihood, one of the effects of such self-disclosure is to boost perceptions of credibility, or competence, of the leader. Generally, self-disclosure on the part of the leader should almost always have some degree of relevance for the couples involved, presumably in the service of making a point more clear and concrete for them.

Furthermore, as expected, leaders who are enthusiastic and empathic, as well as "normalizing" in the face of couples' fears and concerns, are valued by clients (Silliman & Schumm, 1999). Researchers also point out the benefits of collaboration among multiple leaders; such collaboration is viewed positively by couples and it reduces the workload for any one provider (Silliman & Schumm, 1999). Although leader qualifications play a role in the success of an intervention workshop, the relationship between a couple and the leader might play an even greater role in level of satisfaction with the workshop.

Enhancing the Accessibility of Prevention Programs—Promotion. Researchers and clinicians alike are beginning to realize that although having an attractive and effective divorce prevention program is important for getting couples to participate, it is often not sufficient. First, those most at risk for marital distress are often those couples most reluctant to seek help, or even information about available programs. Second, many individuals are uncomfortable with research or academic environments, where many prevention programs are offered. Therefore, many researchers in divorce prevention are beginning to focus on disseminating their programs in the community via agencies that are more approachable and accessible to a greater number of people. We believe that providers of divorce prevention need to approach couples in a community-based effort, while retaining the program's attractiveness and effectiveness.

One research program that has been disseminated into the community is PREP. Markman, Stanley, and colleagues at the University of Denver have begun to test the effectiveness of their intervention (PREP; Markman et al., 1994) when it is delivered through community religious organizations (ROs). The rationale for selecting an RO as a suitable conduit of dissemination is explained fully elsewhere (Stanley et al., 1995). These researchers, acknowledging the loss of control that occurs with such expansion (Stanley et al., 1995), have nevertheless attempted to reproduce the proven effectiveness of PREP in the community by training clergy to administer the program to couples in their religious settings.

Results, so far, are encouraging. In a comparison between PREP, when delivered by religious leaders, and PREP, when given at the University of Denver, no differences have been found in terms of changes in couple interaction over time nor on couples' ratings of satisfaction with divorce prevention training. The data show that clergy and lay leaders presenting PREP are providing as effective a service as the university staff—at least with regard to changes in couple functioning. Whatever these community leaders may have lacked in experience with this specific program seems to have been offset by their skill at marriage education, the user-friendly program format, and the fact that they were working in settings familiar to them and the couples they serve (Stanley, Markman, Prado, Olmos-Gallo, Tonelli, St. Peters, Leber, Bobulinski, Cordova, & Whitton, in press). Such data is promising given that clinicians interested in broad-based divorce prevention will almost necessarily have to coordinate with outside community agencies when promoting divorce prevention programs.

TIPS FOR SELECTING PREVENTION PROGRAMS TO USE

Within this chapter we have discussed the necessity of primary divorce prevention programs and have stressed the importance of selecting programs with empirical foundations. We have also outlined several programs and have discussed various facets of program dissemination and marketing. Although several programs have been described in detail, we believe it is important to enumerate some criteria for choosing a sound prevention program to use within your work with couples.

- Choose a program that incorporates strategies based in research on the factors essential to maintaining a healthy marriage. Examine the evidence regarding the effectiveness of the program you are considering—has it been empirically evaluated? Has it been shown to result in improved marital interaction, enhanced relationship satisfaction, or lower divorce rates?
- Recognize the importance of using a skills-based program to ensure that discussions of relationship issues are re-enforced with skills couples can put into action.
- Consider using a program that is compartmentalized to ensure flexibility in both selecting the desired components and in choosing the format of the program.
- Know who you want to reach—the more broad-based your target population, the more considerations should be made regarding cultural sensitivity, socioeconomic status, and so forth.
- Timing of training should be considered—avoid the period just prior to the wedding.
- The length of the program should be long enough to be comprehensive and seem credible, but short enough to be bearable.
- Coordinate with agencies in communities who work with couples regularly.
- Keep up on the current research in the field by reading journals and reviewing articles on marriage preparation programs.
- Adapt or change your program if new evidence suggests that an unused strategy is effective or if a technique you are currently using has not been demonstrated to be beneficial to couples.
- Consider holding booster sessions so that couples have an opportunity to brush up on what they have learned.

- Evaluate your own program's effectiveness to make it better in the future—often, getting feedback from couples themselves is a good way to test your program.

A FINAL NOTE

The consequences of marital distress and divorce are numerous. As clinicians, we do have the opportunity to reach couples before they are in serious distress. By implementing divorce prevention programs in our community clinics, religious organizations, and private practices, we can help many couples and families to avoid the devastation associated with divorce.

REFERENCES

Addis, M. E., Wade, W. A., & Hatgis, C. (1999). Barriers to dissemination of evidence-based practices: Addressing practitioners' concerns about manual-based psychotherapies. *Clinical Psychology: Science and Practice, 6*, 430–448.

Amato, P. R., & Keith, B. (1991). Parental divorce and the well-being of children: A meta-analysis. *Psychological Bulletin, 110*, 26–46.

Arcus, M. E., & Thomas, J. (1993). The nature and practice of family life education. In M. E. Arcus, J. D. Schvaneveldt, & J. J. Moss (Eds.), *Handbook of family life education: The practice of family life education* (Vol. 1, pp. 229–249). Newbury Park, CA: Sage.

Avery, A. W., Ridley, C. A., Leslie, L. A., & Milholland, T. (1980). Relationship enhancement with premarital dyads: A six month follow-up. *American Journal of Family Therapy, 3*, 23–30.

Bagarozzi, D. A., & Bagarozzi, J. I. (1982). A theoretically derived model of premarital intervention: The making of a family system. *Clinical Social Work Journal, 10*, 52–56.

Bagarozzi, D. A., Bagarozzi, J. I., Anderson, S. A., & Pollane, L. (1984). Premarital Education and Training Sequence (PETS): A 3-year follow-up of an experimental study. *Journal of Counseling and Development, 63*, 91–100.

Bagarozzi, D. A., & Rauen, P. (1981). Premarital counseling: Appraisal and status. *American Journal of Family Therapy, 9*, 13–30.

Baucom, D., & Epstein, N. (1990). *Cognitive–behavioral marital therapy.* New York: Guilford.

Bechtold, D., & Rebol, A. (1988). *Cleveland diocese evaluation for marriage.* Cleveland: Diocese of Cleveland.

Blood, R. O., & Wolfe, D. M. (1960). *Husbands and wives.* New York: Free Press.

Booth, A., & Edwards, J. (1985). Age at marriage and marital instability. *Journal of Marriage and the Family, 47*, 67–75.

Bumpass, L. L., Martin, T. C., & Sweet, J. A. (1991). The impact of family background and early marital factors on marital disruption. *Journal of Family Issues, 12*, 22–42.

Burnett, C. K., & Sayers, S. L. (1988). *PMI profile handbook.* Chapel Hill, NC: Intercommunications.

Butler, M. H., & Wampler, K. S. (1999). A meta-analytic update of research on the couple communication program. *The American Journal of Family Therapy, 27*, 223–237.

Center for Marriage and the Family. (1995). *Marriage preparation in the Catholic Church: Getting it right.* Omaha, NE: Creighton University.

Christensen, A., Jacobson, N. S., & Babcock, J. C. (1995). Integrative behavioral couple therapy. In N. S. Jacobson & A. S. Gurman (Eds.), *Clinical handbook of couple therapy* (pp. 31–64). New York: Guilford.

Clements, M. L., Stanley, S. M., & Markman, H. J. (1998). *Prediction of marital distress and divorce: A discriminant analysis*. Manuscript submitted for publication.

Coie, J. D, Watt, N. F., West, S. G., Hawkins, J. D., Asarnow, J. R., Markman, H. J., Ramey, S. L., Shure, M. B., & Long, B. (1993). The science of prevention: A conceptual framework and some directions for a national research program. *American Psychologist, 48*, 1013–1022.

Cordova, A. (2000). *Teamwork and the transition to parenthood*. Unpublished dissertation, University of Denver.

Corey, S., & Corey, G. (1992). *Groups: Process and practice* (4th ed.). Pacific Grove, CA: Brooks/ Cole.

Cutrona, C. E. (1996). *Social support in couples*. Thousand Oaks, CA: Sage.

DeVita, C. J. (1996, March). The United States at mid-decade. *Population Bulletin, 50(4)*. Washington, DC: Population Reference Bureau.

Doherty, W. J. (1986). Marital therapy and family medicine. In N. S. Jacobson & A. S. Gurman (Eds.), *Clinical handbook of marital therapy*. New York: Guilford.

Eisenberg, N., & Miller, P. A. (1987). The relation of empathy to prosocial and related behaviors. *Psychological Bulletin, 101*, 91–119.

Emery, R. E. (1982). Interparental conflict and the children of discord and divorce. *Psychological Bulletin, 92*, 310–330.

Fincham, F. D., & Beach, S. R. H. (1999). Conflict in marriage: Implications for working with couples. *Annual Review of Psychology, 50*, 47–77.

Fincham, F. D., & Bradbury, T. N. (1989). The impact of attributions in marriage: An individual difference analysis. *Journal of Social and Personal Relationships, 6*, 69–85.

Forthofer, M. S., Markman, H. J., Cox, M., Stanley, S., & Kessler, R. C. (1996). Associations between marital distress and work loss in a national sample. *Journal of Marriage and the Family, 58*, 597–605.

Fournier, D. G., & Olson, D. H. (1986). Programs for premarital and newlywed couples. In R. F. Levant (Ed.), *Psychoeducational approaches family therapy and counseling* (pp. 194–231). New York: Springer.

Fowers, B. J., Montel, K. H., & Olson, D. H. (1996). Predicting marital success for premarital couple types based on PREPARE. *Journal of Marital and Family Therapy, 22*, 103–119.

Giblin, P., Sprenkle, D. H., & Sheehan, R. (1985). Enrichment outcome research: A meta-analysis of premarital, marital, and family interventions. *Journal of Marital and Family Therapy, 11*, 257–271.

Glenn, N. D., & Kramer, K. B. (1987). The marriages and divorces of the children of divorce. *Journal of Marriage and the Family, 49*, 811–825.

Gottman, J. (1994). *Why marriages succeed or fail*. New York: Simon & Schuster.

Gottman, J. M., & Krokoff, L. J. (1989). Marital interaction and satisfaction: A longitudinal view. *Journal of Consulting and Clinical Psychology, 57*, 47–52.

Guerney, B. G. (1977). *Relationship enhancement*. San Francisco: Jossey-Bass.

Halford, K. W. (1998). The ongoing evolution of behavioral couples therapy: Retrospect and prospect. *Clinical Psychology Review, 18*, 613–633.

Halford, K. W., Osbargy, S., & Kelly, A. (1998). Brief behavioural couples therapy: A preliminary evaluation. *Behavioural and Cognitive Psychotherapy, 24*, 263–273.

Harris, T. (1967). *I'm OK—You're OK*. New York: Harper and Row.

Hartman, S. G., Stanley, S. M., & Markman, H. J. (2000). *The role of joint activity in promoting marital satisfaction and commitment: Personal and social determinants of an overlooked protective factor*. Manuscript in preparation, University of Denver.

Hartman, S. G., Whitton, S. W., Markman, H. J., & Stanley, S. M. (in press). Premarital intervention. In W. E. Craighead & C. B. Nemeroff (Eds.), *The Corsini encyclopedia of psychology and neuroscience, Third Edition*. New York: Wiley.

Heaton, T. B., & Pratt, E. L. (1990). The effects of religious homogeny on marital satisfaction and stability. *Journal of Family Issues, 11*, 191–207.

Heitland, W. (1986). An experimental communication program for premarital dating couples. *The School Counselor, 34*, 57–61.

Holman, T. B., Busby, D., & Larson, J. H. (1989). *PREParation for Marriage*. Provo, UT: Brigham Young University, Marriage Study Consortium.

Hughes, R. (1994). A framework for developing family life education programs. *Family Relations, 43*, 74–80.

Jacobson, N. S., & Addis, M. E. (1993). Research on couples and couple therapy: What do we know? Where are we going? *Journal of Consulting and Clinical Psychology, 61*, 85–93.

Jones, E. F., & Stahmann, R. F. (1994). Clergy beliefs, preparation, and practice in premarital counseling. *Journal of Pastoral Counseling, 48*, 181–186.

Kaiser, A., Hahlweg, K., Fehm-Wolfsdorf, G., & Groth, T. (1998). The efficacy of a compact psychoeducational group training program for married couples. *Journal of Consulting and Clinical Psychology, 66*, 753–760.

Karney, B. R., & Bradbury, T. N. (1997). Neuroticism, marital interaction, and the trajectory of marital satisfaction. *Journal of Personality and Social Psychology, 72*, 1075–1092.

Kurdek, L. A. (1993). Predicting marital dissolution: A 5-year prospective longitudinal study of newlywed couples. *Journal of Personality and Social Psychology, 64*, 221–242.

L'Abate, L. (1990). *Building family competence: Primary and secondary prevention strategies*. Newbury Park, CA: Sage.

Larson, J. H., Holman, T. B., Klein, D. M., Busby, D. M., Stahmann, R. F., & Peterson, D. (1995). A review of comprehensive questionnaires used in premarital education and counseling. *Family Relations, 44*, 245–251.

Levenson, R. W., & Gottman, J. M. (1985). Physiological and affective predictors of change in relationship satisfaction. *Journal of Personality and Social Psychology, 49*, 85–94.

Lyster, R. F., Russell, M. N., & Hiebert, J. (1995). Preparation for remarriage: Consumers' views. *Journal of Divorce and Remarriage, 24*, 143–157.

Maneker, J. S., & Rankin, R. P. (1993). Religious homogeny and marital duration among those who file for divorce in California, 1966–1971. *Journal of Divorce and Remarriage, 19*, 233–247.

Markey, B., Micheletto, M., & Becker, A. (1985). *Facilitating Open Couple Communication, Understanding, and Study (FOCCUS)*. Omaha: Archdiocese of Omaha.

Markman, H. J. (1981). Prediction of marital distress: A 5-year follow-up. *Journal of Consulting and Clinical Psychology, 49*, 760–762.

Markman, H. J., & Hahlweg, K. (1993). The prediction and prevention of marital distress: An international perspective. *Clinical Psychology Review, 13*, 29–43.

Markman, H. J., Renick, M. J., Floyd, F. J., Stanley, S. M., & Clements, M. (1993). Preventing marital distress through communication and conflict management training: A 4- and 5-year follow-up. *Journal of Consulting and Clinical Psychology, 61*, 70–77.

Markman, H. J., Stanley, S. M., & Blumberg, S. L. (1994). *Fighting for your marriage*. San Francisco: Jossey-Bass.

Matthews, L. S., Wickrama, K. A. S., & Conger, R. D. (1996). Predicting marital instability from spouse and observer reports of marital interaction. *Journal of Marriage and the Family, 58*, 641–655.

McCullough, M. E., Worthington, E. L., Jr., & Rachal, K. C. (1997). Interpersonal forgiving in close relationships. *Journal of Personality and Social Psychology, 73*, 321–336.

Miller, S., Nunally, E. W., & Wackman, D. B. (1976). Minnesota Couples Communication Program (MCCP): Premarital and Marital Groups. In D. H. Olson (Ed.), *Treating Relationships* (pp. 12–25). Lake Mills, Iowa: Graphic Publishing.

Monarch, N. D., Stanley, S. M., & Markman, H. J. (2000). *The Role of Commitment in Marital Satisfaction*. Manuscript in preparation, University of Denver.

Morris, M. L., Cooper, C., & Gross, K. H. (1999). Marketing factors influencing the overall satisfaction of marriage education participants. *Family Relations, 48*, 251–261.

Notarius, C., & Markman, H. J. (1993). *We can work it out: Making sense of marital conflict.* New York: Putnam.

Olson, D. H. (1983). How effective is marriage preparation? In D. R. Mace (Ed.), *Prevention in family services: Approaches to family wellness* (pp. 65–75). Beverly Hills, CA: Sage.

Olson, D. H., Fournier, D., & Druckman, J. (1986). *PREPARE*. Minneapolis: PREPARE/ENRICH.

Pasch, L. A., & Bradbury, T. N. (1998). Social support, conflict, and the development of marital dysfunction. *Journal of Consulting and Clinical Psychology, 66*, 219–230.

Pribilovics, R. M. G. (1985). Marketing mix case study: Family service agency of San Francisco. *Health Marketing Quarterly, 2*, 75–87.

Renick, M., Blumberg, S. L., & Markman, H. J. (1992). The Prevention and Relationship Enhancement Program (PREP): An empirically based intervention program for couples. *Family Relations, 41*, 141–147.

Ridley, C. A., & Bain, A. B. (1983). The effects of a premarital relationship enhancement program on self-disclosure. *Family Therapy, 1*, 13–24.

Ridley, C. A., Jorgensen, S. R., Morgan, A. G., & Avery, A. W. (1982). Relationship enhancement with premarital couples: An assessment of effects on marital quality. *The American Journal of Family Therapy, 10*, 41–48.

Ridley, C. A., & Nelson, R. R. (1984). The behavioral effects of training premarital couples in mutual problem solving skills. *Journal of Social and Personal Relationships, 1*, 197–210.

Rogge, R. D., Cobb, R., Bradbury, T., Lawrence, E., & Johnson, M. (2000). Modifying pro-social behaviors to prevent adverse marital outcomes. In A. S. Gurman & N. S. Jacobson (Eds.), *Clinical Handbook of Couple Therapy* (pp. 340–351). New York: Guilford.

Russell, M., & Lyster, R. F. (1992). Marriage preparation: Factors associated with consumer satisfaction. *Family Relations, 41*, 446–451.

Russo, F. (1997). Can the government prevent divorce? *The Atlantic Monthly, 280*, 28–35.

Sayers, S. L., Kohn, C. S., & Heavey, C. (1998). Prevention of marital dysfunction: Behavioral approaches and beyond. *Clinical Psychology Review, 18*, 713–744.

Silliman, B., & Schumm, W. R. (1999). Improving practice in marriage preparation. *Journal of Sex and Marital Therapy, 25*, 23–43.

Silliman, B., Stanley, S. M., Coffin, W., Markman, H. J., & Jordan, P. L. (in press). Preventative interventions for couples. In H. Liddle, D. Santisteban, & J. Bray (Eds.), *Family psychology intervention science*. Washington, DC: APA Publications.

Spilka, B., Hood, R., & Gorsuch, R. (1985). *The psychology of religion: An empirical approach*. Englewood Cliffs, NJ: Prentice-Hall.

Stanley, S. M., & Markman, H. J. (1992). Assessing commitment in personal relationships. *Journal of Marriage and the Family, 54*, 595–608.

Stanley, S. M., & Markman, H. J. (1998, July). *Acting on what we know: The hope of prevention*. Paper presented at the Smart Marriages Conferences, Washington, DC.

Stanley, S. M., Markman, H. J., Prado, L. M., Olmos-Gallo, P. A., Tonelli, L., St. Peters, M., Leber, B. D., Bobulinski, M., Cordova, A., & Whitton, S. (in press). Community Based Premarital Prevention: Clergy and Lay Leaders on the Front Lines. *Family Relations*.

Stanley, S. M., Markman, H. J., St. Peters, M., & Leber, D. (1995). Strengthening marriages and preventing divorce. *Family Relations, 44*, 392–401.

Stroup, A. L., & Pollock, G. E. (1994). Economic consequences of marital dissolution. In C. A. Everett (Ed.), *The economics of divorce: The effects on parents and children* (pp. 119–134). New York: Haworth.

Thomson, E., & Collela, U. (1992). Cohabitation and marital stability: Quality or commitment? *Journal of Marriage and the Family, 54*, 259–267.

Van Lange, P. A. M., Rusbult, C. E., Drigotas, S. M., Arriaga, X. B., Witcher, B. S., & Cox, C. L. (1997). Willingness to sacrifice in close relationships. *Journal of Personality and Social Psychology, 72,* 1373–1395.

Van Widenfelt, B., Markman, H. J., Guerney, B., Behrens, B. C., & Hosman, C. (1997). Prevention of relationship problems. In W. K. Halford & H. J. Markman (Eds.), *Clinical handbook of marriage and couples interventions* (pp. 62–81). London: Wiley.

Whitton, S. W., Stanley, S. M., & Markman, H. J. (2000). *Sacrifice in romantic relationships.* Manuscript in preparation, University of Denver.

Wilkins, T. A. (1999). Self-disclosure and working alliance related to outcome in premarital training with couples. Unpublished doctoral dissertation, University of Denver, Denver, CO.

Williams, L. M., Riley, L. A., Risch, G. S., & Van Dyke, D. T. (1999). An empirical approach to designing marriage preparation programs. *American Journal of Family Therapy, 27,* 271–283.

12

Integrating Insight-Oriented Techniques Into Couple Therapy

Douglas K. Snyder
Texas A&M University

Karen and David held hands as they sat on their couple therapist's couch. Karen quietly wept and painfully described how their second son had been stillborn just 2 months earlier. The trauma of their loss and the events that followed, including lost lab reports and endless tests to determine causes of the stillbirth and Karen's difficulty in maintaining a pregnancy to full-term, had overwhelmed the young couple. They had struggled during the past several years as David had pursued a doctoral program in education but had been terminated after obtaining his master's degree. Karen had tried to interweave part-time secretarial work with her responsibilities as a mother to their 4-year-old son, Daniel. The couple had struggled for the past 2 years to conceive; Karen's pregnancy had been a blessing, now lost.

They had managed to keep their marriage together despite financial hardships and growing emotional distance between them. Karen longed for the emotional closeness she had anticipated her marriage would offer and that she had enjoyed with her sister growing up. Instead of drawing closer over the years, David seemed increasingly distant and aloof. Her efforts to draw him nearer and her complaints about his emotional detachment seemed to drive them further apart. David wished he could be more the kind of husband that Karen wanted, but her unhappiness with him was apparent and his feelings of inadequacy in the marriage compounded the inadequacy he felt across most areas of his life. He had cried only briefly following their son's stillbirth. David tried to invest more time and energy with Daniel, but his efforts admittedly felt half-hearted. He empathized with Karen's unhappiness, felt largely to blame, but he found it difficult to approach her given the increasing resentments she seemed to harbor toward him.

INSIGHT-ORIENTED COUPLE THERAPY
WITHIN A PLURALISTIC MODEL

What did Karen and David most need as they entered couple therapy? Would interventions emphasizing developmental origins to the couple's difficulties have been successful in reducing their initial distress? Probably not. The couple was far too distressed and too psychologically defended to tolerate or make use of interpretive techniques early in their therapy. Could they have benefited from interpretive strategies aimed at identifying recurrent dysfunctional relationship patterns later in their couple therapy? Perhaps. Not all couples require exploration of early traumatic or problematic relationship experiences to recognize and modify maladaptive patterns in their marriage. Among those that do, not all are able or willing to engage in such an exploration process. Then, what role should insight-oriented techniques assume in couple therapy? When should couple therapists integrate interpretive affective and developmental methods into their overall strategy and what model can they draw on to guide the content, pacing, and sequencing of their interventions?

Snyder (1999a, 1999b) proposed a pluralistic, hierarchical model for organizing interventions when working with difficult couples (see Fig. 12.1). The six components comprising this model, in order of sequence, include: (a) developing a collaborative alliance, (b) containing disabling relationship crises, (c) strengthening the marital dyad, (d) promoting relevant relationship skills, (e) challenging cognitive components of relationship distress, and (f) examining developmental sources of relationship distress. Therapy generally proceeds from initial interventions emphasizing a collaborative alliance fundamental to working with all couples, to interpretive interventions involving increasing depth and emotional challenge. Whereas interventions lower in the hierarchy are nearly always necessary and are sometimes sufficient to produce reliable reductions in couples' distress, some couples require the explication and resolution of longstanding maladaptive relationship patterns to successfully resolve current relationship difficulties.

Such was the case with Karen and David. Both partners were emotionally battered and bruised by the loss of their second child and by the medical mismanagement Karen encountered following this tragedy. Admonitions by her family physician to "get some mental counseling" after Karen lost her patience one afternoon in his office contributed to a vigilant, mistrustful stance that the couple brought to the initial interview with their therapist. What they needed most were interventions aimed at fostering

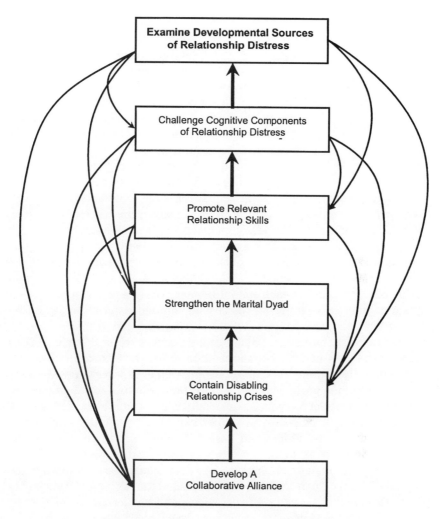

FIG. 12.1. An hierarchical model for a pluralistic approach to couple therapy. From *CaseBook in Family Therapy, 1st edition*, by D. M. Lawson and F. Prevatt © 1999. Reprinted with permission of Wadsworth, an imprint of the Wadsworth Group, a division of Thomson Learning. Fax 800 730-2215.

safety and collaboration—achieved in part by providing a secure atmosphere for each to discuss their hurts and disappointments without attacking the other, deriving a formulation of their difficulties that emphasized stressors outside as well as within their marriage, and identifying both individual and relationship strengths that had sustained them through years of struggle and could be mobilized to reverse the growing despair each had experienced in the past few months.

Only after Karen and David felt secure in their therapist's concern and expertise in treating relationship distress were they able to make use of more directive interventions targeting their bereavement and efforts to strengthen their marriage. Karen needed extended opportunities to express her grief to David, but fear of his own emotional brittleness initially impaired his ability to respond empathically to her hurt. He was able to hear her anguish when this was softened by the therapist's reflections, and gradually David was able to share his own grief and the immobilization he experienced when he thought about their loss. Both partners became better able to draw on each other for comfort around this tragedy. However, in other areas of their relationship and in his own personal life, David remained paralyzed by feelings of inadequacy. His passivity antagonized Karen, who felt increasingly desperate for David to rescue her from her own depression. Their marital tensions diminished as the therapist helped each of them to confront individual and relational challenges—David in managing responsibilities of a new teaching position; Karen in adjusting her work demands and finding more reliable child care for Daniel; and the couple in blocking out one evening each week to engage in an activity outside their home and another evening for discussing mutual aspirations and low-conflict concerns.

Similar to most couples entering therapy, Karen and David each demonstrated deficiencies in their communication skills. David's skill deficits revolved primarily around difficulties in emotional expressiveness and in processing and then paraphrasing feelings that Karen disclosed. In part because of emotional detachment in his family growing up, he lacked an ability to recognize and label his own inner experiences—and this deficiency hindered his ability to understand Karen's feelings and to convey this understanding verbally. Although emotionally more astute, Karen frequently felt overwhelmed by her own distress; her desperate needs for soothing often escalated to a demandingness that precluded the very comfort from David that she sought. Learning to regulate her own affect more effectively and to approach David in a less confrontive manner allowed him enough security to risk more emotional engagement from his end. Although their contrasting emotional styles persisted, their differences lessened and their degree of polarization and accompanying antagonism diminished.

However, despite their successful bereavement and the diminishing of their chronic antagonism and alienation, David and Karen remained vulnerable to episodic outbursts of conflict and withdrawal. Karen continued to feel frustrated by David's lack of initiative in pursuing greater emotional intimacy through protracted discussions, and she attributed his reticence to a lack of caring and passion. The loneliness she experienced in their marriage sometimes felt intolerable, and she acknowledged difficulty in understanding David's comfort with emotional separation as well as confusion about the intensity of her own feelings. David struggled with Karen's vision of intimacy. His own concept of intimacy involved images of relaxed comfort with a partner, unspoken but implicit understandings of one another, and most importantly an uncritical acceptance of the other and an embracing of differences in interpersonal style.

Examining their differences in assumptions and expectancies about relationship intimacy helped Karen and David to label their differences in a less personalized, less blaming manner. Adopting an alternative attributional framework that emphasized cognitive processes rather than deficits in caring or commitment to their marriage helped to reduce the hurt that accompanied their frustrations. However, both Karen and David found it difficult to translate this understanding of their differences in relationship assumptions and standards into accommodations that reduced these differences or the tensions accompanying them. As therapy progressed, it became increasingly evident that both partners' tenacious efforts to persuade the other to adopt their own vision of intimacy, and the deep hurt each experienced when their differences persisted, reflected deeper relationship needs and anxieties they had not been able to identify or resolve.

That became the moment to integrate insight-oriented techniques into their couple therapy.

PRINCIPLES OF INSIGHT-ORIENTED COUPLE THERAPY

Theoretical Assumptions

There is not one approach to insight-oriented couple therapy, but many. Theoretical approaches emphasizing affective and developmental components of couples' distress emphasize recurrent maladaptive relationship patterns that derive from early interpersonal experiences either in the family of origin or within other significant emotional relationships (Meissner, 1978; Nadelson & Paolino, 1978). Diverse approaches to examining maladaptive relationship patterns can be placed on a continuum from traditional psychoanalytic techniques rooted primarily in object relations theory to schema-based interventions derived from more traditional cognitive theory (see Fig. 12.2). These approaches vary in the extent to which they emphasize the unconscious nature of individuals' relational patterns, the developmental period during which these maladaptive patterns are acquired, and the extent to which interpersonal anxieties derive from frustration of innate drives. However, these approaches all share the assumption that maladaptive relationship patterns are likely to continue until they are understood in a developmental context. This new understanding and explo-

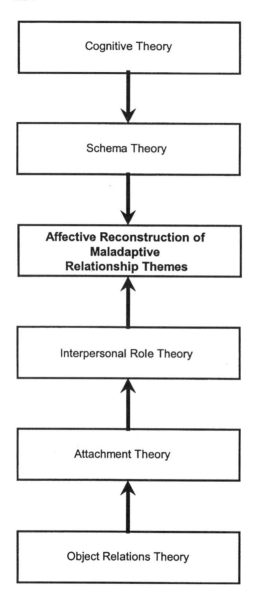

FIG. 12.2. Theoretical approaches emphasizing affective and developmental components of couples' distress.

ration serves to reduce the couple's attendant anxiety in current relationships and permits them to develop alternative, healthier relationship patterns.

Object Relations Theory. Traditional object relations theorists (Fairbairn, 1952; Klein, 1950) argue that the primary drive in infants is to secure attachment to the mother. From interactions primarily with the mother, they develop internalized images of the self, images of significant others, and sets of transactions connecting these images or objects. From an object relations perspective, maladaptive relationship patterns of adults reflect enduring pathogenic introjects that give rise to inevitable frustration when these are projected onto relationships with significant others (Scharff, 1995). In a distressed marriage, partners' pathogenic introjects interact in an unconscious, complementary manner resulting in repeated disappointments culminating in persistent conflict (Dicks, 1967). Consequently, the goal of psychoanalytically oriented marital therapy is helping partners to modify each other's projections, to distinguish these from objective aspects of their own self, and to assume ownership of their own projections.

Attachment Theory. Evolving from object relations theory, attachment theory (Bowlby, 1969) emphasizes the importance of emotional closeness to others as an innate survival function from which infants develop information-processing capabilities and emotional responses intended to foster secure emotional bonds. From an attachment perspective, difficulties in intimate adult relationships may be viewed as stemming from underlying insecure or anxious models of attachment. Partners' dominant emotional experiences drive reciprocal feedback loops maintaining such behaviors as excessive clinging or avoidance (Johnson & Whiffen, 1999). The goal of emotion-focused couple therapy (EFT; Johnson & Greenberg, 1995), reformulated from an attachment theory perspective, is to help partners gain access to their history of attachment experiences stored in schematic memory and to use this information in moving toward more accurate working models of self and partner. Johnson and Greenberg (1995) describe EFT as "one of the few psychodynamic approaches to marital therapy that has been empirically validated" (p. 121).

Interpersonal Role Theory. Interpersonal role theory (Anchin & Kiesler, 1982) regards the persistence of maladaptive interpersonal patterns as resulting from their reinforcement by the responses of significant others. This emphasis involves an important shift from the initial internal object relations giving rise to these patterns to the current interpersonal exchanges perpetuating them. The concept of role complementarity derived from interpersonal theory accounts for some of the same phenomena addressed by early object relation theorists but in a language more closely linked to current events and at a lower level of abstraction. Thus, rather than stressing constructs of projective and introjective identification, interpersonal theory emphasizes the unconscious assignment of specific roles to oneself and others ". . . in which feared and anticipated relational events tend to be elicited and enacted by the individual in his or her interactions with others, who, in turn, will tend to respond in ways complementary to the interpersonal actions of that individual" (Messer & Warren, 1995, p. 120).

Schema Theory. Schema theory (Horowitz, 1988; Young, 1994) emphasizes relationship schemas extending beyond attachment to the mother (object relations theory) or significant others (attachment theory) to consider more generally how early relationship experiences influence adult intimate relationships. For example, Young (1994) conceptualizes early maladaptive schemas as enduring themes initially developed in childhood that serve as a set of expectancies or "template" for processing interactions of oneself with the environment. The greater the conflict between the desired and the anticipated or feared interpersonal state, the more rigid and maladaptive the scripted expression of those expectancies is likely to be. Young conceptualizes his work as an extension of cognitive therapy, but his model overlaps considerably with psychodynamic relational models in its: (a) emphasis on interpretation of interpersonal exchanges within the therapy session as a vehicle for change; (b) attention to affect during the processing of schema-related events; and (c) emphasis on the childhood origins of maladaptive schemas and the emotional reformulation or reworking of these early experiences.

Affective Reconstruction of Maladaptive Relationship Themes. Drawing on earlier psychodynamic formulations, Snyder and Wills (1989) examined the efficacy of an insight-oriented approach to couple therapy emphasizing affective reconstruction of previous relationship injuries resulting in sustained interpersonal vulnerabilities and related defensive strategies interfering with emotional intimacy. In affective reconstruction, developmental origins of interpersonal themes and their manifestation in a couple's relationship are explored using techniques roughly akin to traditional interpretive strategies promoting insight but emphasizing interpersonal schemas and relationship dispositions rather than instinctual impulses or drive derivatives (Snyder, 1999a). Previous relationships, their affective components, and strategies for emotional gratification and anxiety containment are reconstructed with a focus on identifying for each partner consistencies in their interpersonal conflicts and coping styles across relationships. In addition, ways in which previous coping strategies vital to prior relationships represent distortions or inappropriate solutions for emotional intimacy and satisfaction in the current relationship are articulated.

Snyder and Wills (1989) compared their insight-oriented approach to couple therapy with a traditional behavioral approach emphasizing communication skills training and behavior exchange techniques. At termination after approximately 20 sessions, couples in both treatment modalities showed statistically and clinically significant gains in relationship satisfaction compared to a wait-list control group. However, at 4 years following treatment, 38% of the behavioral couples had experienced divorce, in contrast to only 3% of couples treated in the insight-oriented condition (Snyder, Wills, & Grady-Fletcher, 1991a). Based on these findings, Snyder and colleagues argued that spouses' negative views toward their partner's behavior "are modified to a greater degree and in a more persistent manner once individuals come to understand and resolve emotional conflicts they bring to the marriage from their own family and relationship histories" (Snyder, Wills, & Grady-Fletcher, 1991b, p. 148).

Common Tenets. Each of the relational models described here emphasizing developmental components to individuals' maladaptive relationship themes has special relevance to couple therapy. First, in couple therapy data reflecting current expression of persistent dysfunctional patterns of interpersonal relating are not confined to the individual's interactions with the therapist but extend more visibly and importantly to in vivo observations of the individual and his or her significant other. Thus, core conflictual relationship themes having greatest relevance to each partner are more likely to be apparent than in the context of individual therapy. Second, individuals' understanding of maladaptive relationship themes and their reformulation of these in less pejorative terms may extend beyond their own dynamics to a more benevolent reinterpretation of their partners' more hurtful behaviors. That is, both individuals can be helped to understand that, whereas certain relational coping strategies may have been adaptive or even essential in previous relationships, the same interpersonal strategies interfere with emotional intimacy and satisfaction in the present relationship. Finally, in couple therapy the "corrective emotional experience" (Alexander, 1956) of disrupting previous pathogenic interpersonal strategies and promoting more functional relational patterns has an opportunity to emerge not only between the individual and therapist, but between the individual and his or her partner. Thus, interpretation of maladaptive interpersonal themes in the context of couple therapy affords unique opportunities for affective reconstruction of these patterns in individuals' primary emotional relationships.

Therapeutic Techniques

For interpretation of maladaptive relationship themes to be effective with couples, the therapist needs to attend carefully to both partners' preparedness to examine their own enduring relational dispositions. Distressed couples often suffer from a long history of exchanging pejorative attributions for each other's behaviors, furthering their initial resistance to clinical interventions emphasizing early maladaptive schemas underlying relationship distress. The sequential model presented earlier conceptualizes examination of developmental sources of relationship distress as a higher-level intervention more typically undertaken during the latter stages of couple therapy—building on previous interventions establishing a foundation of emotional safety, partners' trust in the therapeutic process, the couple's ability to respond empathically to feelings of vulnerability exposed by their partner, and an introspective stance initially prompted by examining dysfunctional relationship expectancies and attributions residing at a more conscious level.

For affective reconstruction to be effective, both partners must be open to examining current relational difficulties from a developmental perspective. Both should exhibit some capacity for introspection, be open to examining feelings, and be able to resurrect affective experiences from previous relationships on a conscious level. Each partner needs to have established a basic level of trust with the therapist, experiencing the exploration of cyclical maladaptive patterns as promoting the individual's own relationship fulfillment. Moreover, both individuals need to exhibit both a level of personal maturity and relationship commitment that enables them to respond to their partner's intimate disclosures with empathy and support, rather than seizing details of previous relationships as new and more potent ammunition in a mutual blaming process.

Identifying Core Relationship Themes. An essential prerequisite to affective reconstruction of relational themes is a thorough knowledge of each partner's relational history. Critical information includes not only the pattern of relationships within the family of origin but also relational themes in the family extending to prior generations. Beyond the family, intimate relationships with significant others of both genders from adolescence through the current time offer key information regarding such issues as perceived acceptance and valuation by others, trust and disappointment, stability and resilience of relationships to interpersonal injury, levels of attachment and respect for autonomy, and similar relational themes. Some of this information may be gleaned from earlier interventions linked to establishing appropriate boundaries with families of origin, discussion of partners' expectancies regarding parenting responsibilities acquired during their own childhood and adolescence, or disclosures of traumatic experiences with significant others previous to the current relationship.

Initially, previous relationships are explored without explicit linkage to current relational difficulties, to reduce anxiety and resistance during this exploration phase. Often, individuals are readily able to formulate connections between prior relationships and current interpersonal struggles; when this occurs, it is typically useful for the therapist to listen empathically, encouraging the individual to remain "intently curious" about their own relational history but to refrain from premature interpretations that may be either incorrect, incomplete, or excessively self-critical. Just as important is for the individual's partner to adopt an accepting, empathic tone during the other's developmental exploration, encouraging self-disclosure in a supportive but noninterpretive manner.

Provided with relevant developmental history, the therapist encourages each partner to identify significant relational themes, particularly with respect to previous relationship disappointments and injuries. Gradually, as the couple continues to explore tensions and unsatisfying patterns in their own relationship, both partners can be encouraged to examine ways in which exaggerated emotional responses to current situations have at least partial basis in affective dispositions and related coping styles acquired in the developmental context. Developing a shared formulation of core relationship themes is a critical antecedent to subsequent linkage of these themes to current relationship exchanges. Both individuals can be helped to understand that, whereas certain relational coping strategies may have been adaptive or even essential in previous relationships, the same interpersonal strategies interfere with emotional intimacy and satisfaction in the present relationship.

Linking Relationship Themes to Current Conflict. In couple therapy, the therapist's direct access to exchanges between partners affords a unique opportunity for linking enduring relationship themes to current relationship events. Rather than interpreting transferential exchanges between either partner and the therapist, the focus is on partners' own exchanges in the immediate moment. Interpretations emphasize linkage of each partner's exaggerated affect and maladaptive responses to his or her own relationship history, emphasizing the repetition of relationship patterns and their maintaining factors in the present context. Guidelines for examining cyclical maladaptive patterns in the context of individual therapy (Binder & Strupp, 1991; Luborsky, 1984) readily lend themselves to couples work. How does the immediate conflict between partners relate to core relationship themes explored earlier in the therapy? What are each person's feelings toward the other and their desired response? What impact do they wish to have on the other in this moment? How do their perceptions regarding their partner's inner experience relate to their attitudes toward themselves? What fantasies do they have regarding their partner's possible responses? What kinds of responses from their partner would they anticipate being helpful in modifying their core beliefs about their partner, themselves, and this relationship?

It is essential that the therapist recognize each partner's core relationship themes, that developmental interpretations link relational themes to a current relationship conflict, and that therapy focus on a few select relationship themes until some degree of resolution and alternative interpersonal strategies are enabled. It is also important that the extent and complexity of interpretations take into account: (a) the affective functioning of the individual and his or her ability to make constructive use of the interpretation, (b) the level of insight and how near the individual is to being aware of the content of the proposed interpretation, and (c) the level of relationship functioning and the extent to which developmental interpretations can be incorporated in a mutually supportive manner.

From a psychodynamic perspective, cognitive linkage of relational themes from early development to the current context is frequently insufficient for reconstructing or modifying these interpersonal patterns. The affective component of interpretation is seen in the reconstruction of these critical emotional experiences in the immediate context; new understanding by both partners often promotes more empathic responses toward both themselves and the other, facilitating more satisfactory resolutions to conflict. Often, the individuals must be encouraged to work through previous relationship injuries, grieving losses and unmet needs, expressing ambivalence or anger toward previous critical others in the safety of the conjoint therapy, and acquiring increased differentiation of prior relationships from the present one. Similar to individual therapy adopting a relational model, the therapist serves as an "auxiliary processor" helping to "detoxify, manage, and digest" the partners' relationship themes in a manner that promotes interpersonal growth (Messer & Warren, 1995, p. 141).

Promoting Alternative Relationship Behaviors. From a relational model perspective, affective reconstruction makes possible but does not inevitably lead to changes in maladaptive relationship patterns. In addition to interpretive strategies, interventions must promote spousal interactions that counteract early maladaptive schemas. Thus, the couple therapist allows partners' maladaptive patterns to be enacted within limits, but then assists both partners in examining exaggerated affective components of their present exchange. Partners' exaggerated responses are framed as acquired coping strategies that interfere with higher relationship values. Interpretations of the developmental context underlying the current unsatisfactory exchange help both partners to depersonalize the noxious effects of the other's behavior, to feel less wounded, and consequently to be less reactive in a reciprocally negative manner.

Both individuals are encouraged to be less anxious and less condemning of both their own and their partner's affect and are helped to explore and then express their own affect in less aggressive or antagonistic fashion. Throughout this process, each individual plays a critical therapeutic role by learning to offer a secure context in facilitating their partner's affective self-disclosures in a softened, more vulnerable manner. The couple therapist models empathic understanding for both partners and encourages new patterns of responding that enhance relationship intimacy. That is, by facilitating the nonoccurrence of expected traumatic experiences in the couple's relationship, both individuals are able to challenge assumptions and expectations comprising underlying maladaptive schemas. Thus, therapeutic change results from the experiential learning in which both partners encounter relationship outcomes different from those expected or feared. In response, partners' interactions become more adaptive and flexible in matching the objective reality of current conflicts and realizing opportunities for satisfying more of each other's needs.

Although affective reconstruction seeks to promote new relationship schemas facilitating more empathic and supportive interactions, couples sometimes need additional assistance in restructuring longstanding patterns of relating outside of therapy. In the pluralistic hierarchical model for sequencing interventions advocated here, couples already will have been exposed to communication and behavior-exchange techniques characterizing traditional behavioral approaches. Consequently, alternative relationship behaviors can often be negotiated more readily after schema-related anxieties and resistance to changing enduring interaction patterns have been understood and at least partially resolved.

Therapeutic Impact

Affective reconstruction strives to bring about critical changes in how individuals view themselves, their partner, and their relationship. In examining recurrent maladaptive relationship themes, both partners gain increased understanding of their own emotional reactivity and exaggerated patterns of interacting that contribute to their own unhappiness. Increases in partners' self-understanding can lead to diminished confusion and anxiety about their own subjective relationship experiences. Moreover, insight into developmental influences contributing to current difficulties often facilitates an optimism regarding potential for self-change and restores hope for greater emotional fulfillment in the relationship. Affective reconstruction of maladaptive schemas promotes resolution of persistent dysfunctional relationship patterns through redirected cognitive and behavioral strategies.

When conducted in the context of couple therapy, affective reconstruction offers unique advantages over similar therapeutic strategies conducted with individuals. Specifically, as participant–observer in their partner's work on developmental issues, individuals frequently come to understand their partner's behaviors in a more accepting or benign manner—attributing damaging exchanges to the culmination of acquired interpersonal dispositions rather than to explicit motives to be hurtful. This new understanding often facilitates within-session exchanges challenging existing relationship schemas, reducing defensive behaviors, and promoting empathic and mutually supportive interactions.

CONCLUSIONS

How did Karen and David, the couple introduced at the beginning of this chapter, benefit from integrating insight-oriented techniques into their therapy? As Karen explored her early family relationships, she noted that her parents had divorced after many years of conflict during which her father had numerous affairs but her mother remained in the marriage "for the sake of the children." Although Karen had initially been very close to her father, his unhappiness in his marriage generalized into an emotional abusiveness toward the children as well. Because she had idealized her father, his subsequent abandonment and betrayal of his wife and daughters felt acutely painful. Karen had tried to reconcile with her father a few years earlier, but he rebuffed her efforts and predicted that Karen's marriage would end up as his own had.

Karen's relationship with her mother was similarly ambivalent. Karen's mother tried to repress and contain most of her unhappiness in life—her extreme disappointment and resentment in her marriage, her needs for affirmation from her children—but would episodically become verbally abusive and cruel toward her daughters. Karen and her sister were quite close and used each other as an emotional confidante. Karen became the "adult child" in her home—the vigilant, responsible, and caring one. She recalled both her mother and sister approaching her late at night and for hours disclosing their emotional struggles and seeking Karen's advice and support.

As couple therapy progressed, Karen recognized that she had developed a personal coping strategy of "toughening up," determined not to allow anyone to control her life and also vowing to express her frustrations and feelings as she experienced them. Although in the past this had served her well, it also contributed to a "bristly" presentation and rendered her less approachable by David, who was anxious and avoidant of conflict and feelings in general. Karen acknowledged her tremendous fear of being alone with her feelings and being abandoned by David, much as she was abandoned in part by her mother and more dramatically by her father. She was able to accept an interpretation that some of her hurt when David did not respond emotionally in the way that she wanted was related to the urgency of her emotional needs stemming from the abandonment she experienced growing up.

With time, Karen began to re-examine the criteria by which she judged David's behaviors as an expression of his caring, recognizing that these were so narrow and so rigid that she ended up dismissing or rejecting many of his efforts to please her or show her that he cared. She also became clearer about her unfinished emotional business in dealing with both her parents. About 6 months into the couple therapy, Karen engaged in some confrontive dialogue with her sister and mother regarding their early family life, and these discussions helped her to gain some emotional resolution to the deep relationship disappointments she had experienced growing up. Karen set clearer boundaries with her mother, and began to assume less responsibility for resolving her mother's emotional struggles during the week. Karen also worked through some of her anger toward her father, relinquished her fantasies that her father would express remorse and that they would ultimately reconcile, and more effectively limited his ability to intrude in Karen's marriage with his prophesies of its demise.

As David explored his own early relationship experiences, he recognized that emotional nonexpressiveness was the norm throughout both his parents' families for the last several generations. David began to describe his father not only as "unexpressive" but also as a critical man who disparaged and dismissed most of the ideas expressed by his wife and sons. David learned not to share his own thoughts or feelings because he did not want to expose them to judgment or ridicule. Now as an adult, when trying to express himself to Karen, he felt inarticulate and stupid—leading to defensive retreat.

Because his father was particularly cold and aloof, David came to rely exclusively on his mother for emotional closeness. However, he also recognized that he feared his mother's disappointment in him because she tended to withdraw from David and others when she felt let down. Throughout his adolescence, David recognized his parents' detachment and felt painfully responsible for his mother's emotional well-being. At the same time, he felt inadequate to the task of measuring up to either parent's expectations. He and his younger brother both adopted strategies to avoid failure, disapproval, or any level of conflict. David began to recognize that for much of his life he had set unrealistically high standards for himself and that he tried to avoid disappointing others by withdrawing before encountering failure. He also began to understand that this overt behavior was misinterpreted by others (including Karen) as reflecting a nonchalance when, in fact, his behavior was governed by masked anxiety.

With time, David was able to increase his engagement with Karen during times of emotional conflict. He began to appreciate that, although Karen's need for closeness at times felt similar to his mother's need for David's emotional support, it was David's retreat rather than any specific act of commission that triggered her disappointment and subsequent anger. He began to examine other ways in which he responded to Karen in ways similar to his mother—for example, worrying about her reaction if he anticipated getting home late and thus not calling her in advance. Gradually, he developed a higher tolerance for talking with Karen when she was upset. As Karen developed greater trust in David's willingness to engage in discussions, her own distress and use of anger as a means of engaging him diminished.

David also began to challenge assumptions conveyed by his father that everything in life needed to be done "correctly" and that anything less than perfection was unacceptable. A critical incident occurred during therapy when David's parents conveyed that he and Karen were expected to spend Thanksgiving with them when, instead, Karen had hoped they and Daniel would not travel but would relax at home with close friends. David chose this opportunity to appropriately assert his and Karen's needs to his parents, tolerate their disapproval, and affirm to Karen his commitment to supporting her needs. As therapy approached its conclusion, both partners reported experiencing greater understanding of themselves and each other, a stronger sense of commitment to their marriage, and less negative reactivity during times of external stress or relationship disagreements.

Karen's and David's gains in response to insight-oriented techniques are common among couples exposed to this approach. When individuals examine their own developmental sources of relationship distress they often experience diminished confusion and anxiety about their own emotional reactivity and restored hope for achieving harmony and intimacy in their relationship. Frequently, they are able to resolve or substantially modify longstanding conflicts and dysfunctional relationship patterns that, prior to affective reconstruction, had been resistant to cognitive and behavioral interventions. Moreover, by achieving a greater understanding of their partner's behaviors from a developmental perspective, individuals are more apt to achieve enhanced empathy for their partner's emotional distress, experience reduced defensiveness, and take advantage of opportunities to provide emotional and strategic support.

An important source of marital difficulties includes previous relationship injuries resulting in sustained interpersonal vulnerabilities and related defensive strategies interfering with emotional intimacy. Integrating insight-oriented techniques into a pluralistic approach to couple therapy affords partners a unique opportunity to free themselves from recurrent maladaptive relationship patterns and pursue the rich emotional rewards that intimate relationships offer.

REFERENCES

Alexander, F. (1956). *Psychoanalysis and psychotherapy.* New York: Norton.

Anchin, J. C., & Kiesler, D. J. (Eds.). (1982). *Handbook of interpersonal psychotherapy.* New York: Pergamon Press.

Binder, J. L., & Strupp, H. H. (1991). The Vanderbilt approach to time-limited dynamic psychotherapy. In P. Crits-Christoph & J. P. Barber (Eds.), *Handbook of short-term dynamic psychotherapy* (pp. 137–165). New York: Basic Books.

Bowlby, J. (1969). *Attachment and loss: Vol. 1. Attachment.* New York: Basic Books.

Dicks, H. V. (1967). *Marital tensions: Clinical studies towards a psycho-analytic theory of interaction.* London: Routledge & Kegan Paul.

Fairbairn, W. R. D. (1952). *Psychoanalytic studies of the personality.* London: Routledge & Kegan Paul.

Horowitz, M. (1988). *Introduction to psychodynamics: A new synthesis.* New York: Basic Books.

Johnson, S. M., & Greenberg, L. S. (1995). The emotionally focused approach to problems in adult attachment. In N. S. Jacobson & A. S. Gurman (Eds.), *Clinical handbook of couple therapy* (pp. 121–141). New York: Guilford Press.

Johnson, S. M., & Whiffen, V. E. (1999). Made to measure: Adapting emotionally focused couples therapy to partners' attachment styles. *Clinical Psychology: Science and Practice, 6,* 366–381.

Klein, M. (1950). *Contributions to psychoanalysis.* London: Hogarth.

Luborsky, L. (1984). *Principles of psychoanalytic psychotherapy: A manual for supportive–expressive treatment.* New York: Basic Books.

Meissner, W. W. (1978). The conceptualization of marriage and family dynamics from a psychoanalytic perspective. In T. J. Paolino & B. S. McCrady (Eds.), *Marriage and marital therapy: Psychoanalytic, behavioral, and systems theory perspectives* (pp. 25–88). New York: Brunner/Mazel.

Messer, S. B., & Warren, C. S. (1995). *Models of brief psychodynamic therapy: A comparative approach.* New York: Guilford Press.

Nadelson, C. C., & Paolino, T. J. (1978). Marital therapy from a psychoanalytic perspective. In T. J. Paolino & B. S. McCrady (Eds.), *Marriage and marital therapy: Psychoanalytic, behavioral, and systems theory perspectives* (pp. 89–164). New York: Brunner/Mazel.

Scharff, J. S. (1995). Psychoanalytic marital therapy. In N. S. Jacobson & A. S. Gurman (Eds.), *Clinical handbook of couple therapy* (pp. 164–193). New York: Guilford Press.

Snyder, D. K. (1999a). Affective reconstruction in the context of a pluralistic approach to couple therapy. *Clinical Psychology: Science and Practice, 6,* 348–365.

Snyder, D. K. (1999b). Pragmatic couple therapy: An informed pluralistic approach. In D. M. Lawson & F. F. Prevatt (Eds.), *Casebook in family therapy* (pp. 81–110). Pacific Grove, CA: Brooks/Cole.

Snyder, D. K., & Wills, R. M. (1989). Behavioral versus insight-oriented marital therapy: Effects on individual and interspousal functioning. *Journal of Consulting and Clinical Psychology, 57,* 39–46.

Snyder, D. K., Wills, R. M., & Grady-Fletcher, A. (1991a). Long-term effectiveness of behavioral versus insight-oriented marital therapy: A four-year follow-up study. *Journal of Consulting and Clinical Psychology, 59,* 138–141.

Snyder, D. K., Wills, R. M, & Grady-Fletcher, A. (1991b). Risks and challenges of long-term psychotherapy outcome research: Reply to Jacobson. *Journal of Consulting and Clinical Psychology, 59,* 146–149.

Young, J. E. (1994). *Cognitive therapy for personality disorders: A schema-focused approach* (rev. ed.). Sarasota, FL: Professional Resource Press.

13

Forgiveness: Toward a Public Health Approach to Intervention

Frank D. Fincham
The State University of New York at Buffalo

Steven R. H. Beach
University of Georgia

There are few certainties in life. But one certainty is that romantic partners are not perfect despite our tendency to idealize them (e.g., Murray, Holmes, & Griffith, 1996); it is a rare person who does not, at some point, feel hurt, let down, betrayed, disappointed, or wronged by his or her relationship partner. Such events have the potential to corrode, disrupt, and even end relationships. Understanding how partners react to them is therefore fundamental to understanding how relationships are maintained. Romantic relationships may also provide a context for devastating emotional wounds that may initially seem to be beyond repair. Such wounds either end the relationship, change it forever, or are overcome through processes that remain little discussed by marital researchers. How is it that some partners are able to overcome hurt prompted by a negative partner behavior and resume positive interactions whereas others remain hurt and engaged in negative interactions or even avoidance of the partner?

Psychologists have paid considerable attention to negative, potentially destructive behavior in relationships, particularly their role in relationship dysfunction. For example, it is well established that negative reciprocity (increased likelihood of negative behavior following negative behavior by the partner) and negative reactivity (suppression of positive behaviors below base rates following negative behavior by the partner) characterize distressed relationships (e.g., Margolin & Wampold, 1981). Likewise, we know that inhibiting the tendency to respond negatively to a partner's bad behavior and responding constructively instead, a process called *accommodation*, is related to relationship commitment, greater interdependence between persons, and having plentiful time, rather than a limited time, to respond (e.g., Rusbult, Verette, Whitney, Slovik, & Lipkus, 1991; Yovetich & Rusbult, 1994). The proximal determinants of accommodative behavior are perceived "reasons for the event" (e.g., Rusbult, Yovetich & Verette, 1996, p. 79), a finding consistent with growing evidence that explanations for relationship events predict partner responses to the events (for a review, see Fincham, in press). Thus, we have a growing literature that ties together negative relationship events, explanations for those events, and reactions to the events.

Although important, such findings provide only a partial understanding of how relationships are maintained in the face of negative partner behavior, and they seem particularly inadequate to explain reactions to serious relationship transgressions. Consider the case of an extramarital affair where the perceived reason for the affair is the adulterous spouse's selfish focus on their own immediate wishes. Assuming equal levels of commitment, what happens in one marriage that allows the betrayed partner to overcome his or her anger and resentment and behave in a conciliatory manner towards the spouse whereas in another marriage the relationship remains tense for years? As they remain constant in this example, neither the major relationship macromotive (commitment) nor the proximal determinant (reasons for the event) identified in research on accommodation can help in providing an answer. This example highlights the need for a new category of relationship process that may follow the transgression and the initial hurt engendered by it, but that may also influence the aftermath of the event. We examine forgiveness as one process that may be useful in distinguishing between couples with different outcomes

Although it is a complex construct without a consensual definition, at the center of various approaches to forgiveness is the idea of a motivational transformation toward a transgressor in which motivation to avoid or retaliate against the transgressor is relinquished. Forgiveness therefore sets the stage for possible reconciliation with the transgressor, suggesting that it may have substantial implications for long-term relationship outcomes as well as short-term patterns of interaction.[1] At the same time, forgiveness has the potential to provide closure with regard to a painful or disturbing relationship event and so may have substantial implications for individual well-being and health, as well as implications for other family subsystems.

---

[1]It is critical to distinguish the achievement of relationship reconciliation from the granting of forgiveness. Reconciliation, or the re-establishment of trust between partners, is an *interpersonal* process in which the behavior of both parties is necessary for its accomplishment, whereas forgiveness is an *intrapersonal* process that focuses on the interpersonal but in which only the behavior of the forgiver is necessary for its accomplishment (relinquishing of motivation to avoid or retaliate). In short, forgiveness is important for understanding relationship maintenance because it can provide a platform for reconciliation between partners.

This chapter therefore examines the potential importance of forgiveness in close relationships and is divided into two major sections. In the first, we examine objections to forgiveness before reviewing evidence suggesting that it might have beneficial direct and indirect relationship effects. In view of such effects, we briefly summarize research on how forgiveness can be facilitated. This serves as a springboard for the second section in which we argue that existing methods used in forgiveness intervention research cannot address the public health problem posed by transgressions in close relationships. We therefore suggest that an alternative approach is required and outline a new way of addressing the public health problem that can be delivered on the scale that is needed. The chapter concludes by summarizing major arguments and identifying future challenges.

FORGIVENESS IN CLOSE RELATIONSHIPS

Forgiveness is widely accepted as a positive event. However, it is important to consider potential negative connotations to forgiveness that may either provide obstacles to forgiveness or alert us to negative outcomes that could occur if forgiveness were advocated in a careless manner. Therefore, we begin our discussion by considering explicitly several important objections to forgiveness, each of which presents a way in which forgiveness could be seen as harmful.

Forgiving Is Harmful

Forgiving Is Weak. Nietzsche (1921) argued that forgiveness is a sign of weakness and, from this perspective, may have adverse implications for the self. Likewise, many who might otherwise contemplate forgiving a partner might be held back by the potential implication that to do so would be an admission of their own weakness. Accordingly, the perception that forgiveness is a "weak" response may be a significant impediment to forgiveness in close relationships. In considering how to counter the charge that forgiveness is a sign of weakness, it is critical to note that forgiveness requires the victim to acknowledge adverse treatment that entitles him or her to justifiably feel negatively towards the transgressor who, in turn, has no right to expect the victim's empathy. Forgiveness thus requires the strength to assert a right, the right to better treatment than that shown by the transgressor. Absent such assertion, conciliatory actions can reflect factors such as condoning of the transgressor's behavior, a strategic ploy, a desire to appease the transgressor, and so on. Accordingly, some behaviors that may be labeled "forgiveness" might need to be distinguished from "true forgiveness" if we are to avoid confirming the perception that forgiveness is for the weak. Conciliation in the absence of affirming one's right to better treatment may indeed reflect weakness but this should not be confused with forgiveness. In addition to asserting one's claim to a position of moral authority vis-à-vis the transgressor, forgiveness requires the strength to relinquish this position of moral authority and release the transgressor from the debt they incurred by the transgression. As anyone who has attempted to forgive knows, forgiving is not an easy option but is instead extraordinarily difficult because it involves working through, not avoiding, emotional pain.

Forgiving Creates Danger. It can be argued that forgiving creates danger in two ways. First, it prevents people from experiencing appropriate anger and pain and thereby robs them of the motivation to communicate overtly to others that they do not tolerate or find acceptable transgressions against them. From this viewpoint, forgiveness may prevent honest communication and many persons may feel reluctant to forgive because it does not feel "honest" to do so. Indeed, "instant" forgiveness for transgressions may not be beneficial for either victim or transgressor as it may not reflect an honest attempt to move past the hurt. However, as noted before, forgiveness does not preclude experiencing anger and communicating one's right to better treatment. Second, it can be argued that forgiving exposes one to potential revictimization. Many persons report reluctance to forgive precisely because they feel the perpetrator needs to be dissuaded from engaging in the behavior again. But exposure to revictimization is not a necessary part of forgiving. There is nothing inconsistent with forgiving a transgression and, at the same time, taking reasonable measures to prevent a reoccurrence of the transgression, including breaking off all contact with the transgressor if it is prudent to do so. Likewise there is nothing inconsistent about forgiving a transgression while clearly asserting the expectation of better treatment and that a recurrence of the transgression will not be tolerated. To the extent that forgiveness leads to a restored relationship it may be seen as setting the stage for revictimization, but revictimization in romantic relationships can occur, and may be more likely to occur, while the partners are disengaged.

Forgiving Creates Injustice and Inequity. It can be argued that forgiving subverts the course of justice and that when forgiveness occurs, justice is not served. In the aftermath of a transgression, it is commonplace for victims to experience a "moral injury" in the sense that their beliefs about what is right and wrong have been assailed. This experience may lead to a strong desire to set the scale of justice back in balance through some process of retribution or some consequences for the transgresssion. Such consequences (e.g., appropriate punishment, compensation) might be justified on numerous grounds such as a necessary corrective to shape future behavior, to protect others from danger, and so on. Importantly, natural consequences of destructive behavior are not precluded by forgiveness, even when these are the behavioral reactions of the victim. For example, there is no particular reason to expect "trust" to re-emerge quickly in the aftermath of a relationship transgression even if forgiveness has occurred. It has also been argued that forgiveness creates inequity in a relationship. Kelln and Ellard (1999) assert that forgiveness is an unsolicited gift that creates "inequity distress" because a transgressor motivated to relieve his or her guilt can no longer simply compensate the victim but must reciprocate the forgiveness. In a laboratory study, they showed that transgressors were more likely to comply with a requested favor following forgiveness than retribution, both forgiveness and retribution, and a control condition in which neither occurred. As the interdependence in close relationships can be viewed in terms of high "indebtedness" between partners, inequity distress is unlikely to be significant in this context.

Some Events Should Not Be Forgiven

It can be argued that some events should not lead to forgiveness (e.g., rape, severe domestic violence). When not based on the earlier discussed objections to forgiveness, this view is predicated on moral assumptions about behavior and about forgiveness as a moral act. A variant of this view is that humans should not concern themselves with forgiveness as only God can forgive. Once the moral and religious assumptions supporting this viewpoint are adopted, the viewpoint can be compelling. In principle, however, an individual can choose to forgive any transgression. In general, more severe transgressions are harder to forgive and some acts are so heinous that it can be hard to imagine how a victim can forgive them, yet there are documented, compelling examples of forgiveness for such terrible acts (e.g., the murder of a child, see Jaeger, 1998). In addition, the potential positive consequences of forgiveness for the self may pertain even in cases of severe transgressions.

Coda. The arguments offered so far are theoretical and do not preclude forgiveness having a downside in regard to actual, lay conceptions of the construct. For example, some people may link strongly, or even equate, forgiveness and reconciliation and may therefore, by virtue of forgiving someone, place themselves in danger of future harm. This possibility is consistent with the results of a recent study. Katz, Street, and Arias (1997) found that women who forgave a dating partner for hypothetical episodes of relationship violence decreased the stated likelihood that they would leave the relationship. One implication is that therapeutic attempts to facilitate forgiveness should include an educational component to ensure that participants understand fully what forgiveness does and does not entail. It may also be necessary to assess perceived negative consequences of forgiving the partner before we attempt to encourage forgiveness. At the same time, any discussion of facilitating forgiveness is predicated on the assumption that forgiveness is valuable for the individual or the relationship. Before turning to existing literature on intervention, therefore, we first examine whether forgiveness is associated with positive relationship outcomes.

Forgiveness Improves Relationships Indirectly by Promoting Individual Well-being

Physical Health. The belief that forgiveness can improve physical health is found in religious writings and in the recommendations of some health professionals (see Thoresen, Harris, & Luskin, 2000). This link appears to be an intuitive one; forgiveness results in decreased hostility, and there is documented evidence that chronic hostility is associated with adverse health outcomes (Miller, Smith, Turner, Guijarro & Hallet, 1996). In a similar vein, forgiveness can facilitate the repair of supportive close relationships and such relationships are known to protect against negative health outcomes. For example, marital conflict is associated with poorer health (Burman & Margolin, 1992; Kiecolt-Glazer et al., 1988) and with specific illnesses such as cancer, cardiac disease, and chronic pain (see Schmaling & Sher 1997), and hostile behaviors during conflict relate to alterations in immunological (Kiecolt-Glaser et al., 1997), endocrine (Kiecolt-Glaser, Glaser, et al., 1997; Malarkey, Kiecolt-Glaser, Pearl, & Glaser, 1994), and cardiovascular (Ewart, Taylor, Kraemer, & Agras, 1991) functioning. Nonetheless, the *direct* evidence linking forgiveness and physical health is limited to anecdotal accounts and a few cross-sectional correlations. At the present time, "no controlled studies have demonstrated that forgiveness affects physical health" (Thoresen, Harris, & Luskin, 2000, p. 254). Absence of evidence, however, is not evidence of absence and laboratory research supports theoretical linkages between forgiveness and physical health. Specifically, vanOyen Vitvliet and Ludwig (1999) show that engaging in forgiving imagery (empathizing with the offender, granting forgiveness), relative to unforgiving imagery (rehearsing hurts, nursing grudges), decreased physiological indicators of stress (heart rate, blood pressure, and skin conductance). It is quite possible therefore that, over the long-term, forgiveness protects against stress-related health problems.

Mental Health. vanOyen Vitvliet and Ludwig (1999) also showed a link between forgiveness imagery and emotional responses, namely, reported anger and sadness. This finding is consistent with correlational research linking forgiveness and psychological symptoms. For example, Tangey, Fee, and Lee (1999) found a negative relation between a dispositional tendency to forgive others and depressive symptoms and hostility; forgiving oneself as a transgressor was also inversely related to depressive symptoms and positively related to overall psychological adjustment. Symptoms of anxiety, depression, and anger have also been shown to decline following a forgiveness intervention (e.g., Freedman & Enright, 1996). Likewise, to the extent that forgiveness helps enhance relationship quality, it may be associated with improved mental health because of links between overall relationship quality and mental heath. For example, the link between relationship quality and depression is increasingly well established (see Beach, Fincham, & Katz, 1998) and a link with eating disorders has been documented (see Van den Broucke, Vandereycken, & Norre, 1997). Similarly, associations have been noted for physical and psychological abuse of partners (e.g., O'Leary, Malone, & Tyree, 1994), male alcoholism (e.g., O'Farrell et al., 1991) and early onset drinking, episodic drinking, binge drinking, and out-of-home drinking (see Murphy & O'Farrell, 1994). These findings are promising, but again compelling, direct evidence documenting a causal link between forgiveness and mental health is lacking. It would therefore be premature to conclude that forgiveness improves individual well-being. Nonetheless, recognition of the negative physical and mental health outcomes associated with processes that can occur in the absence of forgiving (e.g., preoccupation with blame, rumination) appears to sustain theoretical attempts to identify processes linking forgiveness and physical and mental health. This effort is also supported by findings linking forgiveness and relationship well-being, a topic to which we now turn.

Forgiveness Improves Relationships Directly

Basic Research. Indirect evidence regarding the importance of forgiveness for relationships abounds. For example, experiencing resentment and hurt towards one's partner is probably incompatible with feeling supported by him or her. Lack of support is associated with lower relationship satisfaction and supportive close relationships, in turn, are known to protect against negative health outcomes (though it is not clear whether this happens directly or indirectly through relationship satisfaction; Cutrona, 1996). It is equally hard to imagine resentment or anger towards the partner as engendering feelings of intimacy or producing the beneficial effects that flow from being in an intimate relationship.

Yet, there is direct evidence on the importance of forgiveness in close relationships. Initial evidence shows that forgiveness is related to relationship well-being. For example, McCullough, Rachal, Sandage, Worthington, Brown, and Hight (1998) found that a composite measure of relationship commitment and satisfaction was negatively related to reported avoidance and revenge following a recent hurt and the worst relationship hurt as identified by participants in a romantic relationship. Fincham (2000) also found that forgiveness and marital satisfaction were related and went on to show that forgiveness accounted for variance that was independent of marital satisfaction in predicting overall behavior towards the partner and in reported retaliatory and conciliatory responses to a partner transgression. Moreover, forgiveness fully mediated the relationship between responsibility attributions for partner behavior and reported behavior towards the partner. Importantly, McCullough, Rachal, Sandage, et al. (1998) show that pre- and posttransgression closeness are related, in part, through forgiveness. Worthington (1998), presenting a regression analysis of the same data, shows that forgiveness accounts for variance in current relationship closeness after relationship length, pretransgression closeness, characteristics of the hurt (impact and depth) and events since hurt (apology and time since transgression) are entered into the regression equation. Thus, forgiving does appear to promote reconciliation (closeness). Complementing these findings is the fact that partners themselves acknowledge that the capacity to seek and grant forgiveness is one of the most important factors contributing to marital longevity and satisfaction (Fenell, 1993).

Documenting the association between forgiveness and relationship satisfaction and relationship behavior is an important, preliminary step in showing that forgiveness improves relationships. However, longitudinal data that speak directly to this causal assumption are not yet available. In the interim, we can turn to research on forgiveness interventions for relevant data provided we recognize that any causal relation discovered is not necessarily characteristic of what happens in the normal course of events absent intervention.

Intervention Research. Intervention research also provides useful evidence regarding the effects of forgiveness on close relationships. Because such studies are often experimental in design, they are an important test of the hypothesis that facilitating forgiveness may cause benefits in romantic relationships rather than merely being associated with beneficial relationship outcomes. Since Close (1970) published a case study on forgiveness in counseling, various models of forgiving have emerged in the counseling and psychotherapy literature. However, with the exception of Enright's work (e.g., Enright & Coyle, 1998) the impact of these models on clinical practice has been questioned (McCullough & Worthington, 1994). Where there has been an impact, model builders have skipped the task of validating their models and proceeded directly to intervention outcome research (Malcolm & Greenberg, 2000). Perhaps more importantly, the psychotherapy literature has far outstripped empirical data on forgiveness, leaving us in the position of attempting to induce forgiveness without knowing a great deal about how forgiveness operates in everyday life or in close relationships.

Nonetheless, we examine the small body of data on forgiveness interventions that is beginning to emerge.

Of the 14 available studies, all but 2 (Coyle & Enright, 1997; Freedman & Enright, 1996) are group interventions. Worthington, Sandage, and Berry (2000) summarize these interventions (delivered to 393 participants) by showing that there is a linear dose–effect relationship for the effect sizes they yield. Specifically, clinically relevant interventions (defined as those of 6 or more hours duration) produced a change in forgiveness (effect size = .76) that is reliably different from zero, with nonclinically relevant interventions (defined as 1 or 2 hours' duration) yielding a small but measurable change in forgiveness (effect size = .24). These authors tentatively conclude, "that amount of time thinking about forgiveness is important in the amount of forgiveness a person can experience" (Worthington, Sandage & Berry, 2000, p. 234). Because effect size and proportion of males in the study were negatively related, they also conclude that men are more "substantially at risk for holding onto unforgiveness than are women" (p. 241). Finally, they note that one study produced a negative effect (Al-Mubak, Enright, & Cardis, 1995, Study 1) that is most likely due to participants being given time to think about their hurt without being induced to think about forgiveness.

The analysis summarized here demonstrates that we have made good progress in devising interventions to induce forgiveness, but this is analogous to focusing on a manipulation check in experimental research. What about the dependent variable; does inducing forgiveness produce positive psychological outcomes? Here, results are more mixed. For example, Hebl and Enright (1993) showed that their forgiveness intervention produced significantly greater forgiveness in elderly females than a placebo control group but that both groups showed significant decreases in symptoms of anxiety and depression. In contrast, Al-Mubak et al. (1995) found that, relative to a placebo control group, their forgiveness intervention produced significant increases in forgiveness and hope and a significant decrease in trait anxiety among college students emotionally hurt by a parent. However, the groups did not differ in depressive symptoms following intervention. A problem with these, and many of the other available studies, is that the interventions are delivered to samples that are either asymptomatic or show limited variability in mental health symptoms, making it difficult to demonstrate intervention effects on these variables.

It is therefore encouraging that in an intervention study where participants (adults who had experienced sexual abuse as children) were screened to show psychological distress prior to the intervention (Freedman & Enright, 1996), the intervention produced significantly greater forgiveness, hope, and self-esteem and decreased anxiety and depression relative to a wait list control group. Intervention with the wait list control group showed a significant change for the group relative to the time the group had served as a control condition and made the group indistinguishable from the experimental group. These changes were maintained over a 12-month period.

Summary and Critique. Systematic data are emerging to supplement clinical insights (see Fitzgibbons, 1986) and phenomenological studies of forgiveness (Rowe, Halling, Davies, Leifer, Powers, Van Bronkhorst, 1989). The demonstration of dose-dependent effects is encouraging even though it is mitigated somewhat by the heavy reliance on self-selected participants who do not exhibit clinically significant symptomatology. Because interventions are a relatively blunt experimental manipulation that may influence a number of variables, it will be important in future intervention studies to show that changes in forgiveness are correlated with changes in psychological well-being. Perhaps most importantly in the current context, intervention research has thus far focused on the individual experience of forgiving and not the interactions that occur around forgiveness. The result is that most intervention research tells us little about how to help couples negotiate forgiveness in their relationships (Worthington & Wade, 1999). This is an important omission because repentance and apology (phenomena that involve interpersonal transactions) facilitate forgiveness and because, in the context of a relationship, forgiveness may involve numerous transactions between partners.

The limitations of the available data are more understandable when one recalls that, less than a decade ago, pioneering publications did not contain reference to any published empirical research on forgiveness (e.g., Hebl & Enright, 1993; Mauger, Perry, Freeman, Grove, McBride, & McKinney, 1992). Clearly research on forgiveness is in its infancy and the jury is still out on the case for the importance of forgiveness in maintaining relationships and promoting relationship well-being. This is not to imply that the case lacks evidentiary support. However, we believe that the existing database is most consistent with a view of the problem addressed by forgiveness, and how forgiveness might be promoted, that is different to what is typically found in the literature. We therefore turn to consider how relationship transgressions that give rise to forgiveness can be conceptualized and addressed as a public health problem.

RELATIONSHIP TRANSGRESSIONS AS A PUBLIC HEALTH PROBLEM: THE WAY FORWARD

Relationship transgressions have a significant impact on public health. For example, more people seek professional help for relationship problems than for anything else (Veroff, Kulka, & Douvan, 1981). In a similar vein, it can be noted that while the divorce rate has stabilized in the 1980s and trended downwards since then, it is still high (4.4 per 1,000 population; National Center for Health Statistics, 1995). Not all of these events are due to the inability to come to terms with a relationship transgression but even if only a small proportion are, it would reflect a significant public health problem.

Perhaps this is best illustrated by considering a particular relationship transgression, the extramarital affair, an event that can severely rupture a marriage or even end it (Spring, 1996). A nationwide survey shows how ubiquitous such affairs might be. A sample of 3,432 respondents aged 18 to 59 years was asked: "Have you ever had sex with someone other than your husband or wife while you were married?" On average, 25% of men and 15% of women answered in the affirmative. However, 37% of men aged 50 to 59 years and 19.9% of women aged 40 to 49 years answered yes, suggesting that for lifetime prevalence the figures are higher. Considering the 20% refusal rate to answer the question, the figures may even be higher (Laumann, Gagnon, Michael, & Michaels, 1994). As these considerations make clear, many people will be touched by this serious breach of trust in their marriage as well as by other serious relationship transgressions. Given the potential for such events to precipitate serious mental health consequences (e.g., Cano & O'Leary, in press), the result is a widespread and important public health problem. Indeed, the magnitude of the problem is extensive enough to overwhelm traditional approaches to treatment delivery.

Our point is not to highlight the impact of extramarital affairs, serious though the effects may be. Rather, we hope to illustrate a simple point: Traditional counseling approaches cannot meet the public health challenge posed by this single relationship transgression. Assuming just 5% of marriages were impacted by an affair and required intervention, this would have yielded 2,799,950 cases at the time the survey was conducted. Assuming just 6 sessions of counseling, 13,550 therapists would be needed to work full-time (24 hours of weekly client contact at 50 weeks a year) on this issue alone. Even if these resources were made available, many couples would by default (e.g., lack of financial resources, availability of counselor in geographical area) or desire (one or both partners find counseling unacceptable) not benefit from them, and hence a different means of addressing this problem would be required. As these considerations suggest, we cannot rely on traditional models of therapeutic intervention alone if we are to address forgiveness in relationships in a meaningful way.

Characteristics of a Viable Intervention Approach

Before turning to an alternative intervention approach, we briefly highlight some characteristics of a viable intervention for addressing the ubiquitous problem we have identified.

First, persons in need of help forgiving a partner may not be seeking help. This suggests that the traditional "waiting mode" familiar to counselors needs to be replaced by the "seeking mode" embraced by the community mental health movement (Rappaport & Chinsky, 1974). In contrast to waiting for clients to present at the office for diagnosis and treatment, the interventionist in seeking mode moves into the community, taking on such nontraditional roles as developer of community programs, consultant to local groups, and evaluator of intervention efforts. A shift to seeking mode points to the importance of harnessing community resources in both identifying participants and in delivering the intervention. In the present context, this is particularly important because many potential beneficiaries of a forgiveness intervention are likely to be reached through natural community groups (e.g., religious organizations).

Second, persons in need of help forgiving may not have the financial resources to obtain professional help or be located in areas served by mental health care providers or persons who specialize in relationship problems. Therefore, any forgiveness intervention should be designed to reach people in a variety of settings (including rural and geographically isolated settings) and be viable for use in these settings. Thus, at a minimum, the intervention should be easily implemented, reasonably brief, and economic to implement. Ideally, it should involve a familiar process that occurs naturally in the community. This means that there is likely to be a need to look to a broader range of persons (e.g., media specialists) and modes of delivery (e.g., distance learning) than is typical in traditional psychotherapy.

Third, at the same time as speaking to the previous considerations, ethical considerations require that any intervention should represent best practice in terms of what is currently known scientifically about forgiveness and its facilitation. Perhaps two of the most important considerations here are that the intervention should:

(a) require the participants to spend time thinking about forgiveness as this seems to be related to the occurrence of forgiveness (with the corollary that simply exposing people to the transgression they experienced without facilitating forgiveness may be iatrogenic; Worthington, Sandage, & Berry, 2000); and

(b) include a psychoeducational component about what forgiveness does and does not entail. This is a common ingredient of forgiveness interventions that can serve both to avoid dangers likely to result from misconceptions about forgiveness (e.g., returning to a dangerous situation because reunion is confused with forgiveness) and to relieve psychological distress when someone feels the need to forgive a transgressor but finds themselves unable to do so because forgiveness is confused with something they may not want to do either consciously, or more often, unconsciously (e.g., condone transgressor's action).

Finally, it is important to remind ourselves that any intervention must lend itself to evaluation, for without evaluation no program can be assumed to be effective. The notion that "something is better than nothing" is simply misguided, no matter how well intentioned the intervention. Bergin (1963) noted long ago than any intervention that has the power to help people has the potential to hurt them, and the first principle of good practice is to avoid harm.

Toward a Public Health Forgiveness Intervention

Just the few considerations outlined in the last section make the development of an appropriate forgiveness intervention a challenging task. However, two observations take us a great deal of the way toward making it an achievable reality by helping to identify the form such an intervention might take.

Form of the Intervention. First, as Gordon, Baucom, and Snyder (2000) insightfully note, forgiveness in relationships is occasioned by transgressions that disrupt a partner's beliefs about the relationship, the partner, or the self and that such disruption is similar to that which occurs when a person experiences a traumatic life event (Janoff-Bulman, 1992). For example, on discovering an extramarital affair, the betrayed spouse's assumptions are often disrupted (e.g., that the partner is trustworthy) and they may well feel that their world has become less predictable and controllable, putting them at-risk for (mental and physical) health problems that are known to be provoked by traumatic experiences (Pennebaker, 1995). We do not share the view that forgiveness is only relevant to such contexts, but we do agree that traumatic relationship experiences are most likely to lead partners to think explicitly about forgiveness (forgiveness may occur implicitly and ubiquitously in response to a broader range of negative partner behaviors). Nonetheless, Gordon, Baucom, and Snyder's (2000) observation is particularly helpful because it points us in the direction of the literature on trauma and how it can be treated.

Second, there is a growing body of research showing that writing about past traumatic experiences has beneficial effects on mental and physical health (see Esterling, L'Abate, Murray, & Pennebaker, 1999). This is particularly important as it speaks to several of the criteria we have identified for a public health forgiveness intervention. Writing, in the form of keeping a journal, is familiar and occurs naturally in the community, may be acceptable to people who would not consider counseling, is something to which most people have access, is cost effective, and can be tailored to allow people to deal with transgression at their own rates. Furthermore, a programmed writing intervention can be delivered broadly through traditional print media and also lends itself to delivery via the Internet. This latter medium of delivery is particularly exciting because of its growing penetration of households throughout the world and because it allows greater control over the delivery of the intervention (time spent writing can be monitored precisely, writing can be analyzed online, and so on).

Having identified the form that the intervention might take we now need to specify the nature of the intervention. Yet, any intervention is necessarily predicated on an underlying model of forgiveness, and hence we turn briefly to this issue before specifying the nature of the intervention.

Model of Forgiveness Informing Intervention. We have already offered several important observations about forgiveness. These include the need to acknowledge a transgression, identify that it is appropriate to feel negatively about being victimized, assert the right to better treatment, and a willingness to relieve the debt incurred by the transgressor. Moreover, we clearly distinguish forgiveness from related constructs such as reconciliation and reunion, on the one hand, and from forgiveness transactions between partners on the other. As a more detailed analysis is available elsewhere (Fincham, 2000), we limit ourselves to highlighting additional issues central to the proposed intervention.

Fundamental to the intervention is our analysis of forgiveness as a process that occurs over time and is characterized by a decrease in the probability of negative feelings, thoughts, and behaviors towards the transgressor and an increase in their positive counterparts. However, this is not a linear, mutually exclusive process where, for example, positive thoughts replace negative ones. Rather, consistent with our research on relationship quality, positive and negative dimensions are viewed as relatively independent (see Fincham, Beach, & Kemp-Fincham, 1997). Important determinants of these probabilistic intra- and interpersonal manifestations of forgiveness are the perceived nature of the injury, attribution of responsibility for the injury, the (individual and relationship) context in which it occurs, and the extent to which the hurt is related (consciously or unconsciously) to past injuries and ongoing partner behavior allowing, at one extreme, hurt to be occasioned by the mere presence of the partner. Each of these determinants can be further elaborated. For example, avoidance and revenge motives are increased when injury to self-image is greater, if moral injury (i.e., moral order has been slighted) is greater, when the injury arises from an intentional act in the absence of mitigating factors rather than a negligent act, when the transgression is viewed (symbolically or in concrete terms) as similar to past ones, and so on (see Fincham, 2000). Where appropriate we elaborate on these determinants in outlining the nature of the proposed intervention.

In light of this model, we argue that avoidance and revenge are not a viable means of lessening hurt because they do not help the victim to (a) create a broader framework within which the behavior of the partner can be reinterpreted or reattributed, (b) integrate information in a manner that allows injury to self-image to be repaired, or (c) incorporate new information about the perpetrator's perspective that allows moral injury to be decreased. In addition, avoidance and revenge do not allow the victim to grapple with new information at a sufficiently detailed level that the particular incident can be viewed on its own merits rather than "bundled" with many other incidents. Our analysis suggests that forgiveness might be facilitated by providing a structured set of exercises that facilitate detailed emotional processing of the transgression and one's own reaction to the transgression. Although there are a number of possible pitfalls in emotional processing of partner transgressions, it may be a necessary (if not sufficient) component for true partner forgiveness

Nature of Intervention

The intervention we envisage is one that could be administered with guidance from paraprofessionals in the community and in a self-help format.

Getting Started: Is This Program for You? Whatever the format, the first component of the intervention would (a) screen out participants for whom the intervention is not appropriate and (b) help potential participants understand what is and is not offered by the intervention. Specifically, checklists that help determine the presence of psychopathology (e.g., Beck Depression Inventory) and relationship violence (e.g., Conflict Tactics Scale) should be completed and participants with scores above certain cutoffs advised of the need to obtain professional help. Although the determination of who will benefit is ultimately an empirical question to be resolved by appropriate research, it is important to have initial starting assumptions about the factors most likely to influence success. Because we view forgiveness as involving movement along two dimensions (avoidance and approach), and because we view the ease of forgiveness as being determined in part by explanations and degree of injury to self-evaluation, these dimensions seem particularly important to monitor in future investigations of forgiveness. Persons who are unable to imagine giving up their avoidance and/or punishment of the partner, for example, may be less able to benefit from a highly structured, self-guided approach to facilitating forgiveness. Likewise, persons with extreme attributions of blame or who have suffered extreme injury to self-evaluation may require preliminary activities before they are ready to benefit from the proposed intervention. Accordingly, in addition to screening for mental health and relationship problems requiring treatment, it would also be desirable to screen participants on dimensions that may be related to readiness for a structured, self-guided intervention.

Following initial screening, potential participants can be asked to write a brief statement of what it is they wish to achieve from participating in the program. This exercise helps clarify for the participant what it is they are looking for and sets the stage for the two remaining elements of this first component of the program: a guided evaluation of whether the program is likely to be able to meet their needs and basic education about what forgiving another does and does not entail. These evaluation and education elements would be realized through use of the Socratic method. Having written down what it is they are seeking, participants review their statement with the help of a set of guided questions. Is there a specific hurt that the person is having difficulty overcoming? Or is the person seeking to come to terms with a relationship full of hurts that have accumulated over time and are still ongoing? If the latter, the person would be advised that the program is unlikely to meet their needs. In this case, they might be advised to either break the pattern of hurtful behavior into several particular illustrative incidents that might be more amenable to the current approach, or to pursue couple work with their partner to help address the pattern in some way before attempting to put the past behind them. Is the person seeking reconciliation? If so, they might be advised that forgiveness is different than reconciliation and encouraged to first work through the process of forgiveness fully before deciding if they truly wish to reconcile. They might also be advised that a more complete discussion of the costs and benefits of reconciliation will be provided after the forgiveness intervention. This would also provide an opportunity to present to participants information about the value of forgiveness to them individually, regardless of any effect on the relationship. As such, it provides an excellent opportunity for education about the nature of forgiveness.

A final component of the orientation phase of the intervention therefore would be to provide participants with a model of forgiveness that describes forgiveness as an act of strength and courage but one that is often difficult and may take time. This may be a critical element of the intervention because persons who do not forgive from a position of strength may not forgive in a way that is helpful to them or to their relationship with the partner. Accordingly, a brief educational element would be an important final aspect of the orientation.

Getting Started: Laying the Groundwork for Forgiveness. Consistent with our analysis of forgiveness, and building on the first component of the program, the next component is designed to help the participant write about the transgression and the hurt it engendered. Participants are encouraged to include details about sensations, thoughts, and feelings they may have had at the time. One goal of the exercise is to have participants confront directly any aspect of the event that might otherwise be avoided and so serve as a reason to continue avoiding the partner. Exposure therapies have been very successful in dealing with other patterns of avoidance and a writing format is common in such approaches (e.g., Calhoun & Resick, 1993). A second goal is to have the person acknowledge the hurt, recognize that it is undeserved, and embrace the view that they have a right to better treatment. They would also be encouraged to identify and write about the negative emotions prompted by the transgression. It is recommended that this exercise is done at a time when they feel calm and relaxed and that they attempt to retain this state during the writing. However, a relaxed state may be less important than the participant being able to write fully about the event, particularly about their feelings in regard to those aspects of the transgression that were most damaging to their self-evaluation or their sense of justice in the world. It is likely to be less helpful if participants write only of their conclusions about the perpetrator or the actions they have taken since the event to cope.

Two observations are important here. First, a moderate amount of negative emotion words in writing about trauma benefits health (high and low levels correlate with poorer health; Pennebaker, 1997). Second, simply thinking about or ruminating over the hurt may be iatrogenic (Worthington, Sandage, & Berry, 2000). Hence, a goal throughout the intervention is to facilitate writing that will prompt use of positive emotion words. Thus, in the context of embracing their right to better treatment, respondents are encouraged to highlight positive feeling about the self. In a similar vein, they are asked to write about the constructive ways in which they have coped with the transgression and the feelings that their coping has engendered. The elicitation of positive emotion is not only important because of the research on trauma; it is also important to ameliorate the fact that, by definition, transgressions denigrate the worth of the victim, and repairing injury to self-image is likely to be an important part of being able to forgive.

Although positive feelings about the self are important, in the context of relationships, positive feelings about the partner are also relevant. The next writing task addresses this issue. An important part of laying the groundwork for forgiveness is to (a) weaken the link between partner and the injury they caused and (b) to induce the victim to see the partner as a whole person and not just someone who transgressed against them. Weakening the link between partner and injury involves altering (but not severing) attributed responsibility. Attributed responsibility involves linking the partner to their action and linking their action to the injury (partner → act → injury; see Fincham & Jaspars, 1980).

Weakening of the link between partner and act is addressed by asking the participant to write about the reasons for the partner's action assuming reasonable motives on the part of the partner. How did the partner view the situation and what was s/he thinking and feeling? How did the partner's experiences in life (e.g., in past relationships) influence his/her behavior? Weakening the second link between partner act and injury is addressed by asking participants to write down as many possible outcomes, both foreseen and unforeseen, of the partner's action as they can imagine. The victim is also asked to write about what s/he brings to the situation, particularly thoughts and past experiences that may not be known to the partner or recently communicated to him or her, that make the act especially hurtful to the victim.

In weakening both the partner–act and act–injury links participants are encouraged to write about the immediate situational context and the relationship context in which the act and injury occurred. According to the discounting principle in attribution theory, the extent to which alternative causes are present (e.g., work pressure, relationship tension) certainty as to the operation of the original cause (e.g., partner malice) will be lessened (Kelley, 1972). We also know that an increase in causal and insight words in the course of writing about a traumatic event is associated with improved health (Pennebaker, Mayne, & Francis, 1997) and hence the goal here is not only to change attributed responsibility but also to increase insight into the event.

Finally, in preparing the ground for forgiveness, it is important for the victim to see the partner as a whole person. A final exercise in this component of the program is therefore to write about the partner first from the perspective of a friend or acquaintance who admires or likes the partner, and then to write about positive experiences with the partner. The victim is also prompted to develop a list of the partner's strengths and weaknesses. To ensure some balance, they can start with a weakness and be instructed that they should not add another until they have identified an initial strength and to continue in similar vein until the list is completed.

Getting Started: Adopting a Forgiveness Orientation. Thus far, the issue of forgiveness has been addressed only in the initial phase of the program and only the groundwork for forgiveness laid. To facilitate the emergence of a forgiveness orientation, the issue of forgiveness again needs to be addressed explicitly along with what it does and does not mean to forgive. Here the victim's own humanity is important. S/he is asked to write about events when s/he hurt another and was grateful to be forgiven by the victim. What was it like to know that the victim has been hurt by his/her action? And how did the victim's forgiveness alter these feelings? If participants cannot identify actual events, they can be asked to imagine whether they might have hurt, or are likely to ever hurt, someone without knowing about the harm that they caused. How would that feel? And what if they were to learn about the consequences of their action? And then how would it feel to be forgiven for what they did? The goal here is to help participants experience the ease with which they could occupy the role of perpetrator and how forgiveness not only liberates them from their own negative affect but also lays the groundwork, in conferring a gift on the perpetrator, for relationship reconciliation if that is a desired and prudent goal.

The next step is to actually commit to forgiving. In one intervention program, this takes the form of writing a letter of forgiveness as if the victim were going to send it to the perpetrator, by having the victim write a certificate stating the date of forgiveness, and by having the victim make a public statement about forgiving (Worthington, 1998). With the cautions that forgiveness is not granted on a given date (it is ongoing; only the decision to forgive can occur on a given date) and that a public commitment should only involve a trusted friend or confidant, we see considerable merit in incorporating such processes in our proposed intervention. Our certificate would be carefully crafted to help inoculate the participant from relapse by including statements that recognize the ongoing nature of the process and the steps that will be taken when the inevitable relapses occur in the process. This brings us to the final component of the intervention concerning persistence in the effort to forgive.

Maintaining Momentum: Forgiveness Calls for Persistence. The final component of the intervention is primarily future-oriented in that it encourages writing about challenges to forgiveness. Thus, participants write about how they might react when they re-experience negative feelings and hurt associated with the transgression following their commitment to forgive. The idea is to plan for such lapses to mitigate their impact and to allow for further education about forgiveness (e.g., that periodic thoughts and feelings about the transgression are normative and are not the same as unforgiveness, that emotions cannot be ended through a decision to end them, but they can nonetheless be controlled when they occur).

Participants will also be encouraged to write about their experience of forgiving. This serves several functions. First, it serves to remind them of the task at hand. Second, it allows for reaffirmation of their commitment through reference to their certificate and written letter. Third, it allows participants to cycle back through earlier exercises if needed. Fourth, structured questions probe the person to think about whether the experience they are having pertains to the original transgression or whether additional transgressions are influencing their experience and might point to the need for professional help.

Two further written exercises are likely to be a particularly important. The first requires participants to write about what they have learned through experiencing the transgression and is designed for them to find meaning in what they have suffered. This builds on prior writing exercises and is designed to help the person develop a coherent narrative about their experience, something that is known to be beneficial in responses to traumatic events (Esterling et al., 1999). A second, related exercise is to write about the changes they have experienced as a function of the decision to forgive, a task that is designed to reinforce forgiving in drawing attention to the release from (often persistent) negative affect.

Strengths and Limitations of Intervention. We have already noted several strengths of the proposed intervention, including its flexibility in both the mode of delivery (print media and electronic media) and adaptability to participant need (progress can be determined by responses to critical questions), its cost effectiveness, its similarity to a process that occurs naturally (keeping a journal), its adaptation to and delivery through community organizations, and its ease of evaluation (especially if delivered electronically). However, the program also exhibits the major weakness of extant forgiveness programs: It does not speak to the issue of forgiveness transactions between partners. Indeed, it does not capitalize on the fact that the transgression occurs in an ongoing relationship where the victim has direct access to the transgressor. This seems to be a serious omission and therefore deserves brief comment.

In the absence of research on forgiveness transactions, and without any knowledge of the participant's partner, it would be unwise to build any exercises into the intervention that includes interaction with the transgressor for at least two reasons. First, the transgressor may not view him/herself as having committed a wrong and therefore needing forgiveness. Any forgiveness transaction in such circumstances could easily promote conflict. Second, even where the transgressor acknowledges the transgression, the details of what happened are likely to differ between transgressor and victim as we know both engage in systematic, but differing, distortions of the original event (see Stillwell & Baumeister, 1997). Again, this creates the potential for conflict. Perhaps the best that can be done in this circumstance, is to have a parallel set of writing exercises designed to promote understanding of what people experience and what they go through when they feel they have been wronged by a partner. A transgressor could be referred to these exercises not because of their need for forgiveness but "to better understand their partner." At the same time, this concern raises the likely need to develop a companion writing program for perpetrators that could be pursued by persons coping with the fact that they might have committed a relationship transgression that has caused considerable distress to another.

CONCLUSIONS

In this chapter, we have identified forgiveness as a mechanism in the maintenance of relationships, explored objections to forgiving a partner's transgression, reviewed available evidence on the benefits of forgiving and summarized research on interventions designed to facilitate forgiveness. We then argued that transgressions in relationships pose a public health problem and to identify an approach to forgiveness might address this problem. The next step is to develop a detailed treatment protocol and to investigate the proposed intervention. Although this presents a major challenge, the potential payoff is great as the program is well suited to take advantage of the technological revolution that is afoot. The possibility of delivering an intervention to millions of couples throughout the world via the Internet is makes the road ahead both an exciting and daunting path to travel.

ACKNOWLEDGMENTS

The preparation of this manuscript was supported by a grant from the National Science Foundation award to Steven R. H. Beach and by a grant from the Templeton Foundation awarded to Frank Fincham and Steven R. H. Beach.

REFERENCES

Al-Mubak, R., Enright, R. D., & Cardis, P. (1995). Forgiveness education with parentally love-deprived college students. *Journal of Moral Education, 14*, 427–444.

Beach, S. R., Fincham, F. D., & Katz, J. (1998). Marital therapy in the treatment of depression: Toward a third generation of outcome research. *Clinical Psychology Review, 18*, 635–661.

Bergin, A. E. (1963). The effects of psychotherapy: Negative results revisited. Journal of Counseling Psychology, 10, 244–250.

Burman, B., & Margolin, G. (1992). Analysis of the association between marital relationships and health problems: An interactional perspective. *Psychological Bulletin, 112*, 39–63.

Calhoun, K. S., & Resick, P. A. (1993). Post-Traumatic Stress Disorder. In D. H. Barlow (Ed.), *Clinical handbook of psychological disorders* (pp. 48–98). New York: Guilford.

Cano, A., & O'Leary, K. D. (in press). Humiliating marital events precipitate major depressive episodes and symptoms of non-specific depression and anxiety. *Journal of Consulting and Clinical Psychology.*

Close, H. T. (1970). Forgiveness and responsibility: A case study. *Pastoral Psychology, 21*, 19–25.

Coyle, C. T., & Enright, R. D. (1997). Forgiveness intervention with post-abortion men. *Journal of Consulting and Clinical Psychology, 65*, 1042–1046.

Cutrona, C. E. (1996). *Social support in couples.* Thousand Oaks, CA: Sage.

Enright, R. D., & Coyle, C. T. (1998). Researching the process model of forgiveness within psychological interventions. In E. L. Worthington (Ed.), *Dimensions of forgiveness: Psychological research and theological perspectives* (pp. 139–161). Philadelphia: Templeton Press.

Esterling, B. A., L'Abate, L., Murray, E. J., & Pennebaker, J. W. (1999). Empirical foundations for writing in prevention and psychotherapy: Mental and physical health outcomes. *Clinical Psychology Review, 19,* 79–96.

Ewart, C. K., Taylor, C. B., Kraemer, H. C., & Agras, W. S. (1991). High blood pressure and marital discord: Not being nasty matters more than being nice. *Health Psychology, 103,* 155–163.

Fenell, D. (1993). Characteristics of long-term first marriages. *Journal of Mental Health Counseling, 15*(4), 446–460.

Fincham, F. D. (2000). The kiss of the porcupines: From attributing responsibility to forgiving. *Personal Relationships, 7,* 1–23.

Fincham, F. D. (in press). Attributions in close relationships: From balkanization to integration. In G. J. O. Fletcher & M. S. Clark (Eds.), *Blackwell handbook of social psychology: Interpersonal processes.* Oxford: Blackwell.

Fincham, F. D., Beach, S. R., & Kemp-Fincham, S. I. (1997). Marital quality: A new theoretical perspective. In R. J. Sternberg & M. Hojjat (Eds.), *Satisfaction in close relationships* (pp. 275–304). New York: Guilford.

Fincham, F. D., & Jaspars, J. M. (1980). Attribution of responsibility: From man the scientist to man as lawyer. In L. Berkowitz (Ed.), *Advances in experimental social psychology* (Vol 13; pp. 81–138). New York: Academic Press.

Fitzgibbons, R. P. (1986). The cognitive and emotive uses of forgiveness in the treatment of anger. *Psychotherapy, 23,* 629–633.

Freedman, S. R., & Enright, R. D. (1996). Forgiveness as an intervention goal with incest survivors. *Journal of Consulting and Clinical Psychology, 64,* 983–992.

Gordon, K. C., Baucom, D. H., & Snyder, D. K. (2000). Forgiveness in marital therapy. In M. E. McCullough, K. Pargament, & C. Thoresen (Eds.), *Forgiveness: Theory, research and practice* (pp. 203–227). New York: Guilford.

Hebl, J. H., & Enright, R. D. (1993). Forgiveness as a psychotherapeutic goal with elderly females. *Psychotherapy, 30,* 658–667.

Jaeger, M. (1998). The power and reality of forgiveness: Forgiving the murderer of one's child. In R. D. Enright & J. North (Eds.), *Exploring forgiveness* (pp. 9–14). Madison: University of Wisconsin Press.

Janoff-Bulman, R. (1992). *Shattered assumptions: Toward a new psychology of trauma.* New York: Free Press.

Katz, J., Street, A., & Arias, I. (1997). Individual differences in self-appraisals and responses to dating violence scenarios. *Violence and Victims, 12,* 265–276.

Kelley, H. H. (1972). Causal schemata and the attribution process. In E. E. Jones, D. E. Kanouse, H. H. Kelley, R. E. Nisbett, S. Valins, & B. Weiner (Eds.), *Attribution: Perceiving the causes of behavior* (pp. 151–174). Morristown, NJ: General Learning Press.

Kelln, B. R. C., & Ellard, J. H. (1999). An equity theory analysis of the impact of forgiveness and retribution on transgressor compliance. *Personality and Social Pscyhology Bulletin, 25,* 864–872.

Kielcolt-Glaser, J. K., Glaser, R., Cacioppo, J. T., MacCullum, R. C., Snydersmith, M., & Malarkey, W. B. (1997). Marital conflict in older adults: Endocrine and immunological correlates. *Psychosomatic Medicine, 59,* 339–349.

Kiecolt-Glazer, J. K., Kennedy, S., Malkoff, S., Fisher, L., Speicher, C. E., & Glaser, R. (1988). Marital discord and immunity in males. *Psychosomatic Medicine, 50,* 213–229.

Laumann, E. O., Gagnon, J. H., Michael, R. T., & Michaels, S. (1994). *The social organization of sexuality.* Chicago: University of Chicago Press.

Malarkey, W. B., Kielcolt-Glaser, J. K., Pearl, D., & Glaser, R. (1994). Hostile behavior during conflict alters pituitary and adrenal hormones. *Psychosomatic Medicine, 56,* 41–51.

Malcolm, W. M., & Greenberg, L. S. (2000). Forgiveness as a process of change in individual psychotherapy. In M. E. McCullough, K. Pargament, & C. Thoreson (Eds.), *Forgiveness: Theory, research, and practice* (pp. 179–202). New York: Guilford.

Margolin, G., & Wampold, B. E. (1981). Sequential analysis of conflict and accord in distressed and nondistressed marital partners. *Journal of Consulting and Clinical Psychology, 49*, 554–567.

Mauger, P. A., Perry, J. E., Freeman, T., Grove, D. C., McBride, A. G., & McKinney, K. E. (1992). The measurement of forgiveness: Preliminary research. *Journal of Psychology and Christianity, 11*, 170–180.

McCullough, M. E., Worthington, E. L., Jr., & Rachal, K. C. (1997). Interpersonal forgiving in close relationships. *Journal of Personality and Social Psychology, 73*, 321–336.

McCullough, M. E., Rachal, K. C., Sandage, S. J., Worthington, W. L., Brown, S. W., & Hight, T. L. (1998). Interpersonal forgiving in close relationships. II: Theoretical elaboration and measurement. *Journal of Personality and Social Psychology, 75*, 1586–1603.

McCullough, M. E., & Worthington, E. I. (1994). Models of interpersonal forgiveness and their application to counseling: Review and critique. *Counseling and Values, 39*, 2–14.

Miller, T. Q., Smith, T. W., Turner, C. W., Guijarro, M. L., & Hallett, A. J. (1996). Meta-analytic review of research on hostility and physical health. *Psychological Bulletin, 119*, 322–348.

Murphy, C. M., & O'Farrell T. J. (1994). Factors associated with marital aggression in male alcoholics. *Journal of Family Psychology, 8*, 321–335.

Murray, S. L., Holmes, J. G., & Griffin, D. W. (1996). The benefits of positive illusions: Idealization and the construction of satisfaction in close relationships. *Journal of Personality and Social Psychology, 70*, 79–98.

National Center for Health Statistics. (1995). Advance report of the final divorce statistics for 1989 and 1990. *Monthly Vital Statistics Report, 43(9)*, Supplement. Hyattsville, MD.

Nietzsche, F. W. (1921). *The genealogy of morals*. New York: Boni & Liveright.

O'Farrell, T. J., Choquette, K. A., & Birchler, G. R. (1991). Sexual satisfaction and dissatisfaction in the marital relationships of male alcoholics seeking marital therapy. *Journal of Studies of Alcohol, 52*, 441–447.

O'Leary, K. D., Malone, J., & Tyree, A. (1994). Physical aggression in early marriage: Prerelationship and relationship effects. *Journal of Consulting and Clinical Psychology, 62*, 594–602.

Pennebaker, J. W. (1995). Emotion, disclosure, and health: An overview. In J. W. Pennebaker (Ed.), *Emotion, disclosure, and health*. Washington, DC: American Psychological Association.

Pennebaker, J. W. (1997). Writing about emotional experiences as a therapeutic process. *Psychological Science, 8*, 162–166.

Pennebaker, J. W., Mayne, T. J., & Francis, M. E. (1997). Linguistic predictors of adaptive bereavement. *Journal of Personality and Social Psychology, 72*, 863–871.

Rappaport, J., & Chinsky, J. M. (1974). Models for delivery of service from a historical and conceptual perspective. *Professional Psychology, 5*, 42–50.

Rowe, J. O., Halling, S., Davies, E., Leifer, M., Powers, D., & Van Bronkhorst, J. ((1989). The psychology of forgiving another: A dialogic research approach. In R. S. Valle & Steen Halling (Eds.), *Existential–phenomenological perspectives in psychology: Exploring the breadth of human experience* (pp. 28–42). New York: Plenum.

Rusbult, C. E., Verette, J., Whitney, G. A., Slovik, L. F., & Lipkus, I. (1991). Accommodation processes in close relationships: Theory and preliminary empirical evidence. *Journal of Personality and Social Psychology, 60*, 53–78.

Rusbult, C. E., Yovetich, N. A., & Verette, J. (1996). An interdependence analysis of accommodation processes. In G. J. O. Fletcher & J. Fitness (Eds.), *Knowledge structures in close relationships: A social psychological approach* (pp. 63–90). Hillsdale, NJ: Lawrence Erlbaum Associates.

Schmaling, K. B., & Sher, T. G. (1997). Physical health and relationships. In W. K. Halford & H. J. Markman (Eds.), *Clinical handbook of marriage and couples intervention* (pp. 323–345). London: Wiley.

Spring, J. A. (1996). *After the affair*. New York: HarperCollins.

Stillwell, A. M., & Baumeister, R. F. (1997). The construction of victim and perpetrator memories: Accuracy and distortion in role-based accounts. *Personality and Social Psychology Bulletin, 23,* 1157–1172.

Tangey, J., Fee, R., & Lee, N. (1999, August). *Assessing individual differences in the propensity to forgive.* Paper presented at the 107th Annual Conference of the American Psychological Association, Boston, MA.

Thoresen, C. E., Harris, A. H. S., & Luskin, F. (2000). Forgiveness and health: An unanswered question. In M. E. McCullough, K. Pargament, & C. Thoreson (Eds.), *Forgiveness: Theory, research, and practice* (pp. 254–295). New York: Guilford.

Van den Broucke, S., Vandereycken, W., & Norre, J. (1997). *Eating disorders and marital relationships.* London: Routledge.

vanOyen Vitvliet, C., & Ludwig, T. E. (1999, August). *Forgiveness and unforgiveness: Responses to interpersonal offences influence health.* Paper presented at the 107th Annual Conference of the American Psychological Association, Boston, MA.

Veroff, J., Kulka, R. A., & Douvan, E. (1981). *Mental helath in American patterns of help seeking from 1957–1976.* New York: Basic Books.

Worthington, E. L. (1998). The pyramid model of forgiveness: Some interdisciplinary speculations about unforgiveness and the promotion of forgiveness. In E. L. Worthington (Ed.), *Dimensions of forgiveness: Psychological research and theological perspectives* (pp. 107–137). Philadelphia: Templeton Press.

Worthington, E. L., Sandage, S. J., & Berry, J. W. (2000). Group interventions to promote forgiveness. In M. E. McCullough, K. Pargament, & C. Thoreson (Eds.), *Forgiveness: Theory, research, and practice* (pp. 228–253). New York: Guilford.

Worthington, E. L., & Wade, (1999). The psychology of unforgiveness and forgiveness and implications for clinical practice. *Journal of Social and Clinical Psychology, 18,* 385–418.

Yovetich, N. A., & Rusbult, C. E. (1994). Accomodative behavior in close relationships: Exploring transformation of motivation. *Journal of Experimental Social Psychology, 30,* 138–164.

PART

IV

COMMENTARIES

Maintaining Relationships in the Millennium

Pepper Schwartz
University of Washington

The past 100 years have witnessed major changes in the way men and women interact, bond, and stay happy. For uncountable years, male and female relationships have been organized around the premise of male dominance over female submission and support. Modifications of that system have sporadically appeared, but consistent change has been slow in gaining traction. Volumes of research have been published on why changes in gender enactment have been so intransigent but there is general agreement that important variables have been:

- lack of enthusiasm for change by any advantaged stakeholder,
- cultural norms and values, including religious values that have held back change, and
- the biological assignment of childbearing that has made women uniquely vulnerable to threats and withholding of resources and has also made it harder for them to go after resources themselves.

Even so, a great shift in the conceptualization of relationships happened toward the middle of the 20th century. Male leadership in marriage and intimate relationships became legitimated by cooperation and collaboration rather than by fiat or force. The vision of the "companionate marriage" became normative. Father may still have had male only roles, but now it was acceptable and desirable to have him help occasionally with the dishes. Men retained leadership and veto power over decisions, but it became

303

counternormative to be autocratic. Still, it was understood that the relationship had a captain and women were never supposed to rise above the rank of lieutenant.

It wasn't until the end of the 1960s that the entire idea of hierarchy was attacked on many fronts by a variety of feminist theorists and fledgling political groups. The broadside came from renewed feminism across the United States and in Europe as well. This century's incarnation of feminism, like some earlier ones, located the cause of women's subordinate position in society in familial servitude—and young and some older women in North America and Europe wrote treatises about the injustices of marriage. After years of bitter recriminations and spiked divorce rates, real changes occurred in the relationships of men and women. Women went into paid jobs and professional schools in increasing numbers, sexual prerogatives became more jointly held, and lifestyles of men and women increasingly looked more similar. This trend has only increased over time and yet, strangely enough, the pull toward traditional roles in marriage still exists and the incapacity (or lack of desire) to change from a companionate marriage to an egalitarian one, has been marked. Modern marriage still remains more of an equity model than an equality model.

The differentiation between equity and equality is not always easy to make. But for the purposes of this chapter let us say that an equity model is a relationship based on fairness. People want a fair deal, but they believe that deal can be made in different coin. For example, having a wife who stays home with young children is a fair exchange of value for a man who wants to work outside the home yet still be able to start a family. The idea is that if the two people feel it is fair, the deal is inherently stable because each person is getting what he or she wants—even if they are not exchanging the same thing, even if it is not a deal that might be experienced as fair by two other people who constitute their exchange according to different tastes and values.

Of course this vision of equity: of exchanging unlike services of value for a good deal was the key mechanism of the traditionally married. It was supposed to give dignity to each person's contribution and bond the two people through mutual need for each other's talents and services. Theoretically it should have worked—but of course the modern divorce rate, hovering somewhere around 50% of all marriages, came primarily from traditional marriages. Domestic labor was not really considered the equal of the paid workplace—and women were further disadvantaged by the fact that they could not translate household skills into readily acquired jobs in the capitalist marketplace. Therefore, a number of women chose to flee the equity model and opt for an equality model.

The equality model exchanges like thing for like thing. This obviates figuring out if 5 hours of childcare equals 5 hours of selling cars; rather, tasks are just split in half so that couples are sharing childcare or perhaps swapping night shifts versus day duty. Thus men came back into the home and women joined men in the workplace. Women who pressed for this new deal wanted it so that they might also earn the economic rewards and personal respect and power that they felt men had monopolized. However, the problem with this model was that some women preferred to stay in the home, specializing in childrearing and domestic work, and even when women started out wanting less traditional role assignments, roles often slid back into traditional niches because most men and women naturally went back to the skills they had been with and the roles that therefore felt most "natural." Even if this were not the case, there was a tendency to return to equity, if only for practical reasons. Without a great deal of communication and negotiation, the equality model encourages redundancies (e.g., both persons shopping on their way home from work) that couples can ill afford in this work and role stressed world. Most critically, the egalitarian marriage does not release at least one person in the couple for unfettered achievement in the financial marketplace. Most wives and husbands, not to mention in-laws and other family members, had trouble living with the reality of compromised economic opportunity. Thus, many men and women ultimately rejected equality as a marital theory or withdrew from an equality experiment because they felt defeated by the exigencies of everyday life. A common adaptation was a hybrid marriage based on some elements of equity and other elements of equality.

Another modern adaptation has been avoiding marriage all together until childbearing and future building became more desirable. Cohabitation, an intensely individualistic way of setting up a household, has become more popular as equity has come to the fore as a culturally accepted value. Cohabitation has grown from about 18% of all biographies in America in the early 1970s to its present upward climb, resting temporarily at about 50% of men and women's romantic histories. Cohabitation is not one clear model of relationship (it can be anything from sharing an apartment in college until graduation to a commitment for life), but in general, it is comprised of two persons who share living quarters and are lovers but who do not combine their economic resources and who have not promised each other a lifetime of obligation or love. These relationships look different from marriage and even look different from long-term same-sex relationships in that the longer they are together, the more separate the partners may become (*American Couples*, 1983). Unless they are people who are ideologically opposed to marriage but are otherwise "married," the lesser commitment of the two individuals makes the relationship inherently less stable. Still, the popularity of this form of relationship tells us something about what young people in North America and Europe want. It would seem they want romance, they want each person to carry his or her own weight, and if the deal is not "good enough," they want to keep their options open until they are absolutely sure this is the best deal they can get.

The popularity of cohabitation and the reworking of marriage make the meaning of intimacy a bit fuzzy these days. For example, it is fair to say that in today's world, we really have no archetype of marriage. We have no new hegemonic model such as the Traditional Marriage of the 1950s. Modern marriage is jerryrigged from spare parts that people pick up and put into their marital design. Like all mongrels, each marriage is different—potentially vigorous and smart—but all are successful or unsuccessful based on their own individual experiment. It is hard to imagine a way to make all modern marriages look fundamentally alike ever again.

Still, it seems to this writer, having read all the chapters in this volume, that all modern relationships struggle with at least a few similar aspirations: Each marriage hopes that the relationship will consider individual needs and that each person's contribution will be appreciated and appropriately rewarded. Partners want intimacy and not just day-to-day companionship. Shared power may not be required in all marriages, but when it is absent, feelings of deprivation are likely—and corrosive. The desire for romance, although tempered with time and experience, is still yearned for and the marriage is vulnerable when romance is missing. The need for collaboration of the heart and spirit has become part of the modern conceptualization of what maintains an ongoing relationship.

That is, of course, why relationships are so hard to maintain today. Even without some of the considerable challenges addressed in this book (alcoholism, depression, the institutionalization of a second marriage, or the conflicts often aroused by different parenting techniques or values) the weight placed on marital or intimate provisions is daunting. In fact, regardless of which place on the liberal–conservative continuum a marriage occurs the reader will find a general desire to find a "soulmate." The differences occur over the best way to go about that task. Traditionalists believe that the best way to maintain intimate relationships is still the lock and key vision of adult cooperation, that is, that people have to fill in each other's gaps in order to provide satisfaction and stability. In other words, an equity model, perhaps more subtly and respectfully done than in the past, is what we have to reinstate. Feminists and younger men and women are more likely to believe in new, more egalitarian gender roles as the key to intimacy and stability and the power to resist the centrifugal force that tears and seduces men and women from their original romantic commitment. Liberals say that traditional marriage cannot provide the satisfactions modern men and women seek and that these marriages will ultimately self-destruct. Traditionalists say that modern marriage has fared no better than traditional marriage and that some tinkering can change traditional marriage so that it will ultimately provide the best way for relationships to prosper.

My own studies comparing traditional and egalitarian marriage (called Peer Marriage to avoid using a word that connotes an exact fifty–fifty split of duties) make me bet on the side of more equality with some nod to equity in the pursuit of everyday life's pragmatics. However, let me hasten to add, not too much of a nod. When I studied couples who were trying to be more egalitarian but had failed at it because, for example, his paycheck was so much larger than her's that it made sense for her to be the only child caretaker, I found that these were the most unhappy couples I studied. Why? Because they had an ideology they could not fulfill. The equity model does seem to make good sense when couples have unequal opportunities in the marketplace and many modern couples slide into traditional marriage even if they have no intentions of doing so. Equity is invoked—respect is promised—but sooner or later, the lack of a fair deal becomes a problem for many people who intended to be full partners in every sense of the word. Perceived lack of equal vesting in the relationship, and a loss of intimacy because of unequal roles, destabilizes the relationship.

If, however, equality is a better fit with the new values and purposes of marriage, cohabitation and same-sex relationships, why then does it still seem to be a minority marital form? Cohabitation is increasing and it is definitely a more egalitarian bargain. Most studies of cohabitation show that the division of household labor is far more shared than in marriage (although still not equal between men and women) and that decision making is more negotiated. In fact, it seems to have an impact on marriage itself. A recent dissertation by Teresa Ciabattari (2001), "Institutions, Contracts and Housework: The Division of Labor in Marriage, Remarriage and Cohabitation," indicated that not only do male cohabitors do more housework; but men who marry who previously cohabited (or remarry after a cohabitation) do more housework than other men. If cohabitation creates a new vision of equality (or people who cohabit are more prone toward egalitarian household arrangements) why is equality still rarely promoted as a relationship maintenance strategy?

I have mentioned some answers to this question earlier, but I would like to look at some reasons that are not so much a result of pragmatics as they are deeper beliefs of our culture in what makes marriage and commitment last.

THE PERCEIVED COSTS OF EGALITARIAN COUPLES

The Presumption That Similarity Breeds Instability

The philosophy of "yin" and "yang"—of opposites creating unity, of job specialization, and of maternal, rather than paternal, fitness for childraising, encourages couples to discount couple teamwork on parenting, household labor, equality in workplace commitment and ambition, and other egalitarian endeavors. The Parsonian pronouncement of family stability through task socioemotional specialization may no longer be in fashion in sociology but it is still embraced by many men and women as the most reasonable, indeed the most "natural," allocation of men and women in the family. Religion may not only bolster this opinion, it may command it. Personal history, the roles taken in one's family origin, make similarity seem strange, even sexually unappealing. Modern culture still makes much of men's and women's biological differences, and the public appetite for this viewpoint, as demonstrated by the monster success of the *Men Are from Mars, Women Are from Venus* series of books, is undeniable. While couples seem to feel drawn together by feeling empathy and comfort, and dating tends to be egalitarian, strongly ingrained feelings about men's and women's spheres still guide spouses into highly differentiated family roles.

The Ill Fit Between Work Conditions and Personal Ideology

I have mentioned that couples may give up trying to find a job that fits with their egalitarian needs because they decide they cannot afford the economic compromises that an egalitarian family system may require. Most men still earn more than most women, and couples follow a strategy to maximize family income that ultimately organizes the household around the man's work schedule and options. What may be less obvious, however, is that even if women are capable of maximizing income equivalent or superior to a man's, there is still the deeply held belief by many women that a man should be the major breadwinner and that hierarchy, or at least a slight bit of hierarchy, is the appropriate organization of the sexes. Many women still want their man to outshine them; men, unless they are quite liberated about gender, expect to be the lead earner. Women are more likely to see work as voluntary or flexible and expect it to be bent around child raising; men are more likely to see work as inflexible, and less responsive to child raising needs.

Possible Habituation and "Incest Taboo" in Sex Life

Another more subtle problem is the fear of de-eroticization of relationships—a fear that may have basis for some couples. One interesting issue that can occur when couples mesh daily life is that their day-to-day camaraderie takes on an almost sibling-like cast. Individuals who like the mystery of different gender characteristics may find themselves unprepared for a relationship that has less differentiation. Peer couples I interviewed reported more communication and affection in these relationships than previous marriages or cohabitations, but they also surprised me with lower than expected rates of sexual intercourse. It may be that sex is used in more traditional relationships to bridge gaps in intimacy and communication and becomes less necessary as a consolation and communication technique in egalitarian relationships. Well-functioning couples of all kinds may find that less turmoil or emotional distance modifies the need for sexual intercourse and indeed, my research of lesbian couples (*American Couples*, 1983) found that lesbians had much less genital sexuality than other couples, but reported far more acts of affection such as kissing, hand holding, etc. Folk wisdom has long predicated sexual attraction on a yin–yang vision of the sexes and while that may overstate the case, it may be true that many individuals are drawn to relationships that have more differentiation turmoil and consequently, passion. Men and women are still trying on the eroticization of gender similarity for size—some like it, some find it wanting.

THE POSSIBLE BENEFITS OF EGALITARIAN MARRIAGE

The Avoidance of Parallel Lives

There is however, a pull toward egalitatianism—even the serious problems listed above, notwithstanding. Inasmuch as modern marriage is based on a high standard of intimacy, but modern life is driving both men and women out of the home to be coworkers and perhaps dual providers for the family, there is a marital paradox. At the same time people want more intimacy, they have less time together. That time has got to come from somewhere and it has been suggested that perhaps the technological revolution with its possibilities of home-based work will be that savior. Perhaps it will. But it is also possible a global marketplace could be a countervailing force. A retreat from work would help of course, but it is also possible that some remediation of intimacy could come from couple participation in household and child raising so that the temptation to live parallel lives is less successful. The basis of a marital system based mostly on equality has couples doing the same thing in the same way. Although that could be claustrophobic in a world where couples were isolated, that is hardly the likely problem in today's world. Rather, anything that pulls the couple together is a positive intimacy maintenance technique. After all, couples have to remember why they need each other; why they want to be together.

Increased Intimacy

Most happy couples are likely to describe their partner as their "best friend." This is the mantra of today's relationships and it would be an unusual person who would leave this out of the list describing their partner unless the relationship is in crisis. But empirically, a lot of the marriages that give this answer would not be able to support the claim. Highly differentiated lives may be efficient, but not necessarily close. If we compare the situation to the creation of close friendships among same-sex friends it is clear that the differentiation model is not used for nonsexual friendship. Friendships occur and deepen because friends share important parts of their life. Likewise, friendship is built in marriage and cohabitation because partners do family and work tasks together that build camaraderie. Intimate friendships require empathy—understanding each other, being the "right person to go to" on a given issue, having a deep enough connection and depth of knowledge about a person's thoughts, needs, and history so that one is able to understand the situation and give comfort or advice. Egalitarian couples report an increase in empathy, respect, and negotiating skills—all elements of successful friendship and traits that most psychologists believe help create a better functioning relationship.

The Stability Gained Through Joint Parenting and Housekeeping

In the research I did on "peer marriage" (*Love Between Equals*, 1994) I found that the singlemost important bond between egalitarian couples was their pleasure at providing support for each other and support for their children through joint parenting. There are, of course, voices that counter this finding, particularly among working-class men (see Crouter, Jenkins, Huston, & McHale, 1996). However, I believe that preponderance of studies, especially those that use a middle-class sample, find large numbers of men whose egalitarian participation in the home brings them higher marital satisfaction (e.g., Yogev & Brett, 1985). There is no doubt, of course, what it does for women. Having a partner who does more than assist with childcare and household management has a huge impact on women's satisfaction with their marriage. Traditional division of labor and lack of child-raising participation is linked to women's disappointment with their marital choice (Grote, Frieze, & Stone, 1996). If parenting duties are not shared women, depending on their values and ideology, can experience overall unhappiness with their lives (White, Booth, & Edwards, 1997). On the other side, it seems obvious that the addition of male parenting adds stability and emotional satisfaction to marriage, no matter what class is surveyed. For example, Rosin (1987) showed that a significant number of working-class mothers interpreted their husband's participation with the children and household as a sign of their love and commitment. A very important study by Lye and Mogan (1992) found that men who had more than superficial interaction with their children had lower divorce rates. Thus, if egalitarian relationships include father participation there is every reason to believe that this will strengthen both the family and the relationship.

Individual Growth

In *The Passionate Marriage*, the psychologist David Schnarch (1997) builds a theory of deep bonding based on the psychological proposition that only differentiated individuals are secure enough to allow themselves to have intense emotional and physical connection. Being able to share parenting or providership without being threatened by the other person's expertise takes a mature person, but it may also help create a mature person. And, after all, what is more important to relationship maintenance than a person who can concentrate on the issues rather than take any conflict or negotiation as a rejection or an attack? The importance of respect for the other person and self-esteem for oneself cannot be underestimated. The theory of partnership, of colleagueship in marriage, is that it is here, in a marriage between equals, that the self is given room to grow and flourish.

Conclusion

Relationships, once contracted, can never be on automatic pilot. The best relationship in the world needs aggressive monitoring, and mechanisms for constructive correction. People change, often developing bad habits, or sustain permanent losses of previous capabilities. Children change the focus of the adult relationship and even ordinary transitions, such as from dating to commitment or cohabitation to marriage, change interaction and create new pressure. The myth of "happily ever after" is just that, a hope, a dream, but a vision that has little to do with reality. Those of us who spend a lifetime studying adult intimacy have two approaches to sustaining relationships and both are necessary. One, which I have talked about in this chapter, is to create a foundation for the relationship that bonds and supports the couple. The other, present in many of the chapters of this volume, looks at different stages and situations in a couple's life and offers insight into ways that problems can be solved or modified and strengths can be noted and sustained.

Because relationships are always affected by culture and cultural change, no answer to any relationship question is chiseled out of stone. The suggestions and observations in this chapter and others in this volume, are always thoughts and findings in progress. The glory—and challenge—of human beings is that we modify who we are and what we want in almost every decade. What remains is the almost universal desire to couple, and the deep need to love and to be loved, for a lifetime.

REFERENCES

Blumstein, P., & Schwartz, P. (1983). *American couples: Money, work and sex.* New York: Morrow.

Ciabattari, T. (2001). *Institutions, contracts and housework: The division of labor in marriage, remarriage and cohabitation.* Unpublished doctoral dissertation, University of Washington.

Crouter, A. C., Jenkins, R., Huston, T. L., & McHale, S. (1996). Processes underlying father involvement in dual earner and single earner families. *Developmental Psychology, 23,* 431–440.

Grote, N., Frieze, I., & Stone, C. (1996). Children, traditionalism in the division of family labor and marital satisfaction: What's love got to do with it (Vol. 3, No. 3).

Rosin, E. (1987). *Bitter choices: Blue collar women in and out of work.* Chicago: University of Chicago Press.

Schnarch, D. (1997). *The passionate marriage.* New York: Norton.

Schwartz, P. (1994). *Love between equals.* New York: Free Press.

White, G. D., Booth, A., & Edwards, J. N. (1997). Children and marital happiness: Why the negative correlation? *Journal of Family Issues, 7,* 131–147.

Yogev, & Brett, (1985). Perceptions of the division of housework and child care in marital satisfaction. *Journal of Marriage and the Family, 47,* 609–618.

The Relevance of the Biological Dimension and Biopsychosocial Therapy in Maintaining and Enhancing Close Relationships

Len Sperry
Medical College of Wisconsin

A Clinician's Guide to Maintaining and Enhancing Close Relationships is a very important book, and co-editors John H. Harvey and Amy Wenzel are to be heartily congratulated. Relational distress and enhancement is a cutting edge topic today and the editors have invited a group of experts to present their work at the at the interface of research and clinical practice. Any clinician working with couples will surely find these chapters conceptually interesting and clinically relevant. Some chapters offer very specific clinical guidelines and treatment strategies, and others offer clinically useful information about the recognition and diagnosis of topics that will be new information to most clinicians, that is, treatment of postpartum depression, forgiveness as an intervention strategy, and the impact of social phobia on relational dynamics. I read these chapters with great interest, I learned much, and I believe that my therapeutic work with couples will be greatly enhanced as a result.

Probably because of my medical training, I am attuned to conceptualizing and formulating conditions and concerns from a biopsychosocial perspective. As a result, I am likely to plan interventions that emphasize biopsychosocial therapy. Interestingly, I found that there was little, if any mention, of the biopsychosocial perspective or the biological dimension in the papers I reviewed.

For instance, in "Postpartum Depression," Larsen and O'Hara offer a psychosocial formulation of this debilitating condition. They cite studies of postpartum women that indicate that decreased sexual satisfaction is commonly reported and suggest that it "may be related to decreases in sexual desire/interest and activity/frequency, as well as increases in sexual problems." From a biopsychosocial perspective, decreased sexual satisfaction could also be directly related to hormonal changes. Now, although sexual desire/interest and sexual activity/frequency is known to involve psychosocial factors, it also involves biological factors, such as hormone levels. Accordingly, sexual desire and activity in women can be increased with hormone injections just as medications, such as Viagra, can increased sexual desire and activity in men.

Similarly, in "The Empirical Underpinnings of Marital Therapy for Depression," Banawan, O'Mahen, Beach, and Jackson offer a strictly psychosocial formulation of depression. They describe stress generation theory as a reasonable explanation for the link between depression and marital discord and review several studies of cognitive and behavioral approaches to marital therapy. Unfortunately, no description of the criteria used for determining the type and severity of depression were provided. Rather than a single, undifferentiated entity, depression can be conceptualized in several ways, that is, as a symptom, as an acute disorder, or as a chronic condition, with or without psychotic features. Depression is a multifaceted condition, and the efficacy of its treatment is contingent on the "match" between the type of depression and the type and intensity of the treatment.

No mention was made of the use of biological modalities in the treatment of depression, nor whether individuals or couples being treated with various types of cognitive therapy were also receiving medication. Neither was there any mention of the growing literature on integrated or combined treatment, that is, combining medication and therapy to treat depression in individuals and couples. A basic tenet of integrated or combined treatment is that treatment must be tailored to type and degree of severity of the depressive condition. The recently reported prospective study of combined treatment of depression by Keller et al. (2000) supports the use of tailored treatment. Cognitive Behavioral Analysis System of Psychotherapy (CBASP) is a manual-based approach that integrate elements of cognitive behavioral and interpersonal therapy to help chronically depressed individuals to develop needed problem-solving and relationship skills. CBASP was shown to be as effective as medication treatment in a 12-site national, prospective study with 681 chronically depressed outpatients. Even more significant, a combination of CBASP and the antidepressant nefazadone produced a response rate of 85% as compared to 50% response rate with either medication or CBASP alone. This research protocol conceptualized and treated depression from a biopsychosocial perspective, and appears to challenge the adequacy of psychosocial formulations of depression that Banawan et al. and other researchers espouse.

Although not directly specifying the biological dimension, Wenzel, in "Characteristics of Close Relationships in Individuals with Social Phobia," does note that the majority—up to 99%—of individuals with social phobias have psychiatric comorbidities, and that up to 70% meet criteria for major depression. Heavy genetic loading is associated with major depression and most of the anxiety disorders, so the biological dimension should be part of both research and clinical treatment formulations. Nevertheless, Wenzel's finding that socially anxious partners generally have close, satisfying relationships and that focusing treatment on attribution style should be a treatment focus will be encouraging to clinicians who tend to believe that social phobias and social anxiety disorders are difficult to treat.

Dolan and Nathan's chapter, "When One Partner Is an Alcoholic," did recognize a biological dimension for relational difficulties in couples where alcohol was involved. They reported differences in marital satisfaction between and Type II subgroup of alcoholics. They noted that couples in which Type I (early onset and higher genetic loading for alcoholism) was present appeared to have higher levels of marital satisfaction than in couples in which Type II (later onset and lower genetic loading) was present. They hypothesize that marital satisfaction may be a function of the stabilizing or destabilizing effect that alcohol has on the relationship. Alcohol appears to have a stabilizing effect in close relationships when it has present early or even prior to the relationship, and a more destabilizing effect if it is late onset. Because the necessary coping skills for dealing with alcohol are not in place in these later onset couples, the relationship are less stable and less satisfying. Fortunately, they point out that therapy, that is, Alcohol Behavior Couples Treatment, is effective and efficacious with these couples. To their good favor, these authors did note a biological dimension, and while not overtly recognizing the biopsychosocial perspective, they implied its presence.

THE BIOLOGICAL DIMENSION AND THE BIOPSYCHOSOCIAL PERSPECTIVE

Now why might the biological dimension be a worthwhile consideration in a book on relationship maintenance and enhancement? Because biological factors are often present in individuals in marriage and other close relationships who seek or are in individual psychotherapy, couples therapy, or marriage enrichment. Typically, these individuals meet formal criteria for diagnoses such as depression, bipolar disorder, eating disorders, panic disorder, obsessive–compulsive disorder, or other anxiety disorders. Accordingly, when biological factors are suspected, it is incumbent on clinicians—

whether they are medical or nonmedical clinicians—to formulate the case in biological as well as psychosocial terms. Such biopsychosocial formulations may lead to treatment plans that combine biological interventions with psychosocial interventions. Biological interventions are quite broad and range from medication or hormone replacement therapy to providing biofeedback training or making suggestions about exercise or synchronizing sleep–wake cycles. The clinician may provide such interventions or arrange a referral for such treatment when the intervention is outside the clinician's scope of practice. Even though a referral is made, collaboration between the clinicians is essential. Increasingly, nonmedical clinicians begin working with an individual or couple with biological factors, make an appropriate medical or psychiatric referral, and then continue their psychotherapeutic interventions in isolation from the medical clinician's intervention. Issues such as responsibility for after-hours and vacation coverage, the patient's safety and legal liability, as well as 'splitting' may never be discussed by the various providers. Biopsychosocial Therapy (Sperry, 1988, 1998, 1999, 2000) emphasizes the dimension of collaborative clinical practice between and among various providers.

The biopsychosocial perspective is a holistic and systems perspective for understanding the person and the relationship of the system outside and inside the person that influences both health and illness (Engel, 1977; Sperry, 1988). The model proposes that a person can only be adequately understood if the therapist considers all levels of a patient's functioning: biological, psychological, and social. Biological functioning refers to all peripheral organ system functions as well as to all autonomic, neuroendocrine, and central nervous system functions that are subcortical—that is, to all processes that are automatic and outside conscious awareness. Psychological functioning refers to the self-conscious inner world that directs information processing and communication from and with the outside world. It basically involves cortical structures and conscious awareness. It also includes the internal representation of self, the world, and personal goals, which reflects aspirations, ideals, needs, and the cognitions and strategies that govern behavior. Social functioning refers to the person's behavior in relation to family, friends, authorities, peer group and cultural expectations, as well as community institutions that influence and are influenced by the individual.

THE RETRIEVAL OF THE BIOLOGICAL DIMENSION IN PSYCHOLOGY

Until recently, training in psychology and the behavioral sciences has almost exclusively been directed at the psychosocial dimension of behavior. In the past decade, however, this has begun to change. Training programs in the behavioral sciences, particularly graduate programs in psychology, have begun to require some training in biology, that is, the biological bases of behavior, neuropsychology, cognitive neuroscience, psychopharmacology, and so on. This is occurring for at least two reasons: first, because of advances in our understanding of brain–mind interactions on behavior and the retrieval of the temperament dimension of personality; and second, because the professional practice of psychology has shifted its identity from being a mental health specialty to a health care specialty.

The "Decade of the Brain" did sensitize many clinicians, researchers, and theorists to the biological dimension of psychotherapy. It was not too long ago that psychotherapy was understood to be the treatment of choice for "psychologically based" disorders, or neurosis, and medication was believed to be the treatment of choice for "biologically-based" disorders, or psychosis. Today, this distinction, and the dualistic model of mind–brain relationship on which it is based, is considered not only inconsistent with the basic tenets of Integrative Psychology but also with emerging data from the neurosciences. Research is increasingly demonstrating that psychotherapy affects the brain, by significantly impacting neurotransmitter systems, genetic expression, and various brain structures (Kandel, 1998). Some have gone so far as to proclaim that psychotherapy is essentially a biological treatment intervention, yet others note that it is not longer possible to separate the biological perspective from the psychosocial perspective (Gabbard, 1996). The result is that biopsychosocial thinking is rapidly replacing other more parochial perspectives. It is interesting to note that while the American Psychiatric Association has championed the biopsychosocial perspective for at least the past 2 decades, the American Psychological Association has begun endorsing the biopsychosocial perspective in the past 2 years.

THE BIOPSYCHOSOCIAL PERSPECTIVE

The biopsychosocial model is a holistic and systems perspective for understanding the person and the relationship of the system outside and inside the person that influences both health and illness. Even though this comprehensive model has a long and venerable history, it has only recently gained widespread acceptance following the publication of George Engel's classic article (1977). The biopsychosocial model is a conceptualization that includes all the factors that impinge on the whole person and contribute to changes in health or mental health status. Because it is holistic and comprehensive, this model differs from reductionistic perspectives such as the systems model, the biomedical model, the psychodynamic model, and the behavioral model, to name a few. Rather, the biopsychosocial model integrates several concepts from many of these models (Sperry, 1988b).

The biopsychosocial model proposes that a person can only be adequately understood if the therapist considers all levels of a patient's functioning: biological or physical, psychological, and social. Physical functioning refers to all peripheral organ system functions as well as to all autonomic, neuroendocrine, and central nervous system functions that are subcortical—that is, to all processes that are automatic and outside conscious awareness. Psychological functioning refers to the self-conscious inner world that directs information processing and communication from and with the outside world. It basically involves cortical structures and conscious awareness. It also includes the internal representation of self, the world, and personal goals, which reflects aspirations, ideals, needs, and the cognitions and strategies that govern behavior. Social functioning refers to the person's behavior in relation to family, friends, authorities, peer group, and cultural expectations, as well as community institutions that influence and are influenced by the individual. Some might add that a truly holistic approach would include the spiritual or life-meaning dimension of functioning.

BIOPSYCHOSOCIAL THERAPY

Biopsychosocial therapy is an integrative approach for conceptualizing and implementing treatment when biological factors present along with psychological and social–systemic factors. Biopsychosocial therapy is an integrative approach in two regards: first, it integrates or strategically *combines* various treatment modalities—couple therapy and medication—as well as various methods—dynamic, cognitive–behavioral, systemic and psychoeducational; and second, it integrates and *tailors* these modalities and methods to the needs, styles, and expectations of the client, be it individual or couple.

A basic tenets of biopsychosocial therapy is that without treatment compliance or adherence there is very little correlation between a prescribed treatment and its outcome. Take medication for example; psychotropic agents have significantly impacted treatment outcomes. It is estimated that antipsychotics, antidepressants, and antimanics have an efficacy of 70% which means that about 70% of symptomatic patients can expect to achieve moderate to total symptom remission. This percentage is often compared to the rather dismal figure of 30% to 40% efficacy of other medical treatments. What is less well known and understood is that the actual efficacy of psychotropics is in the same range as other medical treatments. This is because of high rates of noncompliance, relapse, and recurrence, as well as biological factors such as receptor downregulation. Nevertheless, in "treatment-receptive" couples, the use of medication alone or in combination with other treatment modalities can quickly and effectively ameliorate symptoms of most Axis I disorders, and sometimes with Axis II conditions. For this reason, one of the essential strategies of Biopsychosocial Therapy with couples focuses on enhancing compliance and preventing relapse and recurrence.

REFERENCES

Engel, C. L. (1977), The need for a new medical model: A challenge to biomedical medicine, *Science, 196*, 129–136.

Gabbard, G. (1996). Clinical psychiatry in transition: Integrating biological and psychosocial perspectives. In J. Oldham (Ed.), *Review of psychiatry. Volume 15* (pp. 527–548). Washington, DC: American Psychiatric Press.

Kandel, E. (1998). A new intellectual framework for psychiatry. *American Journal of Psychiatry, 155*(4), 457–469.

Keller, M., McCullough, J, Klein, D., Arnow, B. et al. (2000). A comparison of nefazodone, the cognitive behavioral-analysis system of psychotherapy, and their combination for the treatment of chronic depression. *New England Journal of Medicine 342*(20), 1462–1470.

Sperry, L. (1988). Biopsychosocial therapy: An integrative approach for tailoring treatment. *Individual Psychology, 44*(2), 225–235.

Sperry, L. (ed). (2000). *Integrative and biopsychosical therapy: Maximizing treatment outcomes with individuals and couples.* Alexandria, VA: American Counseling Association Books.

Author Index

A

Abrams, D., 222, 225, 228
Abramson, L. Y., 202, 213
Acitelli, L. K., 2, 10, 13, 16, 18, 22, 23, 24, 37
Adams, W. J., 164, 172
Addis, M. E., 234, 249, 254, 256
Adelstein, D., 162, 174
Agras, W. S., 190, 195, 282, 298
Ahrons, C. R., 34, 37, 116, 122, 123, 126
Ainsworth, M. D. S., 63, 64, 65, 76
Albus, K. E., 69, 77
Alden, L. E., 211, 212
Alexander, F., 267, 274
Alexandra, H., 158, 160, 173
Alfano, M. S., 142, 154
Almgren, P. E., 170, 171, 175
Al-Mubak, R., 285, 297
Al-Reda, M. R., 224, 227
Altendorf, D. M., 32, 33, 34, 35, 37
Amato, P. R., 86, 101, 122, 123, 126, 233, 254
Amirkhan, J., 47, 62
Anchin, J. C., 265, 274
Anders, S. L., 70, 79
Anderson, J. Z., 117, 126
Anderson, P., 142, 154
Anderson, S. A., 240, 254
Angenendt, J., 181, 190, 196
Ansell, E., 45, 61
Appel, A. E., 86, 101
Arcus, M. E., 251, 254
Arditti, J. A., 122, 123, 128
Arend, R., 68, 76
Argyle, M., 22, 37
Arias, I., 139, 151, 281, 298
Arizzi, P., 18, 40

Armstrong, W., 48, 62
Arnow, B. A., 190, 195, 314, 319
Aron, A., 2, 10, 15, 37
Aron, E., 2, 10, 15, 37
Arriaga, X. B., 235, 258
Arrinell, W. A., 181, 195
Arthur, J., 139, 154
Asarnow, J. R., 234, 235, 236, 255
Asmussen, L., 18, 40
Attridge, M., 36, 37
Avery, A. W., 242, 254, 257
Avery-Leaf, 140, 153

B

Babcock, J. C., 246, 255
Bagarozzi, D. A., 192, 195, 239, 240, 254
Bagarozzi, J. I., 240, 254
Bain, A. B., 242, 257
Bakeman, R., 139, 152
Bakenstrass, M., 139, 155
Baker, S., 222, 229
Baldwin, M. W., 68, 76
Ballard, C. G., 166, 172
Ballenger, J. C., 179, 195
Banawan, S., 201, 213
Banks, S. P., 32, 33, 34, 35, 37
Bar Tal, D., 146, 152
Barber, J. G., 223, 227
Barling, J., 86, 102
Barlow, D. H., 178, 190, 193, 195, 196, 201, 212
Barrera, M., 134, 140, 152
Barrett, G., 164, 173
Barrett, K. C., 65, 77
Bartholomew, K., 57, 60, 66, 67, 68, 69, 71, 76, 77, 78, 79, 145, 152, 206, 209, 210, 212

Bates, G. W., 210, 213
Battaglia, D. M, 33, 37
Baucom, D. H., 59, 61, 150, 152, 184, 188, 192, 195, 204, 207, 213, 235, 254, 289, 298
Baumeister, R. F., 35, 37, 60, 296, 200
Baxter, L. A., 2, 10, 18, 20, 23, 29, 32, 33, 35, 41, 37
Beach, S. R. H., 134, 135, 136, 138, 139, 142, 143, 146, 147, 148, 149, 152, 153, 154, 155, 201, 212, 213, 234, 236, 246, 255, 283, 290, 297, 298
Bechtold, D., 238, 254
Beck, A. T., 145, 152, 202, 203, 212
Becker, A., 238, 256
Beckett, C., 117, 128
Behrens, B. C., 234, 258
Bejlovec, R. A., 34, 40
Bell, R. A., 19, 28, 37
Beloch, E., 200, 213
Belsky, J., 85, 88, 101
Benazon, N. R., 141, 143, 153
Bera, S., 72, 73, 78
Berenson, D., 219, 229
Berg, B. J., 139, 153
Berger, P., 119, 126
Berger, S. H., 110, 126
Bergin, A. E., 289, 297
Bernstein, A., 116, 117, 121, 126
Berry, J. W., 285, 288, 293, 300
Berry, S., 142, 155
Berscheid, E., 21, 37, 45, 61, 206, 212
Biglan, A., 139, 141, 152, 154
Binder, J. L., 269, 275
Birchler, G. R., 283, 299
Bitter, M., 190, 196
Blair, R. A., 163, 173
Blatt, S. J., 145, 152
Blehar, M., 63, 64, 65, 76
Blood, R. O., 235, 254
Blowers, C. M., 190, 195
Blum, T. C., 134, 135, 152
Blumberg, S. L., 138, 155, 215, 227, 233, 235, 236, 238, 239, 240, 244, 245, 246, 250, 252, 256, 257

Bobulinski, M., 252, 257
Bohman, M., 220, 227
Bombar, M., 19, 37
Bond, A., 159, 160, 170, 175
Bookwala, J., 71, 76
Booth, A., 44, 60, 111, 126, 235, 254, 310, 312
Borkovec, T. D., 203, 213
Bowers, T. G., 224, 227
Bowlby, J., 63, 64, 66, 69, 73, 76, 180, 195, 265, 275
Bowman, M. E., 122, 126
Boyce, P., 158, 165, 166, 173
Bradbury, T. N., 84, 101, 142, 144, 153, 154, 205, 212, 235, 236, 240, 246, 255, 256, 257
Brandeth, Y., 123, 129
Brant, H. J., 164, 174
Braver, S., 123, 126
Braverman, J., 163, 173
Bray, J. H., 110, 112, 121, 123, 126
Brennan, K. A., 68, 69, 76, 79, 210, 212
Brett, 309, 311 (init)
Brody, G. H., 88, 103, 106, 126
Bronkhorst, J., 286, 299
Brooks, A. E., 139, 152
Brough, D. I., 163, 170, 176
Brown, G. W., 140, 152
Brown, H. S., 110, 129
Brown, L., 216, 227
Brown, P., 33, 37
Brown, S. W., 29, 39, 59, 61, 283, 284, 299
Browning, S. W., 124, 125, 126
Bruce, M., 136, 155
Bruch, M. A., 200, 212
Bruess, C. J. S., 19, 37
Brumley, H. E., 158, 169, 174
Buchanan, C. M., 123, 126
Bucher, J., 159, 160, 170, 176
Buehler, C., 122, 127
Buerkel-Rothfuss, N., 19, 28, 37
Bulik, C. M., 75, 79
Bullis, C., 18, 37
Bumpass, L., 105, 127, 235, 254

Burge, D., 69, 77
Burgess, R. L., 21, 37
Burke, M., 88, 103
Burleson, B. R., 16, 23, 37
Burman, B., 84, 87, 88, 102, 282, 297
Burnam, M. A., 142, 155
Burnett, C. K., 238, 254
Burns, D. D., 136, 152
Burt, M., 109, 120, 125, 127
Burt, R., 109, 120, 125, 127
Burton, T., 190, 96
Busby, D. M., 238, 256
Butler, M. H., 243, 254
Byng-Hall, J., 74, 75, 77
Byrne, C. A., 182, 197

C

Cacioppo, J. T., 282, 298
Cahn, D. D., 26, 27, 29, 38
Calarco, M. M., 143, 153
Calhoun, K. S., 293, 297
Callan, V. J., 68, 70, 78
Campbell, S. B., 82, 85, 87, 88, 97,
    98, 101, 159, 163, 166, 170, 173,
    175
Campeas, R., 199, 213
Campos, J. J., 65, 77
Canary, D. J., 13, 25, 26, 27, 29, 38,
    105, 127
Cano, A., 140, 146, 152, 155, 287, 297
Caplan, H. L., 158, 160, 173
Capreol, M. J., 211, 212
Carbaugh, D. A., 32, 33, 35, 41
Cardis, P., 285, 297
Carlson, E. A., 69, 77, 79
Carnelley, K. B., 69, 77, 145, 152
Carro, M. G., 160, 168, 170, 173
Carroll, K., 222, 228, 229
Carson, C. L., 22, 34, 38
Carter, B., 119, 128
Carter, M. M., 178, 181, 194, 195
Cassidy, J., 68, 79
Castle, D., 69, 79
Castle, J. M., 159, 174
Castro Martin, T., 105, 127

Catalan, J., 190, 196
Cate, R. M., 18, 25, 27, 29, 38, 39
Cerny, J. A., 190, 195, 196
Chambless, D. L., 178, 196
Checkley, S., 165, 175
Cherlin, A. J., 105, 119, 127
Chernen, L., 190, 193, 195
Cherry, S., 75, 78
Chevron, E. S., 74, 75, 78, 146, 147,
    148, 153, 171, 174
Childs-Clarke, A., 190, 195
Chinsky, J. M., 288, 299
Choquette, K. A., 218, 225, 229, 283,
    299
Christensen, A., 45, 61, 211, 213,
    246, 255
Christian, J. L., 138, 152
Christian-Herman, J. L., 140, 153
Ciabattari, T., 307, 310
Clark, M. S., 1, 10
Clark, C. L., 67, 77
Clark, L. A., 201, 213
Clark, R., 169, 171, 173
Clarke, J., 203, 213
Clements, M. L., 236, 239, 255, 256
Clingempeel, W. G., 88, 102
Cloninger, C. R., 220, 227
Clore, G. L., 45, 62
Close, H. T., 284, 297
Cloven, D. H., 29, 30, 38, 40
Coale Lewis, H., 113, 121, 127
Cobb, J. P., 190, 195
Cobb, R., 240, 246, 257
Cocco, K., 218, 228
Coche, J., 215, 227
Cody, M. J., 32, 33, 34, 35, 37
Coffin, W., 234, 240, 257
Cogill, S. R., 158, 160, 173
Cohan, C. L., 142, 153
Cohen, E., 203, 212
Cohen, S., 140, 153, 190, 196
Cohn, J. F., 159, 160, 163, 170, 173
Cole, A. L., 122, 127
Cole, C. L., 122, 127
Cole, J. D., 234, 235, 236, 255
Cole-Detke, H., 145, 153

Coleman, M., 59, 60, 105, 109, 110, 111, 112, 113, 114, 115, 119, 120, 127, 128, 129
Collela, U., 235, 257
Collins, A., 45, 62
Collins, J. F., 75, 77
Collins, N. L., 67, 68, 69, 70, 77
Compas, B. E., 160, 168, 170, 173
Conger, R. D., 236, 256
Connor, Y., 163, 173
Conville, R., 33, 38
Cook, S. W., 34, 39
Cooney, N., 222, 228
Cooper, C., 248, 251, 257
Cooper, P. J., 44, 61, 159, 160, 170, 173, 176
Cordova, A., 235, 252, 255, 257
Cordova, J., 146, 150, 153
Corey, G., 251, 255
Corey, S., 251, 255
Couper, D., 60
Cowan, C. P., 83, 99, 100, 101
Cowan, P. A., 83, 99, 100, 101
Cox, A. D., 86, 101
Cox, B. J., 203, 212
Cox, C. L., 235, 258
Cox, J. L., 159, 160, 163, 173, 176
Cox, M. J., 83, 84, 88, 101, 102, 233, 255
Coyle, C. T., 56, 60, 285, 297
Coyne, J. C., 134, 141, 142, 143, 153, 154, 161, 167, 169, 173, 193, 196
Craske, M. G., 177, 179, 185, 190, 191, 194, 195, 196
Craven, L., 111, 127
Critchlow, B., 219, 229
Crohn, H., 110, 129
Crosbie-Burnett, M., 111, 122, 127
Crouter, A. C., 51, 61, 310, 312
Crowell, J. A., 67, 77
Crumley, L. P., 49, 51, 62
Cullen, P., 166, 172
Cummings, E. M., 82, 83, 84, 85, 86, 87, 88, 89, 90, 95, 96, 97, 98, 99, 101, 102, 134, 153, 161, 173

Cupach, W. R., 16, 22, 25, 26, 27, 29, 34, 38, 40
Cutler, L. A., 169, 175
Cutrona, C. E., 140, 153, 158, 162, 173, 246, 255
Cutter, H. S. G., 219, 229

D

Dadds, M. R., 99, 102
Daley, S. E., 69, 77
Dallos, R., 119, 127
Daluto, A. D., 150, 152, 184, 188, 192, 195
Daniels, M., 142, 155
Datteri, D. S., 33, 37
Davidson, R. J., 47, 61
Davies, E., 286, 299
Davies, P. T., 82, 83, 85, 86, 87, 88, 89, 90, 97, 98, 101, 102, 134, 153, 161, 173
Davila, J., 69, 77, 138, 142, 144, 153
Davis, D., 219, 229
Davis, J. L., 2, 10
Davis, K. E., 67, 68, 70, 72, 73, 78
Davis, R., 166, 172
Day, A., 159, 160, 170, 176
de Hann, E., 181, 191, 192, 195
De Lange, I., 181, 196
Dean, R. N. C., 166, 172
Dearth-Pendley, G., 134, 153
Dehle, C., 137, 153
Del Bene, D., 199, 213
Delin, C. B., 216, 227
Denton, W. H., 23, 37
DeVita, C. J., 233, 255
Dicks, H. V., 265, 275
DiClemente, C. C., 222, 228, 229
Dimitrovsky, L., 163, 172, 173
DiNaardo, P. A., 201, 212
Dindia, K., 105, 127
Dion, K. K., 70, 78
Dion, K. L., 70, 78
Direnfeld, D. M., 203, 212
Dobson, K., 147, 148, 154
Docherty, J. P., 75, 77

Doherty, W. F., 234, 255
Dolan, S. L., 217, 26, 227, 229
Dollahite, D. C., 116, 117, 128
Donovan, D., 222, 228
Dornbusch, S. M., 123, 126
Douvan, E., 286, 300
Downey, G., 161, 167, 169, 173
Dozier, M., 69, 77
Drew, J. B., 140, 154
Drigotas, S. M., 235, 258
Druckman, J., 238, 257
Duck, S. W., 15, 16, 22, 23, 24, 26,
    27, 28, 29, 31, 32, 33, 36, 38, 41
Duggan, E. S., 210, 212
Dunn, N. J., 218, 219, 227, 228
Dutton, D. G., 15, 37, 69, 71, 77
Dyer, M., 47, 61

E

Eaton, W. W., 199, 213
Edwards, J. N., 111, 126, 235, 254,
    310, 312
Edwards, M. E., 224, 227
Egeland, B., 68, 69, 77, 79
Eilati, I., 69, 79
Eisen, B., 190, 196
Eisenberg, N., 246, 255
Elicker, J., 68, 77
Elkin, I., 75, 77
Ellard, J. H., 57, 61, 281, 298
Elliott, S. A., 163, 170, 176
Elmore, M., 159, 173
Emanuals-Zuurveen, L., 148, 153
Emerson, R. M., 34, 38
Emery, R. E., 83, 84, 85, 86, 96, 102,
    233, 255
Emmelkamp, P. M. G., 148, 153,
    181, 190, 191, 192, 195
Emms, E. M., 163, 169, 170, 175
Engel, C. L., 316, 317, 319
Engel, T., 110, 129
Englund, M., 68, 77
Enright, R. D., 56, 59, 60, 283, 285,
    286, 297, 298
Epstein, E. E., 220, 224, 226, 227

Epstein, N., 119, 120, 128, 235, 254
Erbaugh, J., 203, 212
Erel, O., 84, 87, 88, 102
Erickson, M. F., 68, 77
Ernst, S., 139, 155
Esterling, B. A., 289, 296, 298
Evans, K., 45, 61
Ewart, C. K., 282, 298
Exline, J. J., 60

F

Fairbairn, W. R. D., 264, 275
Fairburn, C. G., 75, 77
Fallon, B. A., 199, 213
Fals-Stewart, W., 216, 227
Fantauzzo, C. A., 159, 174
Farber, E. A., 68, 77
Farr, R. M., 20, 38
Farrell, J., 110, 111, 127
Fawcet, J., 167, 173
Fedderly, S. A., 169, 171, 173
Fee, R., 282, 300
Feeney, J. A., 68, 69, 70, 71, 77, 78
Fehm-Wolfsdorf, G., 234, 256
Fehr, B., 20, 34, 36, 38, 40, 68, 76
Feingold, A., 20, 22, 38
Felmlee, D., 34, 40
Fenell, D., 284, 298
Ferris, K. O., 34, 38
Fiedler, P., 139, 155
Field, T., 158, 159, 162, 173, 174
Fiester, S. J., 75, 77
Fincham, F. D., 50, 56, 59, 60, 83, 84,
    85, 101, 102, 135, 136, 138, 146,
    149, 152, 153, 205, 212, 234, 235,
    236, 246, 255, 278, 283, 284, 290,
    293, 297, 298
Fine, M. A., 34, 38, 109, 111, 112,
    119, 120, 127, 128
Fischer, M., 181, 190, 196
Fisher, L., 282, 298
Fisher-Nelson, H., 217, 225, 228, 229
Fishman, B., 119, 127
Fisicario, S. A., 140, 154
Fitness, J., 50, 61

Fitzgerald, N. M., 18, 39
Fitzgibbons, R. P., 60, 61, 286, 298
Fivush, R., 146, 154
Flanagan, C., 163, 170, 173
Flanigan, B., 55, 61
Fletcher, G. J. O., 50, 61
Fletcher, J., 163, 169, 170, 175
Flick, U., 20, 39
Floyd, F. J., 219, 229
Floyd, F., 215, 227, 239, 256
Foa, E. B., 181, 196
Folette, W. C., 204, 207, 213
Foley, S. H., 146, 147, 148, 153
Folingstad, D. R., 139, 153
Folkes, V. S., 45, 47, 61, 62
Forehand, R., 106, 126
Forthofer, M. S., 233, 255
Fournier, D. G., 237, 238, 255, 257
Fowers, B. J., 236, 255
Fox, N. A., 47, 61
Fraley, R. C., 67, 77
Francis, M. E., 294, 299
Frankel, O., 65, 79
Frankenstein, W., 218, 219, 227, 228
Frazier, P. A., 34, 39
Freedman, S. R., 283, 285, 298
Freeman, T., 286, 299
Friedman, L., 139, 154
Friedman, S., 190, 193, 195
Frieze, I. H., 146, 152, 310, 312
Frijda, N. H., 47, 48, 57, 59, 61
Fruzzetti, A. E., 147, 148, 154
Fujimoto, K., 182, 196
Fyer, A. J., 75, 78

G

Gabbard, G., 317, 319
Gagnon, J. H., 287, 298
Gaines, C., 167, 175
Galvin, K. M., 44, 61
Ganong, L., 105, 109, 110, 111, 112, 113, 114, 115, 119, 120, 127, 128
Garbin, M. G., 203, 212
Gardner, C. B., 34, 38
Garfinkel, R., 199, 213

Garner, D. M., 163, 175
Gath, D. H., 159, 160, 170, 176
Gee, C. B., 146, 150, 153
Gelder, M., 190, 196
Gelfand, D. M., 158, 161, 174, 176
George, C., 68, 78
Ghodsian, M., 160, 161, 174
Giancola, P. R., 217, 228
Gianetti, C. G., 107, 128
Giblin, P., 242, 255
Gilbertson, R., 223, 227
Gilbreath, J. G., 123, 126
Gilmore, J. S., 163, 173
Gingrich, R., 115, 127
Ginsburg, G. P., 26, 39
Gitlow, A., 199, 213
Glaser, R., 282, 298
Glass, D. R., 75, 77
Glenn, N. D., 235, 255
Goeke-Morey, M. C., 87, 90, 101, 102
Goering, P., 133, 137, 155
Goetz, C., 139, 155
Goffman, E., 15, 33, 39
Goldberg, S., 65, 79
Goldner, V., 121, 125, 128
Goldsmith, H. H., 65, 77
Goldstein, A. J., 178, 196
Goldstein, S., 159, 174
Goodman, S. H., 158, 169, 174
Gordon, K. C., 59, 61, 289, 298
Gore, K., 19, 28, 37
Gorman, L., 171, 175
Gorsuch, R. L., 204, 213, 249, 257
Gotlib, I. H., 136, 137, 141, 142, 144, 153, 155, 158, 159, 160, 163, 168, 169, 170, 171, 173, 174, 176
Gotlieb, I., 210, 213
Gottman, J. M., 17, 18, 19, 29, 39, 85, 89, 102, 236, 239, 255, 256
Grady-Fletcher, A., 267, 275
Graham, E. E., 18, 39
Grant, I., 216, 228
Grant, K. E., 160, 168, 170, 173
Gray, J., 15, 17, 39, 47, 61
Greden, J. F., 141, 153

Greenberg, L. S., 9, 10, 150, 154, 265, 275, 284, 298
Greene, J. O., 32, 33, 34, 35, 37
Greenfield, S., 142, 155
Griffin, D. W., 50, 62, 67, 78, 277, 299
Grigg, F., 50, 61
Gross, K. H., 248, 251, 257
Grote, N., 310, 312
Groth, T., 234, 256
Grove, D. C., 286, 299
Grove, F., 68, 76
Gruen, D. S., 169, 174
Grych, J. H., 84, 85, 102
Guerney, B. G., 234, 239, 240, 241, 255, 258
Guijarro, M. L., 282, 299
Guthertz, M., 159, 174

H

Hafner, R. J., 177, 181, 193, 194, 196
Hahlweg, K., 204, 207, 213, 233, 234, 236, 256
Haley, J., 183, 196
Halford, K. W., 251, 255
Halford, W. K., 150, 154, 215, 228
Hallett, A. J., 282, 299
Halling, S., 286, 299
Hamel, B., 119, 127
Hammen, C. L., 69, 77, 133, 138, 141, 142, 154
Hand, I., 178, 181, 190, 196
Hannon, P. A., 2, 10
Haris, T. O., 140, 152
Harold, G. T., 135, 146, 146, 153
Harris, A. H. S., 282, 300
Harris, L., 33, 39
Harris, T., 243, 255
Hartman, S. G., 235, 255, 256
Harvey, I., 166, 167, 174
Harvey, J. H., 7, 10, 30, 39, 45, 61, 201, 205, 212, 213
Harwood, E. M., 135, 152
Hatgis, C., 249, 254
Hause, E. S., 139, 153
Hautzinger, M., 139, 154

Hawkins, J. D., 234, 235, 236, 255
Hay, W. M., 218, 219, 227, 228
Hayman, P. M., 183, 184, 192, 197
Haynes, O. M., 159, 174
Hays, R. D., 142, 155
Hazan, C., 57, 61, 63, 65, 66, 67, 68, 70, 71, 72, 73, 74, 78, 79, 180, 196
Healy, B., 159, 174
Heatherton, T. F., 35, 37
Heaton, T. B., 235, 256
Heavey, C., 239, 240, 246, 257
Hebl, J. H., 285, 286, 298
Heckelman, L. R., 199, 213
Heimberg, R. G., 211, 212, 213
Heindel, S., 87, 102
Heins, R., 190, 196
Heitland, W., 242, 256
Helgeson, V. S., 34, 39, 47, 61
Helson, R., 72, 78
Heming, G., 99, 101
Henderson, S. H., 121, 128
Henderson, V. K., 88, 101
Hennon, C. B., 119, 120, 128
Hepworth, C., 140, 152
Herbert, T. B., 57, 61
Herzberg, D., 69, 77
Hess, J. A., 59, 61
Hester, R., 222, 228
Hetherington, E. M., 88, 102, 112, 121, 128
Heyman, R. E., 138, 155, 192, 197, 216, 228
Hickle, I., 158, 165, 166, 173
Hiebert, J., 237, 256
Hight, T. L., 29, 39, 56, 61, 283, 284, 299
Himaldi, W. A., 190, 196
Himaldi, W. G., 190, 195
Hirsch, L. S., 220, 227
Hobson, R. P., 69, 79
Hock, E., 163, 166, 168, 174
Hodgson, D., 190, 197
Hoffman, N., 139, 154
Holden, G. W., 86, 88, 101, 102
Hollier, A., 110, 126
Holman, T. B., 238, 256

Holmes, J. G., 50, 62, 74, 78, 277, 299
Holt, C. S., 211, 213
Holtzworth-Monroe, A., 50, 61, 178, 196
Hood, R., 249, 257
Hoodguin, C. A. L., 181, 191, 192, 195
Hooley, J. M., 139, 154, 163, 174
Hope, D. A., 211, 213
Hopkins, J., 159, 173
Hopper, R., 19, 39
Hops, H., 139, 141, 152, 154
Horan, P. M., 135, 152
Hore, B. D., 217, 228
Horesh, N., 69, 79
Horney, K., 47, 61
Horowitz, L. M., 57, 60, 66, 67, 68, 69, 76, 145, 152, 206, 209, 210, 213
Horowitz, M., 266, 275
Hosman, C., 234, 258
Howard, R., 69, 79
Hughes, R., 249, 256
Hummon, N., 218, 227
Hurst, M., 17, 38
Huston, T. L., 18, 21, 37, 39, 45, 51, 61, 204, 213, 310, 312

I

Iannotti, R., 86, 87, 101
Ickes, W., 2, 10
Imber, S. D., 75, 77
Ingham, J. G., 219, 228
Isabella, R., 161, 176
Itskowitz, R., 163, 172, 173
Iverson, A., 15, 37
Iwasaki, Y., 182, 196
Izard, C. E., 159, 160, 174, 176

J

Jackson, P. B., 140, 154
Jacob, T., 218, 219, 227, 228
Jacobson, N. J., 204, 207, 211, 213

Jacobson, N. S., 10, 50, 61, 139, 147, 148, 154, 155, 178, 196, 234, 246, 255, 256
Jaeger, M., 281, 298
Jaffe, K., 69, 77, 145, 152
Jannoun, L., 190, 196
Janoff-Bulman, R., 289, 298
Jaspers, J. M., 293, 298
Jenkins, 310, 312
Johnson, M., 240, 246, 257
Johnson, M. P., 25, 34, 39
Johnson, S. M., 9, 10, 74, 75, 78, 134, 150, 154, 155, 171, 176, 182, 188, 189, 193, 196, 265, 275
Joiner, T. E., 134, 142, 143, 144, 154
Jones, E. F., 250, 256
Jordan, J., 75, 79
Jordan, P. L., 234, 240, 257
Jorgensen, S. R., 242, 257
Jouriles, E. N., 85, 86, 102, 216, 228

K

Kadden, R., 222, 228
Kaflowitz, N. G., 200, 212
Kahn, J., 141, 142, 153
Kaiser, A., 234, 256
Kandel, E., 317, 319
Kaplan, L., 119, 120, 128
Kaplan, N., 68, 78, 79
Karney, B. R., 137, 144, 154, 236, 256
Kasai, S., 182, 196
Kassel, J. D., 145, 155, 210, 213
Katz, J., 135, 138, 142, 149, 152, 154, 281, 283, 297, 298
Katz, R., 160, 173
Kaufman Kantor, G., 217, 218, 228
Keelan, J. P. R., 70, 78
Keith, B., 86, 101, 122, 126, 233, 254
Keller, A., 169, 171, 173
Keller, M., 314, 319
Kelley, H. H., 21, 40, 45, 61, 294, 298
Kelley, P., 117, 128
Kelln, B. R. C., 281, 298
Kelly, A., 251, 255
Kelly, J. R., 58, 61

Kelly, S., 215, 227
Kelvin, P., 47, 61
Kemp-Fincham, S. I., 290, 298
Kendall, R. E., 163, 173
Kennedy, S., 282, 298
Kermeen, P., 164, 174
Keshet, J. K., 107, 128
Kesner, J. E., 69, 71, 78
Kessler, R. C., 66, 69, 79, 141, 153, 199, 213, 233, 255
Kiecolt-Glaser, J. K., 282, 298
Kiernan, K. E., 105, 128
Kiesler, D. J., 265, 274
Kirisci, L., 217, 228
Kirkpatrick, L. A., 68, 71, 72, 73, 74, 78
Kirlike, N., 182, 196
Klein, D., 314, 319
Klein, D. M., 238, 256
Klein, M., 264, 275
Klein, R. C. A., 20, 25, 39
Klerman, G. L., 74, 75, 78, 171, 174
Klohnen, E. C., 72, 73, 78
Knapp, M. L., 19, 39
Knobe, J., 48, 61
Kobak, R., 145, 153
Koester, N. H., 200, 213
Kohn, C. S., 239, 240, 246, 257
Kohn, P. M., 217, 229
Kojima, M., 182, 196
Kotler, M., 69, 79
Kraemer, H. C., 282, 298
Krahn, G. L., 219, 228
Kramer, K. B., 235, 255
Kraus, M. A., 169, 174
Krokoff, L. J., 236, 255
Kroonenberg, P., 65, 79
Kuebli, J., 146, 154
Kuipers, P., 47, 57, 61
Kulka, R. A., 286, 300
Kumar, C., 165, 175
Kumar, R., 158, 160, 163, 164, 167, 170, 171, 173, 174
Kunkel, A. W., 16, 37
Kurdek, L. A., 135, 136, 154, 235, 256

L

L'Abate, L., 45, 61, 246, 256, 289, 296, 298
Lakey, B., 140, 154
Lamb, M. E., 65, 77
Lamontagne, Y., 178, 196
Larson, J. H., 238, 256
Larzelere, R. E., 204, 213
Laumann, E. O., 287, 298
Lawrence, E., 240, 246, 257
Lazarus, R. S., 45, 46, 48, 59, 61
Leach, P., 107, 128
Leary, M. R., 45, 61
Leber, B. D., 247, 248, 252, 257
Leber, W. R., 75, 77
Lee, L., 32, 33, 39
Lee, N., 282, 300
Lee, T. H., 216, 227
Leff, J. P., 139, 155
Legault, F., 169, 175
Leifer, M., 286, 299
Leonard, K. E., 216, 219, 220, 221, 228, 229
Lerner, H. G., 146, 155
Leslie, L. A., 34, 39, 119, 120, 128, 242, 254
Lester, D., 215, 228
Levenson, R. W., 236, 256
Levine, A., 107, 129
Levinger, G., 29, 30, 40, 45, 61
Levinson, S. C., 33, 37
Levy, A. K., 69, 79
Levy, M. B., 67, 68, 70, 78
Lewin, L., 139, 141, 152
Lewinsohn, P. M., 136, 137, 153
Lewis, D. A., 170, 175
Lewis, J. M., 88, 101
Lewis, M. A., 142, 155
Li, S. A., 134, 152
Liebowitz, M. R., 199, 213
Lindberg, N., 69, 77
Linden, M., 139, 154
Lipkus, I., 278, 299
Lipsitz, J. D., 75, 78
Litt, M., 222, 228

Littig, L. W., 19, 37
Litz, B. T., 182, 197
Liu, T. J., 219, 229
Livingston, L. R., 218, 228
Lloyd, S. A., 25, 27, 29, 38, 39
Logan, G. P., 158, 168, 166, 175
Long, B., 234, 235, 236, 255
Lord, C. G., 33, 37
Lovestone, S., 167, 174
Luborsky, L., 269, 275
Lucente, S., 216, 227
Luckman, T., 119, 126
Ludwig, T. E., 282, 300
Lushene, R. E., 204, 213
Luskin, F., 282, 300
Luty, S. E., 75, 79
Lutz, C. J., 140, 154
Lutz, P., 123, 128
Lutz, W. J., 163, 166, 168, 174
Lye, D., 309, 310
Lyster, R. F., 237, 250, 256, 257

M

Maccoby, E. E., 123, 126
MacCullum, R. C., 282 298
Madden-Derdich, D. A., 122, 123, 128
Magee, W. J., 199, 213
Main, M., 65, 68, 78, 79
Maisto, S. A., 225, 228
Malarkey, W. B., 282, 298
Malcolm, W. M., 284, 298
Malkoff, S., 282, 298
Malle, B. F., 48, 61
Malone, J., 283, 299
Maneker, J. S., 235, 256
Manonda, I., 164, 173
Margolin, G., 191, 196, 204, 207, 213, 277, 282, 297, 299
Markey, B., 238, 256
Markman, H. J., 110, 111, 127, 138, 155, 215, 227, 233, 234, 235, 236, 238, 239, 240, 244, 245, 246, 247, 248, 250, 252, 255, 256, 257, 258

Markowitz, J. C., 75, 78, 79
Marks, I. M., 178, 191, 195, 196
Marks, M., 165, 175
Marshall, L. L., 30, 39
Martin, J. K., 134, 135, 152
Martin, M. E., 163, 175
Martin, P., 109, 111, 127
Martin, T. C., 235, 254
Masheter, C., 33, 39, 122, 128
Mathews, A. M., 190, 195
Matias, R., 159, 173
Matsui, T., 182, 196
Matsunaga, H., 182, 196
Matthews, J., 107, 128
Matthews, L. S., 236, 256
Mattick, R. P., 203, 213
Mauger, P. A., 286, 299
Mayne, T. J., 294, 299
McBride, A. G., 286, 299
McCabe, K. M., 140, 154
McCall, G. J., 14, 39
McCann, I. L., 188, 196
McClintock, E., 45 61
McCloud, P., 162, 164, 169, 175
McCrady, B. S., 217, 220, 224, 225, 226, 227, 228, 229
McCullough, J., 314, 319
McCullough, M. E., 29, 39, 51, 59, 61, 62, 247, 256, 283, 284, 299
McDaniel, A. K., 119, 120, 127
McDonald, R., 191, 195
McGoldrick, M., 119, 128
McGonagle, K. A., 199, 213
McGrath, G., 166, 167, 174
McGrath, J. E., 58, 61
McHale, S. M., 51, 61, 310, 312
McIntosh, V. V., 75, 79
McKay, J. R., 225, 228
McKenry, P. C., 69, 71, 78, 116, 128
McKenzie, J. M., 75, 79
McKinney, K. E., 286, 299
McLeod, J. D., 216, 228
Mehta, M., 192, 197
Meissner, W. W., 263, 275
Mellinger, G. D., 29, 30, 40
Mendels, J., 139, 155

Mendelsohn, M., 203, 212
Messer, S. B., 266, 270, 275
Messinger, D. S., 161, 176
Messman, S. J., 25, 26, 27, 29, 38
Metalsky, G. I., 142, 154, 202, 213
Metts, S., 26, 32, 33, 34, 39, 40
Metzger, R. L., 203, 213
Meyer, T. J., 203, 213
Meyers, T., 163, 170, 173
Michael, R. T., 287, 298
Michaels, S., 287, 298
Micheletto, M., 238, 256
Mickelson, K. D., 66, 69, 79
Mikulincer, M., 69, 79
Milardo, R., 20, 25, 33, 39, 40
Milet, T. H., 158, 164, 167, 176
Milgrom, J., 162, 164, 169, 175
Milholland, T., 242, 254
Miller, K. J., 226, 227
Miller, M. J., 203, 213
Miller, P. A., 246, 255
Miller, P. M., 219, 228
Miller, R. B., 122, 126
Miller, S., 240, 242, 256
Miller, T., 219, 228
Miller, T. Q., 282, 299
Miller, W. R., 222, 228
Mills, D. M., 120, 128
Mills, J., 1, 10
Mills, M., 86, 101
Mineka, S., 201, 213
Minuchin, P., 82, 102
Miyata, A., 182, 196
Mock, J., 203, 212
Mohan, 166, 172
Monarh, N. D., 235, 257
Moncher, F. J., 69, 79
Montel, K. H., 236, 255
Montgomery, B. M., 23, 29, 37
Monti, P., 222, 228
Moras, K., 136, 152
Morgan, A. G., 242, 257
Morgan, P., 309, 310
Morris, K. A., 67, 69, 71, 76, 77
Morris, M. L., 248, 251, 257
Morrison, K., 108, 121, 128

Morrow, C., 162, 174
Moscovici, S., 20, 38
Moss, H. B., 217, 228
Mount, J. H., 160, 163, 169, 171, 174
Mueser, K. T., 150, 152, 184, 188, 192, 195
Munby, M., 190, 196
Mundt, C., 139, 155
Murphy, B., 210, 213
Murphy, C. M., 85, 102, 218, 221, 222, 228, 229, 283, 299
Murray, E. J., 289, 296, 298
Murray, L., 158, 160, 161, 173, 175
Murray, S. L., 50, 62, 277, 299
Murstein, B. I., 22, 40
Myers, R. L., 87, 102

N

Nadelson, C. C., 263, 275
Nagyurem J., 51, 62
Nathan, P. E., 183, 197, 217, 218, 219, 226, 227, 228, 229
Negel, L., 45, 61
Nelligan, J. S., 68, 79
Nelson, G. M., 139, 152, 155
Nelson, R. R., 240, 257
Neubaum, E., 106, 126
Neunaber, D. J., 170, 175
Newman, B., 116, 128
Nezlek, J., 21, 40
Nietzsche, F. W., 279, 299
Nilsson, A., 170, 171, 175
Noel, N. E., 217, 225, 228, 229
Nolen-Hoeksema, S., 146, 155
Noller, P., 68, 69, 70, 71, 77, 78
Norman, C. C., 2, 10
Norre, J., 283, 300
Notarius, C., 239, 257
Nowinski, J., 222, 229
Nunally, E. W., 240, 242, 256

O

O'Brien, G. T., 190, 196

O'Farrell, T. J., 218, 219, 221, 222, 225, 228, 229, 283, 299
O'Hara, M. W., 137, 155, 157, 160, 163, 164, 166, 170, 171, 175, 176
O'Leary, K. D., 85, 86, 102, 136, 138, 140, 146, 147, 148, 149, 152, 153, 155, 192, 197, 201, 212, 228, 283, 287, 297, 299
O'Mahen-Gray, H. A., 201, 213
O'Shea, M. W., 163, 173
Oatley, K., 48, 62, 190, 197
Ogawa, J. R., 69, 79
Olmos-Gallo, P. A., 252, 257
Olmsted, M. P., 163, 175
Olsen, N., 2, 10
Olson, D. H., 205, 208, 213, 236, 237, 238, 250, 255, 257
Olson, M. R., 169, 175
Omarzu, J., 7, 10, 201, 205, 212, 213
Omoto, A. M., 206, 212
Onstein, E. J., 190, 196
Orina, M., 2, 10
Orley, J., 139, 154
Ortony, A., 45, 62
Osbargy, S., 251, 255
Osborne, L. N., 85, 102, 135, 136, 146, 153
Osgarby, S. M., 215, 228
Osteen, V., 139, 154
Owen, M. T., 88, 101, 102

P

Paley, B., 69, 77, 83, 84, 101
Paolino, T. J., 263, 275
Papernow, P., 109, 111, 113, 124, 125, 128
Papp, L. M., 87, 90, 101
Parker, G., 158, 165, 166, 173
Parkinson, B., 46, 59, 62
Parks, M. R., 20, 40
Parloff, M. B., 75, 77
Pasch, L. A., 235, 257
Pasley, K., 115, 116, 117, 124, 125, 128, 129
Patrick, M., 69, 79

Patterson, B., 117, 128
Patterson, G. R., 85, 88, 102
Patty, J., 71, 78
Paykel, E. S., 163, 169, 170, 175
Peacock, J., 164, 173
Pearl, D., 282, 298
Pearl, L., 200, 212
Pearlman, L. A., 188, 196
Pearson, J. C., 19, 37
Pellegrini, D., 162, 175
Pennebaker, J. W., 289, 293, 294, 296, 299
Peplau, L. A., 45, 61
Perez-Hirshberg, M., 163, 172, 173
Perlmuter, M. S., 116, 122, 123, 126
Perodeau, G. M., 217, 229
Perrin, F. A. C., 21, 40
Perry, J. E., 286, 299
Peterson, C., 202, 213
Peterson, D., 238, 256
Peterson, D. R., 45, 61
Phillipps, L. H., 160, 164, 175
Phillips, D., 71, 79
Pietromonaco, P. R., 69, 77, 142, 145, 152, 155
Pilkonis, P. A., 75, 77
Pistole, M. C., 71, 79
Plant, M. A., 219, 228
Playfair, H. R., 163, 173
Polek, D. S., 139, 153
Pollane, L., 240, 254
Pollock, G. E., 233, 257
Poppcr, S., 163, 170, 173
Pound, A., 86, 101
Powell, D., 83, 101
Powers, D., 286, 299
Prado, L. M., 252, 257
Pratt, E. L., 235, 256
Pribilovics, R. M. G., 248, 257
Prochaska, J. O., 222, 229
Puckering, C., 86, 101
Putnam, P. H., 159, 174

Q

Quick, D. S., 116, 128

R

Rachal, K. C., 29, 39, 51, 59, 61, 62, 247, 256, 283, 284, 299
Radke-Yarrow, M., 86, 102
Rajab, M. H., 203, 213
Raley, R. K., 105, 127
Rands, M., 29, 30, 40
Raney, S. L., 234, 235, 236, 255
Rankin, R. P., 235, 256
Rappaport, J., 288, 299
Raskin, V. D., 167, 175
Rassaby, E. S., 163, 169, 170, 175
Rauen, P., 239, 254
Rayias, M. F., 159, 174
Read, S. J., 67, 68, 69, 70, 77
Rebol, A., 238, 254
Redman, E. S., 169, 174
Rehm, L. P., 163, 166, 175
Reis, H. T., 21, 40
Renick, M., 238, 239, 250, 256, 257
Resnick, P. A., 293, 297
Revenstorf, D., 204, 207, 213
Rholes, W. S., 68, 71, 79
Richard, F. D., 33, 37
Richman, J. A., 167, 175
Richters, J. E., 162, 175
Ridley, C. A., 240, 242, 254, 257
Riggs, D. S., 182, 197
Riley, L. A., 237, 238, 249, 258
Risch, G. S., 237, 238, 249, 258
Risso, L. P., 136, 149, 155
Ritchie, K. L., 88, 102
Roberts, J. E., 145, 155, 210, 213
Roberts, L. J., 221, 229
Roberts, M. C. F., 219, 229
Robinson, G. E., 163, 175
Robson, K. M., 158, 160, 163, 164, 170, 171, 173, 174
Rodgers, R. H., 123, 126
Rodstein, E., 110, 129
Rogers, W., 142, 155
Rogge, R. D., 240, 246, 257
Roloff, M. E., 29, 30, 38, 40
Roman, P. M., 134, 135, 152
Rook, K. S., 142, 155

Rooney, A. C., 159, 160, 176
Rosen, K. H., 30, 40
Rosenheck, R., 183, 197
Rosin, E., 309, 311
Rothlind, J., 139, 141, 152
Rounsaville, B. J., 74, 75, 78, 146, 147, 148, 153, 171, 174
Roux, J. F., 163, 173
Rovine, M., 85, 88, 101
Rowe, J. O., 286, 299
Rudd, M. D., 203, 213
Rudolph, K. D., 69, 77
Rugg, A. J., 163, 170, 176
Rusbult, C. E., 2, 10, 30, 31, 40, 235, 258, 278, 299, 300
Russel, D. W., 137, 155
Russell, A., 112, 128
Russell, J. A., 20, 38, 40
Russell, M. N., 237, 250, 256, 257
Russo, F., 238, 257
Rustine, T., 216, 227
Rutledge, L. L., 139, 153
Rutt, D. J., 17, 38
Ryan, C., 122, 127
Rychtarik, R. G., 222, 228

S

Sable, P., 180, 197
Sacher, J. A., 34, 38
Sagarese, M., 107, 128
Sager, C. J., 110, 129
Sahlstein, E. M., 2, 10
Salusky, S., 147, 148, 154
Sameroff, A. J., 82, 102
Samter, W., 16, 23, 37
Sandage, S. J., 29, 39, 59, 61, 283, 284, 285, 288, 293, 299, 300
Sanders, M. R., 99, 102
Sandler, I., 123, 126
Saunders, K., 69, 71, 77
Sayers, S. L., 136, 152, 238, 239, 240, 246, 254, 257
Scaturo, D. J., 183, 184, 192, 197
Schaefer, M. T., 205, 208, 213
Schafer, J., 216, 227

Scharfe, E., 68, 69, 79
Scharff, J. S., 265, 275
Scherer, K. R., 45, 62
Schirtzinger, M. B., 163, 166, 168, 174
Schlechte, J. A., 170, 175
Schlee, K. A., 192, 197
Schless, A. P., 139, 155
Schmaling, K. B., 139, 147, 148, 154,
    155, 178, 196, 282, 299
Schnarch, D., 309, 311
Schneier, F. R., 199, 213
Schultz, K. M., 178, 181, 194, 195
Schumm, W. R., 234, 237, 240, 248,
    250, 251, 257
Schwartz, L., 139, 155
Schwartz, P., 309, 311
Schwartz, S., 99, 102
Schweitzer, R. D., 158, 168, 166, 175
Scott, L., 19, 39
Searcy, E., 112, 128
Seeley, J. R., 136, 137, 153
Segrin, C., 15, 40
Seilhamer, R., 218, 227
Seligman, M. E. P., 202, 213
Seltzer, J. A., 123, 129
Semmel, A., 202, 213
Senchak, M., 216, 228, 229
Shapiro, R. J., 224, 229
Shaver, P. R., 47, 57, 61, 63, 65, 66,
    67, 68, 69, 71, 73, 77, 78, 79, 180,
    196
Shea, M. T., 75, 77
Sheehan, R., 242, 255
Sheets, V., 123, 126
Sheldon, C. T., 133, 137, 155
Sher, T. G., 282, 299
Sherman, L., 139, 141, 152, 154
Shifflett, K., 95, 96, 97, 98, 99, 102
Shoham, V., 150, 152, 184, 188, 192,
    195
Sholomaskas, D., 146, 147, 148, 153
Shotter, J., 20, 40
Shure, M. B., 234, 235, 236, 255
Sigvardsson, S., 220, 227
Silliman, B., 237, 248, 250, 251, 257
Silver, R. C., 57, 61

Silverblat, A. H., 110, 126
Simpson, J. A., 2, 10, 58, 62, 67, 68,
    70, 71, 79
Sims, A., 74, 75, 78
Skinstad, A. H., 217, 226, 227, 229
Slovik, L. F., 278, 299
Smith, D. A., 134, 153
Smith, T. W., 282, 299
Snyder, D. K., 59, 61, 260, 266, 267,
    275, 289, 298
Snyder, M., 206, 212
Snydersmith, M., 282, 298
Solano, C. H., 200, 213
Soloman, J., 65, 78
Sommer, K. L., 60
Sotsky, S. M., 75, 77
Spanier, G. B., 17, 40, 204, 213
Speicher, C. E., 282, 298
Sperry, L., 316, 317, 319
Spielberger, C. D., 204, 213
Spilka, B., 249, 257
Spinelli, M. G., 171, 176
Spitzberg, B. H., 15, 16, 22, 24, 27,
    28, 38, 40
Sprague, R. J., 47, 62
Sprecher, S., 34, 36, 40
Sprenkle, D. H., 242, 255
Spring, J. A., 287, 299
Springer, C., 45, 61
Sroufe, L. A., 68, 69, 73, 76, 77, 79,
    80, 161, 176
St. Peters, M., 247, 248, 252, 252, 257
Stafford, L., 13, 38, 105, 127
Stahmann, R. F., 238, 250, 256
Stanley, S. M., 138, 155, 215, 227,
    233, 234, 235, 236, 239, 240, 244,
    245, 246, 247, 248, 250, 252, 255,
    256, 257, 258
Starzomiski, A., 69, 71, 77
Steele, C. M., 219, 229
Steer, R. A., 202, 203, 212
Stein, A., 159, 160, 170, 176
Steinberg, L., 107, 129
Steinberg, M., 226, 227
Steinglass, P., 217, 219, 224, 227, 229
Stenberg, C., 65, 77

Stephens, L. S., 123, 129
Stern, R., 191, 195
Sternberg, R. J., 28, 40
Stewart, A., 142, 155
Stickly, T. R., 150, 152, 184, 188, 192, 195
Stillwell, A. M., 35, 37, 296, 300
Stollman, W., 108, 128
Stone, C., 310, 312
Stoneman, Z., 88, 103
Stout, R. J., 217, 225, 228, 229
Stovall, K. C., 69, 77
Strassberg, D., 158, 168, 166, 175
Strauss, M. S., 217, 218, 228
Street, A., 281, 298
Street, L., 199, 213
Strejc, H., 17, 38
Stroup, A. L., 233, 257
Strupp, H. H., 269, 275
Stuart, S., 171, 175, 176
Sullivan, R. F., 218, 228
Surra, C. A., 18, 39, 40
Swain, A. M., 157, 175
Sweet, J. A., 105, 127, 235, 254
Swinson, R. P., 203, 212

T

Tal, M., 141, 153
Tangey, J., 282, 300
Taylor, C. B., 190, 195, 282, 298
Teasdale, J. D., 139, 154
Teich, J. J., 190, 195
Ter Schur, E., 47, 57, 61
Termine, N. T., 160, 176
Teti, D. M., 158, 161, 174, 176
Thakar, R., 164, 173
Thibaut, J. W., 21, 40
Thomas, C., 48, 62
Thomas, J., 251, 254
Thomas, P. F., 159, 160, 176
Thompson, R. A., 161, 163, 176
Thompson, S. C., 48, 62
Thompson-Guppy, A., 121, 128
Thomson, E., 235, 257
Thoresen, C. E., 282, 300

Tisdall, M. W., 163, 173
Tonelli, L., 252, 257
Tronick, E., 159, 160, 173
Tuchluk, S., 142, 153
Tucker, J. S., 70, 79
Turnbull, J., 141, 153
Turner, C. W., 282, 299
Tyree, A., 283, 299

U-V

Uddenberg, N., 160, 171, 172, 176
Ulrich-Jakubowski, D., 137, 155
Van den Broucke, S., 283, 300
Van Dyck, R., 190, 196
Van Dyke, D. T., 237, 238, 249, 258
Van Ijzendoorn, M. H., 65, 79
Van Lange, P. A. M., 235, 258
Van Widenfelt, B., 234, 258
Vandereycken, W., 283, 300
VanderVoort, L. A., 36, 38
Vangelisti, A. L., 45, 47, 48, 49, 51, 57, 62
Vanni, D., 34, 40
VanOyen Vitvliet, C., 282, 300
Varner, M. W., 170, 175
Vaughn, C. E., 139, 155
Verette, J., 47, 62, 278, 299
Veroff, J., 286, 300
Victor, C., 164, 173
Visher, J. S., 107, 108, 109, 110, 111, 113, 114, 115, 116, 117, 118, 119, 120, 121, 124, 125, 129
Vitanza, S. A., 30, 39
Vivian, D., 138, 152
Vogler, C. C., 218, 229
Volling, B., 88, 101
Von Baeyer, C., 202, 213
Von Sydow, K., 164, 176

W

Wackman, D. B., 240, 242, 256
Wade, 286, 300
Wade, W. A., 249, 254
Walker, L., 110, 129

Wall, S., 63, 64, 65, 76
Wallace, P. M., 160, 163, 169, 171, 174
Wampler, K. S., 243, 254
Wampold, B. E., 277, 299
Ward, C., 203, 212
Ware, J., 142, 155
Warren, C. S., 266, 270, 275
Waters, E., 63, 64, 65, 68, 76, 80
Watkins, J. T., 75, 77
Watson, D., 201, 213
Watson, J. P., 163, 170, 176
Watt, N. F., 234, 235, 236, 255
Weathers, F. W., 182, 197
Weaver, S. E., 115, 120, 129
Webster-Stratton, C., 88, 103
Weinberg, T. S., 218, 229
Weiner, B., 47, 48, 62
Weinfield, N. S., 69, 79
Weiss, R. L., 137, 138, 153, 155
Weissman, M. M., 74, 75, 78, 145, 146, 147, 148, 153, 155, 171, 174
Wells, K. B., 142, 155
Welte, J. W., 217, 229
Wenzel, A., 171, 175, 211, 213
Werking, K. J., 16, 37
West, S. G., 234, 235, 236, 255
Whalen, J., 205, 213
Wheeler, L., 21, 40
Whiffen, F., 9, 10
Whiffen, V. E., 134, 155, 158, 159, 160, 161, 163, 169, 171, 174, 176, 265, 275
Whisman, M. A., 86, 103, 133, 134, 136, 137, 138, 145, 148, 149, 155
White, G. D., 117, 126, 310, 312
Whiteside, M. F., 122, 123, 129
Whitney, G. A., 278, 299
Whitton, S., 235, 252, 256, 257, 258
Wickrama, K. A. S., 236, 256
Widaman, K., 163, 166, 168, 174
Wieck, A., 165, 175
Wieczorek, W. F., 217, 229
Wilke, C., 181, 190, 196
Wilkins, T. A., 251, 258
Williams, L. M., 237, 238, 249, 258

Williams-Keeler, L., 182, 188, 189, 193, 196
Wills, R. M., 266, 267, 275
Wills, T., 140, 153
Wilmot, W. W., 32, 33, 35, 41
Winters, A. M., 23, 29, 41
Wippman, J., 68, 80
Wiseman, J. P., 27, 41, 218, 229
Witcher, B. S., 235, 258
Wittchen, H. U., 199, 200, 213
Wojkiewicz, R. A., 105, 129
Wolchik, s., 123, 126
Wolfe, D. M., 235, 254
Wolkind, S., 160, 161, 174
Wood, J. T., 20, 26, 31, 38, 41, 115, 129
Worthington, E. L., 29, 39, 247, 256, 284, 285, 286, 288, 293, 295, 300
Worthington, W. L., 51, 59, 61, 62, 283, 284, 299
Wortman, C. B., 141, 153
Wrate, R. M., 159, 160, 176
Wright, E. J., 164, 175

Y

Yogev, 310, 312
York, R., 167, 173
Young, J. E., 266, 275
Young, S. L., 47, 48, 49, 57, 62
Youngblade, L., 88, 101
Yovetich, N. A., 278, 299, 300

Z

Zahn-Waxler, C., 86, 87, 96, 101, 102
Zajicek, E., 160, 161, 174
Zdaniuk, B., 71, 76
Zeichner, A., 217, 228
Zeifman, D., 71, 78
Zekoski, E. M., 164, 170, 175
Zelkowitz, P., 158, 164, 167, 176
Zhang, L., 217 229
Zoellner, L. A., 177, 179, 185, 190, 191, 194, 196
Zuroff, D. C., 145, 152
Zweben, A., 222, 228

Subject Index

A

Abandonment
  fear of, 144
Abuse, 30, 31
  alcohol, 216
  child, 69
  physical, 139, 140
  psychological, 138
Adult romantic attachment styles,
  65-76
  anxiety/avoidance factors, 67
  Experiences in Close Relation-
    ships Scale, 67, 68
  self- vs. other models, 66, 67
  similarity to childhood patterns,
    66-68
  sociodemographics and, 66
  three- vs. four-category
    measures, 67
Aggression
  and couple conflict, 87
  nonrelational factors, 30
Agoraphobia
  attachment models, 180, 181
  communication training, 187
  complex agoraphobia model,
    178, 179
  couple therapy and, 185, 186,
    189, 194, 195
  emotionally focused family
    therapy, 188, 189
  in vivo practice (therapy), 187
  partner-assisted exposure, 190,
    191
  psychodynamic models, 179, 180
  stabilization, 188, 189

summarizing self-syndrome, 187,
  188
  therapeutic mechanisms, 191
Alcohol abuse, 7, 8
  aggression and violence, 221, 222
  communication problems, 216,
    218, 219
  family sigma and, 218
  interpersonal factors, 217
  marital dissatisfaction, 215, 216
  marital outcome studies, 219-221
  physical abuse, 216-218
  sexual dysfunction, 218
  treatment for
    Alcoholics Anonymous, 223
    cognitive-behavioral coping
      skills, 222
    motivational enhancement
      therapy, 222
    therapeutic intervention for
      partners, 223-226
    twelve-step facilitation therapy,
      222
Ambiguity of communication, 32
Anger
  see Marital conflict and parenting
Anorexia/bulimia, 69
Anxiety disorders, 6, 7
  agoraphobia, 177-181, 185, 186,
    190, 191, 194, 195
  attachment models, 180
  coping strategies, 186
  interventions, 184-195
  obsessive-compulsive disorder,
    177, 181, 191, 192
  posttraumatic stress disorder,
    177, 182-184, 192, 193

psychodynamic models, 179, 180
relationship factors and, 178
see Social phobia
Attachment
and social phobias, 209-212
see Postpartum depression,
  Social phobia
Attachment and relationship quality
communication patterns, 70
conflict resolution strategies, 71
cross-sectional studies, 70-73
sexuality, 71
see Social phobia
Attachment stability and traited-
  ness, 68-70
and personality traits, 69
and psychopathology, 69, 73-76
Attachment style
depression and, 145
hurtful families, 58, 59
Attachment theory, 4, 5,
and object relations theory, 265
avoidant attachment, 65
change-resistant nature of age, 64
close relationship processes, 63, 64
disorganized attachment, 65
formulation of, 64
strange situation paradigm,
  classification, 64, 65
styles, 9
see Adult romantic attachment
styles, Social Phobias
Attraction research, 20-25
comparison level of, 21, 22
inaccessibility and, 22
presentation of self as partner, 21
shyness, 23
static vs. dynamic beauty, 21
Avoidance strategies, verbal/
  nonverbal, 32

B-C

Blame, 15
Child effects on couples
and marital conflict, 86, 87

as mutually influential, 82-84
child adjustment, 85
clinical implications for child, 91-96
intervention and treatment, 97-100
mediation efforts by child, 95, 96
parent-child interrelations, 84-91
recommendations, 92-94
Child functioning
conflict and, 5
Clinicians' role
see Marital distress, Divorce
  prevention workshops
Commitment factors, 2
Communal behavior, 1, 2
Communication competence
attraction, 21, 22
complexities, 17-20
Communication skills, 17, 20-22
normative appropriateness of,
  24, 25
partners' view of, 23, 24
vs. social skill, 22, 23
Communication style, 3
Communication
ambiguity, 31, 32
and cultural rules, 20
as catalyst, 26
deficiencies, 262
verbal vs. nonverbal dissolution
  strategies, 32
Competence of relational partner,
  16, 17
attraction and, 21, 22
Conflict management, 3, 5
appropriateness of, 25, 29
atypical relationships, 31
avoidant communication, 29, 30
communication in, 27, 28
destructive conflict, 25
intentionality, 27
loss of togetherness (short- or
  long-term), 26
loyalty, 30
Conflict resolution strategies, 71

Couple maintenance
   child adjustment, 85
   child effects, 84-91
   child influence on, 82-85
   marital conflict, 86, 87
Couple therapy
   insight oriented, 8-10
   see Insight-oriented techniques,
     Divorce, Marital Distress

D

Dependency symptoms, 144
Depression and intervention
   methods
   emotion-focused marital therapy,
     150
   integrative couple therapy, 150
   self-regulation couples therapy,
     150, 151
Depression in marriage, 5, 6
   adolescents and, 134
   ambivalent partners, 139
   and therapy, 146-151
   causal models/mediators, 135-138
   coercion, 138
   communication, 138, 139
   disposition to, 145
   family hostility/tension, 139
   gender, 145, 146
   humiliation events, 139, 140
   individual differences and, 144
   interventions, 149-151
   longitudinal investigations, 137,
     138
   loss of emotional support, 140
   marital discord and, 135-137
   negative verbal behavior, 139
   neuroticism and, 144
   obsessive-compulsive symptoms,
     144, 145
   poor role performance, 142, 143
   postpartum, 134
   problem-solving deficits, 138, 139
   psychological abuse, 138, 139

reassurance seeking, 138, 142
   stress generation theory, 141-144
   see Divorce prevention programs,
     Marital distress, Postpartum
     depression
Dissolution
   and individual integrity, 31, 32
   communal skills for, 3, 4, 34
   coparenting partnerships, 34
   cultural scripts, 33
   Face-work Model of
     Disengagement, 33, 34
   four-phase model of, 33
   loss of friends and, 34
   mutuality and, 34, 35
   politeness theory, 33, 34
   process of, 32
   verbal/nonverbal termination
     strategies, 32, 33
   see Divorce, Marital distress
Divorce
   child adjustment and, 86
   coparenting, 34
Divorce prevention programs, 8
   choosing a program, 253, 254
   Compassionate and Accepting
     Relationships Through
     Sympathy, 245-247
   Couples Communication, 242,
     243
   Prevention and Relationship
     Enhancement Program, 244, 245
   program marketing and
     promotion, 247-252
   Relationship Enhancement, 241,
     242
Divorce prevention theory
   assessment and discussion
     approach, 237, 238
   factors related to, 235, 236
   overview of, 235
   program formats, 236-239
   self-report questionnaire, 238
   topic instruction approach, 237
   which factors to address, 236
Dyadic Adjustment Scale, 17

E-F

Empathic accuracy, 2
Families as unique context for hurt,
    44, 45
  and shared history, 45
  appraisals of hurt, 45-47
  as ongoing pattern, 49
  distancing oneself, 49-57
  forgiveness, 55-60
  intentionality, 48, 49
  involuntary nature of, 44, 45
  prolonged influence,
  responses to hurt, 47-49
  vulnerability, 47
Family systems perspective
  see Child effects on couples,
    Couple maintenance
Forgiveness
  and negative reciprocity, 277, 278
  and transgressions in close
    relationships, 279, 287
  as weakness, 279, 280
  as relationship aid, 283, 284
  clinical intervention study, 284-
    296
  dangers of, 280
  events undeserving of, 281, 282
  injustice and inequality of, 280,
    281
  mental health and, 282, 283
  physical health and, 282
Forgiveness strategies, 4, 9

G

Gender differences, 3
  alcohol, 216, 217
  attachment and relationship
    quality, 70, 72
  depression and, 145, 146
  obsessive-compulsive disorder
    and, 181, 182
  see Anxiety, Depression,
    Attachment

H

Hurtful messages
  as ongoing pattern, 49
  background/foreground infor-
    mation, 46
  distancing oneself, 49, 50, 55-57
  family context, 4, 44, 45, 50
  forgiveness, 55-60
  influence of hurtful family
    environment, 50-55
  intentionality, 48, 49
  nature of the interaction, 43, 44
  primary/secondary appraisals of
    hurt, 45-47
  responses to hurt, 47-49
  vulnerability to further harm, 47

I

Insight-oriented techniques
  attachment theory, 265
  identifying core relationship
    themes, 268, 269
  interpersonal role theory, 265, 266
  object relations theory, 264, 265
  pluralistic model, 260-263
  principles of, 263-267
  promoting alternative behaviors,
    270, 271
  reconstructions of maladaptive
    relationship themes, 266, 267
  relationship themes and current
    conflict, 269, 270
  schema theory, 266
  theoretical assumptions, 263, 264
  therapeutic impact, 271, 272
  therapeutic techniques, 267, 268
Interdependence theory, 2

M

Marital conflict and parenting
  clinical implications for child, 91-
    96

constructive vs. destructive
forms, 89, 90
intervention and treatment, 97-
100
mediation efforts by child 95, 96
recommendations for handling,
92-94
Marital distress and divorce
choosing a program, 253, 254
divorce prevention theory, 235
divorce prevention workshops,
234
divorce prevention programs,
239-247
historical intervention approaches,
234
program formats, 236-239
related factors, 235
role of clinicians, 233-254
self-report questionnaire, 238
skills training, 239
Marital transgressions, 26
see Forgiveness, Depression in
marriage
Marriage and depression
see Depression in marriage
Marriage therapy
see Depression in marriage
Marriage
summary perceptions, 14
Mock negativity/warfare, 28
Monogamy, 26

N-O

Neuroticism
and depression, 144
Obsessive-compulsive disorders,
144, 145, 177, 181, 182, 191, 192
Ordinariness of relationship, 13
sameness, 14

P

Parent-child relations, 3-6
nonresidential, 123-126

coparenting, 122, 123
see Child effects on couples,
Stepfamilies
Partnership standards, 16
Personal relationships
as constructs, 35
Postpartum depression, 6
attachment difficulties, 161-163
depressive distortion hypothesis,
162, 163
face-to-face paradigm, 159
genetic component, 170
infant behavior and, 159
males and, 168
men's sex role attitudes and, 166,
167
mother-infant relationships, 158-
163
partner relationship, 163-170
residual effects of, 160, 161
sexual satisfaction, 164
decrease, 165
shared affectivity, 159, 160
women's own parental
relationships and, 158, 170-172
Posttraumatic stress syndrome,
177, 182-184, 192, 193
Prevention of marital distress
see Divorce, Marital distress and
divorce
Prevention/intervention strategies,
3
Profanity, 23, 29
Psychotherapeutic problems and
attachment, 74-76
Public/private behavior, 15

R

Relational maintenance, 13-19
as persistent task, 14
skills of interpersonal relating, 14
see Conflict management
Relationship awareness, 18-20
Relationship distress, 8
Relationship maintenance, 13-15

Relationship
uniqueness of, 15

S

Sexuality
relationship satisfaction, 71
see Depression, Postpartum
depression
Shared meaning, 16
Shyness, 23
depression and, 144
see Social phobia
Skill evaluation, 16-20
Skilled/unskilled behaviors, 15, 16
Social phobias, 7
clinical interventions, 201-209
couples therapy and, 201
Disability Profile, 200
intervention results, 206-209
Liebowitz Disability Scale, 200
psychopathological measurements
Attributional Style Question-
naire, 202
Beck Anxiety Inventory, 202,
203
Beck Depression Inventory, 203
Penn State Worry Question-
naire, 203
Social Interaction Anxiety
Scale, 203
Social Phobia Scale, 203, 204
State-Trait Anxiety Inventory,
204
relationship interference and,
200, 201
relationship measurements
Dyadic Adjustment Scale, 204
Dyadic Trust Scale, 204, 205
Minding Questionnaire, 205
Personal Assessment of
Intimacy in Relationships, 205
Relationship Attribution
Measure, 205, 206
Relationship Closeness
Inventory-Strength Scale, 206

Relationship Questionnaire,
206
see also Anxiety disorders,
Depression
Stalking
former romantic partners and, 34
Stepfamilies, 3, 5
affinity strategies, 109
alternative maintenance strategies, 116, 117
clinical interventions, 107, 108
communication skills, 108, 109
context of new family, 119
coparenting, 122, 123
couple bonding, 109-111
dealing with resentments, 114, 115
differing expectations, 112, 113
differing motivations, 113
helping individuals to cope, 115
mourning losses, 113, 114
nonresidential parent-child
relationships, 123-126
reciprocity, 117, 118
reducing feeling of helplessness,
115, 116
relational maintenance skills,
106, 107
unrealistic expectations, 119, 120
validating feelings, 115
and first marriage family
comparisons, 120-122
Stress generation theory, 141, 151
and communication, 142
and poor role performance, 142,
143
and reassurance seeking, 142
Substance abuse
limitations, 226, 227
treatment for, 222-227
see Abuse, Alcohol abuse

U-V

Unconditional positive regard
idea of, 27
Variability of relationship, 14, 15